COURTS WITHOUT CASES

Since 1875, Canadian courts have been permitted to act as advisors alongside their ordinary, adjudicative role. This book offers the first detailed examination of that role from a legal perspective.

When one thinks of courts, it is most often in the context of deciding cases: live disputes involving spirited, adversarial debate between opposing parties. Sometimes, though, a court is granted the power to answer questions in the absence of such disputes through advisory opinions (also called references). These proceedings raise many questions: about the judicial role, about the relationship between courts and those who seek their 'advice', and about the nature of law.

Tracking their use in Canada since the country's Confederation and looking to the experience of other legal systems, the book considers how advisory opinions draw courts into the complex relationship between law and politics.

With attention to key themes such as the separation of powers, federalism, rights and precedent, this book provides an important and timely study of a fascinating phenomenon.

Courts Without Cases

The Law and Politics of Advisory Opinions

Carissima Mathen

•HART•

OXFORD • LONDON • NEW YORK • NEW DELHI • SYDNEY

HART PUBLISHING

Bloomsbury Publishing Plc

Kemp House, Chawley Park, Cumnor Hill, Oxford, OX2 9PH, UK

HART PUBLISHING, the Hart/Stag logo, BLOOMSBURY and the Diana logo are trademarks of Bloomsbury Publishing Plc

First published in Great Britain 2019

A catalogue record for this book is available from the British Library.

Library of Congress Cataloging-in-Publication data

Names: Mathen, Carissima, author.

Title: Courts without cases : the law and politics of advisory opinions / Carissima Mathen.

Description: Oxford, UK ; Portland, Oregon : Hart Publishing, 2019. | Includes bibliographical references and index.

Identifiers: LCCN 2018052890 (print) | LCCN 2018056242 (ebook) | ISBN 9781509922505 (EPub) | ISBN 9781509922499 (hardback)

Subjects: LCSH: Advisory opinions—Canada. | Judicial power—Canada. | Separation of powers—Canada. | BISAC: LAW / Public.

Classification: LCC KE4775 (ebook) | LCC KE4775 .M38 2019 (print) | DDC 347.71/012—dc23

LC record available at https://lccn.loc.gov/2018052890

ISBN: HB: 978-1-50992-249-9
ePDF: 978-1-50992-251-2
ePub: 978-1-50992-250-5

Typeset by Compuscript Ltd, Shannon

To find out more about our authors and books visit www.hartpublishing.co.uk. Here you will find extracts, author information, details of forthcoming events and the option to sign up for our newsletters.

For my mother, Elsie Mathen

ACKNOWLEDGEMENTS

This book has benefited from the support, advice and encouragement of a great many people.

I presented talks and lectures about the book at a number of institutions, including the ICON Public Law Society gatherings at the University of Copenhagen and the University of Hong Kong; Carleton University; the University of Montreal; Kings College London; the Courts and Politics Research Group gathering at the University of Guelph; and the University of Ottawa. I am grateful to participants and audience members for their thoughtful questions and feedback.

I am fortunate to have wonderful colleagues in the Public Law Group at the University of Ottawa. Former Dean of Law Nathalie Des Rosiers provided early support which was continued in various ways by her successors François Laroque and Adam Dodek. John Mark Keyes, Michael Pal and, especially, Peter Oliver and Vanessa MacDonnell reviewed chapters and provided invaluable advice.

I owe a debt to Benjamin Berger, Dwight Newman, Mark D. Walters and Justice Lorne Sossin. Each of them read the entire manuscript in a very compressed period. Their insights improved the book immeasurably. I benefited, as well, from the helpful suggestions provided by Stephen Bindman, Charles Feldman and Paul Daly; the support of University of Ottawa librarians Emily Landrault and Richard Harkin; and the superb research assistance of Natalya Odorico and Eric McGill.

All remaining errors, of course, are mine.

I very much appreciated the professionalism and courtesy of the associates (former and current) of Hart Publishing including Bill Asquith, Rosamund Jubber, Linda Staniford, Carolyn Fox, Richard Cox and Rose Wood. It has been a pleasure to work with them.

The encouragement of my family and friends during the two years I wrote the manuscript was tremendously important. In particular, I want to acknowledge my father Eusebius Mathen, Elizabeth Benny, Alexis Campbell, David De Marinis, Gerry Kee, Ian Kerr, Don Martin, Charlene Paling, The Honourable Rosalie Abella and The Honorable Michael Moldaver.

Throughout, I have been inspired by the example of my mother, Elsie Mathen, a brilliant literary scholar in her own right.

There remain but two persons to thank. The first is my husband, Jason Kee, for his love and boundless confidence in my abilities. The second is Michael Plaxton, without whom I never would have started, let alone finished, this book. In the true spirit of collegiality and friendship, he travelled with me at every step providing the necessary encouragement or (gentle) admonishment.

A portion of the material in Chapters 3 and 10, and my analyses of the *Patriation*, *Same-Sex Marriage* and *Supreme Court Act References* build on previous publications ('Mutability and Method in the Marriage Reference'; 'The Patriation Reference as Constitutional Method'; 'The Shadow of Absurdity and the Challenge of Easy Cases').

TABLE OF CONTENTS

Acknowledgements .... *vii*
Table of Cases .... *xiii*

Introduction 1

1. Courts *with* Cases 11
   What Do Courts Do? 11
   The Power, and Limits, of Cases 13
   The Separation of Powers 20
   Separation of Powers in Canada 26

2. Apex Courts 31
   The Judicial Committee 31
   'A Judicial Department in Every Well-Organized Government' 37
   A. Confederation 37
   B. Establishment 40

3. Canadian References 45
   Framing the Function 45
   Early Quiet, Early Reform 48
   Squaring Advisory Opinions with a General Court of Appeal 50
   Putting the 'Advisory' in an Advisory Function 58

4. Separate Functions – Separate Powers 61
   Executive Requests and Judicial Resistance 62
   The Lonely Legislature? 70

5. Arbitrating Federalism 79
   Federalism Post-Confederation 79
   A. Treaties 79
   B. Disallowance 83
   C. Marriage 87
   Apex Change – The Revamped Court 90
   A. Natural Resources 91
   B. Inflation and Emergency 92
   C. Inter-provincial Trade 96

Current Battles 98
A. Criminal Law 98
B. Economic Regulation 101
C. Environment and Development 103

6. Rebirth, and Rupture 108
Supreme at Last 108
Constitutional Rebirth 115
A. The Path to Change 116
B. Patriation 118
C. Consequences: Quebec Veto 126

7. Interpretation and Rights 131
Prologue: Process and Persons 132
An Age of Rights 138
A. Fundamental Justice and Criminal Fault (*Motor Vehicle*) 140
B. The Rule of Law (*Manitoba Language*) 144
C. Competing Constitutional Interests (*Bill 30*) 148
D. Revisiting Past Decisions (*Prostitution*) 149
E. The Intersection of Individual Rights, Federalism and Politics (*Same-Sex Marriage*) 152

8. Institutions 158
Rupture, for Real: Quebec Secession 158
Amendment, Actors and Judicial Supremacy 167
A. Frozen in Time: Senate Reform 168
B. Self-entrenchment 172

9. Actors, Advice and Law 180
The Core Tension 180
Why Pursue? 181
A. Doctrinal Guidance 182
B. Co-ordination 183
C. Strategy 184
D. Imprimatur 190
Why Not Comply? 192
Why Comply? 196

10. The Advisory Court 205
Process 207
Authority, Precedent, *Stare Decisis* 213

Providing Answers.....221
A. Abstract Review.....222
B. Answers, Declarations, Remedies.....226

Conclusion.....234

Index.....*237*

TABLE OF CASES

A-G Ontario v. A-G Canada [1947] A.C. 127 [*Re Privy Council Appeals*] 136
A.G. Can. v. A.G. Alta [1916] 1 A.C. 588..........100
Adler v. Ontario, [1996] 3 S.C.R. 609..........149
Alani v. Canada (Prime Minister), 2016 FC 1139 (CanLII)..........172
Att. Gen. of Quebec v. Blaikie et al., [1979] 2 S.C.R. 1016..........136
Attorney General (Ontario) v. Attorney General (Canada) [1896]
A.C. 348 [*Local Prohibition*]..........66
Attorney-General for Ontario v. Hamilton Street R.W. Co, [1903] AC 524..........60
Attorney General of Manitoba v. Forest, [1979] 2 S.C.R. 1032..........145
Attorney General of the Republic v. Mustafa Ibrahim, [1964] Cyprus
Law Reports 19..........146
Attorney-General for Canada v. *Attorneys-General for Ontario, Quebec and Nova Scotia* [1898] A.C. 700..........89
Attorney-General for Manitoba v. Manitoba Egg and Poultry Association et al., [1971] S.C.R. 689..........96, 188
Authority of Parliament in relation to the Upper House, [1980] 1 S.C.R. 54..........115
Baldy v. Hunter, 171 U.S. 388 (1898)..........146
Bank of Montreal v. Hall, [1990] 1 SCR 121..........101
BCGEU v. British Columbia (Attorney General), [1988] 2 S.C.R. 214..........14
Bell Canada v. Quebec (CSST), [1988] 1 S.C.R. 749..........105
Bertrand v. Dussault, January 30, 1909, County Court of St. Boniface
(unreported)..........145
Bilodeau v. Attorney General of Manitoba, [1981] 5 W.W.R. 393..........145
Blackmore v. British Columbia (Attorney General), 2009 BCSC 1299..........1
Borowski v. Canada (Attorney General), [1989] 1 S.C.R. 342..........16
British Coal Corporation v. The King [1935] A.C. 500..........110, 136
Bruker v. Marcovitz, [2007] 3 S.C.R. 607, 2007 SCC 54..........15
Caloil Inc. v. Attorney General of Canada, [1971] S.C.R. 543..........102
Canada (Attorney General) v. Downtown Eastside Sex Workers United Against Violence Society, 2012 SCC 45, [2012] 2 S.C.R. 524..........191, 224
Canada (Attorney General) v. Thouin, 2017 SCC 46, [2017] 2 S.C.R. 184..........25
Canada (Attorney-General) v. Bedford 2013 SCC 72, [2013]
3 S.C.R. 1101..........74–75, 147, 150, 176, 179, 218, 225
Canada (House of Commons) v. Vaid, [2005] 1 S.C.R. 667, 2005 SCC 30..........28
Canada (Minister of Justice) v. Borowski, [1981] 2 S.C.R. 575..........223
Canada (Prime Minister) v. Khadr, 2010 SCC 3, [2010] 1 S.C.R. 44..........20, 29

Canadian Foundation for Children, Youth and the Law v. Canada (Attorney General), [2004] 1 S.C.R. 76, 2004 SCC 4 132
Canadian Western Bank v. Alberta, [2007] 2 S.C.R. 3, 2007 SCC 22 105
Carnation Company Limited v. The Quebec Agricultural Marketing Board [1968] S.C.R. 238 97
Carter v. Canada (Attorney General), 2015 SCC 5, [2015] 1 S.C.R. 331 .... 75–76, 147, 176, 179, 225
Cenac v. Schafer (St. Lucia), [2016] UKPC 25 34
Chaoulli v. Quebec (Attorney General) [2005] 1 S.C.R. 791 224
Charkaoui v. Canada (Citizenship and Immigration), [2007] 1 S.C.R. 350, 2007 SCC 9 14
Chisolm v Georgia 2 US 419 1793 25
Citizens Insurance Company of Canada v. Parsons (1881), 7 App.Cas. 96 (P.C.) 97, 101
Citizens' and The Queen Ins. Cos. v. Parsons; Western Ins. Co. v. Johnston,(1880) 4 S.C.R. 215 210
City of Winnipeg v Barrett, [1892] A.C. 445 210
Constitution Act 1867, ss. 26, 27 and 28 (BC) [1991] 78 DLR (4th) 245 63–64
Cooper v. Canada (Human Rights Commission), [1996] 3 S.C.R. 854 28–29
Crown Grain Co. v. Day, [1908] A.C. 504 101
Dobson v. Dobson and Carter, 1997 CanLII 17827 (NB QB) 36
Dominion Stores Ltd. v. R., [1980] 1 S.C.R. 844 102
Doucet-Boudreau v. Nova Scotia (Minister of Education), [2003] 3 S.C.R. 3, 2003 SCC 62 28–29
Douglas/Kwantlen Faculty Assn. v. Douglas College, [1990] 3 S.C.R. 570 27
Dredd Scott v. Sandford 60 U.S. 393 165
Earth Future Lottery (PEI) [2002] 215 DLR (4th) 656 63
Edwards v Attorney General (Canada) [1930] A.C. 124, 1929 UKPC 86 .... 5, 132, 136
EGALE Canada v. Canada (A.G.) (2003), 13 B.C.L.R. (4th) 1, 2003 BCCA 251 .... 73, 152
Egan v. Canada, [1995] 2 S.C.R. 513 152
Finlay v. Canada (Minister of Finance), [1986] 2 S.C.R. 607 .... 191, 223
Fisheries Case (1898) A.C. 700 90
Fitzpatrick v. Bitzer, 427 U.S. 445 (1976) 25
Ford v Quebec (AG), [1988] 2 S.C.R. 712 .... 126, 196
Freedom of Informed Choice (Abortions) Act (SK) [1985] 25 DLR (4th); 63
Friends of the Oldman River Society v. Canada (Minister of Transport), [1992] 1 S.C.R. 3 104
General Motors of Canada Ltd. v. City National Leasing, [1989] 1 S.C.R. 641 102
Goods and Services Tax [1992] 2 SCR 858 64
Griswold v. Connecticut, 381 U.S. 479 (1965) 141
Halpern v. Toronto (City) (2003), 65 O.R. (3d) 161 (C.A) 73, 152

Hendricks c. Québec (P.G.), [2004] R.J.Q. 851 (C.A.) 73, 152
Highwood Congregation of Jehovah's Witnesses (Judicial Committee) v. Wall, 2018 SCC 26 15
Hollingsworth v. Perry, 133 S. Ct. 2652 223
Home Oil Distributors Limited v. Attorney-General of British Columbia, [1940] S.C.R. 444 97
Horn v. Lockhart, 84 U.S. 570 (1873) 146
Hunter et al. v. Southam Inc., [1984] 2 S.C.R. 145 .... 29, 136
Hussainara Khatoon (I) v. State of Bihar (AIR 1979 SC 1369) 14
Hy and Zel's Inc. v. Ontario (Attorney General); Paul Magder Furs Ltd. v. Ontario (Attorney General), [1993] 3 S.C.R. 675 223
Hyde v. Hyde (1866), L.R. 1 P. & D. 130 .... 73, 152
Imperial Tobacco Limited v Attorney General [1981] AC 718 226
In re Board of Commerce Act, [1922] A.C. 191 (P.C.) 5
In re Canada Provident Assn. 1882 CarswellNat 6 at 1 71
In re Certain Statutes of the Province of Manitoba relating to Education (1894) 22 SCR 577 .... 52, 210
In Re Criminal Code Sections Relating to Bigamy (1897) 27 SCR 461 87
In Re Employment of Aliens, [1922] S.C.R. 293 .... 5, 80
In re Marriage Laws, [1912] 46 S.C.R. 132 .... 87–90, 153
In re Prohibitory Liquor Laws (1895) 24 SCR 170 [*Local Prohibition*] 49
In re References by the Governor-General in Council (1910), 43 S.C.R. 536 at 547 (SCC), aff'd [1912] A.C. 571 (P.C.) [*Reference re References*] 32–34, 48, 51, 53–56, 58, 62, 66, 88–90, 208
In re The Initiative and Referendum Act, [1919] A.C. 935 85
In re The Judiciary Act 1903–1920 and In re The Navigation Act 1912–1920 (1921) 29 CLR 257 3
In the matter of an application by the Northern Ireland Human Rights Commission for Judicial Review (Northern Ireland) [2018] UKSC 27 228
In the Matter of the Jurisdiction of a Province to Legislate respecting Abstention from Labour on Sunday (1905), 35 SCR 581 60
Interpretation of Human Rights Act [1998] 50 DLR (4th) 647 63–64
Japanese Canadians Reference [1947] A.C. 8 93
Johannesson v. West St. Paul, [1952] 1 S.C.R. 292 92
Jones v. Canada (AG) [1975] 2 SCR 182 64
Kerley v. London & Lake Erie Transport Co., [1912] O.J. No. 157 60
Krieger v. Law Society of Alberta, [2002] 3 S.C.R. 372, 2002 SCC 65 28
Labatt Breweries of Canada Ltd. v. Attorney General of Canada, [1980] 1 S.C.R. 914 102
Law Society of Upper Canada v. Skapinker, [1984] 1 S.C.R. 357 .... 136, 139, 142
Legislative Authority of the Parliament of Canada in relation to the Upper House [1980] 1 SCR 54 64

Legislative Privilege (1978) 18 OR (2d) 182....64
Lévis (City) v. Tétreault; Lévis (City) v. 2629-4470 Québec Inc., [2006] 1 S.C.R. 420, 2006 SCC 12 144
Lochner v New York, 198 U.S. 45 (1905) 140–41
Loving v. Virginia, 388 U.S. 1 (1967) 87
Loyola High School v Quebec (Attorney General), 2015 SCC 12, [2015] 1 S.C.R. 613....223
M v. H. [1999] 2 S.C.R. 3 ....152, 207
MacKeigan v. Hickman, [1989] 2 S.C.R. 796....191
MacMillan Bloedel Ltd. v. Simpson, [1995] 4 S.C.R. 725 27
Macnaughton v Macnaughton's Trustees [1953] SC 387 at 392....222
Madzimbamuto v. Lardner-Burke, [1969] 1 A.C. 645 (P.C.) 146
Marbury v. Madison 5 U.S. 137; 1 Cranch 137 (1803) 38, 226
Marine Services International Ltd. v. Ryan Estate, 2013 SCC 44, [2013] 3 S.C.R. 53....105
Marriage Commissioners Appointed Under The Marriage Act (Re), 2011 SKCA 3 (CanLII) 155
Martin v. Hunter's Lessee 14 U.S. 304 (1816)....38
MB (AG) v. Manitoba Egg and Poultry Association [1971] SCR 698....64
McCulloch v Maryland 17 U.S. (4 Wheat.) 316 (1819) 24
McEvoy v. Attorney General (New Brunswick), [1983] 1 S.C.R. 704 67
Miron v. Trudel, [1995] 2 S.C.R. 418 152
Moratorium Legislation Act (SK) [1955] 35 CBR 135 64
Multiple Access Ltd. v. McCutcheon, [1982] 2 S.C.R. 161....101, 105
Munro v. National Capital Commission, [1966] S.C.R. 663....92
Muskrat v. United States, 219 U.S. 346 (1911) 3, 62, 161
Nadan v. The Queen, [1926] A.C. 482 110
New Brunswick (Minister of Health and Community Services) v. G. (J.), [1999] 3 S.C.R. 46 207
New Brunswick Broadcasting Co. v. Nova Scotia (Speaker of the House of Assembly), [1993] 1 S.C.R. 319 28–29
Newfoundland (Treasury Board) v. N.A.P.E., [2004] 3 S.C.R. 381 28
Noble v. Alley [1951] S.C.R. 64....17
Norris v Ireland (1989) 13 EHRR 186 222
Nova Scotia (Board of Censors) v. McNeil, [1976] 2 S.C.R. 265 223
Obergefell v Hodges 576 US _ (2015)....156
Ontario English Catholic Teachers' Assn. v. Ontario (Attorney General), [2001] 1 S.C.R. 470, 2001 SCC 15 149
Ontario Farm Products Marketing Reference [1957] S.C.R. 198 96
Operation Dismantle v. The Queen, [1985] 1 S.C.R. 441....28
Pellant v. Hebert, St. Boniface Co. Ct., (1981), 12 *R.G.D.* 242....145
Proclamations (1611) 12 Co Rep 74 33
Prohibitions del Roy (1607) 12 Co Rep 63....33

Projet de loi fédéral relatif au Sénat (Re), 2013 QCCA 1807 (CanLII) [*Quebec Senate Reference*"] 168–69
Proprietary Articles Trade Association et al v. Attorney-General for Canada et al [1931] A.C. 330. 214
Public Service Employee Relations Act (AB) [1987] 1 SCR 313 64
Quebec (Attorney General) v. A, 2013 SCC 5, [2013] 1 S.C.R. 61 87
Quebec (Attorney General) v. Canada (Attorney General), 2015 SCC 14, [2015] 1 S.C.R. 693 29
Quebec (Attorney General) v. Canadian Owners and Pilots Association, 2010 SCC 39, [2010] 2 S.C.R. 536 105
R v Comeau, 2018 SCC 15 96
R v Demers, [2004] 2 SCR 489 162
R v Director of Public Prosecutions Ex Parte Kebilene [2000] 2 AC 326 28
R v. Blackmore 2018 BCSC 367 .... 2, 190, 219–20
R v. Cyr (1917), 12 Alta. L.R. 320, 38 D.L.R. 601 (S.C.(A.D.)) 133
R. v Big M Drug Mart Ltd., [1985] 1 S.C.R. 295 .... 131, 139, 223
R. v. Bernard, [1988] S.C.J. No. 96, [1988] 2 S.C.R. 833 (S.C.C.) 179
R. v. Butler, [1992] 1 S.C.R. 452 132
R. v. Coffin, [1956] S.C.R. 191 .... 187, 191
R v Comeau, 2018 SCC 15 96
R. v. Crown Zellerbach Canada Ltd., [1988] 1 S.C.R. 401 104
R. v. Cunningham (1986), 31 C.C.C. (3d) 223 (Man. Prov. Ct.) 150
R. v. Downey, [1992] S.C.J. No. 48, [1992] 2 S.C.R. 10 150
R. v. Duke, [1972] S.C.J. No. 67 140
R. v. Forest (1976), 74 D.L.R. (3d) 704 (Man. Co. Ct.) 145
R. v. Hall, [2002] 3 S.C.R. 309, 2002 SCC 64 29
R. v. Hydro-Québec, [1997] 3 S.C.R. 213 .... 93, 104
R. v. Keegstra, [1990] 3 S.C.R. 697 .... 132, 214
R. v. Klassen, (1959) 20 DLR (2d) 406 (Man CA) 102
R. v. Morgentaler [1988] 1 S.C.R. 30 223
R. v. Morgentaler, [1993] 1 S.C.R. 462 95
R. v. Nur, [2015] S.C.J. No. 15, 2015 SCC 15 (S.C.C.) 176
R. v. Oakes, [1986] 1 S.C.R. 103 205
R. v. Oxfordshire County Council ex p. P [1996] ELR 153 222
R. v. Prue; R. v. Baril [1979] 2 S.C.R. 547 141
R. v. Sault Ste. Marie, [1978] 2 S.C.R. 1299 .... 140–41, 215
R. v. Sharpe, [2001] 1 S.C.R. 45, 2001 SCC 2 132
R. v. Sparrow, [1990] 1 S.C.R. 1075 139
R. v. Therens, [1985] 1 S.C.R. 613 .... 131, 205
R. v. Vaillancourt, [1987] 2 S.C.R. 636 214–16
R. v. Wholesale Travel Group Inc., [1991] 3 S.C.R. 154 144
Railway act, Canada v. Canada Pacific Railway [1958] SCR 285 64

Re B.C. Motor Vehicle Act, [1985] 2 S.C.R. 486 .... 5, 28, 136, 139, 141–43, 153, 182, 214–15
Re Brothers of the Christian Schools in Canada, 1876 CarswellPEI 1, Cout. Dig. 1 71
Re Drummond Wren [1945] O.R. 778 (Ont. H.C.) 16
Re Forest and Registrar of Court of Appeal of Manitoba (1977), 77 D.L.R. (3d) 445 (Man. C.A.) 145
Re Manitoba Language Rights, [1985] 1 S.C.R. 721 .... 86, 139, 144–46, 148, 158, 230–31
Re References by Governor-General in Council (1910), 43 S.C.R. 536, aff'd [1912] A.C. 571 [*Reference re References*] 160, 193
Re Regulation and Control of Aeronautics in Canada, [1931] UKPC 93 .... 81–82, 136
Re Residential Tenancies Act, 1979, [1981] 1 S.C.R. 714 .... 27, 95, 142
Re Resolution to Amend the Constitution [1981] 1 S.C.R. 753 .... 5, 38, 115, 121–25, 128–30, 138, 162, 164, 189–90, 203, 220, 227
Re The Educational System in the Island of Montreal, [1926] S.C.R. 246 67
Re: Anti-Inflation Act, [1976] 2 S.C.R. 373 .... 92–95, 142
Re: Authority of Parliament in relation to the Upper House, [1980] 1 SCR 54 .... 67, 142, 171
Re: Objection by Quebec to a Resolution to amend the Constitution, [1982] 2 S.C.R. 793 .... 67, 115, 122–23, 126–29, 159, 166
Reference as to the Legislative Competence of the Parliament of Canada to Enact Bill No. 9 of the Fourth Session, Eighteenth Parliament of Canada, Entitled "An Act to Amend the Supreme Court Act", [1940] S.C.R. 49 [*Privy Council Appeals – SCC*] 111
Reference as to the Validity of the Wartime Leasehold Regulations [1950] S.C.R. 124 93–94
Reference in re Legislative Jurisdiction over Hours of Labour, [1925] SCR 505, 1925 CanLII 77 (SCC) [*Labour Reference*] 81
Reference re Agricultural Products Marketing, [1978] 2 S.C.R. 1198 .... 102, 113
Reference re Amendments of the Constitution of Canada, (1981) 117 DLR (3d) 1, [1981] 2 WWR 193 (MBCA) 120
Reference re meaning of the word "Persons" in s. 24 of British North America Act, [1928] S.C.R. 276 [*Persons Case – SCC*] 133–34
Reference re Amendments to the Residential Tenancies Act (N.S.), [1996] 1 S.C.R. 186 103
Reference re Assisted Human Reproduction Act, 2010 SCC 61, [2010] 3 S.C.R. 457 .... 99–100, 221
Reference Re Bill 30, An Act to Amend the Education Act (Ont.), [1987] 1 S.C.R. 1148 .... 139, 148–49, 229

Reference re Canada Assistance Plan (B.C.), [1991] 2 S.C.R. 525 162
Reference Re Criminal Code (Canada), s. 873(A) (1910), 43 S.C.R. 434 59
Reference re Donald Marshall (1983), 57 N.S.R. (2d) 286 191
Reference re Farm Products Marketing Act [1957] S.C.R. 198 113
Reference re Firearms Act (Can.), [2000] 1 S.C.R. 783 .... 5, 93, 99, 186
Reference re Firearms Act (Can), [1998] A.J. No. 1028 (1998), 219 A.R. 201 (ABCA) 99
Reference re legislative jurisdiction of Parliament of Canada to enact the Minimum Wages Act (1935, c. 44), [1936] S.C.R. 461 82
Reference re Amendments to the Constitution of Canada (1981), 118 D.L.R. (3d) 1, 82 A.P.R. 503, 29 Nfld. & P.E.I.R. 503 *(NLCA)* 120
Reference re Newfoundland Continental Shelf, [1984] 1 S.C.R. 86 92
Reference re Pan-Canadian Securities Regulation, 2018 SCC 48 103
Reference Re Public Service Employees Relations Act (Alta.), [1987] 1 S.C.R. 313 139
Reference re Quebec Sales Tax, [1994] 2 S.C.R. 715 103
Reference re Refund of Dues Paid under s. 47 (f.) of Timber Regulations, [1933] S.C.R. 617 6
Reference re Regulation and Control of Radio Communication, [1931] S.C.R. 541 81
Reference re Remuneration of Judges of the Provincial Court (P.E.I.), [1997] 3 S.C.R. 3 28
Reference re Same-Sex Marriage, [2004] 3 S.C.R. 698 .... 64, 67–68, 73–74, 90, 103, 152–57, 189–91, 216–17
Reference re Secession of Quebec, [1998] 2 S.C.R. 217 .... 5, 27, 29, 57, 62, 67, 129, 158, 160–61, 163–67, 170, 181, 185, 192
Reference re Section 293 of the Criminal Code of Canada, [2011] B.C.J. No. 2211 [*Polygamy Reference*] 151
Reference re Section 94(2) of the Motor Vehicle Act, 1983 CanLII 268 (BC CA), 147 DLR (3d) 539 140–41
Reference re Securities Act, 2011 SCC 66, [2011] 3 S.C.R. 837 .... 29, 93, 101, 176
Reference re Senate Reform, 2014 SCC 32, [2014] 1 SCR 704 [*Senate Reform*] 5, 63, 72, 158, 167–71, 176, 183, 192, 201, 203
Reference re ss. 193 and 195.1(1)(c) of the Criminal Code (Man.), [1990] 1 S.C.R. 1123 [*Prostitution Reference*] 149–51, 182, 218–19
Reference re Supreme Court Act, ss. 5 and 6, 2014 SCC 21 [2014] 1 SCR 433 .... 5, 29, 42–43, 46, 69, 78, 158, 167, 172–76, 178–79, 192, 203, 206, 221, 229

Reference re The Power of the Governor General in Council to Disallow Provincial Legislation and the Power of Reservation of a Lieutenant-Governor of a Province [1938] S.C.R. 71 [*Re Disallowance*] 85–87
Reference re Validity of Section 5(a) of the Dairy Industry Act, [1949] S.C.R. 1 214
Reference re Waters and Water-Powers, [1929] S.C.R. 200 67
Reference Re Workers' Compensation Act, 1983 (Nfld.), [1989] 1 S.C.R. 922 139
Reference re: Anti-Inflation Act (Canada), [1976] S.C.J. No. 12, [1976] 2 S.C.R. 373 .... 174, 183
Reference Re: Offshore Mineral Rights, [1967] S.C.R. 792 91–92
Reference re: Ontario Medical Act, [1906] O.J. No. 147 66
Reference re: Section 293 of the Criminal Code of Canada, 2011 BCSC 1588 [*Polygamy Reference*] 2, 190, 219
Reference Re: Steven Murray Truscott, [1967] S.C.R. 30 .... 94, 191
Reg. v. Brierly, 14 O. R. 525 87
Régie des rentes du Québec v. Canada Bread Company Ltd., [2013] S.C.J. No. 46, [2013] 3 S.C.R. 125 .... 174, 195
Regina (Pretty) v Director of Public Prosecutions [2002] 1 AC 800 226
Regina v. Her Majesty's Attorney General ex parte Rusbridger et al [2003] UKHL 38 .... 19, 222, 227–28
Resolution to amend the Constitution, [1981] 1 S.C.R. 753 64
RJR-MacDonald Inc. v. Canada (Attorney General), [1995] 3 SCR 199 214
Roe v Wade 410 U.S. 113 (1973) 141
Roncarelli v. Duplessis, [1959] S.C.R. 121, at p. 142 146
Rothmans, Benson & Hedges Inc. v. Saskatchewan, [2005] 1 S.C.R. 188, 2005 SCC 13 105
S.P. Gupta v. Union of India, A.I.R. 1982 S.C. 149 223–24
Saskatchewan (Attorney General) v. Lemare Lake Logging Ltd., 2015 SCC 53, [2015] 3 S.C.R. 419 29
Saskatchewan (Human Rights Commission) v. Whatcott, 2013 SCC 11, [2013] 1 S.C.R. 467 132
Saskatchewan Federation of Labour v. Saskatchewan, 2015 SCC 4, [2015] 1 S.C.R. 245 139
Schachter v. Canada, [1992] 2 S.C.R. 679 .... 132, 147
Shannon v. Lower Mainland Dairy Products Board [1938] A.C. 708 97
Smith v The Queen [1960] S.C.R. 776 101
Sobeys Stores Ltd. v. Yeomans and Labour Standards Tribunal (N.S.), [1989] 1 S.C.R. 238 27
Special Reference No. 1 of 1955, P.L.R. 1956 W.P. 598 146
St. Catherines Milling and Lumber Co. v. The Queen (1888), 14 App. Cas., 46 135
Stony Plain Indian Reserve [1981] A.J. No. 1007 64
Sunil Batra v. Delhi Administration (1978) 4 SCC 409 14
Switzman v Elbling, [1957] SCR 285 84

Texas v. White, 74 U.S. 700 (1868)....146
The Attorney General of Ontario v The Attorney General of Canada and others (Canada) [1937] UKPC 11 [*Dominion Trade*]....81
The Attorney General of Ontario v The Attorney General of Canada and others (Canada) [1937] UKPC 6 [*Labour Conventions*]....5, 81–82
The Attorney General of Ontario v The Attorney General of Canada and others (Canada) [1937] UKPC 7 [*Social Insurance*]....81
The Attorney General of Quebec v The Attorney General of Canada & Ors (control of Radio Communication) (Canada) [1932] UKPC 7....81
The Attorney-General of Ontario and others v The Attorney-General of Canada and others and The Attorney-General of Quebec (Canada) [1947] UKPC 1 [*Privy Council Appeals*]....111
The Queen v. *Plowman*, 25 O. R. 656....87
Thorson v. Canada (Attorney General), [1975] 1 S.C.R. 138....27, 223
Tiny Separate School Trustees v. The King [1927] SCR 637....148
Trustees of Dartmouth College v. Woodward, 17 U.S. 518 (1819)....211
Tsilhqot'in Nation v. British Columbia, [2014] S.C.J. No. 44, [2014] 2 S.C.R. 256, 2014 SCC 44 (S.C.C.)....176
Union Colliery Co. v. Bryden [1899] A.C. 580....100
United States v. Insurance Companies, 89 U.S. 99 (1874)....146
United States v. Windsor, 570 U.S. ___ (2013)....87
Upper Churchill Water Rights Reversion Act [1984] 1 SCR 297....64
Validity of a by-law respecting taxi cabs [1958] 16 DLR (2d) 348....64
Vriend v. Alberta, [1998] 1 S.C.R. 493....29
Wells v. Newfoundland, [1999] 3 S.C.R. 199....28
Wilson v. *E. & N. Railway Co.*, [1922] 1 A.C. 202....86
Worcester v Georgia 31 U.S. (6 Pet.) 515 (1832)....24
Workers Compensation Act 1983 (NL) [1989] 1 SCR 922....63

Introduction

In 2007 the Attorney General of British Columbia sought to prosecute two men, Winston Blackmore and James Oler, for actions related to a fundamentalist Mormon sect. In the remote community of Bountiful, Blackmore and Oler exercised broad social and personal power over other people, especially women and children. Many people believed that the men engaged in a variety of criminal behaviours, including sexual exploitation, sexual assault and child abuse, and that they deserved to be prosecuted and punished.

But the BC government had a problem. The most serious of those crimes would be tricky to prove in court without victims who were willing to cooperate. And the government was not confident of securing that cooperation from other members of the Bountiful community.

There was one crime for which a lack of cooperation by the alleged victims would be less significant, however. As fundamentalist Mormons, Blackmore and Oler practised polygamy: they each kept several wives. Polygamy is a crime in Canada[1] and it can be proven with evidence of multiple marriage ceremonies or of multi-person marriage-like relationships. While the testimony of the partners to those relationships would be helpful, their absence was thought to be less fatal to the state's chances. As well, the community in Bountiful has not hidden its way of life. Convictions for polygamy, then, did not pose the same challenges as some of the other crimes being considered for prosecution.

But a polygamy trial would create a new problem. The community in Bountiful practises a particular type of Mormonism under which polygamy is religiously sanctioned or even required. Crown counsel became concerned that the law prohibiting polygamy might infringe the fundamental freedom of religion guaranteed under the Canadian Charter of Rights and Freedoms. Believing that such prosecutions might be unconstitutional, those Crown counsel resisted the idea of framing indictments based upon polygamy.

The Attorney General's attempts to overcome that resistance by its own lawyers tell a sorry tale. The tale includes botched investigations, a carousel of special prosecutors (each of whom the government appointed in the hope of securing an indictment) and significant judicial rebuke.[2] That story is very interesting. But, what I want to stress here is that the government persevered and, in November 2011,

[1] Criminal Code RSC, 1985, c C-46, s 293.
[2] *Blackmore v British Columbia (Attorney General)*, 2009 BCSC 1299.

scored a major victory when the British Columbia Supreme Court stated that the offence of polygamy was consistent with the Canadian Charter and, implicitly, that charges could proceed.[3]

The Court's conclusion, which ran to almost 300 pages, followed a months-long proceeding with thousands of pages of evidence and many days of argument. The presiding judge, Chief Justice Bauman, heard from dozens of witnesses, including some members of the Bountiful community, as well as experts – anthropologists, philosophers, psychologists and economists. Bauman CJ permitted a number of groups to present legal argument as third parties, or interveners, including children's rights groups, civil liberties associations, professional societies and religious organizations. Those groups made submissions about (a) the impact on polygamy on Canadian society and (b) whether criminalising it was constitutional.

Among the numerous witnesses and lawyers, though, there were two notable absences: Winston Blackmore and James Oler. To the casual observer, this may be surprising. After all, the Attorney General had been motivated, in large part, by the desire to prosecute those men, to shine a spotlight on their alleged reprehensible activities, and to send a message that British Columbia would not tolerate the exploitation and abuse of vulnerable persons. There is little doubt that Winston Blackmore and James Oler had a significant interest, and personal stake, in the eventual outcome of the proceeding. Having decided that the polygamy offence was constitutional, the Court effectively permitted the Attorney General to proceed with criminal charges against them.[4]

So, how could such a proceeding possibly take place without them? The answer is that the proceeding was not a trial. It involved no accused persons, defence lawyers or prosecutors. Its outcome was not properly described as a verdict. It was, instead, a reference.[5]

* * *

For the last century-and-a-half Canadian courts have considered questions, heard arguments and issued reasons even when there is no live case and no 'disputants' before them. When Canadian courts perform this role, what they produce is called a *reference* or *advisory opinion*.

[3] *Reference re: Section 293 of the Criminal Code of Canada*, 2011 BCSC 1588 (CanLII).

[4] The Attorney General did just that several years later and a conviction was secured: *R v Blackmore*, 2018 BCSC 367. The relationship between that trial and the prior reference is considered in a later chapter.

[5] The *Polygamy Reference* itself was unusual, because it proceeded before a trial level court. Most Canadian references proceed before provincial courts of appeal or the Supreme Court. Very few jurisdictions even allow for references before lower courts. The British Columbia government selected a trial reference so that it could introduce evidence, including via affidavit and examination of witnesses, that would not be easy to do before an appellate court. Most of the references discussed in this book – and indeed most references anywhere – are issued by appellate courts.

The reference function first appeared in Canadian law in 1875. It was inserted into the federal statute – the Supreme and Exchequer Court Act – that brought into existence the Supreme Court of Canada. The function has remained in place ever since, not just for the Supreme Court but for other courts as well. It sets Canada somewhat apart from similar Anglo-American legal systems.[6] There are few comparators to Canadian references in the United Kingdom,[7] Australia,[8] New Zealand[9] or the US federal judiciary.[10] The function also sets Canada apart from those legal systems with specialist 'constitutional courts'.[11] Numerous countries, in Europe and elsewhere, have instituted courts that are singularly authorised to consider constitutional issues. Those constitutional courts receive issues in numerous ways, including as references.[12] Thus, Canada is not unique in permitting advisory opinions. What is more unusual,[13] however, is to have the same court perform both an adjudicative *and* an advisory function.

[6] The term 'Anglo-American' is intended to denote British heritage, common law tradition, and some influence of American legal history and principles.

[7] The 1988 devolution of powers to Scotland, Wales and Northern Ireland granted a judicial review power to the UK Supreme Court: Scotland Act 1998 (c 46); Northern Ireland Act 1988; Government of Wales Act 2006.

[8] *In re The Judiciary Act 1903–1920 and In re The Navigation Act 1912–1920* (1921) 29 CLR 257; S Crawshaw, 'The High Court of Australia and Advisory Opinions' (1977) 51 Australian Law Journal 112.

[9] No advisory jurisdiction is provided for in the Constitution Act 1986 No 114 or the Senior Courts Act 2016 No 48, Public Act – Part 4: Supreme Court, ss 68–72. Geoffrey Palmer, 'The New Zealand Constitution and the Power of Courts' (2006) 15 Transnational Law & Contemporary Problems 551.

[10] US federal courts may not provide advisory opinions: *Muskrat v United States*, 219 US 346 at 362 (1911). Some states do permit this function: Charles M Carberry, 'The State Advisory Opinion in Perspective' (1975) 44 Fordham Law Review 81; Reuben Goodman, 'Chapter 10: Advisory Opinions', *Annual Survey of Massachusetts Law: Vol 1964*, Article 13 95.

[11] Andrew Harding, Peter Leyland and Tania Groppi, 'Constitutional Courts: Forms, Functions and Practice in Comparative Perspective' 2008 3(2) Journal of Comparative Law 3: 'The essential feature of the constitutional court-based system of judicial review … is that only one court, the constitutional court, has authority to adjudicate questions of constitutional interpretation or to review legislation, and this court is separate from the ordinary judicial system, forming, either by deliberate design or as a practical result, a fourth branch of government'. See also Alec Stone Sweet, 'Constitutional Courts and Parliamentary Democracy' (2002) 25 West European Politics 77–100; Arne Mavcic, *The Constitutional Review* (Den Bosch: Bookworld Publications, 2001); Wojciech Sadurski, *Constitutional Justice East and West: Democratic Legitimacy and Constitutional Courts in Post-Communist Europe in a Comparative Perspective* (The Hague: Kluwer, 2002); Wojciech Sadurski, *Rights Before Courts: a Study of Constitutional Courts in Post-Communist States of Eastern and Central Europe* (New York: Springer, 2002).

[12] Specialist constitutional courts can undertake a variety of tasks including: constitutional drafting; *ex ante* or *ex post* review of legislation; review of government officials and agencies; and review of democratic processes such as elections: Harding et al (n 9) 5. In Anglo-American systems, including Canada, most constitutional review is limited to laws and government action. This book is directed at those particular functions.

[13] India, South Africa and Israel, like Canada, permit advisory opinions. Durga Das Basu, *Introduction to the Constitution of India*, 20th edn (Nagpur: LexisNexis, 2009); Adem Kassie Abebe and Charles Manga, 'The Advisory Jurisdiction of Constitutional Courts in Sub-Sahara Africa' (2013) 46(55) George Washington International Law Review 4; Philip Kurland, *The Supreme Court and the Judicial Function* (Chicago IL: University of Chicago Press, 1975); Richard A Posner, 'Judicial Review, A Comparative Perspective: Israel, Canada, and the United States' (2010) 31(6) Cardozo Law Review 2393.

References resemble cases in a few ways. Like cases, references involve questions about the law, put to law's primary arbiters: courts. References display the procedural trappings of litigation. They feature participants, materials, oral advocacy and written reasons provided by judges. And when the body of references is compared to the body of cases, it can be very difficult to tell them apart, as will be explained in greater detail later in this book.

In at least two respects, though, references and cases are distinct. First, references do not involve a 'plaintiff' in the ordinary meaning of that term. In Canada, a reference is virtually always initiated by the government, but in doing so it does not make a *legal claim* against anyone else. It simply puts questions to a court for an answer. Therefore, it is not accurate to say that the government is the 'plaintiff'; and throughout this book, that term is avoided in favour of the more neutral 'party'. Of course, the government typically offers arguments to assist a court in arriving at an answer and, indeed, often has a clear opinion on what the answer to the questions it has posed should be. And that opinion will tend to correspond with what the government perceives to be in its legal or political interest. Certainly, the actor who initiates a reference is expected to make submissions to the court. But even if it does not, the proceeding can continue. That fact marks a sharp difference from cases. If, in an ordinary case, a plaintiff refused to take a position on one or more of the issues, the opposing party (respondent) almost certainly would prevail. The same does not necessarily apply to references. I say 'not necessarily' because if the initiating government declines to offer any argument on a question, the court may, in turn, decline to provide an answer.[14] But, especially in proceedings where the court has agreed to receive submissions from additional participants, such as other Attorneys General or advocacy groups, the court might well decide to answer the question anyway.

Another distinction between references and cases has to do with the status, in law, of the answers that each proceeding provides. When a court decides a case, it issues a judgment, which binds the parties, and also, in certain instances, binds other courts in how they decide cases – and thus it may be said that it binds generally. If the court is not the highest court in the land, the judgment may be appealed. But, until then, or if no appeal is possible, the judgment, and the reasons supporting it, have the status of 'law' and, indeed, become part of the framework that constitutes a society's commitment to the rule of law. As well, the court's answer may contain a variety of judicial 'remedies', which impose particular consequences on the parties, and those remedies also enjoy legal status.

References do not engage the court's power in the same way. The court provides an *answer* but that answer does not take the form of a *judgment*. The reference, supposedly, is not backed by the power of law and the court is not entitled to directly impose consequences on parties. That does not mean, of course, that

[14] The courts' occasional refusal to answer reference questions is discussed in Chapter 4.

references have no practical consequences. As explored in the chapters below, they do have consequences, sometimes highly significant ones. But the consequences are considered to be ancillary or collateral to what the *court* has done. This distinction is often expressed as the idea that references are not *legally binding*. The soundness of that idea is debated towards the end of the book. The legal status of references, the answers they provide and the true nature of the judicial power that they invoke are the focus of a number of chapters.

References are an important part of Canadian law, especially its constitutional law.[15] They count among the exceptional moments in Canadian legal history.[16] They have been part of Canada's development into a modern nation committed to the rule of law, constitutional order, individual liberties and respect for minorities and other communities. References played a key role in the early battles between the provinces and federal government that shaped the country's particular brand of federalism.[17] They shepherded an approach to constitutional interpretation.[18] The advisory function was pivotal in the debates over the repatriation of Canada's Constitution from the United Kingdom;[19] in path-breaking early decisions concerning the Charter of Rights;[20] and in battles over Canada's status and continued existence. In recent years, advisory opinions have featured in such disputes as whether a province is entitled to secede from Canada,[21] the role of national institutions[22] and the rules of formal constitutional change (amendment).[23]

For all their significance, though, it is necessary to keep the overall role of references in context. This book does not argue that advisory opinions are, necessarily, more important than ordinary constitutional litigation, i.e., constitutional disputes that have been presented to the courts, and considered by them, as cases. For a number of years, references accounted for around one-quarter of the Supreme Court's caseload in constitutional law.[24] That is a significant proportion, but still much less than the total number of cases.

[15] For many years following Confederation in 1867, Canadian cases could be finally appealed to the Judicial Committee of the Privy Council (JCPC). This meant that the JCPC also delivered reference opinions when those were appealed from the Supreme Court of Canada. Both of those routes ended as of 1949, when the Supreme Court became the final court of appeal for all cases arising in any Canadian jurisdiction. For the purpose of this book, I consider the JCPC to be a 'Canadian court' insofar as it considered and delivered arguments in relation to Canadian legal matters.

[16] I am not invoking the idea of an 'exceptional moment' *outside* of law in the sense that Schmitt and Agamben use it. Giorgio Agamben, *State of Exception* (Chicago, IL: Chicago University Press, 2005).

[17] *In re Board of Commerce Act* [1922] AC 191 (PC); *In Re Employment of Aliens*, (1922) 63 SCR 293; *The Attorney General of Ontario v The Attorney General of Canada and others (Canada)* [1937] UKPC 6 [*Labour Conventions*]; *Reference re Firearms Act (Can.)*, [2000] 1 SCR 783.

[18] *Edwards v Canada (AG)* [1930] AC 124, [1929] UKPC 86.

[19] *Re: Resolution to Amend the Constitution*, [1981] 1 SCR 753.

[20] *Re BC Motor Vehicle Act*, [1985] 2 SCR 486.

[21] *Reference re Secession of Quebec*, [1998] 2 SCR 217.

[22] *Reference re Supreme Court Act, ss. 5 and 6*, 2014 SCC 21, [2014] 1 SCR 433.

[23] *Reference re Senate Reform*, 2014 SCC 32.

[24] Barry L Strayer, *The Canadian Constitution and the Courts* (Toronto: Butterworths, 1998) 311. Strayer cites 91 advisory opinions of 352 decisions issued between 1867 and 1986.

Nor do I argue that references are inherently 'weightier' than cases.[25] The Supreme Court exercises a great deal of discretion in deciding which cases to hear.[26] While some cases are guaranteed a hearing, most are not; and the Court selects from among the applications using a somewhat vague criterion of 'national importance' that, because leave decisions are not accompanied by reasons,[27] has never been the subject of authoritative case law. It would certainly seem that the Court *itself* regards the cases it chooses to hear as momentous.

My purpose in this book is different. References, I argue, raise intriguing questions about the legal system in which they operate; about the motivations and strategies of the actors who initiate and participate in them; about the role of the court that produces them; and about the way that a society understands something as being 'law'. Yet, for all their variety, history, singular nature and impact, references have attracted markedly little attention in legal scholarship. To be sure, where individual advisory opinions deal with highly controversial or dramatic issues, they attract attention, scrutiny and analysis. But, with few exceptions, Canadian references are mostly analysed for their content,[28] as opposed to their significance *as* references.[29] They deserve more focussed scrutiny than has been the case.

***

The book proceeds in three general parts.

The first part, spanning Chapters 1–4, provides both conceptual and some historical grounding for the discussion.

Chapter 1 introduces several ideas and concepts. It begins by looking at what courts generally are understood to do: adjudicate cases. Adjudication is linked to the courts' relationship with other arms of the state. That relationship, the separation of powers, has influenced what courts are expected both to do and to refrain from doing. The remaining chapters will show the limitations of that idea.

Chapters 2 and 3 are historical in nature. They situate the advisory opinion in the Canadian legal system, and begin to explain its role. Chapter 2 describes aspects of the British legal tradition that would prove formative to the legal

[25] This was not always the case, particularly in late 19th and early 20th centuries. The *Reference re Refund of Dues Paid under s. 47 (f.) of Timber Regulations*, [1933] SCR 617 concerned a very narrow question regarding the remission of timber duties. In modern times, however, references generally are initiated to address questions that are especially controversial or thought to engage important issues.

[26] SC 1974-75-76, c 18; Supreme Court Act, RSC, 1985, c S-26 s 40.

[27] *Rules of the Supreme Court of Canada* (SOR/2002-156) Part V.

[28] See David Schneiderman (ed), *The Quebec Decision: Perspectives on the Supreme Court Ruling on Secession* (Davidson NC: Lorimer Press, 1999); Sujit Choudhry and Robert Howse, 'Constitutional Theory and the Quebec Secession Reference' (2000) XIII Canadian Journal of Law and Jurisprudence 143.

[29] François Chevrette and Gregoire Charles N Webber, 'L'Utilisation de la Procédure de l'Avis Consultatif devant la Cour Suprême du Canada: Essai de Typologie' (2003) 82 Canadian Bar Review 757.

system ushered in by Canadian Confederation. It discusses the role of the Judicial Committee of the Privy Council and its own advisory function, which provided the template for the Canadian Supreme Court.

Chapter 3 examines the Supreme Court's reference function. It looks at why its inclusion in the 1875 Supreme Court and Exchequer Court Act was controversial. Canadian provinces were gravely concerned that the federal government would abuse it. As well, there was a more fundamental worry about situating an 'advisory' and an 'appellate' function in a single body. The chapter discusses early judicial and legislative decisions that sought both to appease provincial concerns, and to reconcile the divergent functions of 'advice' and 'judgment'.

Taking up in more detail some of the arguments introduced in Chapter 1, Chapter 4 examines how an advisory function can affect the separation of powers. First, in asking or requiring courts to do more than adjudicate live cases, references could extend the judicial function beyond its proper boundaries. The concern is heightened when a court, such as the Canadian Supreme Court, already exerts significant influence in the constitutional order. Second, when the power to initiate references rests exclusively in the executive branch, a sort of 'capture' can result. That can complicate the relationship with the legislature, particularly, as will be explained, in a parliamentary system.

The second part, Chapters 5–8, looks at references as both legally and politically exceptional moments. In many countries, including Canada, the boundaries between law and politics have become blurred. Courts exert great influence over what used to be considered matters solely within the purview of expressly political actors. They frequently consider the limits on the state's ability to frame certain policies; they review state initiatives passed or authorised to achieve those objectives; and they impose judgments that may run contrary to the wishes of democratic majorities.[30]

Applying a thematic approach rooted in the history of a court operating in a specific legal system, these chapters consider how references can not only shape the law, but be invoked *in* political debate as a necessary mechanism to determine – and, in some cases, to predetermine – political accountability. The chapters suggest that the reference function has contributed to the role of the Canadian Supreme Court as a 'provider of answers'. The implications of that role are discussed in the book's final chapter.

Chapter 5 examines the role of references in what the Supreme Court's creators likely assumed would be its chief focus: arbitrating federalism. Examining both early topics such as the scope of disallowance, the location of the treaty

[30] Judicial invalidation of statutes is dramatic whenever it occurs. But such moments should not be overstated. Even in countries with highly active courts, governments tend to prevail in constitutional challenges. See Christopher Manfredi and James B Kelly, 'Misrepresenting the Supreme Court's Record? A Comment on Sujit Choudhry and Claire E Hunter, "Measuring Judicial Activism on the Supreme Court of Canada"' 2004 (49) *McGill Law Journal* 741–64; Christopher Manfredi, 'Conservatives, the Supreme Court, and the Constitution: Judicial-Government Relations, 2006–15' (2015) 52 Osgoode Hall Law Journal 951–83.

power and norms of interpretation, as well as more modern disputes over natural resources and criminal law, the chapter highlights how the Court's arbiter role was abetted by its advisory function.

Chapter 6 discusses how the reference function affected, and even shaped, critical moments in Canada's constitutional development. It begins with the 1949 shift from the Judicial Committee to the Supreme Court as the country's final court of appeal. It then discusses the advisory opinions that ushered in a new constitutional era in 1982, when Canada took full control over the amendment process from the UK and instituted new rights and procedures.[31]

Chapters 7 and 8 discuss advisory opinions post 1982. Chapter 7 looks at the relationship between advisory opinions and constitutional rights. Chapter 8 looks at a number of advisory opinions that have had tremendous impact on certain institutional elements of Canadian constitutional law. These chapters show how the advisory function has cemented the Court's role as a *provider of answers* – one which extends to all of its rulings whether advisory or not.

Alexander Hamilton, an American statesman and one of the 'Founding Fathers' of the United States, famously wrote that the courts have neither the power of the purse, nor the sword.[32] Courts have a special vulnerability: they operate outside the boundaries of practical political power. And yet, when they decide cases, courts do wield considerable authority that is recognised, invoked and respected. Does this authority apply to references in the same way and, if so, why? Is it due simply to the fear of consequences for non-compliance? A political calculation based on the belief that it is best when political opponents agree to respect decisions of external arbiters? Is it what the British legal scholar HLA Hart referred to as the 'internal point of view'[33] analogous to the reasons that players of a game respect the rules? Or, is it something else entirely?

The final part of the book, Chapters 9 and 10, examines more closely the asserted core distinction between advisory opinions and cases. References are said to be 'advisory' rather than binding or coercive. Yet officials and institutions, including courts, do not treat them that way. That is so even when a reference produces a result that the initiating actor finds highly undesirable. That is so even when the court itself is divided about the answer to a reference question. Why? Focussing on, respectively, non-judicial and judicial actors, these chapters suggest broader insights that can be gleaned from Canada's experience with the reference function.

Chapter 9 considers the non-judicial actors who initiate, participate in and react to advisory opinions. It canvasses the reasons that they might trigger an

[31] As a constitutional monarchy, Canada's head of state is still Elizabeth II. However, since 1982 Canada's decision to remain a monarchy or become a republic has been governed by its own constitutional rules, specifically Part V of the Constitutional Act 1982 and constitutional amendment, in particular s 41.

[32] Alexander Hamilton, *The Federalist Papers*, No 78.

[33] HLA Hart, *The Concept of Law* (Oxford: Oxford University Press, 1961) 87.

advisory opinion; and why, having done so, they generally treat the resulting opinion as containing reasons for action. It notes the reasons why one might expect these actors to *decline* to comply, at least on occasion. It concludes, however, that a number of powerful considerations ultimately mean that such actors do, in fact, comply.

One of those considerations is that an advisory opinion is in many respects *indistinguishable* from a decision resulting from the end of ordinary litigation. It makes little difference to a party's legal position, and to likely future consequences, whether a judicial resolution is expressed as one or the other. That is, chiefly, because courts *themselves* do not draw such distinctions. Chapter 10 examines why that is.

Chapter 10 argues that advisory opinions have become part of Canadian constitutional common law.[34] The influence of the common law helps to explain how reference opinions can be captured under the doctrine of *stare decisis*. This probably explains, too, why reference opinions that are themselves divided[35] and not unanimous have little effect on their precedential effect. The chapter explains how such a development occurred, *despite* the insistence in early references that it was 'unthinkable' that courts would ever consider themselves bound by their advisory opinions.

The distinction, in the epistemic sense, between how the legal system *classifies* references versus how it *deals* with them is telling. References suggest where the real power of the court lies. References demonstrate that the true significance of the judicial function is its ability to *provide answers*, to declare what law is – that this is more important even than the ability to compel actors to do, and forbear from doing, certain things. This may be an inevitable result when a common law legal system entrusts questions of legality to the courts.

Advisory opinions are not unique to Canada. As noted above, they are frequently issued by formal constitutional courts, as well by international tribunals. The book occasionally refers to those processes. It also tries to avoid presuming the common law, Anglo-American or Canadian legal experience to be a universal lens for understanding law and legal systems. All the same, the discussion focuses heavily on Canada, its Anglo-American heritage and its common law precepts. A fundamental premise of this book is that 'the law' exists within a particular social, historical and political context. Setting forth that context occupies a good number of the chapters below, but a number of the other chapters aim to show how the Canadian experience contains lessons that go beyond

[34] Canada is bi-juridical: the province of Quebec remains a civilian jurisdiction with regard to its own legal rules. Since 1763, though, the public law has been governed by British rather than French rules. Thus, the term 'common law' is accurate when speaking of Canadian constitutional law, which dominates the vast majority of Canadian advisory opinions.

[35] Unlike the Judicial Committee, the Supreme Court of Canada never observed the practice of issuing a single opinion. The JCPC itself abandoned that tradition in 1966 but by then it had ceased to operate as a court of appeal for Canada.

its own legal borders. In short, this is not a book of comparative law, but it is intended to provide larger insights.

Finally, a note about word usage. This book examines a system and legal tradition in which references and cases are thought to be distinct. Although the book ultimately questions whether that is so, the discussion warrants some precision in terminology. As much as possible, then, cases but not references are referred to as involving 'judgments', 'decisions' and 'verdicts'. Other than to illustrate exceptions, the words 'holding', 'finding' and 'remedy' also are reserved for cases. References are described as 'advising' or 'opining'. I believe that the words 'conclusion' and 'answer' apply to both references and cases. For reasons that are explored in the final chapter, I say the same for the word 'declare' and will use it accordingly.

1

Courts *with* Cases

This book is about what it means for a legal system to permit courts to issue advisory opinions. Drawing on the experience of a particular country, Canada, it contrasts advisory opinions with the other function of courts, namely deciding *cases*. The title of this work, after all, posits the idea of courts 'without' cases. That is an intentional reference to the fact that the advisory function quite often is understood to be separate and apart, in some way, from the case-deciding one.

But why would that be so? Why isn't an advisory opinion just a different *kind* of case? Or, to put it another way, why aren't cases and advisory opinions part of some larger category of legal phenomena?

It will become clear in later chapters that the above questions hint at the better view. That is to say, cases and advisory opinions are, indeed, part of a larger whole. In order, though, to see the strength of that conclusion, it is necessary to address the traditional view that advisory opinions and decisions really are different.

This chapter begins by asking how courts are understood – what they generally *do*. It posits that fundamental to understanding courts is their function of adjudication. The chapter describes that function along with certain assumed defining and limiting features of it. It then suggests that the adjudicative function of courts is linked, at least in part, to the courts' relationship with other arms of the state. That relationship, the separation of powers, has not only influenced what courts are expected to do, but has also shaped beliefs about what they should *not* do. Those expectations encourage the idea not just that advisory opinions and cases are distinct, but that the latter alone is an *appropriate* function for the courts. The remainder of the book will show the limitations of that idea as illustrated by the Canadian example.

What Do Courts Do?

The question of what courts, typically, do is of course difficult to answer in any kind of universal sense. 'What courts do' invariably depends on their broader context and surroundings. For example: does a court operate in a unitary or federal state? What legal tradition (for example, common law or civilian) does it follow? Does the underlying legal system have a Constitution? Is that Constitution written, unwritten or a combination of the two? Does the court operate in a hierarchical relationship with other courts, or as a singular body? Does it exercise jurisdiction over more than one country, like the European Court of Human Rights?

It is not possible to investigate court functions across all of those cross-cutting lines. Nor does this chapter argue that there is one set of features that applies to all courts. Instead it draws upon a particular subset of courts, namely those operating in common law systems (though it does acknowledge others). The subset includes most of the United Kingdom,[1] the United States, Australia, New Zealand, Ireland and of course Canada. Having said that, a number of the observations below would apply to many other courts in many other systems.

Whatever else courts in those systems do, they are closely identified with the function of adjudication. That is, they resolve disputes between parties. They do so through a formalised process. While the active participation of the parties is not necessarily required it is almost always facilitated: parties are afforded some opportunity to advocate for their interests. The person rendering the judgment is a neutral third party – a judge – who occupies that role in a permanent way and who generally does not engage in other activities. The judge is expected to make the decision in accordance with the law. And the judge is expected to offer reasons showing that consistency. The decisions that emerge from the process just defined are understood as cases.

Adjudication, broadly speaking, is a form of dispute resolution. One of the things that makes it distinctive compared to other models of dispute resolution is its coercive character. The consent of the parties is not required for a court's judgment to be enforceable. The court's decision is backed by the power of the state – indeed, as explained further in this chapter, it is appropriate to view the court as an arm of the state.

At least two points bear mentioning. First, this classical understanding of adjudication involves a trial court presided over by a single judge. Of course, in all of the systems being considered, there are other courts; in particular, appellate courts, which exist mainly to review and 'correct' lower court decisions and to set out broader legal principles.[2] The appellate function involves certain variations from ordinary adjudication – for example, a limited ability to review factual questions. Appeals also tend to involve multi-member panels. Throughout this book, the term 'case' nonetheless includes all of the court levels at which that case might be heard before it is considered to be finally resolved.

The second point is that the scope of issues considered appropriate for courts to decide *as* cases varies greatly even in the smaller subset of common law systems noted above, and such variation only increases once other systems are included.

[1] Scotland retains its own civil law system.

[2] Not all case-related decisions can be appealed; nor, in most of the systems being discussed, is there an explicit guarantee of appellate review. Nonetheless, and particularly in criminal cases, most systems do provide a mechanism for error correction.

In particular, the ability of courts to adjudicate issues involving other arms of the state – in other words, judicial or constitutional review – depends on a myriad of other factors. Conversely, advisory opinions commonly *are* sought for issues of constitutional law and most of the topics covered in later chapters are related in some way to constitutional laws and conventions. The idea of a 'constitutional case' is hardly universal. Such cases, though, *are* common in Canada, in many common law systems, and increasingly in other systems as well.

The Power, and Limits, of Cases

All kinds of cases arrive before courts, from the mundane and quotidian to the historic. They include traffic violations, child custody battles, sexual assault trials and constitutional challenges. The adjudicative function, the cases that courts decide, and the parameters under which they decide them, means that courts play an extremely important role in almost every society. Disputes can have high stakes. The parties may be arguing over millions of dollars; the dispute may be a class action involving thousands of people; a person may face life imprisonment. Leaving such cases aside, though, courts are involved in a vast range of disputes that would otherwise be resolved by the parties themselves – and perhaps go unsettled. Almost every society acknowledges that human relations require some sort of regulation by law: to coordinate human interaction for society's benefit and protection; and to provide a means of non-violent, predictable and fair dispute resolution.

Nonetheless, there are limits to the role of courts. For example, courts are essentially *passive* with respect to the cases that come before them. Claims must have an essentially *legal* character. And legal claims must relate to some *dispute* between persons or entities deemed to occupy an *oppositional* or *adversarial* relationship. Further, a court is expected to deliver a remedy that is within the confines of, and *enforceable* in accordance with, law. A few other rules and elements, like the doctrine of standing, will be touched on in later chapters.

Together, these limits inform, and are informed by, the concept of *justiciability*. And the idea of justiciability is built into the concept of the 'case'. To the extent that courts are limited to deciding 'cases', then, their ability to intervene in human disputes and, therefore, to invoke the authority of the law to compel a particular outcome, is constrained.

The justiciability doctrine is thought to ensure, at least in part, that courts stay within their 'proper' boundaries. (It is therefore linked to the separation of powers, discussed below.) It acknowledges the need to limit 'the scope of judicial intervention in social, political and economic life'.[3] If a court routinely sought out

[3] Lorne Sossin, *Boundaries of Judicial Review: The Law of Justiciability in Canada*, 2nd edn (Toronto: Thompson Reuters, 2012) 7.

disputes to decide, if it dispensed with any pretence of requiring a legal basis for its pronouncements, if it eschewed the need to stick at least somewhat reasonably close to what other courts have decided in the past – if it did those things often enough, it would cease to function in the way generally thought necessary for it to be a court. As the Canadian scholar Lorne Sossin puts it, the doctrine of justiciability 'defines the boundaries between our legal and political systems'.[4] It is one way that the courts' otherwise immense power is curtailed, winnowed and made predictable. In the remainder of this section, I will make some brief comments about each of the limitations entailed by the doctrine.

The first element, mentioned above, is that courts are passive. Generally, they do not initiate legal cases.[5] They do not scan the landscape, seize upon a particular issue, and then compel people to appear before them to argue it.[6] It is possible to imagine a system where courts might behave like that, or at least take a more active role.[7] Inquisitorial systems permit a much broader investigatory function for judicial officers.[8] In some systems, ordinary courts may refer constitutional issues to separate constitutional courts. But even those courts generally observe limits to their self-initiated participation.

An important reason why courts wait to be asked is that they are expected to maintain neutrality regarding the disputes and parties before them. Courts may well be 'interested' in the outcome to the extent that they try to ensure that it is consistent with relevant law or legal principles. Otherwise, courts are assumed and expected to be detached from the proceedings. Such detachment would be challenging for a court to maintain, and almost impossible for others to accept, if the court initiated the proceedings in which it subsequently gave judgment.

It is very hard to imagine a circumstance where it would be thought right for a court to initiate a case in which it would then sit as the decision maker. Overwhelmingly, courts do not do that, even if the society in which they are situated is

[4] ibid at 2.

[5] Peter Russell, *The Judiciary in Canada: The Third Branch of Government* (Toronto: McGraw Hill, 1987) 5.

[6] An exception exists for powers deemed essential to the court's ability to maintain control over its processes and which exist independent of statute. Historically, this includes the power to punish for contempt of court and to initiate proceedings to maintain access to the courts, such as when entrance to them is impeded by protestors: *BCGEU v British Columbia (Attorney General)*, [1988] 2 SCR 214.

[7] An example is the Indian Supreme Court's remarkable 'epistolary function': see Michael D Gilbert and Mauricio A Guim, 'Active Virtues' 28 July 2018 (unpublished manuscript on file with author). Responding to the enormous poverty and access to justice concerns in their country, Indian judges began converting letters, postcards and the like into formal petitions for relief. Jamie Cassels, 'Judicial Activism and Public Interest Litigation in India: Attempting the Impossible' (1989) 37 American Journal of Comparative Law 495. See, inter alia, *Sunil Batra v Delhi Administration* (1978) 4 SCC 409; *Hussainara Khatoon v Bihar* AIR 1979 SC 1377.

[8] IF Sheppard, 'The Issue of the Inquisitorial System of Justice' (1999) 31 Australian Journal of Forensic Sciences 19–28; *Charkaoui v Canada (Citizenship and Immigration)*, [2007] 1 SCR 350, 2007 SCC 9 at para 50.

facing a true crisis and many people are clamouring for them to act.[9] The gravity of a particular problem is almost never sufficient justification for the courts to seek to become part of the solution. Courts wait to be asked.[10]

Not only do courts wait to be asked before they take up a dispute, but they generally follow certain additional preconditions. One such precondition is the second limitation mentioned above: courts are creatures of law. Courts render decisions of a particular, legal character. They intervene only in a disagreement that is, in some way, amenable *to* the law.

The second limitation is critical to understanding cases. Human disputes are inherently multifaceted, engaging not just legal concepts, but ethical, moral and factual ones. But not all of those are considered apt for judicial intervention. Conflicts over etiquette or manners, in most societies, are regarded as unsuitable subjects for adjudication. One does not seek an injunction prohibiting a fellow congregant from wearing a baseball hat in church, or damages against a stranger for cutting in line at an amusement park. In 2014 a Canadian man named Randy Wall sought judicial review of a decision by the Judicial Committee of the Highwood Congregation of Jehovah's Witnesses. The Congregation had 'disfellowshipped', or excommunicated, him. Wall argued that the decision, which had caused him both personal and professional harm, was procedurally unfair. Two lower courts thought that the case should be considered on its merits – they were prepared to examine whether the decision had in fact been unfair. The Supreme Court of Canada disagreed. The Court focussed on what it called the theological underpinning of the dispute, namely whether Wall had departed sufficiently from the tenets of his religion to merit the penalty of disfellowship. Such a question, the Court ruled, was non-justiciable. It was not for it to intervene in matters concerning religious doctrine, regardless of whether the particular matter may have been carried out in a way that was procedurally inadequate or, indeed, unfair.[11]

The third general limit on cases follows from the second. Cases must involve a *dispute*. Courts provide one of society's most visible means of dispute resolution. Inasmuch as they are conceived of primarily as providing solutions to *conflict*, courts, and the cases they decide, require an adversarial context. Individuals commonly go to court because they wish to invoke the authority of the law in

[9] A famous illustration of this point is what many consider to be the failure of apartheid-era South African courts to properly respond to the unlawful nature of the regime: Jeremy Sarkin, 'The Common Law in South Africa: Pro Apartheid or Pro Democracy' (1999) 23 Hastings International & Comparative Law Review 1.

[10] This is a feature, as well, of many specialist constitutional courts: Donald P Kommers and Russell A Miller, '*Das Bundesverfassungsgericht*: Procedure, Practice and Policy of the German Federal Constitutional Court' (2008) 3 Journal of Comparative Law 194, 207.

[11] *Highwood Congregation of Jehovah's Witnesses (Judicial Committee) v Wall*, 2018 SCC 26. For a somewhat competing analysis, see *Bruker v Marcovitz*, [2007] 3 SCR 607, 2007 SCC 54 where a majority of the Supreme Court found that a woman could sue her former husband for breach of contract after he refused to grant a previously negotiated Jewish divorce.

order to provide the ultimate vindication of their claims; to secure endorsement of a particular legal position; or to seek recompense of some kind. All of those things involve the individual ranging themselves against someone, or something, else. In that way, one speaks of the courts ensuring that legal rights, obligations, powers and privileges are respected.

In settling disputes, courts help to ensure social peace and harmony. But they do so by intervening in situations where rights, obligations, powers and privileges are in some way threatened or have already been triggered. At that point, one may seek court settlement. Even then, the courts can intervene only so long as the threat is active, or if a past infraction is amenable to a response governed by law. If, by the time the matter reaches a court, intervening events have rendered the core of the dispute no longer active, then, in most systems, a court generally will be expected to decline to hear argument and, consequently, decline to pronounce judgment.[12]

The latter limit can be understood through a number of doctrines including 'ripeness' or 'prematurity' on one hand, and 'mootness' on the other.[13] Their unifying element is that courts generally limit adjudication to live disputes. The distinction between them (ripeness requires a dispute to have arisen, while mootness means that the dispute is no longer a live one) is not pertinent to the current discussion.

The third limitation has different applications depending on whether a case involves only private parties, or the state as well; and, as will become clear throughout this book, the degree to which an 'adversarial' context obtains. Consider, first, how the limit might apply in a private law case. Imagine a dispute between two landowners of adjacent properties. Rachel plans to erect a shed that Steven believes will intrude on his land. Steven initiates a lawsuit in order to stop her. There is a clear dispute between parties who stand in opposition to one another. Steven might secure the assistance of friends or associates to intimidate or prevent Rachel from proceeding. But that would be an undesirable action that would only provoke further conflict and is likely for that reason to be unlawful in itself. Instead, if the two cannot resolve the matter peacefully between themselves, the path open to them is to take the matter to court, present their respective case and receive a legal answer.

If Rachel sells the property and removes all traces of the shed, and assuming that her prior actions have not altered Steven's land, the original boundary dispute will be moot. It will not matter if Steven would much prefer that the case go ahead because he would like to obtain a judicial verdict as to the actual physical boundaries of his property.[14] Nor will it matter if Steven reasonably believes that the

[12] Courts have observed this third limit more or less strictly, depending on the circumstances. For a good overview, see Sossin (n 3) chapters 2 and 3.

[13] See G Nichol, 'Ripeness and the Constitution' (1987) 54 University of Chicago Law Review 153. Canadian cases include *Borowski v Canada (Attorney General)*, [1989] 1 SCR 342.

[14] Occasionally, the law does permit a petition to proceed without an opposing party. See the famous case of *Re Drummond Wren* [1945] OR 778 (Ont HC) where an Ontario court refused to grant the

person to whom Rachel has sold the property will pursue the same shed improvement plan and he, Steven, will face the same headache. The dispute is particular to the conflict between Rachel and Steven and only in the context of its continuing status is the court likely to agree to hear it.[15] Steven is free to retain the services of a land surveyor in order to be armed with evidence in the case of a future transgression. He also may be entitled to file that survey in, say, a land registry that will provide independent proof of his rights. But, because his rights are no longer subject to a continuing *threat*, he is no longer at liberty to seek a court judgment to vindicate them.[16]

In a dispute involving the state, a similar analysis applies although it may involve additional considerations. A good example is criminal justice. Suppose that after the state commences a prosecution for murder the defendant dies. There is no question that the trial will be moot and the Crown will withdraw the charges. This is such a basic principle that, in Canada, it had not been considered necessary to spell it out. The country's Criminal Code has provisions related to the presence of the accused; situations in which the accused may participate through video conference; and the power to continue a trial where the accused has absconded (an accused who has 'absconded' is, by definition, alive).[17] There is even a rule relating to the use of witness testimony after their death. But there is no explicit rule stating that the trial ends if the accused dies prior to the verdict. Nonetheless, it is a virtual certainty that in such a circumstance the case will not proceed.

As with the private law example, it will not matter if the defendant's family or, for that matter, the victim's, fervently desires the trial to continue – because, perhaps, they believe it vitally important to determine what happened. The state's interest in a criminal trial lies not just in ascertaining whether a particular individual is guilty or not guilty, but in providing for a judgment *upon* that person – in visiting consequences upon him or her. Most societies do not turn to the criminal courts to provide legal condemnation, or vindication, of people who are not, at least theoretically, amenable to justice.[18]

Some may find the above analysis unsatisfactory. In the private dispute just discussed, mootness may be a legitimate conclusion because the threat

owner's wish to have a restrictive covenant placed on his land to prevent its eventual sale to 'Jews' or 'other objectionable persons'. Note, though, that the reasoning was considered but not followed in *Noble v Alley*, [1951] SCR 64.

[15] Depending on the jurisdiction, and the extent of pre-trial preparations, Steven might be able to seek reimbursement of his expenses.

[16] I leave aside the particular circumstances in which a party may seek an injunction to constrain future activity.

[17] Criminal Code, RSC 1985 C c-46 ss 560, 475.

[18] More could be said here about the way that death affects legal personality. Certainly, there is a sense in which death does not act as a bar to a person's continued presence in a community. Reputation, legacy and memory matter. There are, as well, ancient proscriptions that accord due respect and dignity to the body of a deceased person that suggest that death does not end one's social value and meaning.

to Steven's property interest vanishes when Rachel decides to sell the property. Assuming that Steven has not suffered any tangible damage, there appears to be *nothing further to be litigated*. But the criminal context seems different. For one thing, a trial always occurs *after* alleged wrongdoing. Even if a defendant has died, there likely is a victim who has suffered a wrong. Calling out such behaviour may be, in itself, a critical role for the criminal justice system. For some, it may be as or even more important than the function of providing specific deterrence to the individual by punishing him. This is especially so when the vast majority of criminal offences are not prosecuted; and those that are often settle prior to trial. It is quite reasonable to think that the resolution that is uniquely provided by the criminal justice system – the finality, solemnity and legal certainty of a verdict – is achievable and legitimate whether the defendant is alive or dead.

This book cannot fully evaluate that objection. There are reasonable arguments for it. The *ex post facto* nature of certain proceedings may affect the analysis of mootness and, consequently, the appropriateness of continued judicial involvement. It may matter, for example, whether the legal system is being harnessed in order to vindicate a wrong that is personal as opposed to societal. When someone alleges that she has suffered a wrong, for which the law offers a remedy, the offender's death will not necessarily vacate her claim. Its continuation will depend, at least in part, on whether the desired remedy can still be enforced. If a plaintiff seeks a personal apology, death bars that possibility. If, however, the plaintiff seeks financial compensation, death may not end the matter. For example, if the alleged wrongdoer has an estate, it is perfectly sensible to argue that legal claims remain open to the plaintiff (at least for a period of time).

Even so, the criminal trial is different. Generally, trials do not vindicate wrongs done to victims. Trials are a social, not personal, enterprise.[19] The manner in which criminal trials seek vindication for societal wrongs demands the accused person's continued existence, if not participation, as a *sine qua non* to the proceeding being understood to *be* a trial. It is, of course, important that the defendant be able to participate because the legal system guarantees to him or her many personal rights and procedural protections that are necessary to trial fairness and, thereby, the integrity of the proceeding. But, additionally, the core function of the criminal justice system is to make individual persons accountable to society for wrongful behaviour. As mentioned above, this is closely tied to the goal of imposing consequences for that behaviour (and is thus linked to remedy, discussed below). That debt cannot be calculated, or repaid, without the defendant.

The criminal trial does not exist as an academic exercise. Perhaps there is a way in which it might do so. One can think of instances in which it might assume

[19] Andrew Ashforth and Jeremy Horder, *Principles of Criminal Law* (Oxford: Oxford University Press, 2013) ch 2. This was not always the case, as made clear by the history of private prosecutions: Peter Burns, 'Private Prosecutions in Canada: The Law and a Proposal for Change' (1975) 21 McGill Law Journal 269; William Searle Holdsworth, 3 *A History of English Law*, 6th edn (London: Methuen, 1938).

such a character[20] or where, at least, the demand that it do so would be understandable. But such possibilities lie far beyond general perceptions of the purpose of a criminal trial, at least in the legal systems familiar to most readers. In those systems, it is unacceptable to continue proceedings where the accused is no longer amenable to justice. In any event, it would be unthinkable for a *judge* seized of the matter to insist on continuing out of some conviction that that is what justice requires.

The final limit is that a court is expected to provide a certain *kind* of resolution to the dispute at hand. When it hears a case, a court is expected to pronounce some kind of *remedy*, or outcome, that is *legally enforceable*. In order to trigger the state's coercive power, a case must be able to provide a resolution that the parties to the dispute are expected, and can be forced, to obey.[21]

There are two related factors at work. First, a claimant can only ask for a remedy that is consistent with the court's character as an institution of, and nested in, law.[22] In the words of one American scholar, he must invoke a 'controversy … which the courts can finally and effectively decide, under tests and standards which they can soundly administer within their special field of competence'.[23]

Examples would include ordering the termination of certain proceedings, or that others begin again (such as a trial or administrative hearing); admitting or excluding evidence; imposing a term of imprisonment; awarding damages; or granting an injunction against certain acts.

In a civil case, a claimant may long for all sorts of things to be done for her, and against her wrongdoer. Even in victory, she is not necessarily entitled to them, even if she has been horribly wronged and the particular remedy she seeks would go far to mitigating her sense of victimisation. For example, in a defamation lawsuit, while the plaintiff may seek a verdict that she has been defamed, she may not seek a general declaration of her good character. In a divorce settlement, while she may seek conditions of support, disposition of assets or custody of minor children, she may not seek an order prohibiting her former spouse from marrying again or having future children.

The second factor relevant to the remedial feature is that there must be legal means to force compliance with whatever the court orders. That requirement arises because the remedy must have a legal character. But it goes further than that. It enjoins a court from imposing a remedy that, in the circumstances, the court has no confidence will be enforced. Such a situation may arise where

[20] For a cautionary tale, consider Russia's posthumous trial of Sergei Magnitsky, which has been condemned as vindictive and politically motivated: www.reuters.com/article/uk-russia-magnitsky-idUKBRE96A09N20130711.

[21] An exception to this is the declaratory action, whereby the Court declares a certain state of affairs but does not join it to a particular order. Such actions are discussed in Chapter 10.

[22] See, eg, *R v Her Majesty's Attorney General ex parte Rusbridger et al* [2003] UKHL 38 at [21].

[23] Alexander Bickel, 'The Supreme Court 1960 Term: Foreword: The Passive Virtues' (1961–62) 75 Harvard Law Review 41, 75.

an entity is not under the court's practical authority. In 2010 the Supreme Court of Canada drew that conclusion in a case involving a Canadian man, Omar Khadr, being held in Guantanamo Bay, Cuba.[24] Khadr sought to have the Canadian government repatriate him back to Canada. For years the federal government refused, notwithstanding that it was generally understood that the United States government was prepared to comply with such a request. While the Supreme Court recognised the underling justice of Khadr's claim, it declined to issue the order because it had no confidence that the order could be satisfied. The Court could order a Canadian official to seek Khadr's return but the physical act of repatriation depended on the cooperation of the US government, over which the Court had no authority. To be sure, the Court *did* grant a remedy of sorts. It issued a declaration that outlined the ways in which Khadr's rights had been infringed, and indicated what would be required to rectify that infringement. But it refused to do anything more.

The above limits are not necessarily universal. They do not apply to every court that exists or that has existed. Nor are they static even within those systems in which they do have purchase. They are dynamic: they expand, or contract, in accordance with how a particular society evolves its understanding of the meaning of 'legality'. Nonetheless, they reasonably describe the function of courts in the ordinary course of adjudication.

Where do the above-noted limits on cases come from? Is it necessarily undesirable for courts to operate in their absence? One answer is that the limits may be prescribed as basic norms, for example, through a Constitution.[25] Often, and especially in common law systems, they are created, and enforced, by the courts themselves. In a deeper sense, the limits arise because of long-standing traditions about how courts ought to behave, not just within their own sphere of activity, but in relation to *other* public institutions. That relationship is understood, generally, as the separation of powers.

The Separation of Powers

The separation of powers is a doctrine that sets out how the various entities that wield state power – including courts – should function, both singly and in relation to each other. There are many different versions of the doctrine, which is inescapably political. But the core of the doctrine, whatever the particular version on offer, is that the state is optimally divided into three branches of government – legislative, executive and judicial – and that each branch should stay in its respective 'lane'. The legislative branch has primary, and usually exclusive, authority to create positive legal rules. The executive branch is charged with

[24] *Canada (Prime Minister) v Khadr*, 2010 SCC 3, [2010] 1 SCR 44.

[25] Article III of the US Constitution, which limits the jurisdiction of federal courts to hear 'cases and controversies', is one of the best examples.

administering those rules, as well as any number of other tasks (which may themselves be either delegated or conferred by statute). Finally, the judicial branch is charged with interpreting and applying legal rules in a variety of contexts.

The concept of separating government functions goes back (at least) to the origins of Western political thought. In the *Politics*, Aristotle identified deliberative, magistral and judicial elements of government action.[26] Even so, the idea of *three* distinct branches of the state was not a common feature of early accounts, which tended not to distinguish between executive and judicial functions.[27] Indeed, American political scientist Martin Shapiro has described the modern focus, in separation of powers doctrine, on the institutional separation of courts as 'the most deviant case'.[28]

In the smaller set of legal systems being considered here, the slow emergence of the judiciary was in part due to the fact that, for centuries, the English King was the 'fount of justice' – 'the head and fountain of the power which governs and executes the established law'.[29] It took time for that power to be dispersed, and this first happened with respect to Parliament (a development discussed in Chapter 2).[30] Indeed, Parliament was itself a kind of court.[31] From that arose the term 'King-in-Parliament': a personage necessary to legislative functions, but largely passive as regards them.[32]

As the law increasingly came to be viewed as a product of 'orders' and not custom,[33] the legislature grew more powerful. In the ensuing tumult, some thinkers and political theorists, fearful of tyranny,[34] increasingly favoured the separation of government functions. Indeed, it is interesting to note that the separation of powers was invoked as a safeguard against untrammelled democracy. Similar fears inspired American founders such as James Madison to propose a representative, rather than direct, system of democratic decision making. That sense, of course, persists today as regards the special province of the courts.

[26] Aristotle, *Politics* IV 14; MCJ Vile, *Constitutionalism and the Separation of Powers* (Oxford: Clarendon Press, 1967) 21–22: 'The major division here between legislation and action was not the modern distinction between legislative and executive, for the Greeks did not envisage the continuous or even frequent creation of new law which is implicit in the modern view of the legislative function'.

[27] Vile (n 26) 28–29, citing Bishop John Poynet, James Harrington, Algernon Sidney and Marchamont Nedham.

[28] Martin Shapiro, *Courts: A Comparative and Political Analysis* (Chicago IL: University of Chicago Press, 1981) 20.

[29] Philip Hunton, *Treatise of Monarchy* 1643.

[30] Vile (n 26) 43: '[The King is bound] for the time being … by the duty of his office, to give his assent to all such laws as by the Lords and Commons assembled in Parliament, shall be adjudged to be for the Good of the Kingdom'.

[31] CH McIlwain, *The High Court of Parliament and Its Supremacy* (New Haven CT: Yale University Press, 1910).

[32] Jeffrey Goldsworthy, *The Sovereignty of Parliament: History And Philosophy* (Oxford: Clarendon Press, 1999) 9. Note John Milton's derision of the term: 'We may conclude that the Kings negative voice was never any law, but an absurd and reasonless Custom': *Eikonoklastes* (London, 1649).

[33] John Austin, *The Province of Jurisprudence Determined and the Uses of the Study of Jurisprudence* (London: Weidenfeld and Nicolson, 1954) 13.

[34] Vile (n 26) 44, 46 quoting *The Royalists Defence* (1648).

The political revolutions in seventeenth- and eighteenth-century Europe produced new models of government, attended by the writings of philosophers such as Locke and Montesquieu. Locke viewed separation as essential to the over-all popular control of government.[35] Noting the 'great temptation of human frailty [that] the same persons, who have the power of making laws, to have also in their hands the power to execute them', he argued that legislative power was best put into the hands of 'divers persons … who are themselves subject to the laws they have made'.[36]

Locke advocated the legislature's 'supremacy'[37] but not its boundless power. The legislature could not, for instance, rule arbitrarily. It was 'bound to dispense justice', as an aspect of natural law. Therefore, it could not be 'judge, interpreter, and executioner' in its own case.[38] In that sense, though he did not discuss the courts extensively, Locke acknowledged their role.

Montesquieu's innovation was to treat the act of judging (*puissance de juger*) as equivalent to other state functions. Judges were to be 'the depository of the laws'. The monarch, thus, could never be a judge without risking 'annihilating … dependent intermediate powers'.[39] He did not, though, think that judges as a class exercised much power. Judges did not decide 'the law' – they decided which facts prevailed so as to merit its application. They did not check other organs of the State, nor were they checked in return.[40]

Note that the above description of the courts evokes a particular kind of isolation in how they function. It carries familiar and modern notions of neutrality, independence and security of tenure. It also creates the expectation that courts will scrupulously avoid political discussions and activities. They will not involve themselves in matters of high policy, of redistribution or of creating positive rules of obligation. The Canadian Supreme Court has observed that the relationship between the executive/legislature and judiciary must be 'depoliticised'.[41] Any hint of political pressure on the judiciary is to be avoided and judges must be discouraged from commenting, outside of decisions, on justiciable matters.[42] Thus, the separation of powers both mandates a zone of non-interference with the judiciary and regulates its relationship with other branches.

[35] John Locke, *Second Treatise on Government* ((Indianapolis, IN: Hackett Publishing Co, 1980) s 143.

[36] ibid.

[37] ibid s 149: '[T]here can be but one supreme power, which is the legislative, to which all the rest are and must be subordinate, yet the legislative being only a fiduciary power to act for certain ends, there remains still in the people a supreme power to remove or alter the legislative, when they find the legislative act contrary to the trust reposed in them'.

[38] ibid s 136.

[39] Montesquieu, *De L'Esprit des Loix*, VI.

[40] Vile (n 26) 93.

[41] ibid.

[42] ibid at para 140.

Montesquieu paved the way for the separation of powers to become 'a universal criterion of a constitutional government'.[43] In England, though, the doctrine emerged through the idea of 'ministerial responsibility' – what the essayist William Bagehot described as the 'fusion' of the legislative and executive powers.[44] On this model, Crown ministers notionally answered to the King but their tenure depended upon the Members of Parliament.[45] The central element of government was the Cabinet – the 'standing committee of the supreme legislature'.[46]

The resulting arrangement produced 'the Matchless Constitution': a theory of government that 'dazzled observers' and for many years remained 'the ideal of foreign constitutionalists, long after it ha[d] ceased to operate in its home country'.[47] But the fusion of legislature and executive raised an obvious question; if they were *jointly* responsible for government acts, 'who was left to exercise the function of control?'[48] Indirectly, the English jurist William Blackstone suggested an answer:

> In this distinct and separate existence of *the judicial power*, in a peculiar body of men, nominated indeed, but *not removeable at pleasure*, by the crown, consists one main preservative of the public liberty; which cannot subsist long in any state, unless the administration of common justice be in some degree separated both from the legislative and also from the executive power.[49]

In America, as in Europe, the separation of powers was the product of revolution. Strong pressure emerged for a rigidly separate and republican model featuring a strict prohibition upon dual membership in the legislative and executive branches. That quality of separation may have been 'the most significant aspect of the doctrine in forming the special character of American government'.[50] Certainly, it is one of the most enduring, although it is not observed in many other systems, including parliamentary ones.

The American system of checks and balances is, of course, famous.[51] It is interesting, then, to note that in the country's early period it became a (negative)

[43] Vile (n 26) 97.

[44] Walter Bagehot, *The English Constitution* (London: CA Watts, 1964) 59.

[45] By this, I mean simply their term of government. Tenure of individual Cabinet members would depend on the Prime Minister.

[46] *A Dialogue on the Best Form of Govt* (London, 1863) 90, cited in Vile (n 23) at 215.

[47] Vile (n 26) 213; Martin Loughlin, *The British Constitution: A Very Short Introduction* (Oxford: Oxford University Press, 2013) citing James Thompson, *Liberty* (1736); see also Martin Loughlin, *Foundations of Public Law* (Oxford: Oxford University Press, 2010) 255–62.

[48] Vile (n 26) 109.

[49] William Blackstone, *Commentaries on the Laws of England* I (Oxford: Clarendon Press, 1765) 7, 269 (emphasis added).

[50] Vile (n 26) 134.

[51] See, eg, Steven G Calabresi, Mark E Berghausen and Skylar Albertson, 'The Rise and Fall of the Separation of Powers' (2012) 106(2) Northwestern University Law Review 527, 536: 'Thus, the President was given a role in the lawmaking function by virtue of his possessing the veto power. The Senate was given a role in the execution of the law through its power to confirm or reject presidential nominees for high office and through its power over treaty ratification – powers that the British Parliament

rallying cry. A key factor was the emergence of a powerful judiciary exercising constitutional review – what President Thomas Jefferson described as 'a very dangerous doctrine indeed'.[52] The judiciary was seen by its supporters as robustly independent while also curiously helpless against the other branches. As Alexander Hamilton observed, the courts wielded neither 'purse' (the power of taxation which is the special province of the legislature) nor 'sword' (the ability to wield force that belongs uniquely to the executive).[53] To detractors, of course, the judiciary's very independence cemented its illegitimacy, particularly when the courts asserted the authority to review acts of Congress for consistency with the Constitution.

The early battles between the United States Supreme Court and various Presidents[54] led to the development of theories such as coordinate construction, which rejects situating constitutional interpretation solely in the courts.[55] The theory has enjoyed something of a resurgence in late twentieth- and early twenty-first-century US political thought;[56] and has also been endorsed by some in Canada.[57] But the understanding of the judiciary as a separate and increasingly powerful branch remains for many a radical and unsettling concept.

The separation of powers strongly influences the notions of justiciability described in the first part of this chapter. The classic concern of courts – adjudication – explains their existence as a separate branch of government with respect to the application of laws made and applied by other arms of the state.

Constitutional disputes complicate the above discussion. Because constitutional rules invariably involve other branches of the state, attempting to determine

had lacked. And, the Supreme Court and the inferior federal courts were arguably given some executive power as a result of their power to issue writs of mandamus to federal executive officials – something that only the Court of King's Bench or the Court of Star Chamber could do in England because of the fiction that the King was a member of the Court of King's Bench and because of the reality of his membership on the Court of Star Chamber'.

[52] Thomas Jefferson, *Letter to William C. Jarvis*, 28 September 1820.

[53] Alexander Hamilton, *The Federalist Papers* No 78.

[54] *McCulloch v Maryland* 17 US (4 Wheat.) 316 (1819); *Worcester v Georgia* 31 US (6 Pet.) 515 (1832); Keith E Whittington, *Political Foundations of Judicial Supremacy* (Princeton NJ: Princeton University Press, 2007).

[55] Andrew Jackson: 'The opinion of the judges has no more authority over Congress than the opinion of Congress has over judges, and on that point the President is independent of both'. Bank Veto Message of 10 July 1833: http://avalon.law.yale.edu/19th_century/ajveto01.asp.

[56] Mark Tushnet, *Taking the Constitution Away from the Courts* (Princeton, NJ: Princeton University Press, 1999); Jeremy Waldron, *Law and Disagreement* (Oxford: Oxford University Press, 1999); Larry D Kramer, *The People Themselves. Popular Constitutionalism and Judicial Review* (New York: Oxford University Press, 2004).

[57] Christopher Manfredi, *Judicial Power and the Charter: Canada and the Paradox of Liberal Constitutionalism*, 2nd edn (Toronto: Oxford University Press, 2001); Janet L Hiebert, *Charter Conflicts: What Is Parliament's Role?* (Montreal: McGill-Queen's University Press, 2002); and James B Kelly, *Governing with the Charter: Legislative and Judicial Activism and Framers' Intent* (Vancouver: University of British Columbia Press, 2005); Dennis Baker, *Not Quite Supreme: The Courts and Coordinate Constitutional Interpretation* (Kingston & Montreal: McGill-Queen's University Press, 2010).

whether particular rules have been breached brings the other branches into the adjudicative context. To the extent that the court purports to issue judgments and grant remedies against its complementary branches, it risks straying outside its 'lane'. Thus, for centuries Crown or sovereign immunity doctrines[58] prevented states or their officials from being sued. In Europe, constitutional review was thought to be incompatible with parliamentary governance and the unitary state.[59]

A federal state with a written Constitution poses the question: who or what body is to determine whether the various orders of government have strayed beyond their authority?[60] In the debates over the American Constitution, which imposed a strong federal structure, Alexander Hamilton famously argued that, as 'the interpretation of the laws is the proper and peculiar province of the courts', and a Constitution is 'a fundamental law', so it also belonged to the courts to 'ascertain its meaning … as well as the meaning of any particular act proceeding from the legislative body'.[61] That argument won the day, with federal courts specifically granted the authority to hear, inter alia, cases arising under the Constitution.[62] But their authority was limited *to* cases (and 'controversies'). The adjudicative features noted earlier have applied to those courts in their strongest sense.[63]

The American model, though, is hardly dominant, even among other federal states. An alternative, adopted in many European countries in the nineteenth century, is generally attributed to the Austrian legal theorist Hans Kelsen.[64] This is the specialist constitutional court deliberately structured as 'an alternative to American judicial review'.[65] Though they take a variety of forms, such courts often occupy a separate position in the machinery of government and, importantly, have only modest links with the ordinary courts. They occasionally are described as a fourth branch of government. In a clear contrast with the American model, such courts may consider constitutionality *prior* to a law's enactment – adopting an explicit posture of 'abstract review'.

[58] The originally very strict approach to Crown immunity has been mitigated over time: *Canada (Attorney General) v Thouin*, 2017 SCC 46, [2017] 2 SCR 184; Crown Proceedings Act 1947 (c 44). In the United States, see *Chisolm v Georgia* 2 US 419 (1793), which inspired the XI Amendment in 1798 that prohibits suing States in federal courts unless they consent to be sued. See also *Fitzpatrick v Bitzer*, 427 US 445 (1976).

[59] Alec Stone Sweet, 'Constitutional Courts and Parliamentary Democracy' (2002) 25 West European Politics 77.

[60] Jean François Aubert, *Traité de droit constitutionnel suisse* (Neuchâtel: Éditions Ides et calendes, 1967).

[61] Hamilton (n 53).

[62] US Constitution, Article III.

[63] Michael C Dorf, 'Abstract and Concrete Review' in Vikram D Amar and Mark V Tushnet (eds), *Global Perspectives on Constitutional Law* (Oxford: Oxford University Press, 2009).

[64] Hans Kelsen, 'Judicial Review of Legislation: A Comparative Study of the Austrian and the American Constitution' (1942) 4(2) The Journal of Politics 183.

[65] Stone Sweet (n 59) 79.

Having briefly described the separation of powers, it remains to consider its role in the Canadian legal system and the degree to which, if at all, it has something to say about the Canadian courts' advisory function. Some of this is addressed below, with the remainder of the discussion in Chapter 4.

Separation of Powers in Canada

It is sometimes said that there is no separation of powers in Canada.[66] It is true that the country does not adhere to the peculiarly strong version of that doctrine that operates in, say, the United States. As a parliamentary democracy influenced by the 'Matchless Constitution', Canada's governance is incompatible with such a rigid division of the state. Instead, there is an explicit connection between the legislature and executive.[67]

The preamble to Canada's Constitution Act 1867 expressed the constituent colonies' 'Desire to be federally united … with a Constitution similar in Principle to that of the United Kingdom'. That phrase brought with it many so-called unwritten aspects of the British Constitution, including Cabinet responsibility and the role and function of the sovereign. At the same time, because Canada did have a written constitutional text, *and* was constituted as a federal state, some notion of judicial review quickly became necessary.[68] That history is recounted over the next two chapters.

Another feature of the Canadian Constitution that may appear to complicate the application of separation of powers doctrine is the fact that the judiciary is appointed exclusively by the executive branch with no formal input from the legislature. Indeed, Canada appears to be virtually alone among constitutional democracies in allocating such a broad appointment discretion to 'the leader of the government'.[69] Much of Canadian constitutional law involves robust judicial review aimed primarily at statutes. In that context, the structural impotence of

[66] Russell (n 5) 89–90.

[67] Peter H Hogg, *Constitutional Law of Canada*, 5th edn (Toronto: Carswell-Thomson Reuters Canada, 2007) ch 9.5(e).

[68] Peter Oliver argues that the preamble has been radically over-interpreted: Peter Oliver, 'Reform of the Supreme Court of Canada from Within: To What Extent Should the Court Weigh in Regarding Constitutional Conventions?' in Jennifer Smith and Nadia Verrelli (eds), *Democratic Dilemma: Reforming Canada's Supreme Court* (Montreal: McGill-Queens, 2013) 161, 167.

[69] Peter H Russell, *A Parliamentary Approach to Reforming the Process of Filling Vacancies on the Supreme Court of Canada, Brief to the Standing Committee on Justice, Human Rights, Public Safety and Emergency Preparedness*, 23 March 2004, p 1, as cited in Erin Crandall, 'Intergovernmental Relations and the Supreme Court of Canada: The Changing Place of the Provinces in Judicial Selection Reform' (2010) Working Paper, Institute of Intergovernmental Relations School of Policy Studies, Queen's University, www.queensu.ca/iigr/sites/webpublish.queensu.ca.iigrwww/files/files/pub/archive/DemocraticDilemma/ReformingTheSCC/SCCpapers/CrandallFINAL.pdf.

the legislature vis-à-vis appointments can become a rallying point in the ongoing debate over the legitimacy of judicial review.[70]

One must be careful, though, not to conflate inter-branch tension with the demands of the separation of powers. Generally, the involvement of one or more branches in judicial appointments is a feature of most modern states, though appointments can be very much affected by particular processes such as arm's-length selection committees.

While appointment of the judiciary's members is important, it also matters what happens once judges are in place. In that respect, Canada observes very strong norms of independence. Judges enjoy security of tenure[71] and the courts are accorded a wide berth for administrative and institutional decisions. Judicial discipline is carried out by councils that are wholly arm's-length from government and that are overseen and staffed by judges themselves.[72] The Canadian Constitution does provide for the removal of judges by Parliament[73] but that is an extraordinary step that to date has never been taken.[74]

At first, Canadian courts did not pay much attention to the separation of powers. The Canadian Supreme Court did not even mention the term until 1975;[75] and only in 1981 did it address the doctrine's role in constitutional terms. The Court's early references tended to be dismissive, noting, for example, that 'there is no general "separation of powers" in the *British North America Act, 1867*' and that the Constitution 'does not separate the legislative, executive, and judicial functions and insist that each branch of government exercise only its own function'.[76]

[70] Judicial appointments are discussed briefly in Chapter 4.

[71] 'The Judiciary Department,' *Federalist* No. 78, 28 May 1788. Hamilton said that security of tenure is 'one of the most valuable of the modern improvements in the practice of government'. He also called an independent judiciary 'the best expedient which can be devised in any government, to secure a steady, upright, and impartial administration of the laws'.

[72] Canadian Judicial Council: www.cjc-ccm.gc.ca/.

[73] Section 99(1): 'Subject to subsection (2) of this section, the judges of the superior courts shall hold office during good behaviour, but shall be removable by the Governor General on address of the Senate and House of Commons'.

[74] It is possible that a parliamentary decision to remove a judge absent prior judicial sanction would be found to violate the separation of powers.

[75] *Thorson v Attorney General of Canada*, [1975] 1 SCR 138. *Thorson* involved a challenge to the constitutional basis for providing moneys to implement the Official Languages Act, RSC 1970, c O-2. The government objected that Thorson lacked standing to bring the suit and the Court's decision to refuse standing formed its first pronouncement on the subject. The Supreme Court's mention of the separation of powers at pp 159–60, is glancing.

[76] *Re Residential Tenancies Act, 1979*, [1981] 1 SCR 714 at 728 ('There is no general "separation of powers" in the *British North America Act, 1867*. Our Constitution does not separate the legislative, executive, and judicial functions and insist that each branch of government exercise only its own function'); *Sobeys Stores Ltd. v Yeomans and Labour Standards Tribunal (N.S.)*, [1989] 1 SCR 238; *Douglas/Kwantlen Faculty Assn. v Douglas College*, [1990] 3 SCR 570 (a rigid separation of powers 'finds no place in the Canadian constitutional structure'); *MacMillan Bloedel Ltd. v Simpson*, [1995] 4 SCR 725 at para 52 ('a strict separation of judicial and legislative powers is not a feature of the Canadian Constitution'); *Reference re Secession of Quebec*, [1998] 2 SCR 217 at para 15 ('the Canadian Constitution does not insist on a strict separation of powers').

After the Constitution Act 1982, the Court started to view the doctrine in starkly different terms: as 'essential',[77] 'defining'[78] and 'fundamental'.[79] In 1993, it said:

> While we do not share the turbulent history of the United Kingdom with respect to the relationships between the different branches of government, there is no question that the maintenance of the independence of the different branches from one another is necessary to their proper functioning.[80]

Much of the understanding of the separation of powers in Canada concerns the judiciary, as opposed to either the executive or legislature. At least in part, that is because the judicial role has greatly expanded, notably following the entrenchment of individual rights and freedoms in 1982. While the articulation of separation of powers concerns has not been limited to cases dealing with rights and freedoms, the Canadian courts acknowledged quite early on that it was that element that had 'added a new dimension'[81] to their role.

Thus, relying upon separation of powers principles, the Canadian Supreme Court has declined to deal with a number of issues that, to go back to an idea articulated above, would risk them straying outside their lane. Those issues have included prosecutorial discretion,[82] parliamentary privileges[83] and Crown

[77] *Operation Dismantle v The Queen*, [1985] 1 SCR 441; *Wells v Newfoundland*, [1999] 3 SCR 199.

[78] *Doucet-Boudreau v Nova Scotia (Minister of Education)*, [2003] 3 SCR 3, 2003 SCC 62 (dissenting opinion but not on this point); *Newfoundland (Treasury Board) v N.A.P.E.*, [2004] 3 SCR 381 [*NAPE*]; *Cooper v Canada (Human Rights Commission)*, [1996] 3 SCR 854.

[79] *Reference re Remuneration of Judges of the Provincial Court (P.E.I.)*, [1997] 3 SCR 3.

[80] *New Brunswick Broadcasting Co. v Nova Scotia (Speaker of the House of Assembly)*, [1993] 1 SCR 319 [*NB Broadcasting*].

[81] *Re B.C. Motor Vehicle Act*, [1985] 2 SCR 486.

[82] Prosecutorial discretion encompasses the Crown's ability to lay criminal charges, frame indictments and offer or withdraw pleas. Courts largely have considered such decisions outside of judicial review, noting that 'Under the doctrine of separation of powers, criminal law is in the domain of the executive': *R v* Power, [1994] 1 SCR 601. See also *Krieger v Law Society of Alberta*, [2002] 3 SCR 372, 2002 SCC 65 at para 45: 'In our theory of government, it is the sovereign who holds the power to prosecute his or her subjects. A decision of the Attorney General, or of his or her agents, within the authority delegated to him or her by the sovereign is not subject to interference by other arms of government. An exercise of prosecutorial discretion will, therefore, be treated with deference by the courts and by other members of the executive'. The approach mirrors that in other systems such as the UK: *R v Director of Public Prosecutions ex parte Kebilene* [2000] 2 AC 326 (absent 'dishonesty or mala fide or an exceptional circumstance' decisions by the Director of Public Prosecutions to consent to a prosecution are not amenable to judicial review).

[83] *NB Broadcasting* (n 80) (refusing to scrutinise a claim that a Speaker's ruling barring third party recordings in the assembly violated the Charter's freedom of expression). See also *Canada (House of Commons) v Vaid*, [2005] 1 SCR 667, 2005 SCC 30: 'Parliamentary privilege … is one of the ways in which the fundamental constitutional separation of powers is respected. In Canada, the principle has its roots in the preamble to our *Constitution Act, 1867* which calls for "a Constitution similar in Principle to that of the United Kingdom". Each of the branches of the State is vouchsafed a measure of autonomy from the others … Parliamentary privilege is a principle common to all countries based on the Westminster system'.

prerogatives.[84] The Court has noted that 'It is fundamental to the working of government as a whole that [the branches] play their proper role …, and that no one of them overstep its bounds, that each show proper deference for the legitimate sphere of activity of the other'.[85]

Those examples demonstrate judicial modesty – a court declining to intervene in affairs it considers to be outside its proper purview. A converse development has been the Canadian Supreme Court's use of separation of powers principles so as to *enhance* its power. Not all of those moments have involved the Court protecting itself *against* interference. For example, the Court has said that it is the 'guardian of the constitution', implying little room for the other branches to participate.[86] It also has asserted its institutional freedom by articulating an 'unwritten constitutional principle' of judicial independence that can impose onerous obligations on the other branches. Most striking of all, it has decided that, even without a moment of explicit entrenchment, it is now protected by the Constitution against a number of changes unless formal amendment procedures are followed.[87]

In short, the separation of powers has featured in too much Canadian jurisprudence[88] to support the claim that it has no purchase. The Canadian Supreme Court has confirmed that the doctrine is now a part of the Canadian constitutional framework. The Court has recognised an important normative and structural imperative towards separation that cashes out in different ways, in various constitutional disputes.

* * *

This book investigates the implication of courts performing a function – issuing advisory opinions – that traditionally has been understood as different from the more 'ordinary' judicial practice of deciding cases. In order to unpack that, this chapter investigated the notion of just what is a 'case'. It suggested that cases are the product of the function of adjudication, which is thought to be the special province of the courts. Adjudication is characterised by a number of features that work to limit what otherwise would be an extraordinary ability to intervene in human

[84] *Canada (Prime Minister) v Khadr*, 2010 SCC 3, [2010] 1 SCR 44. The Court refused to order the executive to seek the repatriation of a Canadian citizen from the United States who was detained in Guantanamo Bay (it did issue a declaration that the individual's Charter rights had been infringed).

[85] *NB Broadcasting* (n 80) 389.

[86] *Hunter et al. v Southam Inc.*, [1984] 2 SCR 145 at 159; *Reference re Supreme Court Act, ss. 5 and 6*, 2014 SCC 21 at para 89. This assertion must be balanced with the Court's fairly consistent embrace of the 'dialogue' model of constitutional relations: *Vriend v Alberta*, [1998] 1 SCR 493; *R v Hall*, [2002] 3 SCR 309, 2002 SCC 64.

[87] *Reference re Supreme Court Act, ss. 5 and 6*, [2014] 1 SCR 433.

[88] Additional cases include *Cooper v Canada (Human Rights Commission)*, [1996] 3 SCR 854; *Reference re Secession of Quebec*, [1998] 2 SCR 217 at para 12; *Doucet-Boudreau v Nova Scotia (Minister of Education)*, [2003] 3 SCR 3, 2003 SCC 62; *Reference re Securities Act*, 2011 SCC 66, [2011] 3 SCR 837, at para 61; *Saskatchewan (Attorney General) v Lemare Lake Logging Ltd.*, 2015 SCC 53, [2015] 3 SCR 419; and *Quebec (Attorney General) v Canada (Attorney General)*, 2015 SCC 14, [2015] 1 SCR 693.

affairs. Those limits may be understood as a doctrine of justiciability. Underpinning those limits is a different doctrine: the separation of powers. We are now in a somewhat better position to see the connection between the two.

The separation of powers shapes the adjudicative function as the particular province of the courts and, importantly, renders others putatively off limits. The courts' principal role is not law making – that is the province of the legislature. Nor are the courts properly concerned with governance through the setting and implementation of public policy – that is a function for the executive. In virtually all legal systems the courts review disputes that raise some legal question related to positive law. In order to perform that function, it is necessary that courts remain passive vis-à-vis the disputes they are charged with settling and do not actively seek out the disputes which they adjudicate.

The separation of powers helps to explain the idea that courts are usually focussed on 'cases'. When courts depart from the role generally associated with it, that often is cause for comment and, even concern. Such departures are most keen when the courts confront questions concerning the other branches of government, for example when those branches allegedly have strayed beyond *their* proper limits, or have violated the Constitution (assuming that one exists). The ways that courts have been empowered (or simply have decided) to respond to actions and decisions of other branches is a major preoccupation of legal scholars and political theorists.In some systems, that reality has spurred the creation of an entirely separate institution such as a constitutional court. The Canadian model combines both concrete and abstract review, in a unified judiciary that renders both adjudicative decisions and advisory opinions: an unusual combination of features.

It may seem reasonable to think that there is a link between the separation of powers and the adjudicative function of the courts being properly limited to cases. But I have not argued that (a) there is something wrong per se with courts doing something other than deciding cases; or (b) that advisory opinions are sufficiently distinct and removed from the adjudicative function so as to be entirely 'not case-like'. As will be explored in the next two chapters, the first premise was considered and firmly rejected by Canadian courts. And in the remaining chapters, the second premise is also found to be wanting in significant ways.

2

Apex Courts

Although advisory opinions may be sought from all Canadian provincial appeal courts (and even, in a few provinces, trial courts),[1] opinions proceeding from the Supreme Court tend to attract the most interest and attention. As the highest court in the country, the Supreme Court's pronouncements have the broadest possible effect (to the extent that advisory opinions have an effect).

In the Canadian context, a focus on 'the apex court' requires some historical context. For 60 years after Confederation, final appeals rested with the Judicial Committee of the Privy Council.[2] Aspects of that Committee's function and scope unquestionably shaped the Canadian Supreme Court. Thus, the Judicial Committee's role merits some attention both in a general sense, and for its specific, advisory role. That is the focus of the first part of this chapter, followed by a brief history of the Canadian Supreme Court.

The Judicial Committee

Traditionally, English law viewed the King as the fountain-head of justice. The King was deemed to possess unique knowledge, fairness and wisdom – qualities that justified an adjudicative role. Over time, successive British monarchs declined to personally exercise this role. They relied instead on a council of advisors – the *Curia Regis* who provided "advice" out of submission and loyalty.[3]

[1] Constitutional Question Act, RSBC 1996, c 68, s 1; Constitutional Questions Act, RSNS 1989, c 89, s 3; Court of Appeal Reference Act, RSQ 1975, c R-23, s 1; Courts of Justice Act, RSO 1990, c 43, s 8(1); Judicature Act, RSA 2000, c J-2, s 26(1); Judicature Act, RSNB 1973, c J-2, s 23(1); Judicature Act, RSNL 1990, c J-4, s 13; Judicature Act, RSPEI 1988, c J-2.1, s 7(1); Constitutional Questions Act, CCSM 2002, c C180, s 1; Constitutional Questions Act, 2012, SS 2012, c C-29.01, s 2(1).

[2] Also referred to as 'Judicial Committee', 'the Committee' and 'the Board'.

[3] Bracton, *Treatise on the Laws and Customs of England*, Twiss ed (1878–83), f 107. The important role of equity, which is omitted from the above discussion, may be found in Johann P Sommerville (ed), *King James VI and I: Political Writings* (Cambridge: Cambridge University Press, 1994) 216, cited in Benjamin L Berger, 'The Abiding Presence of Conscience: Criminal Justice Against the Law and the Modern Constitutional Imagination' (2011) 61 University of Toronto Law Journal 579, 590–93. See also George Burton Adams, "The Descendants of the *Curia Regis*" (1907) 13 The American Historical Review 11; Mark D Walters, "Judicial Review of Ministerial Advice to the Crown" (2016) 25:3 Constitutional Forum 33, 37.

Slowly, the King's power gave way to a competing authority: Westminster Parliament.[4] That included judicial power as 'one after the other of the courts of the Realm gradually hived off from the King's Court' and 'Parliament arrogated to itself ... the ultimate right of appeal'.[5] From the English courts, 'writs of error' went to the House of Lords but the Crown retained the prerogative right to hear appeals from other courts, especially courts in other dominions. Over time, *that* appellate jurisdiction was lodged in a committee of the Privy Council.[6]

There was thus a long history of hearing appeals from dominions and colonies. The Judicial Committee of the Privy Council (JCPC) was created by the Judicial Committee Act (JCA) 1833.[7] The Act substituted a statutory court for any judicial function that remained with the sovereign monarch. It included the following clause:

> 4. It shall be lawful for his Majesty to refer to the said judicial committee for hearing or consideration any such other matters whatsoever as his Majesty shall think fit; and such committee shall thereupon hear or consider the same, and shall advise his Majesty thereon in manner aforesaid.[8]

The marginal note for the section describes it as intended for 'otherwise non-appealable grievances'.[9] Section 4 sets out an advisory function independent of appeals. The words 'in manner aforesaid' appears to mean section 3 of the same Act, which provides for the right of appeal to the Privy Council. Section 3 prescribes how such appeals are to be conducted. The Committee was to render decisions

> in the same manner and form as has been heretofore the custom with respect to matters referred by his Majesty to the whole of his privy council or a committee thereof (the nature of such report or recommendation being always stated in open court).[10]

By 1912, the JCPC was describing such reference opinions as something of an oddity.[11] But it accepted that section 4 reflected an important ancillary function of its members, who, as Privy Councillors, were liable to be called upon by the Crown for advice. Thus, though functioning primarily as a court, the Committee and its members could legitimately be asked questions arising outside of cases. In that 1912 opinion, the JCPC also said that the House of Commons, in its legislative capacity, could exercise the privilege of calling upon its Law Lords to provide

[4] In this chapter, 'Parliament'. Elsewhere in the book, 'Westminster Parliament' or 'the Westminster Parliament' is used to distinguish that body from the federal Parliament in Canada.

[5] See, eg, the abolition of the Star Chamber by the Habeas Corpus Act 1640, 16 Car I, c.10 (Imp).

[6] HH Marshall, 'The Judicial Committee of the Privy Council: A Waning Jurisdiction' (1964) 13 International and Comparative Law Quarterly 697. For an interesting account of appeals from American colonies, see Joseph Henry Smith, *Appeals to the Privy Council From the American Plantations* (New York: Columbia University Press, 1950). Some of this is further discussed in Chapter 10.

[7] An Act for the better Administration of Justice in His Majesty's Privy Council, 1833 c 41.

[8] ibid, s 4.

[9] ibid.

[10] ibid, s 3.

[11] *In re References by the Governor-General in Council*, (1910) 43 SCR 536 at 547 (SCC), aff'd [1912] AC 571 (PC) [*Reference re References*]. The reference is discussed at length in the next chapter.

advice. The Committee was far less sanguine about the prospect of the Executive doing so. It struggled to find a modern example. It could only note, with clear disapproval, an instance in 1760 where a judicial panel had been summoned to provide a legal opinion to the King.[12]

A number of the opinions discussed in this book were issued by the JCPC but they rarely proceeded under the special jurisdiction provided by section 4. They were, instead, the product of appeals from lower court proceedings, which, as will be explained below, include references. They were section 3 appeals, not section 4 references. Section 4 permits 'Her Majesty' to refer to the JCPC a question that has *not* been considered by other courts. The Committee sits as a court of first instance, not as an appellate body.[13]

The relative infrequency of section 4 references inhibited the development of a robust body of jurisprudence. It also attracted relatively little academic or political commentary. The commentary which did emerge struggled to reconcile the JCPC's reference and appellate functions. In 1967, for example, a member of the UK Parliament described section 4 as a mechanism for considering 'cases of constitutional importance ... on a point which cannot be effectively decided in the ordinary courts'.[14]

A similar point was articulated in 1971 during parliamentary debates over whether Britain had a legal obligation to deliver arms to the Republic of South Africa.[15] As the issue was a matter of high controversy, several members of the House proposed to refer it directly to the JCPC. In response, the Lord Chancellor (a very senior UK official and Cabinet Minister)[16] delivered remarks about section 4 of the Act, its history and its modern function. While the comments do not have any particular legal weight, their source (the Lord Chancellor) and their detail make them worthy of consideration.

The Lord Chancellor noted that the JCA 1833's main purpose was 'to create an instrument for the judicial handling of that residuum of cases which remained in the Privy Council after the rest of the judicial system had crystallised'.[17] The JCPC was the only statutory body connected to the Privy Council. Following the

[12] *Reference re References* at 7–8. Interestingly, two of Coke's most famous pronouncements of common and constitutional law were made in response to legal questions put to him, and the other judges, by the King or the Lord Chancellor: Prohibitions del Roy (1607) 12 Co Rep 63; Proclamations (1611) 12 Co Rep 74. See Esther C Cope, 'Sir Edward Coke and Proclamations, 1610' (1971) 15 American Journal of Legal History 215; R G Usher, 'James I and Sir Edward Coke' (1903) 18 English Historical Review 664.

[13] The retention of that original jurisdiction has attracted mention, and even concern, by some UK scholars: Alex Peplow, 'A Curious Jurisdiction – Section 4 of the Judicial Committee Act 1833', *UK Constitutional Law Association*, 7 July 2016: https://ukconstitutionallaw.org/2016/07/15/alex-peplow-a-curious-jurisdiction-section-4-of-the-judicial-committee-act-1833/.

[14] HC Deb 06 March 1967, vol 742 cc 1038–09.

[15] *South Africa: British Obligations on Arms Supply*: HL Deb 21 April 1971, vol 317, cc 754–72: http://hansard.millbanksystems.com/lords/1971/apr/21/south-africa-british-obligations-on-arms ['South Africa Debate'].

[16] At the time the post was occupied by The Right Honourable Quintin Hogg Baron Hailsham of St Marylebone.

[17] South Africa Debate (n 15) at 765.

gradual dismantling of the sovereign's 'judiciary' (the 'King's Council' mentioned above), there yet remained 'a curious residuum' of judicial authority.[18] In creating a statutory court, the JCA 1833 wrested away the final remnants of that power.

The Lord Chancellor observed that the motivation for inserting section 4 into the JCA 1833 was obscure. There was little specific mention of the section in the debates leading to its introduction. After reviewing a number of examples of section 4 proceedings, he concluded that

> [t]he reference under Section 4 is a convenient method of ascertaining the law when no other jurisdiction is available, but only on condition that when it is delivered, after the judicial hearing, the decision is definitive and effective; only when, to quote from the Latin … *Roma locuta est; finita causa est.* It is intolerable for any court of law to be required to adjudicate in a case in which one of the parties affected by the decision has no opportunity of being heard and cannot be expected to treat it as authoritative if it does not agree. I, my Lords, certainly could not be a party to such a constitutional monstrosity.[19]

It is interesting to consider *why* the inclusion of section 4 into the JCA 1833 seemed to attract little attention. Though the Judicial Committee was constituted as a court, it sprang from an institutional and political history of providing advice to the sovereign.[20] Section 4 continued a long-standing tradition. Numerous cases affirm the idea that the judiciary can, occasionally, occupy the role of 'advisor to the Crown'.[21] Indeed, to this day, all of the JCPC's decisions are styled as 'advice' to the Crown.[22] Thus, given the Committee's historical position, it may have seemed both natural and expedient to maintain a route by which the Crown or Parliament could seek advice outside of *inter partes* litigation.

The Lord Chancellor raised a common objection to references: in hearing them, a court might be 'required to adjudicate in a case in which one of the parties affected by the decision has no opportunity of being heard'. In that situation, he claimed, the party could not be expected to abide by an opinion that was negative to that party's interest. Such an expectation would be 'intolerable' and a 'constitutional monstrosity'.[23]

[18] ibid.

[19] ibid. The Latin phrase translates as 'Rome has spoken; the matter is finished'.

[20] Stewart Jay, 'Servants of Monarchs and Lords: The Advisory Role of Early English Judges' (1994) 38 *American Journal of Legal History* 117.

[21] *Reference re References* (n 11).

[22] See, eg, *Cenac v Schafer (St. Lucia)* [2016] UKPC 25 at [36]: 'For these reasons their Lordships will humbly advise Her Majesty that para 6(ii) of the judge's order should be discharged; but that otherwise the appeal should be dismissed'. The broader principle has been stated as: 'Although the Queen is never present at the hearing, or at the rendering of judgments, she is considered, by a fiction of law, as present and presiding over the Court, and the Lords, sitting as judges, are only her advisers'. JJ Beauchamp, *The Jurisprudence of the Privy Council* (Montreal: Periaud, 1891) vii.

[23] South Africa Debate (n 15) at 769.

The Lord Chancellor's concern appeared two-fold. One aspect relates to the appropriate parameters of cases, introduced in Chapter 1. In order for a court to provide results that can be accepted as 'just', parties should not be subject to having their interests decided without an opportunity to participate. Participation is guaranteed by the traditional rules of litigation and civil procedure. In the common law tradition, litigation is highly adversarial.[24] That requires vigorous participation by opposed parties (subject to certain exceptions). A court proceeding that did not offer the opportunity for such participation, yet purported to affect an individual's legal rights, would be inconsistent with that important principle. In effect, the Lord Chancellor appears to be raising a natural justice claim against how references might be pursued.

The second aspect of the Lord Chancellor's unease was the possibility that an individual who was not involved in the reference might feel that they need not *comply* with the ruling. That could raise doubts about the court's authority. Admittedly, the precise source of the Lord Chancellor's anxiety regarding a 'constitutional monstrosity' is ambiguous. It could refer to the breach of the long-standing rule that parties be afforded the opportunity to participate. Or, it could refer to the spectacle of a judicial ruling that exerts no authority. The point is that the concern reflects two distinct aspects of the reference function.

The Lord Chancellor appears to offer as the main justification for the JCPC's advisory function the idea that it will act as a 'last resort'. A reference should be used 'only when no other jurisdiction is available'.

The 'last resort' approach to references can be contrasted with the idea that they should be used whenever they can provide clarity – indeed, that they should be a routine mechanism prior to a law's enactment. The clarification model corresponds to the institution, in some legal systems, of a 'constitutional court' that performs precisely that function. For example, the Federal Constitutional Court of Germany (which has neither appellate nor general jurisdiction) responds to requests by different organs of government to determine the constitutionality of laws and government action.[25]

[24] 'The procedures of this tradition evolved in conjunction with a system of trial by jury in which disputed issues of fact must be established in open court before a panel of lay persons who are responsible for the final verdict'. Peter Russell, *The Judiciary in Canada: The Third Branch of Government*' (Toronto: McGraw-Hill, 1987) 25. See also Patrick Devlin, *The Judge* (Oxford: Oxford University Press, 1979).

[25] German Constitution (*Grundgesetz* – Basic Law) in force 23 May 1949, *Bundesgesetzblatt 1949*, Part IX. The Judiciary, arts 93, 94, 99. In France, the Constitutional Council of the French Republic (*le Conseil Constitutionnel*) supervises the passing of all laws (*ex ante* constitutional review). It also may be requested to consider the constitutionality of a legislative provision already in force, acting on referral by the Conseil d'État or Cour de Cassation, or as raised by a litigant in proceedings before a lower court (*ex post* constitutional review). Constitution du 4 octobre 1958, Title VII: The Constitutional Council, arts 56–63. There are numerous other such courts in Europe, Latin America and Asia: Andrew Harding, Peter Leyland and Tania Groppi, 'Constitutional Courts: Forms, Functions and Practice in Comparative Perspective' 2008 3(2) *Journal of Competition Law* 1.

The foregoing discussion suggests that references under section 4 of the JCA 1833 were thought most appropriate in situations that could not otherwise be resolved through ordinary litigation. Underlying the Lord Chancellor's comments is the sense that there is something *unsettling* about a *court* undertaking an advisory function and that it therefore should do so rarely.[26]

In considering the reference function of Canadian courts, the role it *can* play is at least as important as the role it *does* play. Chapters 9 and 10 suggest that the reference function must be assessed against the broader legal system in which it operates and which provides underlying norms for its use. For now, it will suffice to draw attention to a clear distinction in how the function might be approached.

The idea of 'last resort' judicial reasoning links back to justiciability – that set of principles that operates to limit the jurisdiction of the courts to 'cases'. In ordinary litigation, courts decide only 'live' issues. Additionally, courts generally limit decisions to whatever is necessary to resolve the particular dispute. A court need not always answer all legal questions before it. If a simpler approach will suffice to resolve the claim, the court is entitled to, and on some accounts, should, adopt that approach.

To the extent a court leaves some legal issues unresolved, it can be described as exercising 'restraint' or as 'withholding ultimate constitutional adjudication'.[27] The American scholar Alexander Bickel coined the term 'the passive virtues' to describe the features reflected in an apex court that regularly and predictably adopted that posture.

It can be advisable for a high court to adopt a posture of judicial restraint. Because its decisions will bind all other actors, and are not subject to further appeal, the court may find it prudent to limit the scope of its rulings in order not to restrict unduly the development of the law generally. It may be that a legal argument is quite novel and would benefit from additional consideration among the lower courts which can, say, weigh evidence more thoroughly. This may be especially salient in a federal system with multiple lower courts operating equivalent to one another.

A posture of restraint makes less sense for a lower court which cannot be confident that its conclusion will prevail on appeal. Indeed, lower courts often acknowledge that they should leave an issue to be decided by a higher court.[28] In the example given, a lower court might find in favour of a claimant on one issue, but have that ruling overturned. If the claimant had raised other issues that the lower court declined to consider the case would remain unresolved. In such a circumstance, a higher court would be forced to either consider those additional

[26] James Bradley Thayer. 'The Origin and Scope of the American Doctrine of Constitutional Law' (1983) 7 *Harvard Law Review* 129.

[27] Alexander Bickel, 'The Supreme Court 1960 Term: Foreword: The Passive Virtues' (1961–62) 75 *Harvard Law Review* 40.

[28] See, eg, *Dobson v Dobson and Carter*, 1997 CanLII 17827 (NB QB) at 27: 'This is a question with obvious expanding implications and is one which must ultimately be determined by a higher court of the judicial structure'.

issues as if it were a court of first instance, or remit the matter back for reconsideration. Arguably, neither option is an optimal use of judicial resources.

The judicial restraint or 'passive' model carries with it a number of assumptions about the role of the courts and of other actors. The passive model eschews, or at least is indifferent to, the idea that the judiciary provides a means to safeguard or protect constitutionalism as a social value. It largely dismisses the notion that courts do more than act merely as adjudicators in discrete contexts – that they also provide an important measure of accountability by clarifying the law.[29] Under the restrictive view, the courts' ability to tell the government or legislature what it can and cannot do is an extraordinary thing that it generally should avoid.

Today, Canadian courts regularly articulate societal values and constitutional norms. They also regularly balance state, societal and individual interests. The broader conception of the judicial role often prevails over the narrower one. Certainly, the entrenchment in the constitution of individual rights and freedoms made judicial review of law and government policy somewhat expected (although, in Canada at least, executive and legislative actors did not anticipate the robustness of that review). But the foundation for it was laid much earlier, including the fact that, under the colonial system, domestic laws were subordinate to Imperial ones. As well, a federal system required some means of settling jurisdictional disputes and the courts were identified as the appropriate body to do so. The creation of a particular general court of appeal for that task – the Canadian Supreme Court – is discussed below.

'A Judicial Department in Every Well-Organized Government'[30]

A. Confederation

The Canadian Supreme Court was created some years after Confederation: the union in 1867 of four British provinces into the Dominion of Canada. The idea of the Court reflects two distinct factors. The first was the degree of interest in courts and judicial review in general during the debates over Confederation and the resulting document – the British North America Act (BNA Act).[31] The second is that the prospect of a domestic (rather than Imperial) apex court inspired profound anxieties. While some of those anxieties have dissipated over the intervening century, others have taken their place. Both factors are discussed below.

[29] See Gerald Gunther, 'The Subtle Vices of the Passive Virtues – A Comment on Principle and Expediency in Judicial Review' (1964) 64 *Columbia Law Review* 1.

[30] *Canada Law Journal* (1875) 11, 236. The full quote is as follows: 'It has long been a rule of national policy that, for the security of private rights and the administration of public laws, there should be a judicial department in every well-organized government'.

[31] Constitution Act (CA) 1867 30 & 31 Victoria, c. 3 (UK).

In thinking about the best structure for Confederation, political leaders were certainly aware of the federalism conflicts roiling the United States.[32] In the mid-1800s, the US was mired in battles over the federal courts' interpretation of congressional (and, to a lesser extent, presidential) powers. Their tendency to enlarge, rather than restrict, the scope of those powers was extremely controversial. The US Constitution was drafted primarily to enumerate the function of the federal government. Indeed, the US Constitution states that any unenumerated powers rest with the states.[33] Nonetheless, in numerous cases the Supreme Court of the United States took an unexpectedly broad view of federal jurisdiction and judicial power.[34]

Sir John A Macdonald, Canada's first Prime Minister, was anxious to avoid similar controversy. Thus, for example, the Quebec Resolutions of 1864 (the delegate debates which set the stage for Confederation) and the Constitution Act 1867 granted the residual legislative power to Parliament.[35] Even so, the risk of intergovernmental tension was clear.

Macdonald stated that, in the case of a conflict among the 'numerous subjects which belong, of right, both to the Local and the General Parliaments', the same rule ought to apply as in cases where there was concurrent jurisdiction between the Imperial and colonial Parliaments, namely that the action of the former would overrule the action of the local legislature.[36]

The above reference to the Imperial Parliament seemed to suggest that federal pre-emption would be achieved through disallowance, a prerogative of the Imperial Crown.[37] Under disallowance colonial legislation that conflicted with Imperial

[32] Jennifer Smith, 'Canadian Confederation and the Influence of American Federalism' (1988) 21(3) *Canadian Journal of Political Science* 443.

[33] US Constitution, Am X: 'The powers not delegated to the United States by the Constitution, nor prohibited by it to the states, are reserved to the states respectively, or to the people'.

[34] *Marbury v Madison* 5 US 137 (1803); *McCullough v Maryland* 17 US 316 (1819); *Martin v Hunter's Lessee* 14 US 304 (1816).

[35] See subs 29(37) of the Quebec Resolutions (1864): '... And generally respecting all matters of a general character, not specially and exclusively reserved for the Local Governments and Legislatures'. Compare with s 91 of the CA 1867: 'It shall be lawful for the Queen, by and with the Advice and Consent of the Senate and House of Commons, to make Laws for the Peace, Order, and good Government of Canada, in relation to all Matters not coming within the Classes of Subjects by this Act assigned exclusively to the Legislatures of the Provinces ...' (which is then followed by a list of enumerated heads of power).

[36] *Parliamentary Debates on the Subject of Confederation*, 8th Parl, 3rd Sess, at p 42 (1856) (emphasis added) [*Confederation Debates*]. As Strayer notes, the rule referred to by Macdonald was in fact included in the Quebec Resolutions, but does not appear explicitly in the British North America Act. It survives as the judicially articulated rule of federal paramountcy. Barry L Strayer, *The Canadian Constitution and the Courts*, 3rd edn (Toronto: Butterworths, 1988).

[37] The British North America Act (BNA Act) contains an Imperial power of disallowance: s 56. In 1930 it was agreed that the UK government would not exercise that power; and it has since been rendered null by the Canada Act 1982. Under s 90 of the BNA Act the federal Parliament can 'disallow' provincial laws. The power has not been used since 1943 and owing to modern political realities it is difficult to imagine that it ever would. The Supreme Court of Canada has on occasion referred to the power as having fallen into 'disuse', eg, *Re Resolution to Amend the Constitution*, [1981] 1 SCR 753 at 802. For further discussion, see Gerard La Forest, *Disallowance and Reservation of Provincial Legislation* (Ottawa: Department of Justice, 1955). Disallowance is further discussed in Chapter 5.

laws and was thus legally void could simply be disallowed by the Imperial government (rather than through the cumbersome process of litigation). Macdonald apparently thought that the Canadian Parliament would function in the same way, as 'a sovereign body subject to no external review by the courts'.[38]

Some Confederation leaders *were*, however, thinking about a judicial role in jurisdictional disputes. An exchange between statesmen Antoine-Aimé Dorion and George-Etienne Cartier is illustrative. Dorion demanded to know what authority could intervene in the event of a difference of opinion between the orders of government. Cartier thought such intervention would come from Imperial authorities. Dorion found that unsatisfactory because, in his view, the Imperial government had not been responsive to previous complaints from Lower Canada (today, Quebec).[39] Cartier countered that the Imperial Parliament would rarely be required to 'interfere' because such matters would be taken up by the (domestic) courts of justice. But what, Dorion demanded, would happen in the case of a conflict between different magistrates? Cartier had no clear reply.[40]

One possible answer was to entrench in the Constitution a court that could deal with federal-provincial disputes.[41] At least some viewed such a court as necessary to a uniform system of law and jurisprudence – and to the sort of national identity essential to the new Dominion's success.[42] Ultimately, though, no court of that kind was constitutionally entrenched in the BNA Act.

One reason that the drafters may have abandoned the idea is that the Constitution recognised the Privy Council's continuing authority.[43] The retention of a right to appeal a matter to an Imperial court ensured that parties could receive authoritative decisions in relation to federalism disputes. Another reason is that the prospect provoked powerful regional anxieties. The concerns were most pronounced in Lower Canada – a territory with a distinctive history and legal system that was, after the British conquest, permitted to retain its French civil law.[44]

[38] Strayer (n 36) at 16.

[39] Historically, 'Lower Canada' corresponded to the present-day province of Quebec.

[40] *Confederation Debates* (n 36) at 690.

[41] James G Snell and Frederick Vaughan, *The Supreme Court of Canada* (Toronto: The Osgoode Society, 1985) 4.

[42] ibid at 4.

[43] CA 1867, s.129: 'Except as otherwise provided by this Act, all Laws in force in Canada, Nova Scotia, or New Brunswick at the Union, and all Courts of Civil and Criminal Jurisdiction, and all legal Commissions, Powers, and Authorities, and all Officers, Judicial, Administrative, and Ministerial, existing therein at the Union, shall continue in Ontario, Quebec, Nova Scotia, and New Brunswick respectively, as if the Union had not been made; subject nevertheless (except with respect to such as are enacted by or exist under Acts of the Parliament of Great Britain or of the Parliament of the United Kingdom of Great Britain and Ireland,) to be repealed, abolished, or altered by the Parliament of Canada, or by the Legislature of the respective Province, according to the Authority of the Parliament or of that Legislature under this Act'. It is the reservation of continuing powers that 'are enacted by or exist under' the Imperial Parliament that safeguarded the role of the JCPC.

[44] Quebec Act 1774 (UK).

A bi-jural legal system posed many challenges. French Canadians (or, at least, their political leaders) feared that English Canadians, trained in the common law and adhering to a different religious tradition,[45] would dominate any court of general appeal. As Henri Taschereau noted, Quebeckers would 'be less satisfied with the decisions of a Federal Court of Appeal than with those of Her Majesty's Privy Council'.[46]

The full story of the political sensitivities and rivalries surrounding Confederation is beyond the scope of this book. It suffices to say that the above-noted sensitivities and rivalries made entrenching a high court impossible. Instead, Parliament was permitted to create one. Thus section 101 of the BNA Act provided:

> The Parliament of Canada may, notwithstanding anything in this Act, from Time to Time provide for the Constitution, Maintenance, and Organization of a General Court of Appeal for Canada, and for the Establishment of any additional Courts for the better Administration of the Laws of Canada.[47]

Aside from section 101, the BNA Act contemplated a significant degree of federal control over the judicial branch. The federal government and legislature enjoyed the power to, respectively, appoint and set the salaries for the judges who would sit on most of the country's courts. Federal power was cemented with the establishment in 1875 of a general court of appeal with plenary jurisdiction to hear appeals dealing with federal and provincial issues.

B. Establishment

The creation of a federal state had serious implications for the Canadian legal system. Allocating legislative authority between two orders of government raised questions about their respective jurisdiction; the extent to which one government could affect the authority of another; and how to deal with intergovernmental conflict. The existing legal system could provide some guidance but the existence of multiple orders of law making required an authoritative mechanism to deal with divergent decisions from separate yet equal courts in different jurisdictions.

In 1868 John A Macdonald commissioned lawyer (and future justice) Henry Strong to draft legislation for a court of general appeal for Canada.[48] Strong faced a complex task in designing a judiciary for a federal system that maintained strong ties to a unitary British state.

[45] The French were largely Catholic and the English Protestant.

[46] *Confederation Debates* (n 36) at 897. It is interesting to compare the greater confidence reposed in the Imperial power by linguistic and religious minorities, with the strong sense of connection and direct relationship with the Crown cited by indigenous communities, who to this day trace their relationship with the British monarch to the commitments expressed in the Royal Proclamation of 1763.

[47] BNA 1867 (n 31).

[48] Snell and Vaughan (n 41) 5–6.

The difficulties were compounded by the fact that section 101 of the BNA Act did not qualify the meaning of 'a general court of appeal for Canada'. The section was silent, for example, on the court's jurisdiction. Would the court hear cases pertaining to federal law only, to provincial law only, or both? Macdonald thought that the new court should focus on the provinces, going so far as to say that it 'should stand as regards the Provinces in a position analogous to that of the Queen in Council as regards the Colonies generally'.[49] In Macdonald's vision, the Supreme Court would fulfil the same role for the provinces as the Judicial Committee and the Crown's power of disallowance[50] fulfilled for the Dominion: ensuring that 'subordinate' jurisdictions did not stray too far from their roles.

In an 1869 draft Bill,[51] Henry Strong proposed a court of seven members that would hear civil and criminal appeals from across Canada. Importantly, the court also would have 'exclusive original jurisdiction' in a select number of areas, including with respect to the constitutionality of provincial statutes.[52] Perhaps sensing a contentious debate, Macdonald reassured those who were anxious about the court that the Bill was intended chiefly to promote discussion.

Strong's draft, indeed, almost immediately met with objections. The notion of original jurisdiction was viewed as exceedingly dangerous. Oliver Mowat, a future Premier of Ontario, argued that it would negatively enhance the reach of the central government, which already had significant advantages over the provinces, including disallowance and appointing both the Queen's representatives[53] as well as many judges. Permitting a 'federal' judicial body to also hear cases at first instance would increase that advantage and weaken the superior courts already operating in the provinces.

[49] Sir JA Macdonald Papers no. 64610, Parliamentary Archives Canada, cited ibid at 6. I do not mean to suggest that Macdonald himself collapsed the function of judicial review with the very different power of disallowance. Obviously, disallowance is much broader since it permits the consideration of explicit political factors that would be improper for the courts.

[50] See ss 55–57 of the CA 1867, which permits the Governor General to 'withhold' the Queen's assent for legislation, or to 'reserve' a Bill for further sovereign review. As discussed, below at n 74 and surrounding text, such reservation was, in fact, exercised with respect to the Supreme and Exchequer Court Act, discussed below at n 71. In addition, even after the Governor General gave assent, a power was reserved to the Queen in Council to disallow that assent within two years. A Bill that had been reserved would fail to take effect if assent from the Queen in Council was not received within two years. Disallowance, an extremely powerful symbol of Imperial control that was deeply resented by the provinces, was rarely invoked. There are 21 recorded occasions of a Bill being reserved between 1867 and 1878, and none at all after that: Bourinot, *Parliamentary Procedure and Practice* (2nd edn, 1892) 648–50 as cited in Peter Hogg, *Constitutional Law of Canada*, loose-leaf (Toronto: Carswell-Thomson Reuters Canada, 2007) chapter 3.1. In the Imperial conference of 1930, the United Kingdom agreed to cease exercising the power, though the Constitution Act 1867 did not formally change.

[51] Library of Parliament, House of Commons Bills, Bill 80 (1869), 'An Act to establish a Supreme Court for the Dominion of Canada'.

[52] The Court would also exercise original jurisdiction with respect to enforcement of dominion revenue statutes, treaty disputes and admiralty matters. Ibid.

[53] These are the Governor General for Canada, and the Lieutenant Governors in the provinces.

The Bill was criticised, as well, for failing to acknowledge the need for regional representation on the Court itself. The lack of such consideration resurrected the sorts of anxieties, expressed during the Confederation Debates, that had convinced the drafters not to entrench the Court in the first place.

Macdonald amended the Bill in 1870.[54] Then, politics intervened in the form of a defeat of his government in 1873.[55] A Liberal government, formed under Prime Minister Alexander MacKenzie, took over. But, since the Liberals also favoured the idea, the negotiations continued.

In February 1875 Liberal Minister of Justice Télesphore Fournier[56] introduced the Supreme and Exchequer Court Act. The Bill proposed to establish two courts instead of one: the 'Supreme Court' would hear appeals, and the 'Exchequer Court' would deal with revenue matters. The separation removed the source of one of the objections noted above as the 'general court of appeal' would no longer exercise original jurisdiction at all. The Supreme Court would have six members, five of whom would constitute a quorum (all would simultaneously serve on the Exchequer Court).[57] The Court would also hear appeals from all final judgments of any Canadian court of last resort.

Unlike Strong's version, the 1875 Bill accommodated Quebec's distinctive legal system. First, it excluded from appeals civil matters from the province involving less than 2,000 dollars.[58] Second, it reserved two of the Court's six seats for Quebec appointees.[59]

Quebec Members of Parliament proposed to prohibit appeals in all private law cases from Quebec (excluding commercial law) where two lower courts had reached the same decision.[60] Though it was not sustained, it suggested that some Quebec parliamentarians remained hostile 'to the Supreme Court's review of provincial court decisions, especially [decisions] dealing with Quebec's Civil Code'.[61] Political scientist Peter Russell has described such concerns as 'the central

[54] Library of Parliament, House of Commons Bills, Bill 48 (1870) 'An Act to establish a Supreme Court of Canada'. Particulars of this Bill are discussed in the next section of this chapter.

[55] Macdonald resigned in the wake of the Pacific Scandal because of patronage accusations concerning a railway contract that his government awarded to a financial donor. Macdonald would return to power from 1878 until 1891. Donald Creighton and PB Waite, *John A Macdonald: The Young Politician, The Old Chieftain* (Toronto: University of Toronto Press, 2000) 153–58.

[56] Fournier was appointed to the Supreme Court in September 1875, following which Edward Blake became the Minister of Justice.

[57] Fournier did not explain in any detail the reduction of the Court from seven to six members. After the Bill's first reading, Macdonald noted his curiosity at the change, but it was not otherwise the subject of much discussion. House of Commons Debates, 1875, vol 1, at 289.

[58] Snell and Vaughan (n 41) 8.

[59] Supreme Court and Exchequer Court Act, SC 1875, c 11, s 4. In subsequent versions of the Act, the content of s 4 was divided into two separate provisions (currently, ss 5 and 6) but its content remained largely unchanged: *Reference re Supreme Court Act, ss. 5 and 6*, 2014 SCC 21, [2014] 1 SCR 433 at para 22 [*Supreme Court Act Reference*].

[60] Peter H Russell, *The Supreme Court of Canada as a Bilingual and Bicultural Institution, Volume 1 of Documents of the Royal Commission of Bilingualism and Biculturalism* (Ottawa: Queen's Printer, 1969) 14, citing House of Commons Debates (n 57) at 937.

[61] Russell (n 60) 13. See also the objection by The Honourable Mr Baby, House of Commons Debates, 3rd Parl, 2nd Sess (25 March 1875) at 921–22.

theme of most French Canadian criticism of the Act'.[62] Parliament was attempting to ease those fears.[63] The anxiety over a unitary legal system was deeply regionalist.[64] But the divide between French and English Canada received affirmation in a way that other regional differences did not. For example, an attempt to secure a seat for British Columbia failed.[65]

The relationship between the new court and the Judicial Committee proved equally contentious. Section 129 of the Constitution Act 1867 implicitly recognised the Privy Council's continuing authority to hear appeals of Canadian cases.[66] Strong's 1869 Bill had appeared to do away with them. A Bill introduced in 1870 stated that the establishment of a Supreme Court did not prohibit any subject from further appealing 'to the foot of the throne'.[67]

The Liberal government anticipated that the new institution would be the final court of appeal. Fournier's 1875 Bill did not specify whether Supreme Court decisions could be further appealed to the Judicial Committee. (Under separate Imperial legislation there remained a route for direct (*per saltum*) appeals from the provinces.)[68] The Bill's failure to mention the JCPC created considerable controversy. The federal Minister of Justice, while denying any attempt to *eliminate* such appeals, thought it preferable for the Supreme Court to exercise ultimate and final jurisdiction. He pointed to 'wealthy men and wealthy corporations', who, using their vast resources, had considerably abused JCPC appeals in order to bypass Canadian courts.[69]

Another explanation for the government's reluctance to authorise such appeals was the concurrent effort under way in the UK to transfer the Judicial Committee's jurisdiction over colonial appeals to a new 'Supreme Court of Judicature'. The diminished role for the Committee concerned a number of Liberal MPs. (In the end, the reform came to naught.)[70] But the idea that the Canadian Parliament

[62] Russel (n 60).

[63] In 2014 the Court referred to s 4 as a 'historic bargain'. *Supreme Court Act Reference* (n 59) at para 20.

[64] Bora Laskin, 'The Supreme Court of Canada: A Final Court of and for Canadians' (1951) 29(10) *Canadian Bar Review* 1038, 1041, noting that 'The French-Canadian and English-Canadian components of the population, the Protestant and Roman Catholic persuasion of most of the citizenry, the sectional (and provincial) pressure for representation in central organs of government, were factors to which appointments to the Court gave expression'.

[65] House of Commons Debates, 3rd Parl, 2nd Sess (30 March 1875) at 974 (Mr Bunster).

[66] CA 1867, s 129 (cited in Chapter 1). The provision is reproduced in n 43 above.

[67] Snell and Vaughan (n 41) 7.

[68] Barry Strayer, *Judicial Review of Legislation in Canada* (Toronto: University of Toronto Press, 1968) 23, 25 citing the Judicial Committee Act 1844 and Edward Robert Cameron, *The Canadian Constitution* (Winnipeg: Butterworth, 1915).

[69] House of Commons Debates, Sess 1875, vol 1, at 286.

[70] Snell and Vaughan (n 41) 8. The Supreme Court of Judicature Act 1873 36 & 37 Vict c 66 sought to establish a High Court and Court of Appeal, and to end future appeals to the House of Lords. The UK government fell before the law came into force and the new Prime Minister, Benjamin Disraeli, restored the appellate functions of the JCPC in the Appellate Jurisdiction Act 1876 39 & 40 Vict c 59. The latter act was repealed by the Constitutional Reform Act 2005, c 4, which provided for a Supreme Court of the United Kingdom, and removed most, but not all, of the judicial functions of the Judicial Committee.

could eliminate the Committee's jurisdiction was contested. The British Home Office itself expressed doubts about such a shift.[71] During the debate on first reading, John A Macdonald argued that 'severing the links between [Canada] and the Mother country' could only be done by 'Imperial statute'.[72] After consideration by the UK Queen in Council, the 1875 Act received assent on the understanding that further appeals to the Judicial Committee would not be impeded.[73]

As passed in 1875, the Supreme and Exchequer Court Act set out the following appellate jurisdiction:

> 47. The judgment of the Supreme Court shall in all cases be final and conclusive, and no appeal shall be brought from any judgment or order of the Supreme Court to any Court of Appeal established by the Parliament of Great Britain and Ireland, by which appeals or petitions to Her Majesty in Council may be ordered to be heard: Saving any right which Her Majesty may graciously be pleased to exercise by virtue of her Royal Prerogative.[74]

The insertion of the language relating to the continuing Crown prerogative was a clear capitulation. The Canadian government did not persist in its attempt to wrest full control of the judiciary from Imperial courts. As well, under the Judicial Committee Act 1844, there remained a direct route for appeals to the JCPC that bypassed the Supreme Court altogether.[75] All in all, for a further 60 years, the Committee would continue to play a critical role in the country's jurisprudence.

Chapter 6 will discuss in detail the changes that produced the powerful apex Supreme Court that exists today. The next chapter discusses how the advisory function was incorporated into the Court's role, its early reception and early jurisprudence.

[71] Snell and Vaughan (n 41) 16. The Governor General reserved the Bill, sending it to the Queen's council for a recommendation.

[72] House of Commons Debates, Sess 1875, vol 1, at 289.

[73] Snell and Vaughan (n 41) 16 accurately capture the rather slap-dash nature of the negotiations at 16. At one point, Prime Minister MacKenzie believed that conditional approval had been granted, subject to further amendment. The colonial authorities disagreed with the Prime Minister's assessment. It was only after significant pressure that, on 8 October 1875, the administrator for Canada finally assented to the Bill and swore in the Court's first justices.

[74] Supreme and Exchequer Court Act 1875, s 47.

[75] Peter H Russell, *Leading Constitutional Decisions* (Toronto: McLelland and Stewart, 1973) xiii.

3

Canadian References

The Canadian Supreme Court was created by a new federal state seeking a method of dispute settlement for competing orders of government. While regional concerns had prevented its entrenchment in the BNA Act, the Court emerged relatively soon after. It was granted significant jurisdiction, functioning as a single court of appeal for the entire country – in effect, unifying the judiciary. Though it was but an intermediate court (subject to final appeals to the Judicial Committee) the Supreme Court would play an important role that would dramatically expand over the next 150 years.

Given that the Court had plenary appellate jurisdiction, it could hear appeals of constitutional cases arising between the federal and provincial governments. That, though, did not exhaust its constitutional function. As detailed in this chapter, from the beginning the Court also performed an advisory function. That function, though, came under immediate challenge. The response to those challenges, which were both political and legal in nature, are the focus of this chapter.

Framing the Function

In his 1869 proposal for a 'court of general appeal', Henry Strong had proposed that the Court hear references about the constitutionality of provincial statutes. The suggestion outraged the provinces, which believed that such a power would operate as a prelude to exercises of federal disallowance.[1]

[1] Peter H Russell, *Leading Constitutional Decisions* (Toronto: McLelland and Stewart, 1973) xxiii. The relationship between references and the federal disallowance power was specifically averted to some years later by Edward Blake, who seems to have viewed references as providing a check on federal power:

> Now, Sir, in the exercise of this power of disallowance by the Government, political questions may … arise. Questions of policy may present themselves, that [are] clearly, exclusively for … the political departments of the Government. But it is equally clear that when, in order to determine your course you must find whether a particular act is ultra or intra vires, you are discharging a legal and judicial function.
>
> My own opinion is that whenever … it is contemplated by the Dominion Executive to disallow a provincial Act because it is ultra vires, there ought to be a reference; and also that there ought to be a reference in certain cases where the condition of public opinion renders expedient a solution of legal problems, dissociated from those elements of passion and expediency which are rightly or wrongly too often attributed to the action of political bodies.

HC Deb, Canada, 1890, vol II, 4084–94.

The objection was acknowledged, though not in a way that gave the provinces much comfort. Instead, in 1870 the federal government proposed that the Governor in Council (the federal Cabinet) be able to refer to the Court a much broader array of questions. Still excluded from such review were Acts or Bills of the government of Canada.[2] And the initiation of references remained under the exclusive control of the federal executive.

The 1875 draft Supreme and Exchequer Court Act provided for the hearing of 'special cases on constitutional matters'.[3] The Act contemplated two functions in additional to hearing appeals. First, the Court could hear 'special cases' about the validity of *any* Act or Bill, federal *or* provincial. Importantly, such cases would require the 'advice and consent of the Privy Council'. The special case provisions provided for the automatic, though not mandatory, appearance of federal counsel as well as counsel for affected or interested provinces. They also provided for submissions by other persons 'whose interests may be affected by the Act in question'.

The second function is comparable to the reference jurisdiction as it exists today. Namely, the federal executive could refer a variety of questions including those concerning the BNA Act. That reference function would *not* have depended upon Imperial approval, and it directed the Supreme Court to hear the proceeding and for all judges to provide an opinion on the questions posed.

In the Parliamentary debates, the Justice Minister, Telesphore Fournier, stated that the special case provision 'was framed in order to satisfy a very generally expressed public desire' for judicial review of matters concerning 'the powers of local legislatures'.[4] The Minister identified the Court as a sort of umpire of federal–provincial disputes. The point would prove to have enormous staying power, eventually providing the basis, over a century later, for the Court's assertion that its own status is protected by the Constitution.[5]

Fournier conceded that Parliament could not give the Court original jurisdiction to try constitutional issues.[6] He noted that 'the only power which could be conferred upon the court properly was to try appeals from the decisions of courts of original jurisdiction'.[7] Given those limitations, it would be 'expedient' to provide that 'by the consent of the provincial governments concerned, decisions given by the Supreme Court would have their effect in the cases mentioned as fitted for reference to it'.[8]

[2] James G Snell and Frederick Vaughan, *The Supreme Court of Canada* (Toronto: The Osgoode Society, 1985) 7.

[3] Bill C-31, An Act to establish a Supreme Court, and a Court of Exchequer, for the Dominion of Canada, 2nd Session, 3rd Parliament, 38 Victoria, 1875 (second reading 26 February 1875).

[4] House of Commons Debates, Session 1875 Vol 1 at 286.

[5] *Reference re Supreme Court Act, ss. 5 and 6*, 2014 SCC 21, [2014] 1 SCR 433.

[6] House of Commons debates, Sess 1867, vol 1 at 286.

[7] ibid.

[8] ibid.

Fournier said that the 'opinion' that the Court would certify would be entirely distinct from a verdict in a case. It 'would not bear the character of a judgment, [but] would merely have its *moral weight* in assisting the government to arrive at a determination'.[9] Here, we find a theory about the legal character of reference opinions that has proven to be tenacious (regardless of whether it is borne out in practice). Advisory opinions would have only a 'moral' suasion that would chiefly bear on the (federal) government which would receive and consider them.

The Minister's benign characterisations were intended to diffuse keen anxiety. Some MPs were 'startled' by the scope of the special jurisdiction.[10] Sir John A Macdonald, for example, described the power as requiring 'the gravest consideration', though he apparently was mollified by the idea that it was 'principally for the purpose of informing the conscience of the Government'.[11] Another MP drew an explicit link between the special jurisdiction and the reserve power of the Judicial Committee, noting that, despite the 'extreme' latitude given to the Governor in Council the reference power 'was not unprecedented in England, under the Acts enlarging the power of the Privy Councillors'.[12]

In the end, the advisory function that appeared in the Supreme and Exchequer Court Act was virtually identical to that found in section 4 of the Judicial Committee Act 1833. It read:

> 52. It shall be lawful for the Governor in Council to refer to the Supreme Court for hearing or consideration, any matters whatsoever he may think fit; and the Court shall thereupon hear and consider the same and certify their opinion thereon to the Governor in Council: Provided that any judge or judges of the said Court who may differ from the opinion of the majority may in like manner certify his or their opinion or opinions to the Governor in Council.
>
> 53. The said Court, or any two of the judges thereof, shall examine and report upon any private bill or petition for a private bill presented to the Senate or House of Commons and referred to the Court under any rules of orders made by the Senate or House of Commons.[13]

The Act maintained the advisory function as a creature of Crown discretion. The federal Cabinet, the paramount executive body, was empowered to put questions to the Court without regard to their subject matter. The Act did not exclude from review Bills or Acts of the federal Parliament. But the review was triggered solely by Cabinet.

Section 53 identified an altogether different route for review, allowing for references to 'two or more judges' who would 'examine and report' on any private Bill or related petition put forward by either the Senate or House of Commons

[9] House of Commons Debates, Sess 1875, vol 1 at 286 (emphasis added).
[10] ibid at 750 (Mr Moss).
[11] ibid at 289.
[12] ibid at 750 (Mr Moss).
[13] Supreme and Exchequer Court Act 1875, ss 52–53.

according to rules developed by the respective chambers.[14] Indeed, it bypassed Cabinet altogether.[15] The current version of the provision, which quickly fell into disuse, is discussed in the next chapter. It suffices, for now, to note that the process envisaged in section 53 was different from section 52. It had a much narrower focus (private Bills); and it would not necessarily produce 'opinions' of the entire Court, since it could be satisfied by a 'report' from as few as two judges.

Early Quiet, Early Reform

For a time, the reference function was rarely used.[16] Many perceived it to be inadequate. For one thing, the Supreme Court did not draw any correlation between section 52 of the Act and its more central appellate function. Over the Court's first 15 years, oral argument was only infrequently heard.[17] In addition, following the lead of the Privy Council, the Court sometimes provided a bare answer – a 'yes' or a 'no' – without reasons.[18] Such a practice obviously would fail to provide much guidance. For example, in the *McCarthy Act Reference*,[19] a federal liquor law was deemed to be ultra vires without explanation. That result left the federal government bereft of advice to frame future action other than abandoning the particular law in question.

Indeed, depending on the nature of a question, such an answer could be worse than merely unhelpful. In a *McCarthy Act*-type proceeding, a bare 'no' might suggest that the government ought not to venture into a particular policy area at all, when in fact a number of alternative routes would be constitutionally viable. The bare 'no' could well inhibit government initiative, and, in turn, risk inhibiting worthwhile and constitutionally valid policy.

The procedural defects were noted, rather thunderously, by Attorney General Edward Blake:

> Our present powers [in respect of the Supreme Court], Sir, are wholly inadequate for the effectual execution of the project in hand. There is no certainty – there is in ordinary

[14] The current version of this provision is found at Supreme Court Act (RSC, 1985, c S-26).

[15] The provision was mentioned during the oral argument before the JCPC in *In re References by the Governor-General in Council* (1910), 43 SCR 536 at 547 (SCC), aff'd [1912] AC 571 (PC) [*Reference re References*]. Counsel for the provinces declared that it posed the same concerns as s 52 but that it was not his focus: *The Attorney General for the Province of Ontario and others v The Attorney General for the Dominion of Canada and another (Canada)* [1912] UKPC 35 (16 May 1912), *Proceedings First Day*, 355–56: www.bailii.org/uk/cases/UKPC/1912/1912_35.html.

[16] Barry L Strayer, *The Canadian Constitution and the Courts* (Toronto: Butterworths, 1988) 312.

[17] Barry Strayer, *Judicial Review of Legislation in Canada* (Toronto: University of Toronto Press, 1968) 183.

[18] Strayer (n 16) 3. In fairness, the JCPC apparently offered no objection, which, given the history of references in England, is difficult to explain.

[19] *Sess. Papers* No 85a, 1885 (Can) at 12–13. Bora Laskin, 'The Supreme Court of Canada: A Final Court of and for Canadians' (1951) 29(10) Canadian Bar Review 1038, 1062, provides a helpful summary.

> cases rather an improbability – of our being able to reach the Judicial Committee; and as to all the three possible appeals or references, the Judicial Committee of the Privy Council, the Supreme Court, and the Imperial law officers, the machinery is extremely defective. There is no provision for the representation of the different interests; there is no provision for the ascertainment of facts; there is no provision for the reasoned opinion of the tribunal.[20]

Blake went so far as to call Supreme Court references the equivalent of a 'Delphic oracle'.[21] Seeking to clarify the reference procedure, he clearly hoped to limit it to questions about the federal government's disallowance power.[22]

Though successful in reforming the Act, Blake was less successful at limiting references. Still, it is a testament to his industry that the 1891 amendments have survived largely intact.[23] Under those changes, the Court was still required to 'hear and consider [the reference], and to answer each question so referred';[24] and to certify 'its opinion upon each such question, with the reasons for each such answer'[25] along with any dissents. Now, though, a reference opinion would be 'pronounced in like manner as in the case of a judgment upon an appeal to the Court'.[26]

Another change responded to provincial objections about the perceived imbalance vis-à-vis the federal executive. The Act reverted back to a provision proposed at first reading in 1875 (regarding 'special cases') to the effect that where a reference question concerned the validity of provincial legislation, the Attorney General of that province was deemed to have a 'special interest' in that question and notified of the hearing.[27] The Court additionally could notify or appoint other parties it thought fit to be present, including *amicus curiae*.[28]

The Act as amended in 1891 confirmed a broad range of questions available for review, including "[the] constitutionality or interpretation of any Dominion or provincial legislation"; "[the] powers of the Parliament of Canada, or of the

[20] 2 House of Commons Debates, 6th Parl, 4th Sess, 1890, at 4089–90.

[21] ibid.

[22] Blake also thought that there should be references with respect to the federal power over educational matters: Strayer (n 17) 184.

[23] Supreme Court and Exchequer Act 54–55, Vict, c 25 (1891) (Can).

[24] ibid s 4.

[25] ibid. Unlike the Judicial Committee, which issued a single opinion, the Supreme Court could issue opinions by each judge.

[26] ibid.

[27] ibid.

[28] ibid: '37(5). The Court may in its discretion request any counsel to argue the case as to any interest which is affected and as to which counsel does not appear, and the reasonable expenses thereby occasioned may be paid by the Minister of Finance and Receiver General out of any moneys appropriated by Parliament for expenses of litigation'. The current comparable provision is found in Rule 92, *Rules of the Supreme Court of Canada* (SOR/2002-156). The Court permitted third parties to intervene very early on. For example, in the *Local Prohibition Reference*, it allowed an appearance by the Distillers and Brewers' Association: *In re Prohibitory Liquor Laws*, (1895) 24 SCR 170.

legislatures of the provinces, or of the respective governments thereof"; or "[any] other matter … with respect to which the Governor in Council sees fit to submit any such question."[29]

The 1891 Act also specifically labelled reference opinions as 'advisory'.[30] That nod to the advisory-only nature of references did *not* survive but its disappearance had little effect on how references were and are treated.

In 1922 the Act granted even more scope to the provinces by creating an automatic right to appeal reference opinions issued by provincial appellate courts.[31] The provinces thereby enjoyed nearly equivalent access to the Court as the federal government. It has remained in place ever since. There were no qualms expressed about permitting a party to 'appeal' a reference opinion from a lower court to a higher one. As will be discussed in Chapter 10, this likely contributed to the perception of reference opinions as similar in non-trivial ways to cases.

Today, the scope of the permissible questions, set out in subsection 53(1), mirrors the wording used in 1891. In addition, the Act has retained the Governor in Council's discretion to refer to the Court other questions, legal or factual, that it deems 'important'. The Court is under a 'duty' to hear the reference,[32] to answer each question in 'like manner' to an appeal, and to record the opinions of dissenting judges. The notice provisions remain. As mentioned above, section 36 continues the automatic right of appeal for provinces in respect of opinions they have sought from their own courts.[33]

Squaring Advisory Opinions with a General Court of Appeal

How did references gain such broad acceptance within Canadian legal culture and practice? After all, in Britain, where the function had been in place for centuries,

[29] ibid s 37.

[30] ibid: '37(6). The opinion of the Court upon any such reference, although advisory only, shall, for all purposes of appeal to Her Majesty in Council, be treated as a final judgment of the said court between parties'.

[31] Supreme Court Act 1922 12–13 George V, 14th Parliament, 1st Session C48, s 42A: 'An appeal shall lie to the Supreme Court of Canada from an opinion pronounced by the highest court of final resort in any province on any matter referred to it for hearing and consideration by the Lieutenant Governor in Council of such province whenever it has been by the statutes of the said province declared that such opinion is to be deemed a judgment of the said highest court of final resort and that an appeal shall lie therefrom as from a judgment in an action'. In 1927 the Court increased from six to seven judges: 1926–1927 pt I (Prefix to Statutes; 17 George V, 16th Parliament, 1st Session), assented to 31 March 1927: Chapter 38.

[32] Despite the mandatory wording, the Supreme Court has not always felt obliged to answer – see the discussion in Chapter 4.

[33] Supreme Court Act, RSC, 1985, c S-26: '36. An appeal lies to the Court from an opinion pronounced by the highest court of final resort in a province on any matter referred to it for hearing and consideration by the lieutenant governor in council of that province whenever it has been by the statutes of that province declared that such opinion is to be deemed a judgment of the highest court of final resort and that an appeal lies therefrom as from a judgment in an action'.

advisory opinions ceased to play much of a role beyond the eighteenth century.[34] And yet in Canada the advisory opinion became not only a legitimate route for adjudication but, in some contexts, a preferred one. That point is unpacked over several chapters. Below, I discuss the attempts by both the Judicial Committee of the Privy Council (at the time, recall, Canada's apex court) and the Canadian Supreme Court to wrestle with advisory opinions as distinct legal phenomena.

One starts with the opinion issued in *In Re References by the Governor-General in Council*.[35] Known as the '*Reference re References*', the matter involved a series of federal questions of extraordinary length and complexity[36] about the provincial

[34] Stewart Jay, 'Servants of Monarchs and Lords: The Advisory Role of Early English Judges' (1994) 38 American Journal of Legal History 117.

[35] *Reference re References* (n 15).

[36] ibid at 545–46. I feel obligated to include them in full.

1. What limitation exists under 'The British North America Act, 1867', upon the power of the provincial legislatures to incorporate companies?
   What is the meaning of the expression 'with provincial objects' in section 92, article II, of the said Act? Is the limitation thereby defined territorial, or does it have regard to the character of the powers which may be conferred upon companies locally incorporated, or what otherwise is the intention and effect of the said limitation?
2. Has a company incorporated by a provincial legislature under the powers conferred in that behalf by section 92, article II of 'The British North America Act, 1867' power or capacity to do business outside of the limits of the incorporating province. If so, to what extent and for what purpose?
   Has a company incorporated by a provincial legislature for the purpose, for example, of buying and selling or grinding grain, the power or capacity, by virtue of such provincial incorporation, to buy or sell or grind grain outside of the incorporating province?
3. Has a corporation constituted by a provincial legislature with power to carry on a fire insurance business, there being no stated limitation as to the locality within which the business may be carried on, power or capacity to make and execute contracts—
   (*a*) within the incorporating province insuring property outside of the province;
   (*b*) outside of the incorporating province insuring property within the province;
   (*c*) outside of the incorporating province insuring property outside of the province?
   Has such a corporation power or capacity to insure property situate in a foreign country, or to make an insurance contract within a foreign country?
   Do the answers to the foregoing inquiries, or any and which of them, depend upon whether or not the owner of the property or risk insured is a citizen or resident of the incorporating province?
4. If in any or all of the above mentioned cases (a), (b) and (c) the answer be negative, would the corporation have throughout Canada the power or capacity mentioned in any and which of the said cases on availing itself of the 'Insurance Act', 1910, 9 & 10 Edw. VII, chapter 32, section 3, sub-section 3?
   Is the said enactment, the 'Insurance Act', 1910, chapter 32, section 23, sub-section 3, *intra vires* of the Parliament of Canada?
5. Can the powers of a company incorporated by a provincial legislature be enlarged, and to what extent, either as to locality or objects by
   (a) the Dominion Parliament?
   (b) the legislature of another province?
6. Has the legislature of a province power to prohibit companies incorporated by the Parliament of Canada from carrying on business within the province unless or until the companies obtain a license so to do from the government of the province, or other local authority constituted by the legislature, if fees are required to be paid upon the issue of such licenses?

power to incorporate companies; the competency of the British Columbia government to lease fishing rights in certain provincial waters; and the validity of certain sections of the federal Insurance Act 1910. A number of provinces[37] contested the hearing under what was then section 60 of the Act.[38] They argued, first, that the federal government should not have referred questions about provincial matters;[39] and,

For examples of such provincial legislation see Ontario, 63 Vict. ch. 24; New Brunswick Cons. Stats., 1903, ch. 18; British Columbia, 5 Edw. VII ch. II

7. Is it competent to a provincial legislature to restrict a company incorporated by the Parliament of Canada for the purpose of trading throughout the whole Dominion in the exercise of the special trading powers so conferred or to limit the exercise of such powers within the province?
   Is such a Dominion trading company subject to or governed by the legislation of a province in which it carries out or proposes to carry out its trading powers limiting the nature or kinds of business which corporations not incorporated by the legislature of the province may carry on, or the powers which they may exercise within the province, or imposing conditions which are to be observed or complied with by such corporations before they can engage in business within the province?
   Can such a company so incorporated by the Parliament of Canada be otherwise restricted in the exercise of its corporate powers or capacity, and how, and in what respect by provincial legislation?

The questions referred by order in council, on 29 June 1910, were as follows:

1. Is it competent to the legislature of British Columbia to authorize the government of the province to grant by way of lease, license or otherwise the exclusive right to fish in any or what part or parts of the waters within the 'Railway Belt',
   (a) as to such waters as are tidal, and
   (b) as to such waters as although not tidal are in fact navigable?
2. Is it competent to the legislature of British Columbia to authorize the government of that province to grant by way of lease, license or otherwise the exclusive right, or any right, to fish below low water mark in or in any or what part or parts of the open sea within a marine league of the coast of the province?
3. Is there any and what difference between the open sea within a marine league of the coast of British Columbia and the gulfs, bays, channels, arms of the sea and estuaries of the rivers within the province, or lying between the province and the United States of America, so far as concerns the authority of the Legislature of British Columbia to authorize the government of the province to grant by way of lease, license or otherwise the exclusive right, or any right, to fish below low water mark in the said waters or any of them?

[37] The provinces opposing the reference were Ontario, Nova Scotia, New Brunswick, Manitoba, Prince Edward Island and Alberta. British Columbia consented to the fishing question; and Quebec consented to the fishing and insurance questions. Saskatchewan did not take a position. At the time, there were nine Canadian provinces; today there are 10.

[38] Supreme Court Act, RSC, 1906, c 139. Section 60 was identical to s 37 in the 1891 Act (n 23).

[39] Indeed, the objection was first articulated in *In re Certain Statutes of the Province of Manitoba relating to Education*, (1894) 22 SCR 577 [*Manitoba Education Reference*]. The matter concerned an appeal sought under either the BNA Act or the Act creating the Province of Manitoba, against provincial laws repealing certain statutory rights granted to the Roman Catholic minority to have denominational schools. Interestingly, counsel for Manitoba appeared in court but declined to argue the case, prompting the Court to appoint an *amicus curiae*. In his written opinion, Justice Taschereau expressed doubts about the Court's jurisdiction to hear the matter noting Manitoba's refusal to participate. He went on to say at 678: 'This court is evidently made, in the matter, a court of first instance, or rather, I should say, an advisory board of the federal executive, substituted, *pro hâc vice*, for the law officers of the crown, and not performing any of the usual functions of a court of appeal, nay, of

second, that an advisory function was incompatible with the type of court authorised under section 101 of the Constitution Act 1867.

The provinces noted that section 101 has two clauses. The first authorises Parliament to create 'a general court of appeal for Canada'. The second permits the creation of 'any additional courts for the better administration of the laws of Canada'. The Supreme Court's appellate functions are encompassed by the first clause, they said, but the second clause related only to legal matters pertaining to the laws of the federal order of government.[40] Since an advisory function is not appellate in nature, it could only be authorised by that second clause. Thus, the provinces urged, any court established under it was limited to dealing with questions of federal law.

The Supreme Court dismissed that argument. Writing for a majority of four judges, Chief Justice Fitzpatrick wondered whether 'better words [could have been] used to convey the widest discretion of legislation with respect to the all-embracing subject "the better administration of the laws of Canada"'.[41] The answer, to him, was clear. Nothing in the Constitution Act 1867 suggested that Parliament could not empower a section 101 court to consider references. Indeed, the 'peace, order and good government' clause in section 91 (the section of the BNA Act that enumerates federal legislative authority) supported a reference jurisdiction aimed at construing all laws.[42]

The judges in the majority tended to focus on the functions that Parliament could vest in certain institutions. They did not consider the federalism-related argument that it is inappropriate for one order of government to be able to put to a court, ostensibly under its control, questions pertaining to its jurisdictional rival.

The federalism concerns did strike a chord with the two dissenting judges. Girouard and Idington JJ each reasoned that, to the extent that the federal executive could refer a purely provincial question, the Act was indeed ultra vires. There was a solution, however, if the provinces united with the federal government in submissions. In that case, they said, the Court would be free to answer. Intriguingly, Justice Girouard likened it to an added party intervention in which the resulting decision would be binding upon the parties.[43]

On appeal, the Judicial Committee endorsed the majority view. In allocating legislative authority, it said, a Constitution may be clear or ambiguous.

any court of justice whatever. However, I need not, at present, further investigate this point. It has not been raised, and a similar enactment to the same import has already been acted upon.' The reference is discussed in Chapter 10.

[40] The provinces' argument is best captured in the record of proceedings at the Privy Council: 12 December 1911, at 11; www.bailii.org/uk/cases/UKPC/1912/1912_35(image5).pdf.

[41] *Reference re References* (n 15) (SCC) at 552.

[42] ibid at 553. The provision, known as POGG, states: '91. It shall be lawful for the Queen, by and with the Advice and Consent of the Senate and House of Commons, to make Laws for the Peace, Order, and good Government of Canada, in relation to all Matters not coming within the Classes of Subjects by this Act assigned exclusively to the Legislatures of the Provinces …'.

[43] ibid at 558.

But, 'if the text says nothing expressly, then it is not to be presumed that the Constitution withholds the power altogether'.[44] The division of powers is exhaustive of all potential legislative authority in a given system, for, 'whatever belongs to self-government in Canada belongs either to the Dominion or to the Provinces.'[45]

Given that the BNA Act was silent about a reference function, the issue was whether 'such a power [was] *repugnant* to that Act'.[46] The Committee summarised the provincial argument in these terms:

> [W]hen a Court of Appeal from all the Provincial Courts is authorised to be set up, that carries with it an implied condition that the Court of Appeal shall be in truth a judicial body, according to the conception of judicial character [obtaining in Great Britain] … And they say that to place the duty of answering such questions [on the Supreme Court] is incompatible with the maintenance of such judicial character or of public confidence in it or with the free access to an unbiased tribunal of Appeal to which litigants in the Provincial Courts are of right entitled.[47]

The Committee described the provinces as arguing that when such a court answers reference questions, it 'ceases to be such a judiciary as the Constitution provides for'.[48] Considering that claim required evaluating the provinces' second argument, which, essentially, relied upon the separation of powers and the proper role of the judiciary.

The provinces argued that a reference function should not be invested in a general court of appeal because

> [t]he giving of such advice is no part of the administration of the law … yet it interferes with and hampers that administration. The point involved in such references may afterwards arise in the course of legal proceedings between individuals or between the Provinces and the Dominion.[49]

Sir Robert Finlay, counsel for the provinces, argued that section 101 shows that the Supreme Court was to be a court and a court only. To cast upon it such advisory functions as the Supreme Court Act purported to would be inconsistent with the duties of a Court.[50] The provinces claimed that forcing the Court to provide advice on request of the Executive would 'hamper and interfere' with the proper administration of the law. Such opinions might prove 'highly prejudicial' if the Court later confronted the same issue in a live case.[51] The arguments rest, broadly, on the sorts of justiciability concerns raised in Chapter 1. They echo, as well, the narrower view

[44] *Reference re References* (JCPC) (n 15) at 5.
[45] ibid.
[46] ibid at 6 (emphasis added).
[47] ibid.
[48] ibid.
[49] *Reference re References* (n 15) (PC) (factum of the Appellant at para 12).
[50] Record of Proceedings (n 40) at 16.
[51] *Reference re References* (n 15) (PC) (factum of the Appellant at para 12).

of the judiciary mentioned in Chapter 2. In the case of the Canadian provinces, the argument was advanced to promote and protect regional interests perceived to be at odds with federal ones.

As will be discussed in the next chapter, when Canadian courts believe that they ought not to answer certain questions they have simply refused to answer them. By and large they have not averred the specific federalism concern inherent in permitting one order of government to seek judicial advice about another's laws.

At the hearing for the *Reference re References*, several of the JCPC members were sympathetic to that concern.[52] Ultimately, though, the Committee was not persuaded.

The Committee noted the advisory function's historical precedent: section 4 of the Judicial Committee Act.[53] The section 4 process had been used 'from time to time, though rarely and with a careful regard to the nature of the reference'.[54] Given that the members of the JCPC were themselves Privy Councillors, they were 'bound as such to advise the Crown when required in that capacity'.[55] Indeed,

> [u]pon the whole, it does seem strange that a Court, for such in effect this is, should have been for three-quarters of a century liable to answer questions put by the Crown, and should have done it without the least suggestion of inconvenience or impropriety, *if the same thing when attempted in Canada deserves to be stigmatised as subversive to judicial functions*.[56]

The Committee stated that the advisory function was of long standing and that, in its judicial capacity, the House of Lords could ask the judges any 'such questions as it may think necessary for the decision of a particular case'.[57] But the JCPC was careful to distinguish that function from the House of Lords asking the judges 'what the law is, in order to better inform itself how if at all the law should be altered'.[58] The latter practice had not occurred in 50 years[59] and, in the opinion of the Committee, rested upon an unwritten constitutional privilege.[60]

[52] Record of Proceedings (n 40) at 18 *per* Lord Atkinson: 'I do not see at present how a question on any subject the Governor General chooses to submit can have anything to do with the better administration of the laws of Canada'.

[53] ibid at 7.

[54] ibid.

[55] ibid.

[56] ibid (emphasis added).

[57] ibid.

[58] ibid at 8.

[59] The Judicial Committee appears to have been referring to *McNaghten's Case* (1843) 8 ER 718, where, after the attempted assassination of Prime Minister Sir Robert Peel (and the murder of his secretary), the Lords debated the law of insanity and, in order to guide their discussions, put a set of questions to the judges. *Reference re References* (n 15) (SCC) at 548.

[60] *Reference re References* (n 15) (PC) at 8.

The Committee also cast doubt upon the practice of the Crown – as opposed to Parliament – questioning judges on the state of the law, noting that 'Earlier practice in bad times is of no weight'.[61]

For the Committee, the more pertinent question was how advisory review had evolved *in Canada*. Since 1875, it noted, the Supreme Court of Canada had 'repeatedly' answered such questions and on six occasions those answers had been further appealed to the Committee. Indeed, 'the Acts now alleged to have been *ultra vires*, were in fact acted upon, and so treated as valid, *not only by the Court in Canada but also on appeal in Whitehall*'.[62]

In consequence:

> [It is not easy to believe that] the Judicial Committee would have so often failed even to advert to a departure so serious as is now maintained, from what is due to the independence and character of Courts of Justice. It is clear indeed that no such apprehension ever occurred to any of the great lawyers who heard those cases. And that circumstance militates very strongly against the view now put forward, that it is repugnant to the *British North America Act* and subversive of justice to require the Court to answer questions not in litigation.[63]

In other words, one could not challenge the advisory function without impugning the integrity of numerous prior hearings.

The Committee had not quite finished demolishing the provincial argument. It turned next to the provinces' own histories, noting that nearly all of them had passed reference legislation 'in terms somewhat similar to the Dominion Act which they impugn'.[64] Either the provincial Acts were valid while the Dominion law was not, which 'seems very strange'; or both sets of laws were ultra vires.[65] In any event, it was 'remarkable that for 35 years this point of view has apparently escaped notice in Canada, and a contrary view, *now said to menace the very essence of justice*, has been tranquilly acted upon without question'.[66]

The Committee was neither oblivious to the federalism question, nor uncritical of the federal government's approach. With respect to the federal executive

[61] ibid at 8–9. The JCPC did note a request related to one Lord George Sackville, in command during the Battle of Minden in 1759. Sackville was put to a Court Martial *after* he had resigned his commission. The controversy produced the following comment in the opinion submitted by Lord Mansfield: '[We] see no ground to doubt of the legality of the jurisdiction of a Court Martial in the case put by the above question. But as the matter may several ways be brought, in due course of law, judicially before some of us by any party affected by that method of trial, if he thinks the court has no jurisdiction; or if the Court should refuse to proceed, in case the party thinks they have jurisdiction, *we shall be ready, without difficulty, to change our opinion*, if we see cause, upon objections that may then be laid before us, though none have occurred to us at present that we think sufficient'. Record of Proceedings (n 40) at 26–27 (emphasis added).

[62] *Reference re References* (n 15) at 9–10 (emphasis added).

[63] ibid at 10.

[64] ibid.

[65] ibid.

[66] ibid (emphasis added).

referring provincial questions, the JCPC noted that any answers were merely advisory. It acknowledged that the Act had enabled 'asking a series of questions very difficult to answer exhaustively and accurately without so many qualifications and reservations as to make the answers of little value'.[67] But, 'whether [a] power is rightly or wrongly used'[68] had no bearing on whether it was ultra vires.

In the JCPC's view, it was being asked to say 'that the Canadian Parliament ought not to pass laws like this because it may be embarrassing and onerous to the Court, and to declare this law invalid because it ought not to have been passed'.[69] That was something the JCPC refused to do:

> Their Lordships would be departing from their legitimate province if they entertained the arguments of the Appellants. They would really be pronouncing upon the policy of the Canadian Parliament, which is exclusively the business of the Canadian people, and is of no concern of this Board.[70]

The Committee did though, 'point out the mischief and inconvenience which might arise from an indiscriminate and injudicious use of the Act, and leave it to the consideration of those who alone are lawfully and constitutionally entitled to decide upon such a matter'.[71]

The JCPC roundly dismissed the notion that a reference function is incompatible with the duties of a general court of appeal. The role was firmly established (if infrequently used) in British legal tradition. The provinces were in a poor position to complain, on grounds of judicial propriety, about a function they had vested in their own courts! While there were some risks to such a function, any 'mischief and inconvenience' was best addressed on a case-by-case basis.

Following suit, Canadian courts accepted the reference function as part of their duties. Rather than functioning solely as a 'check' on the executive branch by ruling on the legality of its decisions, the judiciary was occasionally drawn into an altogether different relationship with it.[72] Between 1867 and 1986, references accounted for one-quarter of the Supreme Court's constitutional docket.[73] Since the enactment in 1982 of a constitutional framework that includes an entrenched Bill of Rights, references have not arisen as frequently (a point considered in chapter 7).

[67] ibid at 12. The questions are found above at n 36. The Committee went on to state: 'The Supreme Court itself can however either point out in its answer these or other considerations of a like kind, or can make the necessary representations to the Governor General in Council when it thinks right so to treat any questions that may be put. *And the Parliament of Canada can control the Executive*' (emphasis added). The above ideas are discussed in Chapter 4.

[68] ibid.

[69] ibid.

[70] ibid.

[71] ibid.

[72] This continues through the modern period, as the Supreme Court has noted that the American conception of separation of powers does not find an exact corollary in Canada. *Reference Re Secession of Quebec*, [1998] 2 SCR 217 at para 15 [*Secession Reference*].

[73] Strayer (n 16) 331.

Putting the 'Advisory' in an Advisory Function

One of the most consequential differences between references and live cases is that the former are said to not engage a court's remedial function and therefore are not binding.[74] From the outset, some viewed that feature as functionally inconsistent with a court of general jurisdiction. Justice Taschereau put it rather dramatically in the 1894 *Manitoba Education Reference*:

> We give no judgment, we determine nothing, we end no controversy; and, whatever our answers may be, should it be deemed expedient … by [the] executive to impugn the constitutionality of any measure that might hereafter be taken … whether such measure is in accordance with or in opposition to the answers to this consultation, the recourse, in the usual way, to the courts of the country remains open to them. … For if, as a matter of policy, in the public interest, no action is to be taken upon the petitioners' application, even if the appeal lies, the futility of these proceedings is apparent.[75]

Justice Idington expressed similar sentiments, but in even stronger terms, in the *Reference re References*: 'If we *degrade* this court by imposing upon it duties that cannot be held judicial but merely advisory and especially in the wholesale way submitted herein, *we destroy a fundamental principle of our government*'.[76] As we have seen, the Judicial Committee of the Privy Council (and the majority of the Supreme Court) rejected that view. The advisory nature of references was described by both courts as both useful and consistent with legal tradition.[77]

In early decisions, judges tended to emphasise that references were merely 'advisory'. In *Reference re References*, Davies J stated:

> [T]hese answers are simply to aid the Governor in Council in reaching conclusions for which they must be held entirely responsible. The answers do not bind the Governor in Council. He may act in accordance with them or not, as he pleases, giving them just such weight as he pleases. They are advisory only. They do not bind even this court …. [Nor can they] be said to be in any way binding upon the judges of any of the provincial courts.[78]

This point was echoed by the JCPC:

> It is difficult to resist the conclusion that the point now raised [by the provinces] would never have been raised had it not been for the nature of the questions … But the answers are advisory only and will have no more effect than the opinions of the Law Officers.[79]

[74] Chapter 10 examines this asserted distinction more closely.

[75] *Manitoba Education Reference* (n 39) at 678. The Reference is also revisited in Chapter 10.

[76] ibid at 582 (emphasis added).

[77] *Reference re References* (n 15) (SCC). See also the decisions of Justice Girouard at 558, Justice Davies at 559, Justice Duff at 592 and Justice Anglin at 592. Alone of the *seriatim* opinions, the Chief Justice's did not mention the advisory nature of references, though he did not dispute the point either. Ibid at 11.

[78] ibid (SCC) *per* Davies J at 559.

[79] ibid (JCPC) at 11.

Indeed, the Supreme and Exchequer Court Act itself described reference opinions as 'advisory' though one scholar has suggested that the words were inserted as a precaution, to underline that the opinions did not bind the executive or the Supreme Court in future cases – because that was implicit in the very nature of a reference.[80] The point is borne out by the fact that after the removal of those words in 1956,[81] there was no appreciable effect on reference opinions.

The analysis offered in the *Reference re Criminal Code*,[82] is instructive. The underlying issue concerned the circumstances under which the Crown could prefer an indictment.[83] A man named William Duff was tried in Saskatchewan for importing stolen property into Canada.[84] Immediately following his conviction, the deputy Attorney General for Saskatchewan, who was present in court, preferred a charge under then section 188 (escaping/attempting to escape imprisonment).[85] The trial court held that the second charge was not lawful because the Code limited that decision to judges or the Attorney General himself.

Over strenuous provincial objections, the federal government put a number of questions about the matter to the Supreme Court of Canada.[86] Justice Girouard admitted that he *was* concerned by the prospect of 'sit[ting] in a case which looks very much as if it were an appeal from provincial courts in a criminal matter where the statute says there is no appeal to this court'.[87] Justice Davies and Justice Anglin, in separate opinions, made similar points.[88]

Nonetheless, the Court decided that it could answer the questions. It did so at least in part because it was persuaded that its advice 'has no legal effect, does not affect the rights of parties, nor the provincial decisions, and is not even binding upon us'.[89] Justice Davies said something very similar: 'I do not think this court or its members would feel bound in any concrete case which might arise hereafter by any expression of opinion we may now give on these questions'.[90]

Thus, from the beginning, courts were confident of maintaining a feasible distinction between references and cases. They rarely declined to answer questions.

[80] Gerald Rubin, 'The Nature, Use and Effect of Reference Cases in Canadian Constitutional Law' (1959) 6 McGill Law Journal 168.

[81] 4–5 Eliz II c 48, s 7.

[82] *Reference re Criminal Code (Canada), s. 873(A)* (1910), 43 SCR 434 [*Criminal Code Reference*].

[83] Section 873(a) of the Criminal Code (6 & 7 Edw VII ch 8).

[84] The offence was the then s 398. Criminal Code of Canada RSC 1906, C-146.

[85] ibid.

[86] *Criminal Code Reference* (n 83) at 435.

[87] ibid at 426.

[88] ibid. Justice Davies wrote that the questions '… practically ask us to sit as a court of appeal'. Noting that 'no such appeal is allowed' he stated that 'the better course would be for this court to refer the questions back to His Excellency in Council'. He complained, further, of a lack of argument 'on both sides of the questions'. Justice Anglin noted that since 'a review of the judgment of [the Saskatchewan court] is unavoidably involved', and there had been 'strong disapprobation expressed by the Judicial Committee of the Privy Council of the practice of procuring judicial opinions upon abstract questions', he answered the questions 'with reluctance and diffidence, solely in obedience to the imperative provisions of the statute …' ibid at 454.

[89] The Court answered all of the questions in the negative. Idington J dissented from the answer to Question 1.

[90] *Criminal Code Reference* (n 83) at 437.

Yet, their position did not explain exactly what a court *does* when it issues a reference opinion; or how references would coexist with the many appeals that the Supreme Court also would produce. It also did not answer the reasonable question of what would be the *point* of such non-binding opinions. Courts simply were confident that references would be non-binding.

Chapter 10 will return to that issue. It will do, for now, to note that the tidy distinction never really took hold. The exceptions[91] proved the rule: the Supreme Court and the Judicial Committee cited previous reference opinions in much the same way as cases – indeed, exercising what one scholar has called 'undiscriminating zeal'.[92] As discussed later in this book, that fact would have profound effects on Canadian constitutional law. The next chapter considers how an advisory function can spur separation of powers concerns.

[91] See *Kerley v London & Lake Erie Transport Co.*, [1912] OJ No. 157. In deciding whether a provincial statute purporting to fine a railway company for operating on Sunday was ultra vires, Boyd J noted that both the Supreme Court and the Judicial Committee had previously issued advisory opinions stating that such 'Sunday closing legislation' fell within the exclusive federal competence over criminal law: *In the Matter of the Jurisdiction of a Province to Legislate respecting Abstention from Labour on Sunday*, (1905) 35 SCR 581; and *Attorney-General for Ontario v Hamilton Street R.W. Co* [1903] AC 524. In holding that the impugned law was intra vires, Boyd J noted at para 30: 'I cannot regard the opinion expressed on this head as a judgment binding on me, nor can I accept it as the law'.

[92] Strayer (n 16) 331.

4

Separate Functions – Separate Powers

The previous two chapters explored the advisory opinion's origins in Canada – the primary case study for the book. This chapter considers how the advisory function as practised in Canada raises issues for the separation of powers.

I do not intend here to argue for the independent value of the separation of powers, or that it must take pure, or even robust, form. In Chapter 1, the doctrine was introduced and described as a common feature in many states. Classically, the doctrine has been justified as a safeguard for political liberty – by avoiding the risks of untrammelled power should a single state actor engage in too many government functions. While that account is likely somewhat under-inclusive,[1] I do agree that the separation of powers does have value for governance. Therefore, institutional features which may create tensions or stress in branch relationships are worthy of attention.

Chapter 1 gave an overview of the operation of the separation of powers in Canada. While the doctrine has sometimes been described as having no relevance, that is simply not true. In fact, aspects of the separation of powers have become essential to how the Canadian state is conceived.

This chapter considers two potential problems that the Canadian advisory function poses for the separation of powers. First, by vesting courts with the ability to do more than adjudicate cases, references might be thought to extend the judicial function beyond what many might think to be its optimal boundaries. Second, by concentrating the initiating power for advisory opinions within the executive branch, Canadian references seem to align that branch with the judiciary, and to exclude the legislature, at the same time as the function tends to concern questions related to the latter (ie, statutes).

It should be noted that these problems are not really equivalent. The first, which draws on principles of judicial independence, is more closely correlated with traditional separation of powers concerns. The second problem is complicated by the interdependent nature of the executive and legislative branches in a parliamentary system. The observations offered below are more in the sense of a 'thought-piece' on that way that the advisory function can have effects upon that relationship.

[1] 'Political liberty' would seem to be a classic negative right, ie, one largely dependent on non-interference by state actors. As a goal for governance, it provides little room for, or consideration of, different aims, such as collective goals which might require a sharing of tasks by different actors.

Executive Requests and Judicial Resistance

The first potential problem with advisory opinions is that providing such opinions *outside* the normal boundaries of justiciability threatens the legitimate functions, and legitimacy, of the courts. This was one of the claims in the *Reference re References* previously discussed in Chapter 3.[2] Recall that the provinces had argued that a court of appeal should not exercise an advisory function. (Seventy years later, the argument would be repeated in the *Quebec Secession Reference.*)[3]

That premise has been accepted in certain countries. In 1793 US Supreme Court Chief Justice John Jay refused to accept questions posed by President George Washington's administration regarding US relations with France and Britain during the French Revolution. Jay stated that 'The lines of separation drawn by the Constitution between the three Departments … and our being judges of a court in the last Resort, are Considerations which afford strong arguments against the Propriety of our extrajudicially deciding the questions alluded to …'.[4] In Australia, since the early twentieth century at least, it has been thought improper for courts to go beyond hearing 'facts and law' and, thereby, be 'drawn into the region of political controversy'.[5] And in 2004, when UK parliamentarians debated the creation of that country's Supreme Court,[6] some insisted that it was wrong to 'see the courts as having an advisory function; they are bodies which resolve disputes between people'.[7]

As noted in Chapter 3, Canadian courts have rejected that sort of argument. They largely accept that they may perform functions other than deciding disputes that present as 'cases'. That has had numerous implications for the role of the courts.

An entity that is expected to perform at the command of another could be perceived as being subordinate to it. To be sure, it is common in any system of governance for branches of the state to have to respond to each other as a matter of practical or constitutional reality. In a presidential system, the executive must

[2] *In re References by the Governor-General in Council* (1910), 43 SCR 536 at 547 (SCC), aff'd [1912] AC 571 (PC) [*Reference re References*].

[3] *Reference re Secession of Quebec*, [1998] 2 SCR 217 [*Quebec Secession Reference*] (discussed in Chapter 8).

[4] *Letter from the Supreme Court to President George Washington* (1793). See also *Muskrat v United States*, 219 US 346 (1911).

[5] See the statement from the Chief Justice of the Supreme Court of Victoria known as the *Irvine Memorandum*: 'The duty of His Majesty's Judges is to hear and determine issues of fact and law arising between the King and the subject, or between subject and subject, presented in a form enabling judgment to be passed upon them, and when passed to be enforced by process of law. There begins and ends the function of the judiciary'. Quoted in Sir Murray McInerney, 'The Appointment of Judges to Commissions of Inquiry and other Extra-Judicial Activities' (1978) 52 Australian Law Journal 540, 541–42.

[6] Constitutional Reform Act 2005.

[7] https://api.parliament.uk/historic-hansard/lords/2004/feb/09/supreme-court (Lord Falconer). See also Byron Karemba, 'Brexit, the Reference Jurisdiction of the UKSC and the New Separation of Powers', UK Constitutional Law Blog (30 July 2018): at https://ukconstitutionallaw.org/.

respond to a Bill passed by the legislature, indicating his or her consent (or veto). Such relationships do not necessarily imply subordination. The particular concern here is whether the fact that the court is expected to modify its actions, priorities and tasks because of an executive demand may indicate, in a non-trivial sense, diminished independence. When references are initiated, the courts are expected to respond. The Supreme Court of Canada, for example, must modify its schedule to accommodate the necessary hearings. It must devote both administrative and judicial resources[8] to dealing with the myriad requests that accompany them. And it must allocate time to sifting through the arguments, both written and oral; discussing the issue in conference; and, finally, delivering a written opinion.

Canadian courts do retain a significant degree of control over the process. Under the Supreme Court Act,[9] for example, the Court retains full say over such things as: appointing *amicus curiae*, directing process, deciding on additional participants,[10] assigning the judges who will review and hear the argument, deciding on the content of the opinion and determining the timing of its release.

Such control may help mitigate the perception that Canadian courts, and the Supreme Court in particular, are captive to another branch. Yet, the fundamental character of the reference seems largely unaffected. It is important, then, to consider other responses, by the judiciary itself, that seem intended to resist the limiting effect of a reference on its institutional autonomy. The most important of those is resisting or refusing to provide an answer.[11]

On numerous occasions, the Supreme Court simply has refused to engage with the question posed to it by the executive.[12] At times, the Court has seen fit to *modify* the question in some way; at others, it has declined to respond altogether.

[8] For example, the Supreme Court docket in the *Reference re Senate Reform*, 2014 SCC 32 [*Senate Reform Reference*] indicates at least eight motions between the initial filing in February 2013 and the date of closure in May 2015. The hearing involved 18 participants, all of whom were permitted to file submissions and some of whom were permitted to make oral submissions. Numerous additional parties applied for leave to intervene unsuccessfully. The appeal was heard over three days before the eight sitting members of the Court (Justice Marc Nadon had been sworn in but, because of the challenge to his appointment discussed in Chapter 8 did not participate).

[9] Supreme Court Act RSC, 1985, c S-26.

[10] Under the Supreme Court Act, provincial and federal governments are accorded notice of proceedings, initiated by other actors, that raise constitutional issues and may indicate their intention to intervene.

[11] In a helpful taxonomy, Kate Puddister includes within this broader category those references where the Court declined to answer a question where it was deemed unnecessary by virtue of its answer to another. That most commonly occurs where a reference asks a broad question of validity and then separates out validity into constituent components, for example concerning the division of powers on one hand and the Charter on the other. The discussion in this chapter excludes such instances. Kate Puddister, *Inviting Judicial Review: A Comprehensive Analysis of Canadian Appellate Court Reference Cases*, PhD Thesis, McGill University, Montreal, December 2015.

[12] Puddister, ibid, has identified the following examples from 1949 to 2014: *Earth Future Lottery (PEI)*, [2002] 215 DLR (4th) 656; *Interpretation of Human Rights Act*, [1998] 50 DLR (4th) 647; *Constitution Act 1867, ss. 26, 27 and 28 (BC)*, [1991] 78 DLR (4th) 245; *Workers Compensation Act 1983 (NL)*, [1989] 1 SCR 922; *Freedom of Informed Choice (Abortions) Act (SK)*, [1985] 25 DLR (4th);

The 1981 *Patriation Reference*[13] was initiated in relation to several aspects of the constitutional reform package that eventually would become the Canada Act 1982. The questions included the following:

> Question 2 – Is it a constitutional convention that [the Parliament of Canada] will not request Her Majesty the Queen to … amend the Constitution of Canada affecting federal-provincial relationships or [provincial powers, rights or privileges] without first obtaining the agreement of the provinces?
>
> Question 3 – Is the agreement of the provinces of Canada constitutionally required for amendment to the Constitution of Canada where such amendment affects federal-provincial relationships or alters [provincial powers, rights or privileges] granted or secured by the Constitution of Canada to the provinces, their legislatures or governments?[14]

The Supreme Court justices disagreed on what the questions were asking. Question 3 related to how a constitutional amendment affecting existing provincial powers might occur. At that time, the Canadian Constitution could only be amended by legislation passed by the Westminster Parliament.[15] Seven of the nine justices said that they would consider *only* the Canadian Parliament's ability to *initiate* the process for such a law to be passed by Westminster, but that their answer did not in any way relate to the UK's subsequent *disposition* of that request, which was not a matter 'upon which this Court would presume to pronounce'.[16] Ultimately, the majority concluded, there were *no* legal constraints upon the Canadian Parliament's ability to pass those resolutions.

The two judges in dissent approached the question quite differently. In their view, it was necessary to recognize that Westminster was highly likely to accede to any such request from the Canadian Parliament. Therefore, the issue was whether the Canadian Parliament possessed the legal authority to pass a resolution that would fundamentally change provincial powers without first obtaining those provinces' consent.[17] They found that passing a resolution of *that* kind would be inconsistent with the nature of Canadian federalism.

Upper Churchill Water Rights Reversion Act, [1984] 1 SCR 297; *Legislative Privilege*, (1978) 18 OR (2d) 182; *Jones v Canada (AG)*, [1975] 2 SCR 182; *Validity of a by-law respecting taxi cabs*, [1958] 16 DLR (2d) 348; *Railway Act, Canada v Canada Pacific Railway*, [1958] SCR 285; *Moratorium Legislation Act (SK)*, [1955] 35 CBR 135; *Interpretation of Human Rights Act*, [1998] 50 DLR (4th) 647; *Goods and Services Tax*, [1992] 2 SCR 858; *Public Service Employee Relations Act (AB)*, [1987] 1 SCR 313; *Stony Plain Indian Reserve*, [1981] AJ No 1007; *Legislative Authority of the Parliament of Canada in relation to the Upper House*, [1980] 1 SCR 54; *MB (AG) v Manitoba Egg and Poultry Association*, [1971] SCR 698; *Same Sex Marriage*, [2004] 3 SCR 698; *Constitution Act 1867, ss. 26, 27 and 28 (BC)*, [1991] 78 DLR (4th) 245.

[13] *Resolution to Amend the Constitution*, [1981] 1 SCR 753 [*Patriation Reference*]. The Reference is discussed in detail in Chapter 6.

[14] These questions are taken from the reference initiated by the provinces of Manitoba and Newfoundland to their respective courts of appeal.

[15] Constitutional amendment is discussed in Chapters 6 and 8.

[16] ibid at 774.

[17] ibid at 815.

Question 2 asked whether there existed a *constitutional convention* that the Canadian Parliament would not pass such resolutions without provincial consent.

The panel again divided on the question's meaning. This time, they differed over concerned the *level* of provincial 'agreement' contemplated. Was the question whether *all* of the provinces must agree, or only *some*? In the majority's view:

> It would have been easy to insert the word 'all' into the question had it been intended to narrow its meaning. But we do not think it was so intended. The issue raised by the question is essentially whether there is a constitutional convention that the House of Commons and Senate of Canada will not proceed alone. The thrust of the question is accordingly on whether or not there is a conventional requirement for provincial agreement, not on whether the agreement should be unanimous assuming that it is required. …
>
> If the questions are thought to be ambiguous, *this Court should not, in a constitutional reference, be in a worse position than that of a witness in a trial and feel compelled simply to answer yes or no …*[18]

It ultimately concluded that there *was* such a convention, but one that could be satisfied by securing the 'substantial consent' of the provinces. Exactly how many provinces would be required for consent to be 'substantial', the majority did not say.

The dissent[19] sharply criticised the majority's narrowing of the question. It stated that in 'plain English', the terms 'of the provinces' or 'of the provinces of Canada' means *all* of the provinces of Canada.[20] The Court 'would not be justified in editing the questions to develop a meaning not clearly expressed'.[21] The dissent went on to find that the asserted convention did not exist.

In one sense, the above examples are in line with ordinary legal interpretation. I have highlighted them to demonstrate that the Court clearly did not consider itself bound by either the wording of a particular reference question or the favoured reading of that question by the initiating actor (in this case, the provinces). That the Court felt able to approach a question differently, or even to modify it, suggests that it did not view the reference as significantly different from any other legal proceeding, at least not in that respect. Notwithstanding, then, that a Canadian reference is grounded in an executive request for answers, the Court has asserted a type of firewall against that request.

Perhaps the most dramatic response to a reference question is to refuse to answer it at all. This the Canadian Supreme Court has done on numerous occasions. Although the total number of such refusals is small, they nonetheless represent a considerable assertion of juridical power.

[18] ibid at 875 (emphasis added).

[19] The dissenting jurists on Question 3 were Martland and Ritchie JJ. Laskin CJC and Estey and Martland JJ dissented on Question 2.

[20] ibid at 851.

[21] ibid.

In Britain, judges were often requested by the House of Lords to provide advice on terms that suggested that they were not free to decline.[22] Those judges, too, asserted an occasional discretion to refuse, most often when they anticipated that the same issue would arise in subsequent litigation.[23] Thus, it is not surprising that the JCPC noted that references were vulnerable to 'indiscriminate and injudicious' uses.[24] One instance of evasion is found in the *Local Prohibition Reference*.[25] That Reference was one of several matters arising from the controversial issues of alcohol regulation. At play were federal[26] and provincial[27] statutes containing a 'local option' provision permitting municipalities to adopt a prohibitory scheme via plebiscite. The Supreme Court had issued conflicting judgments about whether such laws could coexist in the same locality.

Much of the opinion[28] was taken up with whether Ontario had the jurisdiction to impose a local option. The Judicial Committee advised that the provincial Act was intra vires 'subject to this necessary qualification, that its provisions are, or will become, inoperative in any district of the province which has already adopted, or may subsequently adopt[,] the second part of the [federal law]'.[29]

With regard to the other six questions,[30] the Committee stated that they related 'to *matters which may possibly become litigious in the future, but have not as yet given rise to any real and present controversy*'. They were 'better fitted for consideration of officers of the Crown, than of a court of law'.[31] The Board noted, as well, that its answers would not have 'the weight of a judicial determination'.[32] It nonetheless proceeded to answer some of the remaining questions, though it determined that the two did not require a 'categorical reply'.[33]

Similar refusals would recur over the ensuing decades. In the memorable words of one judge, a court need not provide '[an] answer to such questions, for instance, as "whether the moon is made of green cheese"'.[34] The Supreme Court has given

[22] See the discussion in Chapters 2 and 10.

[23] E Foster, *The House of Lords 1603–1649* (Chapel Hill, NC: North Carolina Universiy Press, 1983) 79–82; E Coke, *The First Part of the Institutes of the Laws of England* L.2, C 10, § 164 n.5 (13th edn, 1823); W Jones, Politics and the Bench (1971) 62, cited in Stewart Jay, 'Servants of Monarchs and Lords: The Advisory Role of Early English Judges' (1994) 38 American Journal of Legal History 117.

[24] *Reference re References* (n 2) at para 16.

[25] *Attorney General (Ontario) v Attorney General (Canada)* [1896] AC 348 [*Local Prohibition*].

[26] Canada Temperance Act, RSC 1887 c 106.

[27] Local Option Act, SO 1890 c.56.

[28] The questions may be found at *Local Prohibition* (n 25), Appellant's Case.

[29] The JCPC upheld the law as being in relation to either 'property and civil rights in the province' or 'matters of a merely local or private nature in the province', ie, s 92(13) or (16) of the BNA Act.

[30] Above note 25.

[31] *Local Prohibition* (n 25) at 20 (emphasis added).

[32] ibid.

[33] Questions 5 and 6 asked specifically about the remaining powers of prohibition available to Ontario should the Board find that the local-option provision was ultra vires. The Board found that its answer to Question 7 was sufficient and further elaboration was not required.

[34] *Reference re: Ontario Medical Act*, [1906] OJ No 147, per Meredith JA at para 68. The judge went on to suggest that the broad power granted to the Lieutenant-Governor of Ontario by RSO (1897),

that idea much greater heft. The Court has cited as reasons to refuse mootness,[35] lack of specificity,[36] vagueness[37] and the risk of creating legal uncertainty.[38]

In examining the Supreme Court's assertion that it may refuse to answer a reference question, several points are noteworthy. The first point is that the stated reasons for refusal constitute, for all intents and purposes, a doctrine of 'reference justiciability'. Mootness, prematurity, insufficient factual context, lack of specificity – all of these reasons constrain the courts' intervention in issues that do not correspond to the limits, integral to the separation of powers, that are imposed on the court in view of their role as *legal* arbiters. Thus, reference justiciability plausibly demonstrates an intention by the Court to retain first and foremost a *legal* role.

The second point is that the Supreme Court sometimes asserts the *ability* to refuse while not actually doing so. For example, in the *Quebec Veto* Reference Quebec argued that the Constitution Act 1982 had proceeded contrary to constitutional convention because the proposal sent to Westminster had not included its agreement.[39] By the time the reference arrived at the Supreme Court, the Queen had proclaimed in force the Constitution Act 1982. While the matter was indisputably moot, the Court nonetheless concluded that it was 'desirable that the constitutional question be answered in order to dispel any doubt over it'.[40] The Court would employ similar reasoning in the *Quebec Secession Reference*[41] against the *amicus curiae* who urged the Court to refuse to answer the questions. The Court decided that it would answer, but not before noting two circumstances in which it might be appropriate to refuse, namely where the Court believed that to answer would stray 'beyond its own assessment of its proper role in the

ch 84 – essentially, the provincial advisory function – was nonetheless restricted to '(1) legal questions; (2) respecting matters within the jurisdiction of the Court; and (3) of Provincial concern', ibid.

35 *Re Objection by Que. To Resolution to Amend the Constitution*, [1982] 2 SCR 793, 806 [*Quebec Veto*]. The reference is further discussed in Chapter 6.

36 *Re Authority of Parliament in Relation to the Upper House*, [1980] 1 SCR 54 [*Upper House Reference*]. The Court declined to answer several questions relating to possible changes to the Senate of Canada 'in the absence of a factual context or actual draft legislation'. See also *Re The Educational System in the Island of Montreal*, [1926] SCR 246 at 270; *Reference re Waters and Water-Powers*, [1929] SCR 200 at 224.

37 *McEvoy v Attorney General (New Brunswick)*, [1983] 1 SCR 704 at 707. In considering the validity of establishing a 'unified criminal court' within a province, the Supreme Court noted the lack of 'draft legislation' or 'even any draft proposals to infuse the three questions which, in our view, suffer from excessive abstractness'. It complained of being forced to 'speculate as to the form the legislative schemes contemplated by the questions might take'. It continued, at 714–17, that, 'while we deprecate the practice of bringing before the Court as important constitutional questions as are raised in this case on extremely flimsy material, we would not abort the appeal on this ground', 714–15.

38 *Reference re Same-Sex Marriage*, [2004] 3 SCR 698 [*Same-Sex Marriage*].

39 *Quebec Veto* (n 35). See also Chapter 6.

40 ibid at 805–06.

41 Above n 3. The *Secession Reference* is discussed in Chapter 8.

constitutional framework of our democratic form of government'; or where the question fell outside of the Court's core area of expertise, which it defined as legal interpretation.[42]

For at least two reasons, this second point is significant. First, it finds a counterpart in the Court's approach in ordinary cases. Especially since 1982, the Court has entertained cases that strictly speaking, were moot, because it determined that the hearing would serve some additional interest.[43] In so doing, the Court acknowledges limits to its jurisdiction while retaining the authority to determine what those limits are. To be sure, this is common to many types of judicial craft. In the context of references, though, which strain the ordinary understanding of what a court does, it is noteworthy that the Supreme Court does not consider itself bound to observe what *another* branch wants it to do. In other words, while the refusal seems on the surface an acknowledgment of the *limits* of judicial power, in practice it may serve to *enhance* it, by both entrenching a certain type of interpretative role and highlighting the court's independence.

The third point is the most striking. The Court has never *explained* the source of its discretion. Nor has it reconciled such refusals with the plain, mandatory language of its enabling statute. Section 53(4) of the Supreme Court Act proclaims, inter alia, that 'it is the *duty* of the Court to hear and consider it and to answer each question so referred, and the Court *shall* certify to the Governor in Council, for his information, its opinion on each question …'.[44] The section clearly fames the reference function as an *obligation* imposed upon the Court. Yet, the Court has never mentioned that aspect of its reference function.

At times, the omission seems deliberate. For example, in the *Same-Sex Marriage Reference*, the Court 'reproduced and interpreted the first three subsections of section 53 of the Supreme Court Act which detail the authority of the Governor General in Council to refer questions to the Court' but did not mention 'the fourth subsection detailing the Court's duty on a reference'.[45] One would have thought that final subsection particularly material to the Court's decision to decline to answer Question 4.

What can explain such a pattern?

It may be that even though section 53(4) of the Supreme Court Act squarely articulates a 'duty', the Court does not feel that the language is material. It may be that no one has ever put the question squarely to the Court. Or, it may be that the Court believes that it is operating in a different register – one where its institutional and functional independence supersedes any countervailing directive from another branch.

[42] ibid at para 26.
[43] See the discussion in Chapter 10.
[44] Supreme Court Act, RSC, 1985, c S-26 (emphasis added).
[45] John McEvoy, 'Refusing To Answer: The Supreme Court and the Reference Power Revisited' (2005) 54(29) University of New Brunswick Law Journal 37; *Same-sex Marriage Reference* (n 38).

The latter point seems the most likely. That is, the Court has never explicitly considered the obligation framed in section 53(4) because the Court does not consider it relevant to its current context, a context that, at least in part, presumes that its institutional independence must prevail.

The Supreme Court functions as the chief constitutional arbiter and the primary interpreter of its norms; and it enjoys independence from the other branches. Any doubts about that independence appear to have been laid to rest by the 2014 *Supreme Court Act Reference*.[46] Discussed more fully in Chapter 8, the Court stated that it is no longer a creature of statute that can be repealed at Parliament's command. Rather, because of the integral role that it plays in Canada's underlying legal and political arrangements, the Court's 'composition' and 'essential features' are protected against unilateral change at the federal level. Such changes require constitutional amendment.

The *Supreme Court Act Reference* arose because of a question about the eligibility requirements for judges appointed to the Court. But to the extent that the Court's conclusion rests on the need to maintain its status as an independent arbiter, it might well resist an expectation to answer a reference question it views as inappropriate.[47] To be sure, the matter is not black and white. For one thing, the *Supreme Court Act Reference* related to Parliament's ability to *change* aspects of the current Act, while the mandatory duty to answer has been part of the Act since 1875.

For another, there are separate aspects of the Court's appellate jurisdiction, such as criminal appeals as of right, that are not wholly under its control.[48] There, however, the Court's appellate jurisdiction is triggered because Parliament has judged that certain circumstances warrant, in the interests of justice, a final determination from the country's apex court. At the very least, the *executive* capture of the Court by forcing it to submit to questions would seem to be of a very different character. And that prospect seems to have inspired the Court on numerous occasions to assert that it has the right to refuse to engage.

Thus, the unwritten constitutional principle of judicial independence, articulated as an aspect of the separation of powers, best explains the Court's repeated insistence that it can not be *compelled* to answer any reference question the executive chooses to put before it. The doctrine insulates the Court from being in a truly subordinate position to the executive, and provides a check of sorts on the latter. This is not, of course, to say that refusal doctrine is a cure-all for the political *consequences* of the advisory function. But it is an important part of the fuller picture of executive–judicial relations when an advisory function is in play.

[46] *Reference re Supreme Court Act, ss 5 and 6*, 2014 SCC 21, [2014] 1 SCR 433 [*Supreme Court Act Reference*].

[47] The extent to which the *Supreme Court Act Reference* complicates the Court's current appellate jurisdiction remains an outstanding question.

[48] Criminal Code of Canada, RSC 1985 c C-46 s 691 (granting an accused person an automatic right of appeal in certain circumstances).

The relationship between the judiciary and executive is one facet of the separation of powers that is affected, in intriguing ways, by the advisory function. Another, not entirely symmetrical, facet is the fact that the *initiation* of advisory opinions is vested in the executive alone. That issue is explored below.

The Lonely Legislature?

When it comes to Canadian advisory opinions, the legislative branch seems to be left out of the process. On one view, that may be unsurprising. As discussed in a previous chapter, English courts were initially conceived of as advisers to the sovereign. The advisory function is perhaps the last vestige of that historical role. In addition (and leaving aside administrative tribunals) the judiciary is institutionally associated with the interpretation of statutes. The judiciary and legislature perform distinctive functions related to positive law. In that sense, they stand somewhat apart from the executive, which primarily approaches law and legal norms as tools for operationalising policy.

In other words, it may be more tolerable for the judiciary to act as adviser to the executive than to the legislature. To draw the legislature and judiciary too close together risks undermining the latter's independence and complicating the former's work. Of course, the Canadian legislative branch is bound by constitutional norms and limits. But it enjoys a significant degree of latitude in how it interprets them. Inserting a pre-emptive judicial opinion into such matters could well represent an unwise intrusion.

Nevertheless, there is an argument to be made that the Canadian advisory function privileges the executive branch at the legislature's expense. By granting the executive special access to the Court outside of the ordinary litigation process, the advisory function draws the executive and judiciary into a relationship that not only affects future judicial review, but may give the executive a significant strategic advantage. It is noteworthy that, compared with other countries that authorise the provision of advisory opinions, Canada is unusual in limiting them to executive requests.[49]

[49] Peter H Russell, 'A Parliamentary Approach to Reforming the Process of Filling Vacancies on the Supreme Court of Canada, Brief to the Standing Committee on Justice, Human Rights, Public Safety and Emergency Preparedness', 23 March 2004, p 1, as cited in Erin Crandall, 'Intergovernmental Relations and the Supreme Court of Canada: The Changing Place of the Provinces in Judicial Selection Reform' (2010) Working Paper, Institute of Intergovernmental Relations School of Policy Studies, Queen's University, www.queensu.ca/iigr/sites/webpublish.queensu.ca.iigrwww/files/files/pub/archive/DemocraticDilemma/ReformingTheSCC/SCCpapers/CrandallFINAL.pdf. See also Peter H Russell, *The Judiciary in Canada: The Third Branch of Government* (Toronto: McGraw-Hill Ryerson, 1987) ch 5.

Here, several caveats require mention. First, section 54 of the Supreme Court Act does permit the Houses of Parliament to seek a specific advisory opinion. It provides:

> The Court, or any two of the judges, shall examine and report on any private bill or petition for a private bill presented to the Senate or House of Commons and referred to the Court under any rules or orders made by the Senate or House of Commons.[50]

The above provision was virtually identical to a practice that persisted in the UK House of Lords for centuries.[51]

Section 54 is a most interesting clause. First, it restricts the advisory function to 'private bills' or petitions of same. The term 'private bills' does not mean 'private members' bills'. In Canadian parliamentary practice, they are laws intended to 'confer special powers or benefits (in excess of or in conflict with the general law) upon one or more persons or group of persons (including corporate entities) or to exempt them from the application of a statute'.[52] They are, in other words, laws directed at private parties. Historically, such Bills tended to be introduced in the Canadian Senate. Second, section 54 refers to 'rules or orders' made by either chamber, suggesting that both retain the authority to determine the procedure by which a request may be made.[53] Third, it can be satisfied by a 'report' issuing from as few as two members of the Court. The provision does not require an opinion, a hearing or notice to other parties, perhaps because of the latitude granted to the legislative branch to frame the process.

There have been very few section 54 references. The last one was in 1882.[54] All proceeded from the Senate rather than the House of Commons: *An Act to Incorporate the Brothers of the Christian Schools in Canada* (1876);[55] *Quebec Timber Company* (1882);[56] and *Canada Provident Association* (1882).[57] Two were reported as opinions; one was not. Note that, in the *Brothers* case, the Minister of Justice raised a concern that the Bill might be ultra vires, and offered to refer the matter himself. The Senate did not take up the offer.[58] That may well have reflected a latent separation of powers concern: the idea that it would be unseemly for

[50] Supreme Court Act RSC, 1985, c S-26.

[51] William Blackstone, *Commentaries on the Laws of England* (Oxford: Clarendon Press, 1765) 175–76, noting that 'In the house of lords, if the bill begins there, it is (when of a private nature) perused by two of the judges, who settle all points of legal propriety'. See also the discussion in Jay (n 23).

[52] www.parl.gc.ca/procedure-book-livre/document.aspx?sbdid=da2ac62f-bb39-4e5f-9f7d-90ba3496d0a6&sbpidx=3.

[53] The current Senate practice is covered by Senate Rule 11-18: https://sencanada.ca/en/about/procedural-references/rules/11/.

[54] Charlie Feldman, 'Legislative Vehicles and Formalized Charter Review' (2016) 25(3) Constitutional Forum 79, 83.

[55] *Re Brothers of the Christian Schools in Canada*, 1876 CarswellPEI 1, Cout Dig 1.

[56] Senate, *Journals of the Senate*, 4th Parl, 4th Sess, vol 1 (30 March 1882) at 158.

[57] *In re Canada Provident Assn.* 1882 CarswellNat 6 at 1.

[58] *Debates of the Senate*, 3rd Parl, 3rd Sess, vol 1 (4 April 1876) at 287 (Hon Mr Bellerose).

a Minister to intervene to secure the aid of the court for a Bill that was the product of the Senate.

After 1882, the practice fell into disuse. But, even if section 54 was revived, its limitation to 'private bills' severely constrains the possibility that it might enable a comparable role for the Court as does section 53. One might argue that that constraint is justified on the basis that, where a Bill is introduced by the executive, another branch should not have the freedom to seek a judicial opinion about it. But is that persuasive? Given that enacting such a Bill into law is within the peculiar province of Parliament, it is difficult to see why seeking advice about it ought to be confined to the executive.

In any event, such a concern as applied to the House clearly does not obtain for the Senate or at least not to the same degree. The Senate of Canada was mandated as a second chamber of 'sober second thought'.[59] While politically partisan for much of its history, the chamber was not intended to be partisan as such.[60] Thus, any alleged unwarranted imbalance as between the executive and House of Commons, in respect of the advisory function, is heightened in respect of the Upper House.[61]

The second caveat, of course, is the overlap between the executive and legislature in a system of responsible government. The precise make-up of the Commons, and of the government, may vary, but the necessary relationship does not. In an archetypal majority government, where the executive's members come from a single party controlling a majority of seats, the decision to refer advisory opinions may not pose cause for concern, or, indeed, for comment.[62] Over much of Canada's history, that appears to have been be the case. In majority Parliaments, references are initiated based on the executive's say-so, with input mostly from Cabinet and little concern, or even notice, from the caucus or the House. Of course, that does not prevent the opposition from suggesting that a reference occur and even bringing the matter to a vote.

A minority government creates greater opportunity for conflict.[63] That is because, while the *executive* continues to be drawn from only one party, the House of Commons is not, and the Cabinet thus cannot count on party discipline to control outcomes. The primary 'check' available to MPs is to bring down the government and history shows that non-ruling parties approach the question of confidence with caution. It seems unlikely that, outside of an extraordinary circumstance, a decision simply to *initiate* a reference would itself qualify as

[59] *Re Upper House* (n 36) at 76.

[60] *Reference re Senate Reform*, 2014 SCC 32 at para 57.

[61] I leave, for now, the prospect that such a change to s 54 is now impossible absent a formal constitutional amendment. That point is taken up in Chapter 8.

[62] But see Motion reading in part 'the House call on the government to refer the Comeau decision and its evidence to the Supreme Court for constitutional clarification of Section 121'. Defeated 184–131: www.ourcommons.ca/DocumentViewer/en/42-1/house/sitting-72/journals.

[63] I will not discuss the potentially special situation posed by a coalition government that draws from more than one party to populate the executive.

sufficiently serious to risk bringing down a Ministry. However, it may be that in such cases the parties work towards forcing a reference indirectly.

For example, the opposition might seek to insert a provision that certain portions of the legislation will not operate until such time as a reference opinion confirms their validity.[64] Though such provisions are rare, one was recently proposed in the Canadian Senate to address concerns over the constitutionality of government legislation in respect of medical assistance in dying.[65]

There have been occasions on which the reference function *was* affected by minority dynamics. A good example is the *Same-Sex Marriage Reference*.[66] There, the court was asked a series of questions about a proposed federal law, the Civil Marriage Act,[67] which sought to confirm a gender-neutral definition of 'marriage'.[68] The law was proposed after several provincial courts ruled that the common law definition of marriage violated the Charter of Rights and Freedoms.[69]

In 2003, while those rulings were being appealed in Quebec, Ontario and BC, the federal Minister of Justice announced a standing committee of Parliament would conduct hearings on the issue. A discussion paper was released. Hearings were held across the country.[70] Then, after two provincial courts of appeal confirmed the lower court rulings, the federal government (which held power in a minority parliament) announced that it would not seek an appeal to the Supreme Court of Canada.[71] It declared instead an intention to legislate the effects of the BC and Ontario decisions.

The government referred that legislation to the Supreme Court in draft form.[72] The initial questions concerned the division of powers and protection of religious freedom. No question was posed about whether the existing common law definition of marriage was consistent with the Charter – a curious evasion of the central issue. When, after significant criticism and political pressure, the government did pose that question, it declined to offer any arguments about it.[73]

Some viewed the government's determination to trigger a reference as a problematic intrusion into what was, at bottom, an issue peculiarly within the province

[64] An Act to amend the Liquor License Act 1883, 47 Vic, c 32.

[65] *Journals of the Senate of Canada*, 42nd Parl, 2nd Sess, 17 June 2016, Issue 52.

[66] Above n 38.

[67] Bill C-38, An Act respecting certain aspects of legal capacity for marriage for civil purposes, 1st Sess, 38th Parl, 2005.

[68] SC 2005, c.33.

[69] *Hendricks c Québec (PG)*, [2004] RJQ 851 (CA); *Halpern v Toronto (City)*, (2003) 65 OR (3d) 161 (CA); *EGALE Canada v Canada (AG)*, (2003) 13 BCLR (4th) 1, 2003 BCCA 251. At common law, marriage was defined as 'the union of one man and one woman for life, to the exclusion of all others': *Hyde v Hyde*, (1866) LR 1 P & D 130 at 133.

[70] Canada, Standing Committee on Justice and Human Rights, *Evidence of 34th Meeting*, 37th Parl, 2nd Sess (8 April 2003); see also House of Commons, News Release, 'Justice Committee's Tentative Cross-Canada Travel Plans' (28 February 2003).

[71] Kim Lunman, 'Ottawa backs gay marriage: Court decisions won't be appealed', *The Globe and Mail* (18 June 2003) A1.

[72] The draft legislation is discussed in Chapter 7.

[73] The questions and their answers are discussed in Chapter 8.

of Parliament. At the time, the lower courts' redefinition of marriage had become a lightning rod.[74] Many Canadians, suspicious of the idea that abstract rights theory could mandate the reordering of long-standing social mores, were threatened by the prospect of changing the definition of marriage. When the reference cut short parliamentary committee work on the very issue, it exacerbated existing tensions. To critics, it appeared that the executive had seized the issue out of Parliament's hands.[75] The minority government was criticised as having politicised the issue. The Leader of the Opposition, Stephen Harper, accused the federal government of no less than a conspiracy to further a 'hidden agenda'.[76]

The revolutionary change in Canada's marriage laws is a testament to focussed constitutional rights advocacy. But the *Same-Sex Marriage Reference* can be critiqued for contributing to the phenomenon of 'democratic debilitation' – encouraging the legislature to withdraw from constitutional deliberation in favour of judicial pronouncements.

Reasonable people can disagree on the utility or principles behind the government's strategy. The point is that, where the reference function appears politicised, it can create resistance to laudable law reform, give opportunities for mischief in public debate, and draw the Court into tricky institutional conflicts. The *Same-Sex Marriage Reference* demonstrates the power inherent in framing a reference, and determine (at least initially) its focus, over significant objections by a good number of legislative branch members.

At the opposite end of the spectrum, the *failure* to seek an advisory opinion can also spur political controversy. That may arise if Parliament is considering legislation about which there is a credible constitutional concern. In that case, a reference might seem like a principled alternative to simply ploughing ahead.

In recent years, parliamentarians have urged the executive to pursue references before passing controversial legislation. For example, in *Bedford v Canada*, the Supreme Court concluded that several prostitution-related criminal offences violated the Charter.[77] One of the noteworthy aspects of the decision was the Court's repeated emphasis of the fact that the actual exchange of sex for money had never been the subject of criminal prohibition in Canada.[78] At points in its decision, the Court appeared to imply that if prostitution *itself* were to be prohibited,

[74] The push for marriage equality was very new. As recently as 1999, the federal Cabinet had acquiesced in a House of Commons motion 'that marriage is and should remain the union of one man and one woman to the exclusion of all others, and that Parliament will take all necessary steps to preserve this definition of marriage in Canada'. Hansard (8 June 1999) 15960.

[75] C Mathen, 'Developments in Constitutional Law – The 2004–2005 Term: A Court in Transition' (2005) 50 Supreme Court Law Review 89, 137.

[76] Alexander Panetta, 'Harper accuses Liberals of setting up court losses on gay marriage' *Canadian Press* (4 September 2003) (ProQuest) quoting Harper: 'I think it's a typical hidden agenda of the Liberal party. They had the courts do it for them [change the definition of marriage], they put the judges in they wanted, then they failed to appeal – failed to fight the case in court. I think the federal government deliberately lost this case in court and got the change to the law done through the back door'.

[77] *Canada (Attorney-General) v Bedford* 2013 SCC 72, [2013] 3 SCR 1101 at para 2 [*Bedford*].

[78] ibid at paras 5, 87.

a different balancing of constitutional interests would ensue.[79] The Conservative federal government responded with a series of sweeping changes to Canada's prostitution laws that went some way to doing that.[80] In response, several MPs proposed that prior to its passage, the government should seek further clarification from the Supreme Court, and were highly critical when the government failed to do so.[81]

Another example involves a case called *Carter v Canada*. There, the Court held that sections 14 and 241 of the Criminal Code (which, respectively, bar anyone from consenting to their own death, and from assisting in another's suicide) are unconstitutional to the extent that they apply to competent adults who are suffering from irremediable conditions (for example, amyotrophic lateral sclerosis) and wish for medical assistance in dying.[82] In response, the government proposed amending the Code to exempt such cases from criminal punishment, but it made the exemption subject to a number of additional limitations and qualifications. Many persons argued that the new provisions fell short of the Court's ruling in the *Carter* case.[83] Once again, the government faced calls to return to the Court for an opinion about the proposed legislation. And it was criticised when it did not.[84]

The converse is also true. In 2017, Parliament passed S-201, An Act to prohibit and prevent genetic discrimination. The law prohibits requiring an individual to undergo a genetic test or disclose the results of a genetic test as a condition of providing goods or services, including contracts of insurance. The Bill originated in the Senate and was co-sponsored by a Liberal backbencher. It was, thus, a private

[79] ibid at para 5:

> Under the existing regime, Parliament has confined lawful prostitution to two categories: street prostitution and 'out-calls' – where the prostitute goes out and meets the client at a designated location, such as the client's home. This reflects a policy choice on Parliament's part. Parliament is not precluded from imposing limits on where and how prostitution may be conducted, as long as it does so in a way that does not infringe the constitutional rights of prostitutes.

[80] Bill C-36, An Act to amend the Criminal Code in response to the Supreme Court of Canada decision in Attorney General of Canada v Bedford and to make consequential amendments to other Acts, 2nd Sess, 41st Parl, 2014. The law adopted an asymmetrical approach, criminalising the buying but not the selling of sex, enacting limits to discourage as much as possible what it termed the 'commodification' of sex and the 'objectification' of the human body. In the Bill's preamble, the government explicitly articulated a commitment to the values of 'equality and human dignity' and the belief that prostitution is inconsistent with both.

[81] *Debates of the House of Commons*, 42nd Parl, 2nd Sess, No 74, 16 June 2016 at 4634 and 4616. Cited in Charlie Feldman, 'Parliamentary Timing and Federal Legislation Referred to Courts: Reconsidering C-14' [2017] Canadian Parliamentary Review 18.

[82] *Bedford* (n 77) at para 4.

[83] *Carter v. Canada (Attorney General)*, 2015 SCC 5, [2015] 1 S.C.R. 331. The government included two threshold criteria – that the condition be 'incurable' and that death be 'reasonably foreseeable' – that appear to interfere with medical aid against the prior ruling. That said, any judicial consideration of the new law would have to consider the law's purported objective, which could affect the section 7 analysis and the degree to which further limits could be found to be over-broad.

[84] Charlie Feldman points out that the *Carter* case was complicated by the fact that the Supreme Court suspended the effect of its ruling for one year. Some might argue that it was inappropriate to use the reference function when Parliament was operating under a 'deadline'. Feldman (n 81) 23.

members' Bill, which ordinarily is not subject to party discipline – so government caucus members could vote as they wished.

The federal Minister of Justice expressed concern that, in its extension to insurance contracts, S-201 was ultra vires. Insurance regulation has long been held to be a matter of provincial jurisdiction, and so, she believed, Parliament lacked the jurisdiction to intervene.[85] The Bill's supporters claimed that Parliament was well within its criminal law powers[86] to target discriminatory behaviour for punishment. (When the Bill was examined by parliamentary committees, expert opinion on the issue was mixed.)

Ultimately, the Bill was passed but the entire Liberal Cabinet voted against it.[87] Such an unprecedented result was the product of diverse motivations: honest support for the Bill among many MPs, but also a willingness on the part of opposition parties to exploit a division within the governing Liberals.

A few days after the law's passage, the Minister of Justice announced that she would seek a reference opinion on its validity.[88] The juxtaposition of that decision together with her refusal to seek a similar opinion on the *Carter* legislation was attacked as a 'glaring inconsistency'.[89] The Minister was perceived to be acting purely politically, in tension with the broader role she also performs as Attorney General wherein she must dispassionately assess the validity of laws submitted to Parliament.

On S-201, the reference function provided the executive with a highly potent tool to advance its concerns about the law. For one thing, seeking a reference could effectively encourage a delay in the law's implementation. For another, it would grant the executive the critical advantage of setting the questions.[90] That could well make a difference if, for example, Cabinet asked the Court to advise on the law's general validity versus its potential intrusion into provincial jurisdiction over insurance.

At the time of writing, the federal Cabinet had not referred the matter to the Supreme Court. That may be, in part, because Quebec initiated its own reference about the Bill to its Court of Appeal.[91]

Had the federal government acted before Quebec did, some unusual questions would arise. Normally, the executive defends laws passed by the legislature

[85] *Debates of the House of Commons* 42nd Parl, 1st Sess, No 77, 20 September 2016 at 1810.

[86] Under s 91(27) of the Constitution Act 1867 Parliament has exclusive authority over 'the Criminal Law'.

[87] The vote was 222–60.

[88] Joan Bryden, 'Bill S-201: Government Seeking Supreme Court's Advice on Genetic Discrimination Bill', *Canadian Press*, 10 March 2017, www.huffingtonpost.ca/2017/03/10/bill-s201-supreme-court-advice_n_15283628.html.

[89] ibid.

[90] The advantage of setting reference questions is elaborated in Chapter 9.

[91] Order in Council of the Government of Quebec #522-2017, *Reference to the Court of Appeal of Quebec concerning the Genetic Non-Discrimination Act enacted by sections 1 to 7 of the Act to prohibit and prevent genetic discrimination* (7 July 2017).

from all attacks on their validity. One wonders whether the Minister of Justice would so do in this circumstance. It is arguable that a Minister who has good-faith, serious doubt as to a law's validity cannot defend it in court and should resign before doing so. It also is unclear that the government must defend every law passed by Parliament. Would it be proper, though, for the government, to actively argue *against* validity? Although there is no obvious legal barrier to it doing so, such a move would highlight the division between the executive and legislative branches in an unprecedented way. It might in fact, be highly relevant that such a rift would occur in the context of an advisory opinion as opposed to a live case.

Could some of the issues discussed above be mitigated? Perhaps one could lessen the degree of executive control by permitting the legislature to decide that a reference (that is more expansive than the current section 54) ought to proceed. The House of Commons or Senate might be authorised to initiate a proceeding on a majority resolution of members.[92] Or, such a power could fall to either a standing committee of Parliament or an independent parliamentary officer. Perhaps, as occurs in France, a reference could be triggered if a certain number of parliamentarians petitioned the Court after passage of a Bill to ensure its validity prior to its coming into force.[93] One could even simply ensure a method for providing for legislative input into reference questions or hearings, such as granting automatic intervenor status to the Senate or House of Commons.

To be sure, such changes would pose issues. They would add time to the legislative process. A government might regard a legislative reference launched in defiance of its wishes as a confidence matter. Preventing a new law from taking effect where the old one has been found unconstitutional could create a legislative vacuum. A reference also could delay other matters within the machinery of government – such as regulations.

An expanded function might also make more sense if Parliament were able to maintain independent carriage of the subsequent litigation – currently, such litigation is undertaken by government lawyers subject to the direction of the Minister of Justice (in her executive rather than legislative capacity). A litigation guardian could be appointed by the Court or managed by a parliamentary actor. Nonetheless, in a parliamentary system, there may well be limits to the degree of legislative independence that is feasible.[94]

Such operational constraints aside, expanded parliamentary references might exacerbate the existing difficulties in determining legislative intent. A Bill's sponsor might have had a different vision in mind than her colleagues and all of them might be opposed to the government. In references requiring some investigation of legislative intent (as many constitutional questions do) a court

[92] One could extend this to the Senate.

[93] Constitutional Revision 1974. See the discussion in Alec Stone, 'In the Shadow of the Constitutional Council: The "Juridicisation" of the Legislative Process in France' (1989) 12(2) West European Politics 12.

[94] I am grateful to Aniz Alani and Charles Feldman for their very helpful discussion of this issue.

may face a difficult situation if it has before it, say, Senate and House sponsors who present different explanations for a law; or who depart from interventions they made in their respective chambers, interventions that might otherwise be relied upon.

A more general complication, which cannot be further explored here, is whether such attempts at reform could be enacted through ordinary legislation. That is because of the uncertain implications of the 2014 *Supreme Court Act Reference* with respect to any changes to that Act, or to the Court's functions.[95]

* * *

This chapter has focussed on the Canadian experience with the separation of powers. In other systems, the balance of factors will be different, as will the corresponding issues. In countries with specialist constitutional courts, to cite one example, it is common for 'ordinary', non-constitutional courts to be able to refer constitutional questions.[96]

As discussed in Chapter 1, the separation of powers is an important Canadian principle despite the country's adherence to Parliamentary democracy and to the conventions of responsible government. The idea that the separation of powers has no application in Canada does not hold given the specific features of the Canadian Constitution that assume in at least some respects a separation of government functions. In addition, the Supreme Court has repeatedly confirmed that the doctrine has non-trivial significance. This chapter has highlighted possible separation of powers implications of an advisory opinion function. It does not argue that these issues are symmetrical. The effect on the judiciary of an advisory opinion is different from the relationship that it may promote between the explicitly political branches. Nor do I mean to suggest that the issues described above are somehow fatal indictments of the advisory function.

Nonetheless, the Canadian experience shows how references can present challenges to inter-branch relationships. It is noteworthy that the Supreme Court has engaged in 'self-help' – relying on separation of powers principles to mitigate the most extreme of those challenges. Where those challenges relate to the tension that emerges between the executive and legislative branches, however, there are few obvious escape routes if an executive actor is determined to press its advantage.

[95] See n 46 above.

[96] Spain and Italy employ this type of reference: Tania Groppi, 'The Italian Constitutional Court: Towards a Multilevel System of Constitutional Review' (2008) 3 Journal of Comparative Law 100.

5

Arbitrating Federalism

This chapter examines one of the primary roles of Canadian advisory opinions – providing settlement in federal–provincial disputes. Though advisory opinions may have come to Canada via a largely moribund British tradition, they quickly came to be viewed as a way of doing the business of federalism. The resulting references constitute both vertical and horizontal dialogue, that is to say, between orders *and* branches of government. In providing answers to these sorts of disputes, the court performs one of its essential functions: an arbiter of Canadian federalism and national power.

Taking a rough historical approach, this chapter traces the use of advisory functions in several discrete areas. It first addresses issues arising relatively soon after Confederation. It then looks at opinions arising just after the Supreme Court became the apex court in 1949 (that shift is discussed in Chapter 6). Finally, it examines a number of more recent disputes.

Throughout, a few themes are highlighted. The courts quickly assumed the position of interpreter that could fill in 'gaps' in existing constitutional text. They supplanted more overtly political mechanisms such as federal disallowance. In addition, federalism itself assumed a more fundamental character – as part of the process of nation-building. Far from a departure from the business of federalism, advisory opinions became essential to it.

Federalism Post-Confederation

A. Treaties

In many contexts, treaties are a defining feature of sovereignty.[1] The ability to enter into agreements with other nation states that will be binding under international law marks a clear, understandable and politically salient division between

[1] In Canada, treaties carry additional significance in the context of aboriginal peoples who have executed numerous treaties with the Canadian Crown. Here, the term is used to describe arrangements between states at the international level.

state and non-state actors.[2] For an emergent federal state with multiple sites of authority, it is especially important to confirm the identity of its treaty makers or signatories.

The British Empire retained full control over international affairs, including those that involved colonies So it is not surprising that the BNA Act omitted treaty making as a subject matter. Section 132 did grant the federal Parliament the power to implement treaties, but only those conducted between 'the British Empire' and 'Foreign Countries'.[3] No provision was made for treaties entered into by Canada of her own accord.

Treaties had a serious effect on federal–provincial relations. For example, in *In re Employment of Aliens*,[4] a British Columbia law[5] restricting the employment of Chinese and Japanese persons conflicted with the Japanese Treaty Act 1913.[6] After objections were received from the Consul General of Japan, the federal government referred the provincial law to the Supreme Court, which concluded that it was ultra vires.

The wording of section 132 suggests that Britain did not expect Canada to become fully independent.[7] But, over the next several decades, the Empire became increasingly fragile. The Balfour Declaration of 1926 confirmed the British Dominions as 'equal in status … [with] the power to negotiate, sign and ratify treaties …'.[8]

As a result, Canada pursued more of its own international agreements, which, to be effective, required enforceable domestic laws. In the United States, treaties approved by the Senate become part of that country's 'supreme law'.[9] The Canadian Constitution provided a somewhat comparable mechanism (though it was not mandatory and involved Parliament as a whole, not just one chamber) for Imperial treaties. But what about treaties conducted by the federal government (in this context, Canada)?

The matter came to a head when Canada joined the International Labour Organization (ILO).[10] A 1925 Supreme Court reference had concluded that labour

[2] For a less state-centric view, see the analysis of Hugo Cyr in *Canadian Federalism and Treaty Powers: Organic Constitutionalism at Work* (Brussels: PIE-Peter Lang, 2009).

[3] Constitution Act 1867, s. 132.

[4] *In Re Employment of Aliens*, [1922] SCR 293.

[5] An act to Validate and Confirm Certain Orders in Council and Provisions Relating to The Employment of Persons on Crown Property (BC) 1921, 11 Geo V c 49.

[6] Section 3 of the Treaty Act provided that the Japanese would have '[most favoured nation status] in all that relates to the pursuit of their industries, callings, professions and educational studies'.

[7] There are different interpretations of the section. FR Scott, for example, wrote that through it 'The Fathers of Confederation established Canadian unity in face of the outside world'. FR Scott, 'The Consequences of the Privy Council Decisions' (1937) 15 Canadian Bar Review 485.

[8] Peter H Hogg, *Constitutional Law of Canada*, 5th edn (looseleaf) (Toronto: Carswell Thomson Reuters, 2007) ch 11.5(b). Canada's independence was confirmed in the *Statute of Westminster*, but s 132 was not changed.

[9] US Constitution, Articles II and VI.

[10] The International Labour Organization (ILO) is a United Nations agency initially formed through the League of Nations in the aftermath of World War I. Canada was a founding member. Government of Canada: www.labour.gc.ca/eng/relations/international/forums/index.shtml.

relations lay within provincial jurisdiction, and the prospects for federal legislation seemed dim.[11] An earlier reference on aeronautics[12] had confirmed the validity of federal legislation enacted in compliance with the Paris Convention of 1919, but under section 132.[13]

A reference[14] about the International Radiotelegraph Convention of 1927 produced a similar result. There, the federal government had 'leapfrogged' an existing Quebec reference[15] with one to the Supreme Court.[16] The Court advised that jurisdiction over radio communications is federal, citing several possible anchors in section 91.[17] The JCPC agreed with the outcome but not the reasoning. Canada had entered the Convention under its own name, so section 132 was inapplicable. Instead, the Committee said, federal legislation to implement the treaty was valid under the 'peace, order and good government' power of section 91.[18]

Nevertheless, Canada referred five laws[19] implementing the ILO conventions prior to their enactment. The Judicial Committee found all of the relevant legislation to be ultra vires.[20] The Judicial Committee noted that Canada had entered the conventions 'by virtue of her new status as an international person'.[21]

[11] *Reference in re Legislative Jurisdiction over Hours of Labour*, [1925] SCR 505, 1925 CanLII 77 (SCC) at 512. The Court recognised an exception for laws applying to federal employees or territories lying outside provincial boundaries.

[12] *Re Regulation and Control of Aeronautics in Canada* [1931] UKPC 93 [*Aeronautics*]. The matter came on appeal from the Supreme Court, which considered an extensive set of questions. Justice Newcombe expressed some irritation at the framing of the questions: [1930] SCR 663, at 696–701. This was endorsed by Lord Haldane for the Judicial Committee, who noted that the 'comprehensive nature of the questions' made useful review 'extremely difficult'. He went on to say: 'The Board certainly has no desire, nor do they conceive it to be part of their function to act as draftsmen for Canadian Acts of Parliament', ibid at 5.

[13] Convention Relating to the Regulation of Aerial Navigation of 1919.

[14] *The Attorney General of Quebec v The Attorney General of Canada & Ors (control of Radio Communication) (Canada)* [1932] UKPC 7 [*Radio Reference* (JCPC)].

[15] *Reference re Regulation and Control of Radio Communication*, [1931] SCR 541 [*Radio Reference* (SCC)].

[16] The questions were: '1. Has the Parliament of Canada jurisdiction to regulate and control radio communication, including the transmission and reception of signs, signals, pictures and sounds of all kinds by means of Hertzian waves, and including the right to determine the character, use and location of apparatus employed? 2. If not, in what particular or particulars or to what extent is the jurisdiction of Parliament limited?'.

[17] *Radio Reference* (SCC) (n 15) at 547. The related powers were: '5. Postal Service; … 7. Militia, Military and Naval Service, and Defence; … 9. Beacons, Buoys, Lighthouses, and Sable Island; … 10. Navigation and Shipping; … and 29. Such Classes of Subjects as are expressly excepted in the Enumeration of the Classes of Subjects by this Act assigned exclusively to the Legislatures of the Provinces'.

[18] *Radio Reference* (JCPC) (n 14) at 3.

[19] The Limitation of Hours of Work Act (1935, c 63), Weekly Rest in Industrial Undertakings Act (1935, c 14), Minimum Wages Act (1935, c 44); the Employment and Social Insurance Act (1935, c 48); and the Dominion Trade and Industry Commission Act (1935, c 25–26).

[20] *The Attorney General of Ontario v The Attorney General of Canada and others (Canada)* [1937] UKPC 6 [*Labour Conventions Reference*]; *The Attorney General of Ontario v The Attorney General of Canada and others (Canada)* [1937] UKPC 7 [*Social Insurance*]; *The Attorney General of Ontario v The Attorney General of Canada and others (Canada)* [1937] UKPC 11 [*Dominion Trade*].

[21] *Labour Conventions Reference* (n 20) at 7.

Therefore, the jurisdiction of the laws in question lay in the division of powers – *not* section 132.

Although the legislation appeared to deal with property and civil rights – an exclusive provincial power – some members of the Supreme Court felt bound by the *Aeronautics* and *Radio* references (in itself an interesting fact about the treatment of references!)[22] to conclude that the laws fell within federal competence because they were enacted in furtherance of treaty obligations.[23] The JCPC disagreed.[24] It stated that although 'treaty-making is an executive act', it is not self-executing.[25] Accordingly, if the federal executive chose to enter a treaty requiring changes to domestic law, it would have to obtain assent of the relevant legislatures.[26]

What of the concern that such a result would render Canada unable to legislate so as to uphold its treaty obligations? Brushing that aside, Lord Atkin offered the metaphor that Canada was a 'ship of state'. While she 'now sails on larger ventures and into foreign waters she still retains the watertight compartments which are an essential part of her original structure'.[27] It was necessary to honour the essential structure, even on the international stage.

The preference to retain integrity in intergovernmental relations – practical implications be damned – was striking.

The *Labour Conventions Reference* has been controversial for eighty years. Praise for it tended to emanate from among Francophone/Quebec scholars, while Anglophone scholars were almost uniformly outraged.[28] Lawyer FR Scott claimed that as a result of the opinion Canada 'cease[d] to be a single nation in the conduct of her international relations'.[29] Many years later, lawyer and scholar Barry L Strayer charged that the reference created 'a continuing source of difficulty in international affairs'.[30] Peter Hogg argued that the 'watertight compartments' metaphor 'typified the narrow and inflexible approach of the Privy Council to the interpretation of the Canadian Constitution'.[31]

The *Labour Conventions Reference* is sometimes cited as an example of how the advisory function enables highly abstract, and therefore problematic, legal

[22] This point is taken up in Chapter 10.

[23] *Labour Conventions Reference* (n 20) at 8, referring to *Reference re legislative jurisdiction of Parliament of Canada to enact the Minimum Wages Act* (1935, c 44), [1936] SCR 461.

[24] The Board distinguished *Aeronautics* because the disputed matter there fell squarely within s 132; and the *Radio Reference* because 'broadcasting' was not mentioned in either s 91 *or* s 92. Since 'treaty making' was not enumerated the allocation of legislative authority would depend on the subject of the particular treaty: *Labour Conventions Reference* (n 20) at 8.

[25] *Labour Conventions Reference* (n 20) at 5.

[26] ibid at 6.

[27] ibid.

[28] Gerard La Forest, 'The Labour Conventions Case Revisited' (1975) 12 Canadian Yearbook of International Law 132; Cyr (n 2); FR Scott, 'Centralization and Decentralization in Canadian Federalism' [1951] Canadian Bar Review 1095, 1112.

[29] Scott (n 7) 485.

[30] Barry L Strayer, *The Canadian Constitution and the Courts* (Toronto: Butterworths, 1988) 327.

[31] Hogg (n 8) C.11.5(c).

reasoning. Strayer queried whether the lack of a factual context could produce a greater tendency to find laws invalid. He conceded, though, that the evidence was equivocal.[32] The issue surrounding 'abstract review' and its connection to references is discussed in Chapter 10.

B. Disallowance

The relationship between the advisory function and the now defunct practice of federal disallowance is another way in which references have featured in federal-provincial disputes.

Federal disallowance, found in section 90 of the Constitution Act 1867, permits the federal government to advise the Queen's representative to withhold royal assent to provincial legislation. Unsurprisingly, it has always been viewed as a symbol of untrammelled federal power.[33]

For some time after Confederation, the federal government regularly disallowed provincial laws. Prime Minister John A Macdonald proposed that it be used where impugned legislation was unconstitutional either in whole or in part; where it conflicted with federal legislation in fields of concurrent jurisdiction; or where legislation 'affected the interests of the Dominion as a whole'.[34] Despite the note of restraint, and the fact that at least some of the criteria were legal standards, the scheme relied heavily on political judgement. As a result, it did little to mitigate provincial concerns.[35]

Attorney General Edward Blake thought that the reference power could alleviate some of that unease. The federal government, he said, should initiate references

[32] Strayer (n 30) 323, citing a failure rate of 53% (cases) versus 35% (references) for provincial laws and 31% versus 22% for cases.

[33] Hogg (n 8) notes that 'If the federal objection to a provincial statute is that it is [unconstitutional] … a court is the appropriate forum to determine the issue. If the federal objection to a provincial statute is that it is unwise, then the provinces may fairly reply that its voters should be left to determine the wisdom of the policies of the government which they have elected. In my view, the provincial case is unimpeachable: the modern development of ideas of judicial review and democratic responsibility has left no room for the exercise of the federal power of disallowance'. It is almost impossible to think that the power could have a resurgence. And yet, during the intense debate over Quebec's Charter of the French Language, CLQR c C-11, Prime Minister Pierre E Trudeau suggested that provincial laws could be disallowed where 'their effect cuts directly across the operations of federal law or creates serious disorder particularly beyond [provincial boundaries]'. Letter from Prime Minister Trudeau tabled in House of Commons, July 21, 1975, *Sessional Papers* No 301-5/185 cited in Hogg, ibid, ch 5 Federalism 5.3(e).

[34] Dominion and Provincial Legislation (1867–1895) (Ottawa, 1896) pp 61–62.

[35] According to JR Mallory, MacDonald's schema meant, in practice, that there were four major grounds for disallowance: (1) threat to 'imperial interests' such as treaty obligations; (2) threat to 'the success of some major national policy or interest'; (3) other situations where the provincial legislation was nonetheless ultra vires provincial powers; and (4) where intra vires provincial legislation 'attacked vested rights in such a way as to be contrary to the principles of sound legislation': JR Mallory, 'Disallowance and the National Interest: The Alberta Social Credit Legislation of 1937' (1948) 14(3) *Canadian Journal of Economic and Political Science* 342 at 354.

to the Supreme Court whenever it believed a provincial law was ultra vires. He also thought that advisory opinions would be helpful in cases where 'public opinion renders expedient a solution of legal problems, dissociated from those elements of passion and expediency which are rightly or wrongly too often attributed to the action of political bodies'.[36]

The legal scholar JR Mallory argued that disallowance was motivated by federal apprehension regarding the impact of certain provincial laws on foreign capital markets.[37] In addition, federal leaders had little respect for their provincial counterparts and, consequently, little hesitation in denying their law-making authority.

At the turn of the nineteenth century, instances of disallowance fell off considerably. Indeed, the federal government refused to use it even for highly controversial laws – including a series of power contract cancellations by the Ontario government, and Quebec's infamous Padlock Act.[38] The shift was motivated in part by growing federal respect for provincial democratic legitimacy. As a result, where certain initiatives appeared unwarranted or unwise, federal actors were content to allow political consequences to flow naturally at the local level. The rise of political parties also played a role – the federal government proved to be less interventionist against provincial governments of the same political camp. Finally, and perhaps most importantly, the practice of judicial review created an alternative. The decidedly robust representation of division of powers issues in early federalism jurisprudence suggested the availability of a neutral arbiter.

Amid the growing federal reluctance to use disallowance, the story of the Alberta Social Credit Legislation stands as a dramatic exception. Following the surprise election in 1935 of a 'Social Credit' government, the new Alberta Premier, William Aberhart, passed several laws aimed at radically re-shaping the economy.[39] Market reaction was severe. The legislation was described as '[pressing] the theory of provincial rights to its utmost extremity' and 'aggressively attempting to modify fundamental national policy', and, in effect, daring the federal government to intervene.[40]

[36] Debates, House of Commons, Canada, 1891, vol I, 3586–87.

[37] Mallory (n 35) 354 citing *Dominion and Provincial Legislation* (1867–1895) (Ottawa, 1896) 376–77.

[38] Act to Prevent the Propagation of Communist Propaganda, RSQ 1941, c 52 made it illegal to use private dwellings for the promotion of Communism. Those found guilty were subject to having their property 'padlocked' against all use. Some 20 years later, in *Switzman v Elbling*, [1957] SCR 285, the Supreme Court held that the law was ultra vires.

[39] Credit of Alberta Regulation Act 1937. As described by Mallory (n 35) 349: 'This Act provided for the licensing of "bankers" within the province by the Social Credit Board, and for the establishment of local directorates to "supervise, direct and control the policy of the business of the Banker in respect of which such Local Directorate has been appointed for the purpose of preventing any act by such Banker or any employee or employees thereof constituting a restriction or interference, either direct or indirect, with the full enjoyment of property and civil rights by any person within the Province"'.

In addition, the Bank Employees Civil Rights Act denied civil rights to any unlicensed employees of a chartered bank. And the Judicature Act Amendment Act required anyone challenging the constitutionality of any Alberta law to first seek the government's permission.

[40] Mallory (n 35) 349.

Prime Minister William Lyon Mackenzie King began with what he surely took to be a conciliatory approach. He offered to refer the matter to the Supreme Court.[41] It was not received well. Aberhart claimed to be 'dumbfounded' at the thought of joining a process that would question his own laws.[42]

Consequently, the federal government disallowed the laws[43] in August of 1937. It called out the province's deliberate attempt 'to interfere with the operation of dominion laws … *[particularly] where the legislature has denied recourse to the courts of justice*'.[44] In other words, Alberta's refusal to sign on to a reference suggested that it could not be reasoned with. That sentiment was bolstered by the province's refusal to publish notice of the disallowance, forcing the federal government to do so in the *Canada Gazette*.[45]

Alberta enacted new legislation.[46] The province omitted all mention of 'banking' (which expressly falls under federal jurisdiction) on the basis that it was 'interested only in the credit of the people'.[47] It introduced, as well, legislation containing particularly stringent measures against the press, including demands for clarification of stories about government activity or policy and the disclosure of confidential sources.

This time, Alberta requested the reference. The federal government quickly complied so that the matter proceeded directly to the Supreme Court. Two sets of questions were posed: one set about the validity of the so-called 'Alberta statutes'[48] and one about the disallowance power.[49]

In relation to disallowance, Alberta argued that section 90 of the BNA Act could no longer apply in its literal sense because the federal disallowance power had fallen into disuse;[50] it was inconsistent with the increasingly recognised equal sovereignty of provinces; and, as any comparable Imperial power had long vanished, it was unthinkable that a colonial representative could exert 'greater power than his master, the King'.[51]

[41] 'Canada and Alberta: The Revival of Dominion Control over the Provinces', p 104. Reprinted from (1939) IV(16) *Politica*.

[42] *Canadian Annual Review*, 1937–38, 471–72.

[43] Mallory (n 35).

[44] Canada, House of Commons Debates, 1938, p 178 (emphasis added).

[45] *Canadian Annual Review*, 1937–38, 111.

[46] 'An Act to Provide for the Regulation of the Credit of the Province of Alberta'; 'An Act to Provide for the Restriction of the Civil Rights of Certain Persons'; and 'An Act to Amend the Judicature Act'. Toronto *Evening Telegram*, 5 October 1937, cited in Mallory, *ibid* at 351.

[47] Toronto *Evening Telegram*, Oct. 5, 1937, cited in Mallory (n 35) 351.

[48] [1938] SCR 100.

[49] *Reference re The Power of the Governor General in Council to Disallow Provincial Legislation and the Power of Reservation of a Lieutenant-Governor of a Province*, [1938] SCR 71 [*Re Disallowance*]. British Columbia attended but did not take part. None of the other Attorneys General, who received notice of the proceeding, participated.

[50] *In re The Initiative and Referendum Act* [1919] AC 935 at [8]: 'a Lieutenant-Governor, when appointed, is as much the representative of Her Majesty for all purposes of provincial government as the Governor General himself is for all purposes of Dominion government'.

[51] Canada, Department of Justice, *Memorandum on Dominion Power of Disallowance of Provincial Legislation*, October 1937 (Ottawa, 1938) p 33, cited in Mallory (n 35) 352.

Noting that many past instances of disallowance and reservation had proceeded solely in conformity with section 90's text, Supreme Court Chief Justice Duff stated that current practice was irrelevant.[52] The answer did not depend on 'constitutional usage'[53] but 'the law' (including section 90 and the Statute of Westminster). None of those assisted Alberta. Indeed, by ending Imperial control over Dominion law the Statute of Westminster suggested the opposite.[54]

The JCPC previously had described disallowance as 'unrestricted'.[55] Did the power admit of *any* limits? Members of the Court preferred to not express an opinion about the issue.[56] Disallowance was a Crown prerogative. The Court was 'not constitutionally empowered'[57] to pronounce on its parameters. In effect, this was a separation of powers response.

The Supreme Court avoided broader philosophical questions about federal–provincial relations. It did, though, recognise a *justification* for disallowance, namely where it proved necessary 'in order to safeguard the unity of the nation'.[58] The threat posed by a Social Credit government, and the resulting federal-provincial tension, appears to have created in the Court an 'unusually keen awareness of the role of disallowance in asserting the paramountcy of the national interest'.[59]

The Social Credit saga is often viewed as an extraordinary circumstance that left the federal government little choice.[60] It seems to have reinvigorated a sense of national identity organised around core economic principles. After a period of somewhat moribund federal policy, the *Disallowance Reference* ushered in distinctly more activist economic regulation.

The advisory function played an important role in the controversy. The federal government sought to obtain the opinion of the Supreme Court as an alternative to disallowance. Only when Alberta rejected a reference did the Prime Minister turn to the 'self-help' provided by the power. Cabinet could have put the questions to the Supreme Court on its own but it evidently did not view a process in which Alberta refused to participate as worthwhile. Arguably, the federal government realised that, in order to have the proper 'weight', the reference would have to have the trappings of an adversarial proceeding.

[52] Mallory (n 35) 77.

[53] ibid at 78.

[54] (1931) 22 Geo V, Imp ch 4 [Statute of Westminster]; *Re Disallowance* (n 49) at 82.

[55] *Re Disallowance* (n 49) at 78, citing *Wilson v E. & N. Railway Co.* [1922] 1 AC 202, at 210.

[56] ibid at 95. This has been interpreted in subsequent jurisprudence as denying to the Court any powers of review over the matter: See *Re Manitoba Language Rights*, [1985] 1 SCR 721 at para 70.

[57] *Re Disallowance* (n 49) at 95.

[58] ibid at 83.

[59] Mallory (n 35) 353.

[60] Mallory, ibid at 356, succinctly sums up the limited political and legal levers, and concomitant political pressure: 'It was all very well to say that the banks had a constitutional remedy in the courts and at the ballot box, but in fact the former had been denied to them by the legislation and the latter was unlikely to give them effective redress in Alberta. The Liberals at Ottawa had nothing to lose by disallowing the legislation since the loss of support in Alberta was negligible set against the loss of prestige and eastern support which would have resulted from a refusal to disallow'.

After adopting an implacable posture with respect to the first set of laws, Alberta changed course. Perhaps it saw merit in taking a more conciliatory approach. Or, it may have perceived some value in being able to articulate its position before a more neutral arbiter than the federal government. Indeed, the Supreme Court singled out Alberta's counsel for diligent and lucid submissions.[61] The reference also permitted Alberta a structured and formal process in which to explain and defend its objectives to its own constituents, political rivals, federal and provincial counterparts, and the nation. These issues are addressed more fully in Chapter 9.

C. Marriage

The state regulation of marriage also became a flashpoint in the first decades after Confederation. The subject inspired two references that, in addition to clarifying legal principles, underscored a growing sense of Canadian sovereignty.

In the BNA Act, authority over 'Marriage and Divorce' is granted to Parliament, while 'The Solemnization of Marriage' belongs to the provinces. Provinces also have power over 'property and civil rights', including the division of marital property, and child custody.[62] The bifurcation is said to reflect the view that family law is best regulated according to local customs and mores, while 'marriage and divorce' benefits from national standards.[63]

Family law cases at the appellate court level are rare, and advisory opinions even more so.[64] Nonetheless, two such opinions were issued around the turn of the twentieth century: *In re Bigamy*;[65] and *In re Marriage Laws*.[66] *In re Bigamy* concerned the federal crime of leaving Canada with the intention of entering into a second marriage.[67] The matter was referred to the Supreme Court after lower courts divided over the law's validity.[68] *In re Marriage* arose in the wake of

[61] *Re Disallowance* (n 49) at 74.

[62] Constitution Act 1867, ss 91(26), 92(12).

[63] Some have suggested that the choice was meant to avoid the disputes such as those that arise in the United States, where, because the Constitution does not enumerate a federal power over marriage, a legal union might not be valid in all states. Article IV states, inter alia, 'Full faith and credit shall be given in each state to the public acts, records, and judicial proceedings of every other state'. This creates a state comity rule for civil marriage but it has been tested in debates over inter-racial marriage and, more recently, same-sex marriage: *Loving v Virginia*, 388 US 1 (1967); Defense of Marriage Act (DOMA) 1 US C §7; *United States v Windsor*, 570 US ___ (2013); Hogg (n 8) ch. 27.2.

[64] A search of the Supreme Court of Canada decisions database reveals some years without any apparent appeals in the family law area, such as 2016, and many years with a single decision, like 2013 (*Quebec (Attorney General) v A*, 2013 SCC 5, [2013] 1 SCR 61).

[65] *In Re Criminal Code Sections Relating to Bigamy*, (1897) 27 SCR 461 [*In re Bigamy*].

[66] *In re Marriage Laws*, [1912] SCR 132 [*In re Marriage* (SCC)].

[67] Criminal Code of Canada, RSC, c 161, s 4.

[68] *Reg. v Brierly*, 14 OR 525 (1887); *The Queen v Plowman*, 25 OR 656 (1894). In the latter case, Chief Justice Armour had said, at 656: 'The Dominion Parliament, being a subordinate legislature, has no such power; and that is the effect of the case of *Macleod v Attorney General for New South Wales*, which covers this case. The second marriage is the offence, and the Dominion Parliament has no power to legislate about such an offence committed in a foreign country'.

a papal decree that, in changing religious marriage laws, exerted great hardship on Canadian Catholics.[69] Parliament drafted a law intended to mitigate (in a civil sense at least) that hardship and referred the law to the Supreme Court.[70]

Both proceedings raised broader questions about advisory opinions. In *In re Bigamy*, no one offered submissions *against* the law's validity, a point that some used to criticise references in general.[71] Perhaps in partial response, in *In re Marriage* Canada appointed two additional sets of counsel. The Attorney General of each province also was given the opportunity to appear.[72] (Today, such matters are governed by the Supreme Court Rules.)

The *Bigamy* reference revealed a fault line about Canada's colonial roots. The underlying issue was whether a dependency of the Crown of the United Kingdom could regulate the conduct of British subjects. In the view of the Chief Justice, it could not.[73] The rest of the panel disagreed, in terms that amounted to a rallying cry for Canadian sovereignty:

> [We] cannot fail to see the manifest intention of the framers of our constitution to have been to give to … the people of Canada, a political status infinitely superior to that of a colony – a national existence in fact as an integral portion of the British Empire – having a constitution similar in principle to that of the United Kingdom and a Parliament … with sovereign jurisdiction over all matters placed by the constitution under their control.[74]

Confederation's hopes and aspirations would be 'utterly disappointed if the Parliament of this great Dominion' were held to not have the power to enact the impugned law.[75]

Turning to *In re Marriage*, because the hearing was so proximate to the *Reference re References*, there was a question over whether the Court ought to hear the

[69] The controversy arose after Pope Pius X, under the decree *Ne Temere*, limited valid Catholic marriages to those contracted before parish priests or their delegates and declared all other marriages canonically void. Existing marriages were annulled. Women, especially, suffered. JS Moir, 'Canadian Protestant Reaction to the *Ne Temere Decree*' (1981) 48 *CCHA Study Sessions*.

[70] The questions were:

1. *(a)* Has the Parliament of Canada authority to enact … 'An Act to amend the "Marriage Act"'? [which purported to deem valid in Canada any law performed in accordance with valid local laws notwithstanding any differences in the faith of the celebrants or officiant.] …
2. Does the law of the Province of Quebec render null and void, unless contracted before a Roman Catholic priest, a marriage that would otherwise be legally binding, which takes place in such province,

   (*a*) between persons who are both Roman Catholics, or,
   (*b*) between persons one of whom, only, is a Roman Catholic?
3. If either *(a)* or (*b*) of the last preceding question is answered in the affirmative … has the Parliament of Canada authority to enact that all such marriages … shall be legal and binding?

[71] *In Re Bigamy* (n 65) at 464.

[72] *In Re Marriage* (SCC) (n 66) at 136–37.

[73] *In Re Bigamy* (n 65) at 471, 474.

[74] ibid at 479–80.

[75] ibid at 480.

matter at all. By the time the matter was argued, however, the JCPC had confirmed the validity of the advisory function. But the broader discussion continued. Some counsel in *In re Marriage* suggested that if the Court concluded that the federal marriage law was ultra vires, then it should decline to answer Question 2. They argued that

> [i]f the Parliament of Canada has no part or parcel in jurisdiction in regard put as for the solemnization of marriage, … why then should the Dominion request your Lordships to answer what the law in any province is[?] … I think the only body that could come before your Lordships for any authority to ask for interpretation of that question would be the body that can … amend or alter or change that law …[76]

The argument reiterated long-standing provincial concerns about the federal government using references to interrogate provincial law without their consent.

During oral submissions, lawyers could not resist commenting on *Reference re References*. Quebec advocate RC Smith was positively acerbic.[77] He took pains to note that the Judicial Committee had recognised the right of the courts to *decline* to answer particular questions[78] and to urge the government to avoid as much as possible 'the mischief and inconvenience which might arise from an indiscriminate and injudicious use of the Act'.[79]

Smith argued that the Court should decline to answer the aforementioned Question 2 because it predominantly affected 'private rights and interests' not currently represented before the Court and was 'purely hypothetical'.[80] Justice Anglin agreed. It was 'difficult to perceive how an answer to [Question 2] can be useful either to Parliament or to the Governor-General in Council'. Depending on the Court's answers to the other questions, it might be 'purely academic'.[81]

For his part, Idington J remained unpersuaded by the Judicial Committee's reasoning about advisory opinions:

> As to the objections strongly pressed by counsel for Quebec that we should not answer the second question, I may observe that incidentally to dealing with the like questions in [the *Reference re References*] I assumed that private rights might be touched and urged all I could in the same direction as counsel do now argue as ground of refusal to answer. The Judicial Committee's judgment indicates such objections were hardly worthy of notice.[82]

[76] ibid at 265 (submissions by Counsel acting for the Government of Canada but appointed to argue against the validity of the Bill (essentially *amicus curiae* for the government); described *ibid* at 136. See also the discussion of procedure in Chapter 10.

[77] ibid at 137–38. 'I suppose I must say frankly that, with regard to the absolute question of jurisdiction, we must accept [the *Reference*] as disposing of the question of jurisdiction and upholding that such a reference is constitutional'.

[78] *Attorney-General for Canada v Attorneys-General for Ontario, Quebec and Nova Scotia* [1898] AC 700, at 717.

[79] ibid at 139–41. See the discussion in Chapter 3.

[80] ibid.

[81] ibid at 421.

[82] ibid at 395.

He again derided the idea that references could ever be merely advisory:

> If I understand their Lordships aright, the statute creates this court *pro tanto* an advisory board. They suggest the answers need not bind. But, I respectfully submit, we and the other colonial courts have been told more than once that their Lordships' judgments bind us at least and we follow them. Hence their judgment in this case must bind us and all colonial courts, notwithstanding the large powers of self government, the judgment informs us Canada is possessed of.[83]

The Court cited prior JCPC cautions about reference questions.[84] Indeed, Anglin J noted that the Board had described the actual questions put in the *Reference re References* as 'very difficult to answer exhaustively and accurately without so many qualifications and reservations as to make the answers of little value'.[85] The current case warranted a similar caution. But, because a majority of his colleagues had decided to answer Question 2, 'in deference to their views'[86] Anglin J proceeded to give his opinion of it.

The Court concluded that Canada did not have the power to pass marriage legislation for the entire country,[87] nor could it declare legal marriages voidable in Quebec on religious grounds.[88] The split attracted controversy because, to some, it appeared to track denominational differences: the three judges who found mixed marriage valid under Quebec law were Protestant; the two who either dissented or demurred were Catholic.[89]

The Judicial Committee upheld the majority opinions.[90] On a 'true construction' of sections 91 and 92, it advised, 'the jurisdiction of the Dominion Parliament ... does not cover the whole field [of "marriage"]'.[91]

The Court would not issue another family law advisory opinion until the *Reference re Same-Sex Marriage*.

Apex Change – The Revamped Court

As recounted in more detail in the next chapter, a combination of international and domestic events inspired Parliament to amend the Supreme Court Act so that

[83] ibid.

[84] *Reference re References*, citing the *Fisheries Case* [1898] AC 700, at 717.

[85] *In re Marriage* (SCC) (n 66) at 423, citing *Reference re References* at 589. This is a fair criticism. The questions themselves were reproduced in Chapter 3.

[86] ibid at 423–24.

[87] Idington J's response was more nuanced, stating that a concurrent scheme of federal-provincial law was preferable *if* it could confirm the validity of past marriages in a way that neither order of government could do on its own. Ibid at 397.

[88] ibid at 456. A majority of the panel thought marriages between Roman Catholics, but not contracted under a Roman Catholic priest, could stand; while one concluded that Quebec law rendered them null; and the Chief Justice, citing the *sub judice* rule, declined to answer. Idington J thought Parliament could so declare 'if and when a province fails to provide adequate means of solemnization'. Ibid at 336.

[89] Moir (n 69) at 88.

[90] *In Re Marriage* [1912] UKPC 63.

[91] ibid at 6.

the Supreme Court would be the final court of appeal for the country. The Court's composition was increased from seven to nine members. Its advisory function remained unchanged.[92]

The three decades between the elimination of Privy Council appeals and the Constitution Act 1982 were marked by increasing federal–provincial conflict. The federal government sought to protect economic interests on a national level, often conflicting with provincial desires, law and policy.[93] During this period, the pattern of Supreme Court decision making was seen as a marked 'course correction' from earlier JCPC jurisprudence.[94]

While the pattern was not perfectly consistent, the Court came to be viewed as significantly more disposed to federal concerns.[95] For example, from 1949 to the late 1970s, the Court heard more than 100 federalism appeals. Forty per cent of the challenges to provincial laws, but only a handful involving federal ones, were successful.[96]

A. Natural Resources

The newly constituted Supreme Court faced its first serious federalism issue in the *Reference re Offshore Minerals*.[97] The matter arose when federal–provincial negotiations[98] failed to resolve the ownership of mineral rights in the territorial sea adjacent to British Columbia. Prime Minister Lester Pearson asked the Court for advice regarding who owned the lands in question; the attendant natural resources; and the continental shelf.[99] British Columbia Premier WAC Bennett called the reference an attempted usurpation.[100] Concerned about the potential implications for their own interests, six provinces participated in the hearing.[101]

[92] The Supreme Court Act does not specify a minimum number of judges for references. In practice, they are usually heard by the full Court.

[93] Hogg is particularly cogent on this: 'The general tendency of technological change is to convert activities which were once local and private, and which could be governed by the private law of contract, tort, and property, into activities which extend across the entire nation, make use of public facilities and require regulation in order to protect the public from predatory or monopolistic practices'. Peter W Hogg, 'Is the Supreme Court of Canada Biased in Constitutional Cases?' (1979) 57(4) Canadian Bar Review 721, 728.

[94] John T Saywell, *The Lawmakers: Judicial Power and the Shaping of Canadian Federalism* (Toronto: Osgoode Society, 2002) 258.

[95] Ken Lysyk, 'Reshaping Canadian Federalism' (1979) 13 University of British Columbia Law Review 1. Lysyk did not allege bias.

[96] For analysis up to 1978, see Hogg (n 93) 726–27. Peter Russell, 'A Political Scientist's View' (1974) 13(2) Osgoode Hall Law Journal 293; Paul Weiler, *In the Last Resort* (Toronto: Carswell, 1974).

[97] *Reference Re: Offshore Mineral Rights*, [1967] SCR 792 [*Offshore Minerals*].

[98] Saywell (n 94) 257.

[99] *Offshore Minerals* (n 97) at 716.

[100] ibid at 257.

[101] In addition to British Columbia, Ontario, Nova Scotia, New Brunswick, Prince Edward Island and Newfoundland participated. Quebec maintained that 'the question had to be settled by political negotiations, not the courts'. Other provinces did not appear. Saywell (n 94) 257.

In a *per curiam* opinion, the Court stated that the term 'ownership' must be given its international rather than common law meaning. As Canada alone was a sovereign state,[102] the provincial claim depended in part on the status of the waters in question at the time that British Columbia entered Confederation.[103] In 1871 the province 'did not have ownership or property in the territorial sea'.[104] With respect, then, to the 'continental shelf', which had not even existed as a legal subject matter, the answer turned on the division of powers.

Offshore Minerals contains important recognition of federal legislative authority with respect to mineral ownership and development in territorial waters. The Court concluded that because the matter corresponded to no provincial head of jurisdiction the concomitant federal jurisdiction lay in the 'gap' and 'national concern' branches of the POGG power (peace, order and good government).[105] This potentially signalled an important break from prior JCPC jurisprudence, which mostly had confined POGG to 'emergency' applications. The Supreme Court had already begun to evince a more open attitude to POGG[106] but *Offshore Minerals* was a particularly dramatic, and politicised, example.[107]

B. Inflation and Emergency

Re: Anti-Inflation Act is a towering advisory opinion. Not only was it a rare example of the use of the 'peace, order and good government' power, it also ushered in an approach to evidence that would have an enormous effect on all constitutional litigation.[108]

The matter arose as a result of the 1975 wage and price controls instituted by Prime Minister Pierre E Trudeau.[109] Structured as a temporary, 'emergency'

[102] *Offshore Minerals* (n 97) at 816: 'There can be no doubt now that Canada has become a sovereign state. Its sovereignty was acquired in the period between its separate signature of the Treaty of Versailles in 1919 and the Statute of Westminster, 1931, 22 Geo. V, c. 4. Section 3 of the Statute of Westminster provides in an absolutely clear manner and without any restrictions that the Parliament of a Dominion has full power to make laws having extra-territorial operation'.

[103] ibid at 800.

[104] ibid at 808.

[105] ibid at 816–17. The 'residuary' theory of POGG in respect of offshore lands was confirmed in *Reference re Newfoundland Continental Shelf*, [1984] 1 SCR 86 at 127 [*Re Continental Shelf*].

[106] Successful POGG cases include *Johannesson v West St. Paul*, [1952] 1 SCR 292 (aviation); and *Munro v National Capital Commission*, [1966] SCR 663 (national capital region).

[107] It would be followed some years later by an equally controversial reference involving the province of Newfoundland and Labrador: *Re Continental Shelf*, above n 105.

[108] *Re: Anti-Inflation Act*, [1976] 2 SCR 373 [*Re Anti-Inflation*].

[109] 1974-75-76 (Can.), c 75. It contained the following long title and preamble:

> An Act to provide for the restraint of profit margins, prices, dividends and compensation in Canada
>
> WHEREAS the Parliament of Canada recognizes that inflation in Canada at current levels is contrary to the interests of all Canadians and that the containment and reduction of inflation has become a matter of serious national concern;
>
> AND WHEREAS to accomplish such containment and reduction of inflation it is necessary to restrain profit margins, prices, dividends and compensation …

measure, the Act provided for guidelines to restrain prices and profit margins, employee compensation, and dividends.[110] The federal government sought to confirm the law's validity. In three separate opinions, a 7–2 majority of the Court concluded that the law was intended to deal with a present and urgent situation as Parliament is entitled to do under the emergency branch of POGG.[111]

Anti-Inflation was a federal victory but, because the use of the 'emergency' branch meant that the law would be time limited, a qualified one. Despite positive applications of the POGG power in earlier opinions, the Supreme Court did not agree with the federal government's suggestion that particular economic challenges could be classed as matters of 'national concern' and, thus, fall under POGG.[112] If anything, *Anti-Inflation* contributed to a narrowing of the scope of the POGG power and in subsequent cases the federal government has been reluctant to invoke it.[113]

The reference has been more consequential for its effect on evidence and litigation. Recall that, where a reference concerns a matter that was not the subject of extensive prior litigation, the more artificial construct can inhibit the judiciary's ability to evaluate and test facts that normally help it reach a decision. It is therefore significant that the Court articulated a rule that enlarged the scope of the record in a reference.

When the majority concluded that the anti-inflation law was a valid exercise of the POGG emergency power, it refused to consider (a) whether the state of inflation in Canada at the time amounted to an *actual* economic 'emergency' or (b) whether the proposed measures in the law would actually *mitigate* such a crisis. Four judges stated that they merely were seeking evidence that Parliament 'did not have a rational basis' for regarding the law as 'temporarily necessary' to meet an economic crisis. The remaining judges were content to conclude that Parliament

[110] The Act automatically expired at the end of 1978. It could, though, be terminated earlier, or extended by Parliament.

[111] Of the seven-judge majority, four held, *Re Anti-Inflation* (n 108) at 425, that the government need only have a 'rational basis' for thinking that it faced an emergency, and the Court need not determine whether that belief was valid. Three judges, at 439, adopted the test articulated in the war measures cases (*Japanese Canadians Reference* [1947] AC 8; *Reference as to the Validity of the Wartime Leasehold Regulations* [1950] SCR 124) that emergency legislation can only be found ultra vires 'by reliance on very clear evidence that an emergency had not arisen when the statute was enacted'. Four judges declined to take a position on whether the law could have been sustained under the POGG 'national concern' branch, in essence leaving the question open, while three (plus the two dissenters) insisted that inflation was not a matter of 'national concern'. The dissenting opinion found that the 'containment of inflation' did not justify such a dramatic federal intrusion into the provincial sphere.

[112] Hogg has questioned the Court's analysis: 'a visitor from another federation would be surprised that permanent wage and price controls cannot be enacted by the federal Parliament. This means, of course, that they cannot be enacted at all, because provincial controls could not be effective while there is free movement across provincial boundaries of personnel, capital, goods and services. The opinions in the Anti-Inflation Reference … abundantly demonstrate the continuing life of the Privy Council extensions of property and civil rights in the province'. Hogg (n 93) 731.

[113] See *Reference re Securities Act*, 2011 SCC 66; *R v Hydro-Québec*, [1997] 3 SCR 213; *Reference re Firearms Act (Can)*, [2000] 1 SCR 783 [*Re Firearms Act*].

was motivated 'by a sense of urgent necessity' and, critically, that those opposed to the law had failed to show 'by very clear evidence that an emergency had not arisen'.[114]

Absent an examination of sources outside of the Anti-Inflation Act itself, a court would be hard pressed to answer *any* of the above questions. And yet, to look at such sources had been out of bounds in advisory opinions. The rule against so-called 'extrinsic evidence' was stated most clearly in *Re Wartime Leasehold Regulation*, where the Supreme Court noted that 'precisely on account of their character the [advisory] opinions are supposed to be given on the material which appears in the Order of Reference and the Court is not expected to look to outside evidence'.[115] Aside from matters of 'common knowledge' or 'judicial notice', Chief Justice Rinfret continued, the Court was 'limited to the statements of fact contained in the Order of Reference'.[116]

In *Re Anti-Inflation* a majority of the Court abandoned the *Re Wartime Leasehold* rule. Instead, it said, when 'an issue is raised that exceptional circumstances underlie resort to a legislative power … [the Court may] consider extrinsic material bearing on the circumstances alleged, both in support of and in denial of the lawful exercise of legislative authority'.[117] The majority hastened to note that such evidence would not be examined in terms of 'whether it provides *proof* of the exceptional circumstances as a matter of fact'.[118] The typical matters at issue in a reference, it said, concern 'social and economic policy and hence governmental and legislative judgment', which would be unsuited to judicial pronouncements.[119] The Court then cited statistics and an academic study describing the economic conditions at the time of the Anti-Inflation Act. That material, the majority found, provided a basis upon which Parliament could have concluded that the economic crisis was urgent.[120]

[114] *Re Anti-Inflation* (n 108) at 439.

[115] *Reference re Wartime Leasehold Regulations*, [1950] SCR 124 at 126 [*Re Wartime Leasehold*]. Note that in *Reference Re: Steven Murray Truscott*, [1967] SCR 309 (a wrongful conviction review discussed further in Chapter 9) the Supreme Court did permit the introduction of new evidence. Kate Puddister describes this as the first time such evidence was received. The Court did not elaborate on the practice at that time, though the particular circumstances (review of the legal basis for conviction) make it appear obvious why the Court would have been open to receiving such evidence when it was not in references per se. Kate Puddister, *Inviting Judicial Review: A Comprehensive Analysis Of Canadian Appellate Court Reference Cases*, PhD thesis, McGill University, Montreal, December 2015, 119,

[116] *Re Wartime Leasehold.* The rule could be traced to the JCPC's initial forays into interpretation of the BNA Act. For criticism of the Committee on this ground, see HA Smith, 'The Residue of Power in Canada' (1926) 4 Canadian Bar Review 432.

[117] *Re Anti-Inflation* (n 108) at 422–23 *per* Laskin CJ. The three concurring judges, in an opinion written by Ritchie J, generally agreed stating at 437–38: 'I think it not only permissible but essential to give consideration to the material which Parliament had before it at the time when the statute was enacted for the purpose of disclosing the circumstances which prompted its enactment'.

[118] ibid at 423 (emphasis added).

[119] ibid.

[120] The Court summarised the material as: submissions by the Canadian Labour congress, including a study by Professor Richard G Lipsey; telegrams from a large number of economists supporting Lipsey's analysis; a transcript of a speech delivered by the Governor of the Bank of Canada; and a comment prepared by the Ontario Office of Economic Policy. ibid at 387.

Anti-Inflation Act concerned the POGG emergency power, which itself is a marked departure from ordinary division-of-powers questions. That might have justified, and provided a natural limit for, the deviation from prior practice. In fairly short order, though, the analysis was expanded beyond that context. In *Reference re Residential Tenancies*,[121] the Court said that Rinfret CJ's blanket statement in the wartime reference could 'no longer be taken as a correct statement of the law'.[122] It would be imprudent to 'enunciate *any* inflexible rule governing the admissibility of extrinsic materials in constitutional references', the effect of which 'might well be to exclude logically relevant and highly probative evidence'.[123] The Court hinted that its analysis could extend beyond advisory opinions.[124] That suggestion was borne out in subsequent rulings, where the Supreme Court confirmed a broad approach to admissibility of a variety of facts in all proceedings (with the weight to be accorded such evidence treated as a separate legal issue).[125]

The nod to extrinsic evidence in *Anti-Inflation* drew the Court further into a political quagmire. No matter how gingerly the Court framed the question to which it would direct its use of such evidence (in *Re Anti-Inflation* itself, the Court applied an exceptionally low 'rational basis' standard), it opened the door to charges of politically motivated reasoning. For example, Laskin J set aside a submission that cited scores of economists who disputed the idea that an inflation rate of 10 per cent could constitute an economic emergency.[126] To be sure, his point was that the soundness of such a conclusion was irrelevant to the precise constitutional question. But the analysis, unsurprisingly, was attacked as selective.

Re Anti-Inflation is significant for its treatment of the emergency power, but the power has not been invoked since.[127] Far more significant is the reference's call for a new approach to constitutional litigation. The Court's choice probably contributed to the collapse of most practical distinctions between references and ordinary cases.[128] The reference presaged the paradigm shift that would occur in 1982, discussed in the next chapter, and the overall approach to constitutional disputes and interpretation, discussed in Chapter 7.

[121] [1981] 1 SCR 714.

[122] ibid at 722.

[123] ibid (emphasis added).

[124] ibid at 723: 'Generally speaking, for the purpose of constitutional characterization of an act we should not deny ourselves such assistance as Royal Commission reports or Law Reform Commission reports … They may carry great, little, or no weight, but at least they should, in my view, generally be admitted as an aid in determining the social and economic conditions under which the Act was enacted. … The mischief at which the act was directed, the background against which the legislation was enacted and institutional framework in which the act is to operate are all logically relevant'.

[125] *R v Morgentaler*, [1993] 1 SCR 462.

[126] *Re Anti-Inflation* (n 108) at 424.

[127] Peter W Hogg, 'Proof of Facts in Constitutional Cases' (1976) 26 University of Toronto Law Journal 386.

[128] See the discussion in Chapter 10.

C. Inter-provincial Trade

Important references also arose regarding inter-provincial trade.[129] In the three or so decades between the abolition of Privy Council appeals and the Constitution Act 1982, political tension emerged over the production, distribution and marketing of agricultural products.[130] The issue has been a particularly thorny one, which reverberates even to the present day.[131]

One of the most significant references involved the so-called 'chicken and egg war'[132] concerning the excess volume of eggs in Ontario and chickens in Quebec. The two provinces enacted controlled marketing schemes with in-province preferences. A federal marketing scheme intended to resolve the problem through a complex process of delegation became bogged down in parliamentary wrangling.[133]

Growing impatient, the province of Manitoba decided to force the issue. It enacted a 'carbon copy' of the Quebec scheme purporting to regulate the marketing of inter-provincial eggs.[134] It then referred the scheme to the Manitoba Court of Appeal.[135] After that Court found the scheme ultra vires, Manitoba was able to appeal as of right to the Supreme Court.[136]

The Court confirmed that the Manitoba scheme (and, thus, all similar ones) was ultra vires. The programme was 'intended to govern the sale in Manitoba of all eggs, wherever produced, by means of quotas, or even outright prohibition'.[137] The Court acknowledged that prior decisions had implied a fairly narrow role for the federal power over trade and commerce, and a significant degree of

[129] The issue is given heightened importance by the presence in the Constitution Act 1867 of s 121: 'All Articles of the Growth, Produce, or Manufacture of any one of the Provinces shall, from and after the Union, be admitted free into each of the other Provinces'. Notwithstanding this, provinces routinely impose such tariffs. The matter came to a head in *R v Comeau* where the Supreme Court confirmed the validity of such laws: 2018 SCC 15.

[130] The earliest example during the period is *Ontario Farm Products Marketing Reference*, [1957] SCR 198. There, a number of the judges hinted that s 91(2) might extend to some transactions wholly in-province.

[131] Geoffrey Mohan, 'Behind Trump's dairy rant, a cheesed-off Wisconsin and Canada's sacred cows', *LA Times*, 12 June 2018: http://www.latimes.com/business/la-fi-dairy-canada-20180612-story.html; Laura Stone, 'Maxime Bernier renews attack on Canada's supply management system amid trade battle with Trump', *Globe and Mail*, 11 June 2018: www.theglobeandmail.com/politics/article-maxime-bernier-renews-attack-on-canadas-supply-management-system/.

[132] Weiler (n 96) 156–57.

[133] ibid.

[134] ibid.

[135] *Order in Council 1083/70 re Provincial Control of Agricultural Products (Re)*, [1971] 3 WWR 204, 18 DLR (3d) 326.

[136] *Attorney-General for Manitoba v Manitoba Egg and Poultry Association et al.*, [1971] SCR 689 [*Manitoba Egg Reference*]. The lengthy Order-in-Council stated that 'many Provinces of Canada, including the Province of Manitoba, have enacted legislation pertaining to the regulation and control of marketing of agricultural products' and that 'doubt exists' concerning their validity. The Court was requested to make a number of assumptions about the regulation of 'the marketing of eggs produced in Manitoba in interprovincial and export trade'.

[137] ibid at 701.

latitude for the provincial one.[138] But the key issue was 'whether [a provincial law or programme] was made in relation to the regulation of *inter*-provincial trade and commerce'.[139] Here, that clearly was the case.[140]

As further explored in Chapter 9, the *Manitoba Egg Reference* demonstrated that proceeding via a reference can have significant advantages. Not only was Manitoba able to seize control of the timing, it crafted a scenario to its greatest advantage: drafting the Order-in-Council to perfectly mimic the scheme it found so objectionable. It also stated a series of factual assumptions to guide the Court. Neither tactic would be easily available, if at all, in ordinary litigation.

Indeed, in his concurring opinion, Chief Justice Laskin complained that the completely abstract nature of the argument 'seriously affected' the reference's utility.[141] As he pointed out:

> Marketing data to illuminate those issues might have been set out in the Order itself …, or in an agreed statement of facts, or, indeed, might have been offered to the court to indicate the circumstances which prompted the questions addressed to it.[142]

Instead,

> I know nothing of the nature of the market for eggs in Manitoba or outside of it, nothing of the production of eggs in that province, nothing of the uses to which the production is put, nothing of the number of producers in Manitoba, nothing of any problems that may have been created in relation to quality, price or otherwise by the entry of out-of-province eggs.[143]

'[T]he absence of relevant data' meant that the legislative scheme and regulations reflected an absurdly broad marketing scheme in order that 'the naked constitutional question [would] be faced'.[144]

Manitoba, plainly, did not wish the putative scheme to be upheld. After all, it had drawn up the Order-in-Council for the sole purpose of showing its constitutional defect! Thus, it carefully avoided putting before the Court any

[138] ibid at 701–02, citing *Citizens Insurance Company of Canada v Parsons*, (1881) 7 App Cas 96 at 113, 51 LJPC 11 [*Parsons*]; *Shannon v Lower Mainland Dairy Products Board* [1938] AC 708 at 719, 2 WWR 604, 4 DLR 81; *Home Oil Distributors Limited v Attorney-General of British Columbia*, [1940] SCR 444, [1940] 2 DLR 609; *Carnation Company Limited v The Quebec Agricultural Marketing Board*, [1968] SCR 238, 67 DLR (2d) 1 [*Carnation*].

[139] *Manitoba Egg Reference* (n 136) at 703 (emphasis added).

[140] ibid: 'It is my opinion that the Plan now in issue not only affects inter-provincial trade in eggs, but that it aims at the regulation of such trade. It is an essential part of this scheme, the purpose of which is to obtain for Manitoba producers the most advantageous marketing conditions for eggs, specifically to control and regulate the sale in Manitoba of imported eggs. It is designed to restrict or limit the free flow of trade between provinces as such. Because of that, it constitutes an invasion of the exclusive legislative authority of the Parliament of Canada over the matter of the regulation of trade and commerce'.

[141] ibid at 704.

[142] ibid at 705.

[143] ibid.

[144] ibid at 704–06.

broader context in which provinces enacting such schemes might be responding to negative circumstances elsewhere.[145] The reference thus impeded those provinces with an interest in preserving such boards – namely Quebec and Ontario – from highlighting additional economic facts that might have explained their protectionism.[146]

For some, the above elements compromised the quality of the opinion. In particular, the reference was criticised for not adequately explaining the Court's shift from earlier jurisprudence, including a 1968 case where the Court upheld a provincial plan controlling the prices of raw milk sold to a company which shipped the bulk of the product intra-provincially.[147]

It is surely an overstatement to blame such doctrinal inconsistency solely on the reference procedure. Nonetheless, Manitoba's tactics illustrate how the advisory function can be manipulated to achieve certain political ends, potentially at the expense of coherent law. The *Manitoba Egg Reference* supports the intuition of some commentators that a hearing cloaked in legal robes, yet disconnected from the broader factual context, cannot truly compete with a live case in terms of providing clarity and precision in adjudication. Acknowledging that the vast majority of 'facts' in litigation are never purely objective, inter partes litigation does provide some constraints that render cases more resistant to bald political manipulation.

Current Battles

In recent years, the Canadian state has faced new challenges to federal–provincial relations. An obvious example is where a threat arises to Confederation itself – for example, when a province seeks to 'secede'. That has been a recurring threat since, at least, the election of a secessionist government in Quebec in 1976. The courts' involvement in that dispute is discussed in Chapter 8. Immediately below are other recent examples. At the time of writing, two had not yet been finally resolved; nonetheless they provide important hints about the motivation of federal and provincial actors (which will be taken up again in Chapter 9).

A. Criminal Law

A number of federal–provincial conflicts have arisen over the scope of Parliament's power to create criminal law. In a society that requires increasingly complex

[145] Kate Puddister notes that Manitoba did not raise the issue of 'the injury caused to Manitoba by agricultural discrimination', Puddister (n 115) 123.

[146] The opinion contains no information regarding the state of affairs in other provinces, such as Quebec and Ontario, and those provinces, being confined to intervenor status, could not present such information.

[147] *Carnation* (n 138).

forms of regulation, the federal government finds itself using criminal law not just to prohibit behaviour outright, but to set boundaries around it. When it does so, it invites challenges that what it produces is not, properly, criminal legislation.

One such reference was *Re Firearms Act*.[148] In 1995 the federal government amended the Criminal Code[149] to include a series of offences relating to firearms registration and licensing. A number of provinces objected and Alberta referred the law's validity to the Court of Appeal. That Court upheld it 2–1.[150]

The Supreme Court agreed. In its view, sub-section 91(27) of the BNA Act (the federal power over 'Criminal Law') provided ample basis for the law. A wish to reduce the public safety risk posed by guns easily met the test for a valid criminal law purpose.[151] The law's complexity and the discretion it reposed in non-judicial actors[152] did not strip it of its criminal character.

The Court emphasised that it was not examining the soundness or efficiency of gun control, but merely whether Parliament had the power to enact it. Gun control is commonly criticised on those bases, though, and the Court's opinion has become part of a political narrative that portrays politically liberal governments as relentlessly urban and out of touch with, or even contemptuous of, rural communities.

A second reference is *Re Assisted Human Reproduction Act*.[153] The Act,[154] which was passed after two years of federal–provincial consultation,[155] completely prohibited human cloning and the commercialisation of human reproductive material. It also created a separate class of 'controlled activities' which could be pursued only in accordance with various regulations.[156]

The Attorney General of Quebec conceded that the absolute prohibitions were valid criminal law but attacked the other provisions. The Quebec Court of Appeal agreed that they were ultra vires. On a narrow, 5–4 split, the Supreme Court largely did as well.

Writing for the four-judge dissent, Chief Justice Beverley McLachlin stated that all of the challenged provisions were acceptable uses of the criminal law: they attacked what Parliament viewed as a 'public health evil'. The legislature's focus,

[148] *Re Firearms Act* (n 113).

[149] Firearms Act, SC 1995, c 39.

[150] *Reference re Firearms Act (Can)*, [1998] AJ No 1028 (1998), 219 AR 201 (ABCA).

[151] *Re Firearms Act* (n 113) at para 33.

[152] The law empowered a chief firearms officer.

[153] *Reference re Assisted Human Reproduction Act*, 2010 SCC 61, [2010] 3 SCR 457 [*Re AHRA*].

[154] SC 2004, c 2.

[155] The Royal Commission on New Reproductive Technologies (the 'Baird Commission') expressed concern about certain practices and recommended that their use be limited. A majority of the Court interpreted the Committee as having made two principal recommendations: that legislation be enacted to prohibit certain activities and that a federal reproductive technology regulator be established. The Commission defended the latter recommendation as an acceptable use of the federal power to regulate for the 'peace, order and good government of Canada': *Proceed With Care: Final Report of the Royal Commission on New Reproductive Technologies*.

[156] Those provisions were followed by numerous sections related to administration and enforcement. *Re AHRA* (n 153) at paras 11–14.

she claimed, was not to regulate assisted reproduction as something good or bad in itself, but to 'prevent or punish practices that may offend moral values, give rise to serious public health problems, and threaten the security of donors, donees, and persons not yet born'.[157] Parliament was entirely competent to do this.

A block of four judges disputed the Chief Justice's characterisation. Instead, they classified the law's 'pith and substance'[158] as 'the regulation of a specific type of health services provided … to individuals who for pathological or physiological reasons need help to reproduce'.[159] As such, those provisions related to the regulation of such activity fell within the exclusive provincial jurisdiction over hospitals, property and civil rights, and matters of a local nature,[160] and were consequently ultra vires Parliament. The ninth judge, who disagreed with the analytical approach of both camps, concluded that fewer provisions were ultra vires.[161] As a result, much of the attempted national regulation of assisted reproduction failed and Canada has a patchwork system under which the provinces regulate such activity very differently if, indeed, they do at all.[162]

Re AHRA was a significant defeat for the federal government. That the loss came in relation to criminal law was all the more striking. Previously, the Supreme Court had been very tolerant of federal attempts to employ criminal prohibitions and related provisions to address large and complex social issues. The reference asserted that there are limits to criminal law's elasticity, and seemed to retrench on the previously broad latitude granted to Parliament.

The matter again came to a head in the debate over Bill S-201: An Act to prohibit and prevent genetic discrimination. Passed in 2017, the law was the first in Canada to deal with genetic testing. S-201 was proposed as a necessary protection against the increasing prominence of the practice and its possible invasion into insurance and employment matters.

The federal Attorney General expressed concerns that, to the extent that it affected insurance contracts, the law was ultra vires. Since 1916, the regulation of insurance has been held to fall outside federal competence.[163] On that basis,

[157] ibid at para 32.

[158] 'Pith and substance' is a term of art developed in division-of-powers jurisprudence. It inquires into the essential gravamen or domain of a particular law. It is the first step in classifying legislation with regard to eventually deciding under what head of jurisdiction (enumerated in ss 91–93 of the CA 1867 it falls). See *Union Colliery Co. v Bryden* [1899] AC 580; Hogg (n 8) ch 15.5(a); WR Lederman (ed), *The Courts and the Canadian Constitution* (Toronto: McLelland and Stewart, 1964) 186.

[159] *Re AHRA* (n 153) at para 227.

[160] ibid at paras 259–73.

[161] ibid per Cromwell J at para 294.

[162] Laura Eggertson, 'Patchwork Regulations Likely Outcome of Reproductive Technologies Ruling' (2011) 183(4) Canadian Medical Association Journal E215–E216; Angela Cameron and Vanessa Gruben, 'Quebec's Constitutional Challenge to the Assisted Human Reproduction Act: Overlooking Women's Reproductive Autonomy?' in Stephanie Patterson, Francesca Scala and Marlene Sokolon (eds), *Fertile Ground: Exploring Reproduction in Canada* (Montreal: McGill-Queen's University Press, 2011).

[163] *AG Can. v AG Alta* [1916] 1 AC 588.

she and fellow Cabinet members voted against the Bill. The vote was not whipped, however, and when 104 members of the governing Liberal Party voted for it, it passed easily.

The result created a conundrum. Shortly after the law's passage in the House, the Attorney General announced that she intended to put a reference to the Supreme Court. She asserted her continuing doubts about the law's constitutionality and her belief that the Court's input was required. Before such a reference was initiated, the Quebec government referred it to its own Court of Appeal. The possible choices facing the federal government were discussed in Chapter 4.

B. Economic Regulation

Advisory opinions have played a crucial if episodic role in financial regulation. In the post-1982 period, one of the most noted is the *Reference re Securities Act.*[164] The purpose of the (proposed) Act was to create a single Canadian securities regulator in order to 'provide investor protection, to foster fair, efficient and competitive capital markets and to contribute to the integrity and stability of Canada's financial system'.[165]

In the past, securities regulation was an area in which the courts recognised what is called 'double aspect', meaning an intersection of federal and provincial jurisdiction that can accommodate laws regulating the same activity.[166] For example, both orders of government have created laws prohibiting creating a false prospectus,[167] or insider trading.[168] In such cases, the laws may coexist so long as they do not conflict. If they do, the courts will apply the doctrine of federal paramountcy so as to render the provincial law 'inoperative' to the extent of the conflict.[169]

Parliament has cited various heads of federal power to justify securities regulation, including its criminal power and company incorporation power. In the *Securities Reference*, it cited sub-section 91(2): 'trade and commerce'. That head of power encompasses two 'branches': the power to regulate inter-provincial and international trade; and a 'general' power to regulate trade, including trade occuring entirely within a province, that affects the country as a whole.[170] In the *Securities Reference*, the federal government said it was legislating under its general power.

[164] 2011 SCC 66, [2011] 3 SCR 837 [*Re Securities*].
[165] ibid at para 29.
[166] Hogg (n 8) ch 15.5(c).
[167] *Smith v The Queen*, [1960] SCR 776.
[168] *Multiple Access Ltd. v McCutcheon*, [1982] 2 SCR 161 [*Multiple Access*].
[169] *Crown Grain Co. v Day* [1908] AC 504; *Bank of Montreal v Hall*, [1990] 1 SCR 121.
[170] *Parsons* (n 138).

The federal trade and commerce power has long challenged federal–provincial relations. Critics tend to view it as a swamp capable of swallowing up provincial jurisdiction. After receiving generally restrictive interpretations from the JCPC, the power enjoyed a resurgence beginning in the 1950s when the Supreme Court and other courts began to uphold various federal laws directed at economic regulation.[171]

Many provinces opposed the idea of a national securities regulator. Ontario alone was in favour. Nonetheless, given the general thrust of the case law, it would have been reasonable for the federal government to anticipate a favourable response from the Court.[172] Instead, in an unsigned *per curiam* opinion, the Court advised that the proposed law would be ultra vires.

Given prior case law,[173] one might have expected the Court to focus on the inability of the provinces to achieve what it could vis-à-vis effective control over the securities market, and the negative repercussions of such inability. It did not. Instead the Court examined the very different question of what can best maintain the appropriate balance between federal and provincial powers.[174] It perceived the proposed legislation as an attempt by the federal government to oust provincial competence altogether – something that it viewed with great concern. Even with respect to a scheme structured as 'opt-in',[175] the Court said 'Parliament cannot regulate the whole of the securities system simply because aspects of it have a national dimension'.[176] The Canadian federal system 'rests on the organizing principle that the orders of government are coordinate and not subordinate one to the other … [and, consequently], a federal head of power cannot be given a scope that would *eviscerate* a provincial legislative competence'.[177]

The Court did note the possibility that the relevant actors could 'exercise their respective powers over securities harmoniously, in the spirit of cooperative

[171] *R v Klassen*, (1959) 20 DLR (2d) 406 (Man CA); *Caloil Inc. v Attorney General of Canada*, [1971] SCR 543; *Reference re Agricultural Products Marketing*, [1978] 2 SCR 1198; *General Motors of Canada Ltd. v City National Leasing*, [1989] 1 SCR 641. But see *Dominion Stores Ltd. v R*, [1980] 1 SCR 844; *Labatt Breweries of Canada Ltd. v Attorney General of Canada*, [1980] 1 SCR 914.

[172] *Re Securities* (n 164) at paras 34–35. In two provincial references, courts of appeal had advised that it was unconstitutional: (2011 ABCA 77, 41 Alta LR (5th) 145); (2011 QCCA 591 (CanLII)).

[173] *Re Securities* (n 164) at para 80, citing *General Motors* (n 171) at 661–62.

[174] Poonam Puri has critiqued the focus on balance: 'Rather than focusing on the preliminary question of whether Parliament has the jurisdiction to enact securities legislation and then moving to a discussion of the application of the "paramountcy" doctrine, the Court immediately engaged in what appears to be a novel discussion of the appropriate balance between federal and provincial power and attempted to ensure that provincial regulatory capacity is not prejudiced by federal action … [T]he decision assumes that the Court's role is to create balance between the provinces and the federal government, while dismissing the concept that such balance is achieved by the proper application of a division of powers analysis'. 'Twenty Years of Supreme Court Reference Decisions: Putting the Securities Reference Decision in Context', in Anita Anand (ed), *What's Next for Canada? Securities Regulation after the Reference* (Toronto: Irwin, 2012) 13, 15.

[175] *Re Securities* (n 164) at para 123.

[176] ibid at para 7.

[177] ibid at para 71.

federalism'.[178] Such an approach could 'ensure that each level of government properly discharges its responsibility to the public in a coordinated fashion'.[179] But,

> [f]ederalism is an underlying constitutional principle that demands respect for the constitutional division of powers and the maintenance of a constitutional balance between federal and provincial powers. The 'dominant tide' of flexible federalism, however strong its pull may be, cannot sweep designated powers out to sea, nor erode the constitutional balance inherent in the Canadian federal state.[180]

The *Securities Reference* is redolent of an older approach to federalism.[181] It showed a court more invested in policing jurisdictional boundaries than permitting legislative powers to adapt to fit current contexts and needs.[182]

Scholars have noted how the reference function itself may have played a role in the result. For example, Poonam Puri argued that the *Securities Reference* is emblematic of a court leaning towards more 'originalist' analysis than it generally has in the Charter of Rights (post-1982) era.[183] Puri also criticised the Court for failing to engage adequately with the materials.[184]

The merits or lack thereof of the *Securities Reference* cannot be addressed here. But the opinion does represent a potentially important turning point in the Court's attitude towards federalism, and a potentially harder line against initiatives perceived to have been crafted outside of federal–provincial cooperation. In that regard, the *Securities Reference* is one of a series of post-1982 reference opinions taking a firm line both on preserving provincial powers against federal encroachment and, further, on staking out the Court's self-described unique role and responsibility to do so. A number of those other references are discussed in Chapter 8.

C. Environment and Development

Another 'emergent' area that has challenged federal–provincial relations is environmental regulation. Public concern for the environment has greatly

[178] ibid at para 9 (emphasis added). Indeed, as this book was going to press, the Court approved a pan-Canadian cooperative scheme: *Reference re Pan-Canadian Securities Regulation*, 2018 SCC 48.

[179] ibid.

[180] ibid at paras 61–62.

[181] See Lorne Sossin's discussion and promotion of an alternate view, called 'purposive federalism' in 'Can Canadian Federalism be Relevant?' in Anand (n 174) 101 citing David Smith, 'National Political Parties and the Growth of National Political Community' in R Kenneth Cart and W Peter Ward, *National Politics and Community in Canada*.

[182] Anand (n 174). David Schneiderman argues that most 'English-speaking constitutionalists' predicted that the Court would side with the federal argument: 'Making Waves: the Supreme Court of Canada Confronts Stephen Harper's Brand of Federalism' in ibid at 75.

[183] Puri (n 174) 23.

[184] ibid. Here, Puri cites *Reference re Quebec Sales Tax*, [1994] 2 SCR 715, *Reference re Amendments to the Residential Tenancies Act* (NS), [1996] 1 SCR 186, and *Reference re Same-sex Marriage*, [2004] 3 SCR 698, 2004 SCC 79.

increased since Confederation but the BNA Act (like most eighteenth- and nineteenth-century documents) does not mention it. It instead recognises diffuse, related areas of jurisdiction belonging in some cases to the federal government (criminal law, fisheries and inter-provincial 'works and undertakings') and in others to provincial governments ('property and civil rights', 'local matters' and 'lands and waters entirely within provincial boundaries'.)

The Supreme Court has been cautious about simply recognising 'the environment' as a 'new matter' that would fall under federal POGG power. It views the environment as 'too diffuse' to fall exclusively under the control of one order of government.[185] At the same time, the Court recognised certain aspects of environmental regulation as falling within federal control, including marine pollution[186] and punishing environmentally harmful behaviour.[187]

Often, disputes over the environment tend to involve disagreement not over the risk posed by such things as climate change, but the appropriate government and legislative response to that risk.[188] A particularly trenchant topic has concerned the imposition of a federal 'carbon tax'. The carbon tax was a key electoral plank of the federal Liberal Party in 2015. Upon assuming power the government set up the structure to institute it. The structure involves numerous motivators[189] for provinces to create and sustain initiatives that can assist reducing the country's total carbon emissions by 2030 in order to honour the 2016 Paris Agreement.[190] However, the federal plan also includes a so-called 'backstop' to impose a carbon tax in those provinces opposed to it.[191]

The plan has generated significant provincial resistance. Some provinces oppose the plan on a policy basis, finding it unlikely to improve environmental outcomes. But more and more, provinces have begun to cite constitutional concerns.

In April 2018 the province of Saskatchewan referred the validity of the federal plan to its Court of Appeal. The government claims that the regulation of carbon emissions falls within provincial jurisdiction. Following an election in June 2018, the country's largest province, Ontario, announced that it would join the proceeding to support Saskatchewan's and it has since launched its own challenge.

[185] *Friends of the Oldman River Society v Canada (Minister of Transport)*, [1992] 1 SCR 3.

[186] *R v Crown Zellerbach Canada Ltd.*, [1988] 1 SCR 401.

[187] *R v Hydro-Québec* (n 113).

[188] Obviously, disputes about the phenomenon itself still remain, with some people displaying marked scepticism towards the idea that climate change is solely, or even primarily, caused by human activity.

[189] The chief such incentive was access to a $1.14 billion 'clean energy fund' available only to those provinces who signed the Pan Canadian Framework on Clean Growth Climate Change: www.canada.ca/en/services/environment/weather/climatechange/pan-canadian-framework.html; /www.cbc.ca/news/canada/saskatchewan/premier-says-sask-should-get-federal-funding-to-reduce-emissions-despite-saying-no-to-carbon-tax-plan-1.4550709.

[190] UN Doc FCCC/CP/2015/L/9, 12 December 2015: https://unfccc.int/process-and-meetings/the-paris-agreement/the-paris-agreement.

[191] At the time of writing, the federal policy was contained in the Greenhouse Gas Pollution Pricing Act contained in Part 5 of Bill C-74: An Act to implement certain provisions of the budget tabled in Parliament on February 27, 2018 and other measures: http://www.parl.ca/LegisInfo/BillDetails.aspx?Language=E&billId=9727472.

It is unclear how other provinces will participate. Manitoba, for example, commissioned a legal opinion from a constitutional law professor who predicted that the Canadian Supreme Court will likely uphold a federal 'carbon tax' as, inter alia, a valid exercise of the federal taxation power which is enumerated in very wide terms. At least initially, Manitoba chose to treat such 'advice' as containing sufficient reasons to frame its policy response accordingly. Other provinces did not consider the opinion important enough to overcome their independent reasons for seeking a judicial answer.

The reference function also can become important as a political tool in its own right – even where the underlying issue is, arguably, neither new nor particularly unsettled (in other words, not especially in need of the court's 'advice'.) An example of this is with respect to the rancorous debate over oil pipelines. Canada has garnered worldwide attention (some of it quite negative) over the Alberta oil sands – the largest known deposits of crude bitumen in the world. The province has been keen to ship this product directly to Canada's west coast for transportation to foreign markets. As a result, there is an initiative to build a new pipeline concurrent to an existing pipeline called Trans Mountain. A proposal was submitted to a federal regulator, the National Energy Board, which approved it subject to a large number of recommendations and required safeguards. The federal Cabinet authorised the so-called 'Trans Mountain Expansion' (TMX) in 2017.

TMX has spurred an extremely bitter dispute among federal and provincial governments. The two provinces most at loggerheads are British Columbia and Alberta. Ironically, in 2018 they had governments belonging to the same political party (NDP). Nonetheless, they are diametrically opposed on the question of whether a second pipeline carrying diluted bitumen should be permitted to proceed.

Under the BNA Act, pipelines are considered a 'local work or undertaking' that fall under the jurisdiction of the territory in which they are situated. Pipelines that extend to two or more provinces fall under federal jurisdiction. There would seem little scope to challenge, on division-of-powers grounds, federal construction of a pipeline than begins in Alberta and ends in British Columbia. Even if the federal government's decision ran entirely contrary to a province's environmental aims, policy and law, the Constitution prevents otherwise valid provincial laws from either impairing federal entities,[192] or rendering federal law nugatory.[193]

[192] This is the result of the doctrine of interjurisdictional immunity: *Marine Services International Ltd. v Ryan Estate*, 2013 SCC 44, [2013] 3 SCR 53; *Quebec (Attorney General) v Canadian Owners and Pilots Association*, 2010 SCC 39, [2010] 2 SCR 536; *Bell Canada v Quebec (CSST)*, [1988] 1 SCR 749.

[193] This is prevented by the doctrine of federal paramountcy: *Rothmans, Benson & Hedges Inc. v Saskatchewan*, [2005] 1 SCR 188, 2005 SCC 13; *Canadian Western Bank v Alberta*, [2007] 2 SCR 3, 2007 SCC 22; *Multiple Access* (n 168).

Yet, the province of British Columbia decided to do just that, initiating a reference to its court of appeal in 2018.[194] The province proposed amendments to its own laws[195] that would authorise the provincial Cabinet to restrict the flow of certain designated substances into the province. To date, the only proposed designated substance is diluted bitumen. Were a court to confirm that authority, it clearly would hamper the primary function of the pipeline. To be sure, the province has articulated a sincere concern about the effect of transporting the substance through its borders, citing the possibility of a spill or tanker accident and the unknown effects given that the substance is relatively unfamiliar. Nonetheless, the province has a weak case in division-of-powers terms. It appears that part of the value to the reference is simply to slow down the pace of the project, while adopting a very reasonable stance of simply seeking 'clarification'.

* * *

As a modern federal state, Canada regularly encounters issues involving complex facts and unclear legal rules. While sometime eclipsed by very high-profile battles over entrenched individual rights and freedoms, the fault lines of federalism continue to require elucidation, to attract rivalries and to spur unsettling national conflicts. Throughout, the advisory opinion has played an important role, at times even superseding parallel ordinary litigation.

The Supreme Court's performance in arbitrating federalism has long been a matter of controversy, including whether the Court had any legitimate role to play.[196] Though that question has been long settled in the affirmative, the Court's decisions have provoked various, often competing, commentary and criticism, often reflecting deeply opposed visions of the federal project.

[194] The questions were as follows.

> On the recommendation of the undersigned, the Lieutenant Governor, by and with the advice and consent of the Executive Council, orders that the questions set out below be referred to the British Columbia Court of Appeal for hearing and consideration under the Constitutional Question Act:
>
> 1 Is it within the legislative authority of the Legislature of British Columbia to enact legislation substantially in the form set out in the attached Appendix?
> 2 If the answer to question 1 is yes, would the attached legislation be applicable to hazardous substances brought into British Columbia by means of interprovincial undertakings?
> 3 If the answers to questions 1 and 2 are yes, would existing federal legislation render all or part of the attached legislation inoperative?

Office of the Premier, 'Province submits court reference to protect BC's coast' https://news.gov.bc.ca/releases/2018PREM0019-000742.

[195] Environmental Management Act, SBC 2003, c 53.

[196] Weiler (n 96).

Throughout that debate, the advisory function has remained a forum for examining fundamental legal principles concerning the division of powers. The references discussed above reflect a broad array of doctrinal, political and real-world issues. Their cross-cutting element is the fact that the judicial branch, at the request of one of the Confederation parties, may be called upon to settle fraught disputes. That role has been enhanced in the current era of high-profile, high-stakes constitutional review.

6

Rebirth, and Rupture

Law performs diverse functions. It aids in social organisation and co-ordination, norms production and values signalling. A more political exercise can scarcely can be imagined. As much of this book demonstrates, advisory opinions are shot through with politics. In that sense, they resemble ordinary constitutional litigation. But there is an additional factor operating in advisory opinions which heightens the political considerations beyond even the most severely contested cases.

The focus of this chapter is a period rife with constitutional significance. Much of the discussion presages the development of the Supreme Court's robust review of issues covering the panoply of Canadian law and social life. The first step in that journey was its shift to a truly final court of appeal in 1949. The second step was the entrenchment of the Constitution Act 1982.

The advisory function was central both to the rebirth of the Constitution with additional norms and guarantees, and a key enabler of the rupture thereby entailed. 'Rupture' may be understood in two senses. The first is the momentous change to the underlying political framework that occurred in the face of objections by one of the nation's key communities (Quebec). The second denotes the Court's emergence as a central constitutional actor – far more than it had been in the past and foreshadowing the role it would play thereafter. A driving theme is the Court's maturation, growing confidence and ever-increasing role.

Supreme at Last

In the mid-twentieth century, the Supreme Court suffered from a marked lack of prestige and even talent. Appointments to it seemed to prioritise political over substantive considerations. The salary was low and the Court was not always able to attract the best candidates.[1] Though some appointments were strong, most did not inspire confidence.

The federal government's attitude added to the sense that the Court was not a priority. Judges were frequently requested to put aside their duties to participate in

[1] James G Snell and Frederick Vaughan, *The Supreme Court of Canada* (Toronto: The Osgoode Society, 1985) 152–55.

non-judicial tasks such as sitting on commissions of inquiry.[2] Today, such assignments (at least at the Supreme Court level) are avoided. Not only would they tear the judges away from their core adjudicative duties, but they would be perceived as creating the potential for conflict.[3]

During the 1930s and 1940s, the Court's composition provoked growing regional discontent. The provinces viewed a seat on the Court as a sign of their status within the federation. It did not help that the Court was perceived as disinterested in the vast swaths of the country outside the main urban centres in Ontario and Quebec. A proposal to have the Court hold hearings outside the national capital (Ottawa) was rejected as impractical. It was offered at the same time as the Supreme Court's invalidation of much of Bennett's New Deal and its negative assessment of Alberta's Social Credit legislation.[4] None of this advanced the Court's image as a national unifier. That said, the number of references, and the potent issues they addressed, increased the Court's profile. Its opinions in those matters were, on the whole, well received.[5]

The Second World War and its aftermath effected a tremendous change to the country's identity and institutions. The Supreme Court benefitted from that new sense of national distinctiveness.[6] 'As Canadians increasingly viewed themselves as self-governing and independent, the judicial tie to Great Britain became a sign of inferiority, a colonial fetter'.[7]

The idea that Canada's general court of appeal should also be its final one was not new. As discussed in Chapter 2, the debates over the court's jurisdiction and position in the judicial hierarchy were key to its creation in 1875. At that time,

[2] In 1934 Chief Justice Duff acted as sole commissioner in the inquiry about former Prime Minister Arthur Meighen and the Ontario Hydro-Electric Power Commission. In 1947 Justice Rand was the Canadian representative on the United Nations' Special Committee of Observation in Palestine. He also arbitrated a Ford Motor Company strike. Justice Kerwin chaired two railway conciliation boards.

[3] Snell and Vaughan (n 1) 156–57. Duff CJ's conclusion that the federal government should be absolved of all liability in the Battle of Hong Kong has been criticised for bias. JL Granatstein, *The Politics of Survival: The Conservative Party of Canada, 1939–1945* (Toronto: University of Toronto Press, 1967); David Williams, *Duff: A Life in the Law.* (Toronto: Osgoode Society, 1984). Perhaps the selection of Supreme Court judges for those rather unorthodox roles was a (positive) sign of their political value. And, in performing such roles the judges did offer valuable service to the country. But their assumption of such duties was not easily reconciled with the judicial function. Today, sitting lower court judges continue to perform that function, arguably raising similar issues although the practice generally has not been viewed as objectionable.

[4] A discussion is found in Chapter 5.

[5] Snell and Vaughan (n 1) 166 cite a *Maclean's Magazine* article on 1 April 1936 which states: 'The Supreme Court of Canada! Truly a term to conjure with. The highest tribunal in our country. It awes one. Even the shoddy little [Supreme Court] building cannot rob the institution of that particular reverence one automatically feels'.

[6] Snell and Vaughan (n 1) 195, note other developments in the move to a stronger nationhood: the Canadian Citizenship Act of 1946; the admission of Newfoundland into Confederation in 1949; the inclusion of a partial domestic amending formula in s 91 of the BNA Act in 1949 (since repealed); and the selection of the first Canadian-born Governor General, Vincent Massey, in 1952.

[7] ibid at 183. For an account of the emergence of a 'new' constitutional law sensibility, see Eric Adams, 'Canada's "Newer Constitutional Law" and the Idea of Constitutional Rights' (2006) 51 McGill Law Journal 435.

the Court's enabling statute did not specify whether the Court's rulings could be further appealed to the JCPC. Only after the UK Home Office objected was that provision read down so that the Committee's place was assured.

Attempts to bolster the Court's authority continued. One initiative terminated the right to further appeal criminal cases.[8] In a 1926 case called *Nadan v The Queen*,[9] the JCPC found that to be ultra vires. The opinion provoked an uproar.[10] One Supreme Court justice was so incensed that he urged the Prime Minister to eliminate *all* appeals to the Committee.[11]

Together with the constitutional crisis known as 'King-Byng',[12] *Nadan* created a demand for greater autonomy. Peter Hogg describes both events as contributing to the 1926–30 Imperial conferences between Britain and its various Dominions. From those conferences came the Balfour Declaration of 1926 affirming the Dominions as 'autonomous communities'; and the Statute of Westminster 1931, under which most Imperial legislation was deemed inapplicable to a Dominion unless it consented.[13] As a result, Canada re-enacted the criminal appeals statute, and the JCPC subsequently advised that it was, indeed, valid.[14]

[8] The provision was then s 1025 of the Criminal Code: 'Notwithstanding any Royal Prerogative, or anything contained within the *Interpretation Act* or in the *Supreme Court Act*, no appeal shall be brought in any criminal case from any judgment or order of any Court in Canada to any court of appeal or authority by which in the United Kingdom appeals or petitions to His Majesty in Council may be heard'.

[9] *Nadan v The Queen* [1926] AC 482. The Board determined that the provision was in conflict with the Judicial Committee Acts of 1833 and 1844 and the 1865 Colonial Laws Validity Act. It stated that the royal prerogative, which included appellate jurisdiction, had evolved into a privilege, open to British subjects, that the Dominion Parliament was incompetent to remove.

[10] Saywell argues that the federal government understood that the JCPC had been trying to pre-empt a similar outcome in Ireland. Still, that 'those less in the know had found it an affront to Canadian nationalism'. John T Saywell, *The Lawmakers: Judicial Power and the Shaping of Canadian Federalism* (Toronto: Osgoode Society, 2002) 199.

[11] Robert J Sharpe and Patricia McMahon, *The Persons Case: The Origins and Legacy of the Fight for Legal Personhood* (Toronto: Osgoode Society, 2008) at 152.

[12] The King-Byng crisis arose when Governor General Lord Byng refused to dissolve Parliament upon the advice of Prime Minster William Lyon MacKenzie King, who was facing an imminent vote of censure. King resigned and Byng called on Conservative leader Arthur Meighen to form a government – which did not hold for more than a week. In the ensuing federal election, King was returned to power. Peter W. Hogg, *Constitutional Law of Canada*, 5th edn (looseleaf) (Toronto: Thomson Reuters Carswell, 2007) 9.7(d); Eugene Forsey, *The Royal Power of Dissolution in Parliament in the British Commonwealth*, PhD thesis, McGill University, 1941, chs 5 and 6: http://digitool.library.mcgill.ca/webclient/StreamGate?folder_id=0&dvs=1486928093119~84&usePid1=true&usePid2=true.

[13] 22 & 23 Geo 5 c 4. In an explicit departure from the Colonial Laws Validity Act, the Statute granted each Dominion the power to repeal or amend imperial statutes which had become part of their law. This applied to Canadian federal and provincial governments within their respective areas of jurisdiction. However, in response to the concerns of Canadian delegates, the Statute exempted from its scope 'the repeal, amendment or alteration' of the BNA Act. It permitted, as well, a dominion Parliament to pass laws having extra-territorial application: s 3.

[14] *British Coal Corporation v The King* [1935] AC 500. Lord Sankey drew on the 'large and liberal' approach to interpretation he had first articulated in the *Persons Case* (discussed in Chapter 7). Applying that approach, he concluded the law was within federal authority: '[The BNA Act] does not

In 1939, the federal government sought to abolish the remaining jurisdiction of the JCPC. Given the changes wrought by the Statute of Westminster, particularly its nullification of section 129 of the BNA Act,[15] there should have been little obstacle to doing so for appeals heard in the Supreme Court. But, the country had always preserved *per saltum*, direct appeals from provincial courts to the JCPC. Did such cases fall within Parliament's authority in section 101 to legislate in respect of 'a general court of appeal for Canada'? Or, did they fall instead under the provincial jurisdiction over 'the administration of justice'?

The Supreme Court advised 4–2 that the legislation was intra vires.[16] Eliminating further appeals did not relate to the 'administration of justice *in the province*'.[17] Moreover, section 101's words 'notwithstanding anything in this Act' gave Parliament the exclusive authority to determine the Supreme Court's jurisdiction.[18] The Statute of Westminster rendered such an amendment wholly within the purview of the Dominion Parliament.[19]

After a delay occasioned by the Second World War, the Judicial Committee released an opinion in January 1947.[20] It surmised that, given that the UK Attorney General took no part in the proceeding, the matter was one wholly internal to Canada.[21] Nonetheless, it recognised the issue as one of 'transcendent constitutional importance'.[22]

empower the elimination of criminal appeals by express terms, but it does so by necessary intendment. Section 91 of the Act, read along with the rest of the Act, is, according to its true construction in their Lordships' opinion, apart from the limitations already referred to, intended to make and is apt to make the Dominion Legislature supreme and endow it with the same authority as the Imperial Parliament, within the assigned limits of subject and area'. Notably, at the end of the opinion the Board clarified that it was dealing only with abolition of criminal appeals. That would prove to be a point of argument in the eventual attempt to abolish all appeals: *Privy Council Appeals* (n 20).

[15] CA 1867, s 129: 'Except as otherwise provided by this Act, all Laws in force in Canada, Nova Scotia, or New Brunswick at the Union, and all Courts of Civil and Criminal Jurisdiction, and all legal Commissions, Powers, and Authorities, and all Officers, Judicial, Administrative, and Ministerial, existing therein at the Union, shall continue in Ontario, Quebec, Nova Scotia, and New Brunswick respectively, as if the Union had not been made; subject nevertheless (except with respect to such as are enacted by or exist under Acts of the Parliament of Great Britain or of the Parliament of the United Kingdom of Great Britain and Ireland,) to be repealed, abolished, or altered by the Parliament of Canada, or by the Legislature of the respective Province, according to the Authority of the Parliament or of that Legislature under this Act'.

[16] *Reference as to the Legislative Competence of the Parliament of Canada to Enact Bill No. 9 of the Fourth Session, Eighteenth Parliament of Canada, Entitled 'An Act to Amend the Supreme Court Act'*, [1940] SCR 49 [*Privy Council Appeals – SCC*]. The relevant statute was RSC 1927 ch 35.

[17] ibid at 56–57.

[18] ibid at 63–65.

[19] Two judges dissented. Crocket J thought the law wholly ultra vires: Parliament could not so fundamentally alter provincial interests, and prerogative powers, by ordinary law. Davis J objected on a narrower basis, singling out the amendment's inclusion of *provincial* appeals authorised by *provincial* laws on *provincial* subject matter. *Privy Council Appeals – SCC* (n 16).

[20] *The Attorney-General of Ontario and others v The Attorney-General of Canada and others and The Attorney-General of Quebec (Canada)* [1947] UKPC 1 [*Privy Council Appeals*].

[21] Ontario, British Columbia and New Brunswick appealed the Supreme Court opinion via special leave, supported by Quebec. Canada, Manitoba and Saskatchewan acted as respondents. The JCPC noted that 'the hearing of the appeal was postponed until the conclusion of the war', ibid at 2.

[22] ibid at 5.

The Committee concluded that Parliament did have the power to eliminate further appeals from Supreme Court decisions. The earlier reference in the Supreme Court Act to a Crown prerogative right of appeal[23] had been required to respect *Imperial* legislation. After the Statute of Westminster, however 'it must be within the power of the Dominion parliament to enact that the jurisdiction of its Supreme Court shall be ultimate'. No other conclusion was 'consonant with the status of self-governing Dominion'.[24]

The Statute of Westminster had a similar effect on the question of provincial appeals. After 1931, any limitations on Parliament's power had to emanate solely from the BNA Act. That Act granted Parliament authority over a general court of appeal 'notwithstanding' anything else, including whether cases dealt with federal versus provincial law, or were heard in 'provincial' versus 'federal' courts.[25]

The Board concluded that it was not useful 'to embark upon a nice discrimination' between the powers in section 91 and section 92 of the BNA Act. Section 101 granted to Parliament plenary authority to create a court with not just 'final' but 'exclusive' appellate jurisdiction. It would be inconsistent with the concept 'embodied in the British Commonwealth of Nations' to preclude a member from setting up a tribunal 'both ultimate and exclusive of another member'.[26] As the Statute of Westminster rendered Canada legally and politically 'equal' to the United Kingdom, the latter could exercise no further control over the former's judicial process.

Thus, the JCPC confirmed that it henceforth would have no role in future Canadian legal proceedings. A momentous change to the legal landscape was confirmed only after the release of an advisory opinion. That presaged a definite pattern: axial moments to which court input was viewed as essential.

Though the path was now clear, not all Canadians were pleased. Some retained strong pro-British sentiment. Others believed there was value in a court that was somewhat removed from regional and linguistic divisions.[27] A further source of concern, especially in Quebec, was that the Supreme Court continued to be under federal control.[28] It was argued, too, that the JCPC had acted as a sort of 'quality control', encouraging Canadian courts to approach decisions with care so as to avoid the embarrassment of negative judicial review.

[23] Supreme Court Act, RSC 1927 s 54. This is the section that Parliament proposed to repeal and replace.

[24] *Privy Council Appeals* (n 20).

[25] The Board also noted and rejected the proposal made by Justice Davis in his dissent that one might craft a different rule for appeals from provincial courts deciding provincial cases (ibid at 7–8). That, it said, would produce the 'strange result' that cases emanating from the same court, and indeed separate issues arising in the same case, would have different routes of appeal.

[26] ibid.

[27] Louis St Laurent advised Prime Minister King that Quebec Liberals would vote for abrogation of appeals in all cases *except* those involving federal–provincial disputes. Snell and Vaughan (n 1) 190.

[28] Jacques Yvan Morin, 'The Quebec Ruling: A Legitimate and Achievable Secession in Theory' in David Schneiderman, *The Quebec Decision: Perspectives on the Supreme Court Ruling on Secession* (Toronto: Lorimer, 1999).

An emergent issue was the weight that should be accorded to prior JCPC opinions dealing with Canadian law. Would they be entitled to deference? Strong views were expressed on both sides.[29] In the end, the Supreme Court Act amendments did not mention the issue. To the extent there was any consensus, it seemed to be that the Court was not operating in a complete *tabula rasa* – that it could not depart from all prior case law.[30]

Proclaimed to have 'exclusive ultimate appellate civil and criminal jurisdiction' with judgments that were 'final and conclusive' the new Court came into effect in June of 1949.[31] An additional clause 'specifically denied that the royal prerogative or any United Kingdom statute permitted appeals to any overseas tribunal'.[32] The Court's composition was increased from seven to nine members, with three seats reserved for Quebec. A few other proposals to increase the Court's status and prestige within the legal profession were rejected.[33]

The advisory function was unaltered.

The Court entered a new era but with few indications that it was prepared for the enormous task that now confronted it. The new Court met for the first time in

[29] See, in this vein, WPM Kennedy: '[Unless] we get rid of past decision … they will hang around the necks of the judiciary … in that uncanny reality with which *stare decisis* seems doomed to rob the law of creative vitality'. 'The British North America Act: Past and Future' (1937) 15 Canadian Bar Review 394, 187; the Canadian Bar Association: 'the rule of *stare decisis* ought to continue to be applied'. See also Saywell (n 10) 239.

[30] Saywell (n 10) 240. See also *Reference re Farm Products Marketing Act*, [1957] SCR 198. The Court finally shed all pretence of following JCPC precedent in 1978: *Reference re Agricultural Products Marketing*, [1978] 2 SCR 1198.

[31] Act to Amend the Supreme Court Act, SC 1949 (2nd sess), c 37, s 3. The relevant provisions were:

1. Section fifty-four of the *Supreme Court Act*, chapter thirty-five of the Revised Statutes of Canada, 1927, is repealed and the following substituted therefor:—

   '54. (1) The Supreme Court shall have, hold and exercise exclusive ultimate appellate civil and criminal jurisdiction within and for Canada; and the judgment of the Court shall, in all cases, be final and conclusive.

   (2) Notwithstanding any royal prerogative or anything contained in any Act of the Parliament of the United Kingdom or any Act of the Parliament of Canada or any Act of the legislature of any province of Canada or any other statute or law, no appeal shall lie or be brought from any court now or hereafter established within Canada to any court of appeal, tribunal or authority by which, in the United Kingdom, appeals or petitions to His Majesty in Council may be ordered to be heard.

   (3) *The Judicial Committee Act, 1833*, chapter forty-one of the statutes of the United Kingdom of Great Britain and Ireland, 1833, and *The Judicial Committee Act, 1844*, chapter sixty-nine of the statutes of the United Kingdom of Great Britain and Ireland, 1844, and all orders, rules or regulations made under the said Acts are hereby repealed in so far as the same are part of the law of Canada'.

2. Nothing in this Act shall affect any application for special leave to appeal or any appeal to His Majesty in Council made or pending at the date of the coming into force of this Act.

[32] Snell and Vaughan (n 1) 190–91.

[33] For example, the deputy minister of justice investigated establishing a 'special permanent committee' of the Canadian Bar Association to work with other organisations to develop 'the good name and reputation of the Court with the public'. Some of the initiatives considered included luncheons, judge-authored articles and a book on the history of the Court. Department of Justice file no 152966; PAC RG13, A5, vol 2073, no 156794, cited in Snell and Vaughan (n 1) 196. While all of these things

early 1950. It also moved into new accommodations – a welcome change from the entirely inadequate building it previously had occupied.[34] That might seem to be a mundane detail, but it represented a significant investment in the institution – for which approval had taken many years. The Court's substandard working conditions had exacted a toll in terms of the justices' productivity and the attractiveness of the position.

In the first slew of post-1949 appointments, Prime Ministers 'showed no special sensitivity or concern for the [Court's]newly won independence'.[35] The 'old established lines', focussing on regional considerations and conservative legal philosophy, were observed. Notwithstanding a few outstanding jurists like Ivan Rand, debates over pending vacancies were consumed by denominationalism (by tradition, the Chief Justice position rotated between a Protestant and Roman Catholic) and, even, patronage.[36]

The rather casual approach to appointments did have one positive result: it spurred public commentary about the Court. The Canadian Bar Association urged the government to treat the Court with more seriousness. Though slow to respond, such critiques would over time work a shift in the executive's attitude – though not before a Conservative government offered the position of Chief Justice to John Diefenbaker in the wake of a parliamentary crisis. Thankfully, Diefenbaker refused but the attempt betrayed a shockingly transactional approach to the Court.

Snell and Vaughan put it well: 'The impression is that federal politicians wanted a truly Canadian final court of appeal, but they were not sure why they wanted it'.[37]

The provinces began to evince more interest in the Court as well. The changes to the Court had been achieved through ordinary federal law, with barely any provincial input. That caused dissatisfaction, particularly in Quebec, where the Privy Council had been viewed as a significant counter-weight to central power. In 1956 a report commissioned on the 'erosion of federalism' recommended that the Court be entrenched in the Constitution; that it focus on review of decisions from provincial courts of appeal; that it be limited to federal matters; and that provinces have input into judicial appointments.[38] While the Report was not taken up by the federal government, it spurred further discussion and provided a template for future constitutional negotiations in which the Court would feature heavily.

inevitably would emerge, they were not part of a concerted, organised effort following the Court's expansion.

[34] The new location, at the corner of Kent and Wellington streets, is the Court's home today. By all accounts, the new building was well received. Snell and Vaughan note that 'It was variously described as "breathtaking", "an architectural spectacle", and "a truly humbling experience"'. Snell and Vaughan (n 1) 177.

[35] ibid at 196.

[36] The best (or worst) example is the 1954 appointment of Douglas Abbott, finance minister from 1945 to 1953. Upon leaving politics Abbott let it be known that he sought a seat on the High Court. He had no judicial experience and was many years removed from active practice. Abbott's was the first court appointment from Cabinet since 1911. It would not be repeated.

[37] Snell and Vaughan (n 1) 203.

[38] *Royal Commission of Inquiry on Constitutional Problems* (Tremblay Report).

Constitutional Rebirth

This section discusses the periods immediately prior to, and following, the entrenchment of the Canada Act 1982.[39] As in the past, the judiciary was called upon to intervene in affairs contested at the highest possible levels – involving what one scholar has termed 'mega constitutional politics'.[40] Invariably, those mega constitutional politics involved advisory opinions. The opinions – *Upper House*,[41] *Patriation*[42] and *Quebec Veto*[43] – confirmed Canada's path to constitutional independence, and cemented the Court's role in that new framework. Their surrounding context, the choices they offered and the path that was selected would prove highly formative.

The tenure of Prime Minister Pierre Elliott Trudeau (1968–79, 1980–84) had a profound effect on the Court. He brought changes to its jurisdiction, process and composition. The effects were important to the Court's expanded constitutional review under the Constitution Act 1982.

A key change was administrative. By the early 1970s, the Court was collapsing under the weight of its docket. Any civil case involving more than $10,000 was appealable as of right and, by one estimate, counted for 70 per cent of all appeals. In 1975, the Supreme Court Act abolished almost all as-of-right appeals except for certain criminal matters.[44] The Court was empowered, instead, to grant leave where

> any question involved therein is, by reason of its public importance or the importance of any issue of law or any issue of mixed law and fact involved in that question, one that ought to be decided by the Supreme Court or is, for any other reason, of such a nature or significance as to warrant decision.[45]

In other words, the Court exercised an ultimate curial function over the cases through which it would shape law. (Advisory opinions, of course, continued to operate 'as of right' although, as discussed in Chapter 4, that does not always guarantee that questions will be answered.)

Trudeau also dramatically changed the character of the court through its jurists. Beginning with his appointment of Bora Laskin, a former law dean and noted constitutional scholar, Trudeau demonstrated an intent to elevate the Court's

[39] Canada Act 1982 c 11.

[40] Peter Russell, *Constitutional Odyssey: Can Canada Become a Sovereign People?* (Toronto: University of Toronto Press, 2004).

[41] *Authority of Parliament in relation to the Upper House*, [1980] 1 SCR 54 [*Re Upper House*].

[42] *Re: Resolution to amend the Constitution*, [1981] 1 SCR 753 [*Patriation Reference*].

[43] *Re: Objection by Quebec to a Resolution to amend the Constitution*, [1982] 2 SCR 793 [*Quebec Veto*].

[44] SC 1974-75-76, c 18. Provincial references may still be appealed as of right. In criminal cases, there is generally an appeal as of right where there is a dissent on a point of law in the ruling from the provincial court of appeal.

[45] Supreme Court Act, RSC, 1985, c S-26 s 40(1). The Act does not require reasons to be given, which has hampered the development of jurisprudence in this crucial area.

intellectual heft. He appointed persons with legal academic backgrounds and diverse philosophical perspectives.[46] While he did not depart from the convention of appointing judges from particular regions, he forever changed the Court by appointing its first Jewish person (Laskin, in 1970) and its first woman (Bertha Wilson, 1982). His selection of William McIntrye and, critically, Brian Dickson (whom he later would elevate to Chief Justice) would also have a profound effect. In fact, some have accused Trudeau of manipulating the composition of the Court in order to ensure a friendly reception to the Constitution Act 1982 and an inclination to favour the federal government.[47] While the charge is probably overstated, there is no question that his appointments would forever change the Court's approach to constitutional law, its relationship to other actors and its place in society.

A. The Path to Change

The BNA Act has been described as an instance of 'ancient' as opposed to 'modern' constitutionalism.[48] It did not rupture an existing state. It was, instead, a request of an Imperial power to make plain the 'continuation of a very old framework'.[49]

The Act's preamble stated that Canada is to have 'a constitution similar in principle to that of the United Kingdom'. The most obvious sign of this was the retention of numerous unwritten rules or conventions. For example, the Act did not enumerate the rules of a parliamentary system, the role of the Prime Minister, the composition of Cabinet or the relationship between the legislature and the executive. As discussed in earlier chapters, the Act was largely concerned with the questions of federalism. Where the Constitution was silent, constitutional convention and Crown prerogative would fill the gaps.

In addition, at least some matters were left to the continued oversight of the Imperial Parliament.[50] The most important of those was the process of amendment. While the BNA Act would be amended several times, such amendment was achieved through the Imperial Parliament acting upon a request from the

[46] See also the appointments of Pigeon (1967), and Beetz and de Grandpré (1974).

[47] Michael Mandel, *The Charter of Rights and the Legalization of Politics in Canada* (Toronto: Thompson Educational Publisher, 1994) chs 1 and 2.

[48] Charles McIlwain, *Constitutionalism: Ancient and Modern* (Ithaca NY: CUP, 1947).

[49] Simone Chambers, 'Contract or Conversation? Theoretical Lessons from the Canadian Constitutional Crisis' (1998) 26(1) *Politics and Society* 143.

[50] Alan C Cairns wrote that one of the resulting effects was 'to place a special responsibility for adjusting the BNA Act on the Privy Council, and then to castigate it for not presiding wisely over the adaptation of Canadian federalism to conditions unforeseen in 1867'. Cairns, 'The Judicial Committee and its Critics' (1971) 3 Canadian Journal of Political Science 301. See also Geoffrey Marshall, *Constitutional Conventions: The Rules and Forms of Political Accountability* (Oxford: Clarendon Press, 1984) 180.

Dominion of Canada that took the form of a joint address of both houses of the Canadian Parliament. The provinces did not uniformly have input. Nonetheless, on many occasions they were duly consulted and did agree to the requested change.[51]

At various points between 1927 and 1982,[52] federal and provincial actors sought to negotiate a change to the BNA Act that would incorporate into it a formal amending formula.

Prime Minister Pierre Trudeau brought renewed attention to the issue. Amending the Constitution no longer was viewed as concerned solely with federalism, but as an important component of a new identity. It was viewed as necessary to move Canada away from the colonial control[53] increasingly at odds with the country. Additionally, Trudeau hoped to diminish the appeal of separatist forces in Quebec by ensuring robust linguistic and cultural protections for minority communities.

The election in 1976 of an openly separatist Quebec provincial government made the situation urgent. Prime Minister Trudeau wrote to the provincial Premiers calling them back to negotiations and threatening that should an agreement *not* be forthcoming, he would approach Westminster on his own.[54] Understandably, the provinces were dismayed at the prospect of dramatic changes to their powers proceeding without their consent. But there was relatively little popular support for their position. The federal government had successfully harnessed public appetite both for an entrenched Bill of Rights (the future Charter) and for strong federal structures capable of dealing with the separatist problem.[55]

In 1978 Trudeau tabled Bill C-60, An Act Amending the Constitution. The Bill sought to use the federal amending power in section 91(1) of the BNA Act, which provided Parliament with the power to amend certain aspects of the Constitution (namely those dealing exclusively with federal matters and having no effect on provincial powers).[56] In particular, the Bill proposed numerous changes to the Senate of Canada.

[51] Nadia Verrelli, 'Searching for an Amending Forumula: The 115-Year Journey' in Emmett MacFarlane (ed), *Constitutional Amendment in Canada* (Toronto: University of Toronto Press, 2016) 19.

[52] Marshall cites eight such attempts (n 50) 181.

[53] Other highly symbolic decisions in the same vein were the adoption in 1965 of the Canadian flag, which has no visible links with UK symbols, and the designation of the anniversary of Confederation (1 July) as 'Canada Day', replacing the previous 'Dominion Day'.

[54] 'But if unanimity does not appear possible, the federal government will have to decide whether it will recommend to Parliament that a Joint Address be passed seeking "patriation" of the BNA Act. A question for decision will then be what to add to that action'. J Peter Meekison (ed), *Constitutional Patriation Letters: the Lougheed-Levesque Correspondence*(Kingston, ON: Institute of Intergovernmental Relations, Queen's University, 1999).

[55] Russell (n 40).

[56] The entire provision read: '1. The amendment from time to time of the Constitution of Canada, except as regards matters coming within the classes of subjects by this Act assigned exclusively to the Legislatures of the provinces, or as regards rights or privileges by this or any other Constitutional Act granted or secured to the Legislature or the Government of a province, or to any class of persons with respect to schools or as regards the use of the English or the French language or as regards the requirements that there shall be a session of the Parliament of Canada at least once each year, and that no House of Commons shall continue for more than five years from the day of the return of the Writs for choosing the House: provided, however, that a House of Commons may in time of real or apprehended

In response to provincial protest, the federal government initiated a reference. Question 1 asked whether Parliament could simply abolish the Senate outright. Question 2 invoked changes to virtually every compositional element and function of the chamber – from name to numbers to method of appointment.[57]

The Court advised that several of the proposed amendments were ultra vires.[58] It refused to recognise a federal power to abolish the Senate of Canada. The power the federal government invoked to make such changes, sub-section 91(1) of the BNA Act, had been instituted in 1949 to obviate the need for the UK Parliament's consent on 'housekeeping' matters.[59] Changes affecting the constitutional position of the provinces lay entirely outside that limited power.[60]

The Court noted that constitutional amendments affecting the powers or status of Canadian provinces traditionally had involved their input. It appeared to accept as an accurate description that (a) the UK would amend the Constitution of Canada only on formal request, (b) the formal request must involve a parliamentary resolution, (c) a mere provincial request would not suffice and (d) that the Canadian Parliament would not request 'an amendment directly affecting federal-provincial relationships without prior consultation and agreement' although 'The nature and the degree of provincial participation' were not easy to define.[61]

The changes proposed in Bill 60 were dramatic. Indeed, they were so dramatic as to resemble a trial balloon. It strains credulity that the federal government actually thought that Parliament could simply abolish the Senate. No doubt, it was useful for the federal government to receive the Court's advice on constitutional amendments and, in particular, the scope of Parliament's amending power. But the Court cast significant aspersions on the government's unilateralism, and strongly affirmed the principle of provincial input into important constitutional matters. Further, the Court declined to answer most of the sub-questions in Question 2 on the basis that they lacked a proper factual context.[62] At least some of the Court's analysis would prove fateful in later disputes.

B. Patriation

After *Re Upper House*, the federal government dropped further mention of Bill C-60. Then, in 1980, events careened wildly off course and a new constitutional

war, invasion or insurrection be continued by the Parliament of Canada if such continuation is not opposed by the votes of more than one-third of the members of such House'. British North America (No. 2) Act 1949, 13 Geo VI, c 81 (UK). Section 91(1) was repealed when the Constitution was repatriated, and replaced by the general amending formula in Part V of the Constitution Act 1982.

[57] *Re Upper House* (n 41).

[58] ibid at 65.

[59] ibid at 65.

[60] ibid.

[61] 'The Amendment of the Constitution of Canada', published in 1965 under the authority of The Hon Guy Favreau [*White Paper*] as cited in the *Re Upper House*, ibid at 64.

[62] *Re Upper House* (n 41) at 75. It declined to answer questions 2(a), (c), (d) and (e)(i) to (iv). See also the discussion in Chapter 4.

agreement became more urgent than ever. A Quebec referendum asking whether the province should pursue 'sovereignty-association' returned highly unsettling results. A significant proportion of voters, though not an outright majority, chose 'yes'.[63] Pierre Trudeau moved quickly to resume constitutional negotiations. But old conflicts emerged and by the autumn of 1980 discussions came to a standstill.

In early October, making good on his earlier threat, Trudeau tabled a resolution before the Parliament of Canada that included an entrenched Bill of Rights and an amending formula. Following consideration by a special joint committee of the House and Senate, Parliament adopted the resolution in April 1981.

Trudeau's unilateralism forced the provinces' hand. Save for Ontario and New Brunswick, all opposed the resolution. The so-called 'Gang of Eight' developed a three-pronged strategy: challenge the constitutionality of the joint resolution; propose an alternative plan; and, if necessary, convince the UK Parliament to reject the resolution.

As discussed in earlier chapters, the Canadian provinces have long argued that their interests and standing in Confederation are structurally vulnerable to an indifferent or hostile federal government. The Prime Minister's decision to seek to amend the Constitution regardless of the provinces' input or wishes perfectly illustrated that point.

The provinces reasonably concluded that a reference would be an effective tool.[64] Seeking an advisory opinion would highlight the question of the appropriate conditions for constitutional change. It would secure a statement from the Supreme Court far more quickly than ordinary litigation (which would be difficult to mount in any event). Further, it would permit running concurrent, and coordinated, proceedings in several lower courts, increasing the chances of an outcome favourable to their position.

So it was that Quebec, Manitoba and Newfoundland initiated references in their respective courts of appeal. Though the wording of the references varied, the core issues did not.[65] The courts were asked (a) whether the proposed amendments

[63] Fifty-six per cent of those who voted rejected the idea, and 44 per cent voted yes.

[64] They were not alone in that view. When it became clear that Trudeau was prepared to proceed, the British government urged him to seek the Court's advice, to no avail. Marshall (n 50) 191.

[65] Manitoba and Newfoundland posed the following questions in common:

> Question 1 – If the amendments to the Constitution of Canada sought in the 'Proposed Resolution for a Joint Address to Her Majesty the Queen respecting the Constitution of Canada', or any of them, were enacted, would federal-provincial relationships or the powers, rights or privileges granted or secured by the Constitution of Canada to the provinces, their legislatures or governments be affected and if so, in what respect or respects?
>
> Question 2 – Is it a constitutional convention that the House of Commons and Senate of Canada will not request Her Majesty the Queen to lay before the Parliament of the United Kingdom of Great Britain and Northern Ireland a measure to amend the Constitution of Canada affecting federal-provincial relationships or the powers, rights or privileges granted or secured by the Constitution of Canada to the provinces, their legislatures or governments without first obtaining the agreement of the provinces?

would affect the constitutional powers of the provinces and (b) whether there was either a constitutional *requirement* or *convention* that provincial agreement be secured before such amendments could be forwarded to Westminster.[66]

The first question was deceptively simple. It queried the impact of the proposed constitutional amendments on provincial powers. Describing the question as 'premature', the Manitoba Court of Appeal declined to answer it. Noting that the proposed amendments might be 'altered, deleted, or supplanted' by others, the Court saw the enterprise as an 'adventure in futility'.[67] The other two courts of appeal did answer it (in the affirmative) although Newfoundland recognised a similar concern to Manitoba.[68]

At the Supreme Court,[69] while not much time at all was spent on the first question, all of the judges answered it in the affirmative. But the provinces had made

> Question 3 – Is the agreement of the provinces of Canada constitutionally required for amendment to the Constitution of Canada where such amendment affects federal-provincial relationships or alters the powers, rights or privileges granted or secured by the Constitution of Canada to the provinces, their legislatures or governments?

Newfoundland submitted an additional question:

> Question 4 – If Part V of the proposed resolution referred to in question 1 is enacted and proclaimed into force could
>
> (a) the Terms of Union, including terms 2 and 17 thereof contained in the Schedule to the British North America Act, 1949 (12–13 George VI, c. 22 (UK)), or
> (b) section 3 of the British North America Act, 1871 (34–35 Victoria, c. 28 (UK))
>
> be amended directly or indirectly pursuant to Part V without the consent of the Government, Legislature or a majority of the people of the Province of Newfoundland voting in a referendum held pursuant to Part V?

Quebec's questions took a different form:

> Question A – If the Canada Act and the Constitution Act, 1981 should come into force and if they should be valid in all respects in Canada would they affect:
>
> (i) the legislative competence of the provincial legislatures in virtue of the Canadian Constitution?
> (ii) the status or role of the provincial legislatures or governments within the Canadian Federation?
>
> Question B – Does the Canadian Constitution empower, whether by statute, convention or otherwise, the Senate and the House of Commons of Canada to cause the Canadian Constitution to be amended without the consent of the provinces and in spite of the objection of several of them, in such a manner as to affect:
>
> (i) the legislative competence of the provincial legislatures in virtue of the Canadian Constitution?.

[66] In the actual references the order of the questions about constitutional convention and legality was flipped.

[67] *Reference re Amendments of the Constitution of Canada*, (1981) 117 DLR (3d) 1, [1981] 2 WWR 193 at para 14.

[68] *Reference re Amendments to the Constitution of Canada*, (1981) 118 DLR (3d) 1, 82 APR 503, 29 Nfld. & PEIR 503.

[69] The three lower-court opinions were appealed as of right to the Supreme Court by the respective provinces, with the remaining provinces intervening supporting either the appellants (members of the Gang of Eight) or the federal government (Ontario and New Brunswick). There was only one additional intervener, the Four Nations Confederacy, which argued in support of the provinces.

their point: the federal government was pursuing a major change to the Constitution of Canada that affected provincial rights, and was seemingly indifferent to their views.

The second and third questions concerned the legal and conventional parameters of constitutional amendment. Chapter 4 discussed the reference's answers, the splits among the panel, and the different ways that the judges read the questions (for example, whether 'provincial agreement' implies that the agreement be unanimous). Recall that a majority of the Court (7 justices) held that provincial agreement was *not* a legal requirement. But a different majority (6 justices) concluded that there was, nonetheless, a *constitutional convention* requiring 'a substantial degree of agreement among the provinces'.[70]

Despite the panel's divisions, no judge declined to answer the questions. The majority justified its answers by adopting the following statement from Justice Freedman in the Manitoba Court of Appeal:

> In my view, the request for a decision by this Court on whether there is a constitutional convention, in the circumstances described, that the Dominion will not act without the agreement of the Provinces poses a question that i[s], at least in part, constitutional in character. *It therefore calls for an answer, and I propose to answer it.*[71]

For its part, the dissent wrote:

> [N]o legal question is raised in the questions under consideration in these reasons and, ordinarily, the Court would not undertake to answer them. Because of the unusual nature of these References and because the issues raised in the questions now before us were argued at some length before the Court and have become the subject of the reasons of the majority, with which, with the utmost deference, we cannot agree, we feel obliged to answer the questions notwithstanding their extra-legal nature.[72]

Note the different factors cited. The majority concluded that its opinion was being sought as a precondition to federal action in a case that was, at least partly, constitutional. The dissent, by contrast, viewed the reference as 'unusual' but noted that

[70] The Court adopted the following definition of a convention from the Manitoba Court of Appeal: 'What is a constitutional convention? There is a fairly lengthy literature on the subject. Although there may be shades of difference among the constitutional lawyers, political scientists, and Judges who have contributed to that literature, the essential features of a convention may be set forth with some degree of confidence. Thus there is general agreement that a convention occupies a position somewhere in between a usage or custom on the one hand and a constitutional law on the other. There is general agreement that if one sought to fix that position with greater precision he would place convention nearer to law than to usage or custom. There is also general agreement that "a convention is a rule which is regarded as obligatory by the officials to whom it applies". There is, if not general agreement, at least weighty authority, that the sanction for breach of a convention will be political rather than legal'. As discussed in Chapter 4, the majority answered the question on the basis that the word 'agreement' did not mean 'unanimous agreement'. The dissent took the view that it did, and found no such convention. *Patriation Reference* (n 42) at 883.

[71] ibid at 884.

[72] ibid at 849.

the issues had received extensive argument in the Court and the majority had already decided to answer the question. In essence, the dissent felt compelled by the majority's choice to answer to do so as well.

The *Patriation Reference* was a game changer.[73] Certainly, it achieved the provinces' prime objective: it forced the Prime Minister to resume negotiations.[74] The resulting process has been exhaustively covered by legal and political scholars.[75] It culminated in a package agreed to by nine provinces, but not Quebec, that became the basis for the UK Canada Act 1982. The proposal included a Charter of Rights, an amending formula, formal recognition of existing Aboriginal rights and a legislative override.

While the Prime Minister was the party most obviously affected by the *Patriation Reference*, the advisory opinion had a significant effect on the provinces as well. For, while the Court indicated that it would be contrary to constitutional convention for Trudeau to approach Westminster without *some* provincial approval, the majority did not prescribe a clear threshold for it. It said simply that the agreement must be 'substantial', which could mean anything from a bare majority of provinces (six) to near unanimity (nine). That left the provinces in a far more constrained position than if the Court had stated that the convention required unanimity. Any province adopting an obstructionist position to the final proposal risked being left out of an agreement that might ultimately be deemed to have satisfied the convention.

The precise sequence of events by which Quebec was presented with what it took to be a fait accompli is hotly debated. But the outcome – Quebec ranged against the nine provinces and the federal government – illustrates the political vulnerability produced by the majority's answer. As it was a convention, the standard of 'substantial agreement' was unenforceable by conventional judicial remedy.

[73] Russell (n 40) c 8.

[74] That is not to imply that the resulting negotiations were easy or collegial. The federal–provincial conference on 1 November 1981 was shot through with distrust. It was unclear how deeply the federal government was motivated to actually reach an agreement. Indeed, the federal government made no move to withdraw its request for a joint resolution. It avowed that it remained prepared to seek patriation alone. Nonetheless, it was clear that a 'made in Canada' solution was the preferred outcome.

[75] Steve Patten (ed), *Patriation and its Consequences* (Vancouver: UBC Press, 2015); GJ Brandt, 'Judicial Mediation of Political Disputes: The Patriation Reference' (1982) 20(1) University of Western Ontario Law Review 101; FL Morton, *Law, Politics and the Judicial Process in Canada* (Calgary: University of Calgary Press, 1992); Carissima Mathen, 'The Question Calls for an Answer, and I Propose to Answer it: The Patriation Reference as Constitutional Method' (2011) 54 Supreme Court Law Review 143; Adam M Dodek, 'Courting Constitutional Danger: Constitutional Conventions and the Legacy of the *Patriation Reference*' (2011) 54 Supreme Court Law Review 117; Jean-Francois Gaudreault-DesBiens, 'The "Principle of Federalism" and the Legacy of the *Patriation* and *Quebec Veto References*' (2011) 54 Supreme Court Law Review 77; Neil Carter and Patrick James, '"Grab the Signatures and Run": Federal Unity Strategy in Canada from the Referendum to Patriation' (2009) 3 International Political Sociology 194; Chambers (n 41); B Pelletier, *La modification constitutionnelle au Canada* (Scarborough: Carswell, 1996); JR Hurley, *Amending Canada's Constitution: History,Processes, Problems and Prospects* (Ottawa: Canada Communication Group, 1996).

It could, at most, lead to the issuance of a further declaration (which occurred, in a sense, in the *Quebec Veto* opinion discussed below). In other words, the provinces were forced to exercise a predictive judgment about the consequences of failing to sign on.[76]

In framing the argument over amendment as at least partly legal in nature, the provinces confirmed the Court's role in settling disputes which were *also* indisputably political. At least some of the provinces' hesitation at the new constitutional package stemmed from the additional powers of judicial review (related to the new Charter) that it mandated. Yet, those same provinces turned to the courts to validate their concerns. That hardly undercut the legitimacy of judicial review writ large and, in fact, may have affirmed it. The supposition is bolstered by the provinces' reception of the opinion and, especially, the fact that a number of them departed from prior positions. Manitoba, Prince Edward Island and Alberta, for example, had insisted that the constitutional convention required *unanimous* agreement. But they were prepared to accede to a package that fell short of it.

The Court's discussion of the asserted convention drew on past political practice (the circumstances under which previous amendments were pursued or abandoned)[77] and a 1965 Federal White Paper.[78] Those precedents did not provide perfect clarity in the sense of specifying a particular number or mathematical fraction of provinces required by the convention. The lack of precision affected the nature of the answer but not its essence. The majority did not go beyond what it took to be the core of those precedents, stating: 'It would not be appropriate for the Court to devise in the abstract a *specific* formula' because 'Conventions by their nature develop in the political field' and it is thus for political not judicial actors 'to determine the degree of provincial consent required'.[79] But the impact of any

[76] For example, in May 1981, a Quebec Minister boasted to his provincial counterparts that the province was in a 'win/win' position. If Quebec did not achieve its preferred constitutional changes, the political backlash would only redound to the separatist government's favour within the province. The comment revealed the lack of any real solidarity between Quebec and the other provinces and probably was a factor leading to the ultimate exclusion. Meekison (n 54).

[77] The majority identified five 'positive precedents' which had directly affected federal–provincial relationships: the British North America Act 1930 (natural resources agreements between the government of Canada and the governments of Manitoba, British Columbia, Alberta and Saskatchewan); the Statute of Westminster 1931; the British North America Act 1940 (unemployment insurance); the British North America Act 1951 (old age pensions); and the British North America Act 1964 (pension supplementary benefits). *Patriation Reference* (n 42) at 861–62. It identified as well certain 'negative precedents' where proposed amendments failed for lack of provincial agreement: one relating to indirect taxation in 1951 and the failure of the Constitutional Conferences of 1960, 1964 and 1971.

[78] *White Paper* (n 61). The *White Paper* articulated a number of principles governing amendment including, most critically for the *Patriation Reference*, the following: '[Fourth,] that the Canadian Parliament will not request an amendment directly affecting federal-provincial relationships without prior consultation and agreement with the provinces. This principle did not emerge as early as others but since 1907, and particularly since 1930, has gained increasing recognition and acceptance. The nature and the degree of provincial participation in the amending process, however, have not lent themselves to easy definition'. The *White Paper* was previously cited in *Re Upper House* (n 41).

[79] ibid at 905.

ambiguity ended there. Certainly, such ambiguity did not affect the Court's judgement that it was proper, in such a momentous case, to affirm the existence of a convention and to articulate it in relatively concrete terms.

Thus, in the *Patriation Reference*, the Court appeared to embrace a political role. Prior to the opinion, the distinction between legal and political principle, between law and convention, was generally accepted (if, perhaps, imperfectly observed). The Court dismantled that distinction. It articulated a rule rooted *solely* in past practice, governing inherently political affairs and decisions, and observed by explicitly political actors.

That is not to say that the opinion lacked legal trappings. After all, it concerned the process for changing a constitutional document. By looking to past practice, the inquiry into convention took the form of common law reasoning. And, the Court noted that one element of the test for identifying convention is the reason or reasons that political actors consider themselves bound to observe it in the first place – in other words, an element of *justification*. That bears some resemblance to a kind of inquiry that is only contingently part of *political* deliberations but commonly present in *legal* ones.[80]

Of course, the content of the answer is also relevant. Eric Colvin wrote that 'the central issue in the legal part of the Constitutional Amendment Reference was surely the circumstances under which the rules of recognition of the Canadian legal system accept enactments of the United Kingdom Parliament as law for Canada'.[81] That is, in the era before the Canada Act 1982, under what circumstances ought such enactments to be accepted? The Court could have specified an exact threshold required by the convention, most easily by adopting a standard of unanimity. Or, it could have specified certain conditions under which the convention would (eight provinces or more) or would not (six provinces or less) be satisfied.

The majority did neither of those things. Instead, it settled upon a broad descriptor ('a substantial degree of consent') that provides clarity only in extreme cases. One could argue that, since a convention is a political benchmark, it should be for political not judicial actors to determine the meaning of 'substantial'; and that a set numerical target would not have been an accurate response to the extent that it implied an unchanging standard. But answering the question in that way was also important, in a strategic sense, for the Court itself. In doing so, it thrust the question back into the political sphere, while also indicating that the Prime Minister's stated plan was unacceptable.[82]

[80] The normative inquiry, though, is to be distinguished from a moral one. The Court is not endeavouring to decide whether the convention is *desirable* per se, but whether it can be said to have a rational explanation that is linked to the overall system in which it operates.

[81] Eric Colvin, 'Constitutional Jurisprudence in the Supreme Court of Canada' (1982) 4 Supreme Court Law Review 3.

[82] According to Russell, the Court spoke 'with a forked tongue', gave 'half a loaf to each side' and provided a 'legal green light but a political red light': Russell (n 40) 118–19.

The majority's decision to address the question of a convention has dominated subsequent discussion of the *Patriation Reference*.[83] But it is worth noting, as well, the somewhat cursory treatment of whether it ought to say anything about the circumstances under which Westminster *should* adopt a unilateral federal request to amend the Constitution. The majority stated simply that its analysis had *nothing to say* about any action by Westminster, and then proceeded to confirm that such a request was perfectly legal.

TRS Allan has critiqued the majority for failing to adequately consider the effect of the Statute of Westminster 1931.[84] The Statute, which expressly carved out from its application any changes to the British North America Acts 1867 to 1930, 'was framed to protect the federal character of Canada by preventing changes being made in the constitutional balance of powers by unilateral action of the federal authorities'.[85] Therefore, it would be 'reasonable to conclude that use of the resolution procedure to procure amendment against the wishes of the provinces was rendered unlawful by necessary implication' and, further, 'that a United Kingdom statute enacted in compliance would be ultra vires and invalid as a matter of Canadian law'.[86]

Indeed, the Newfoundland Court of Appeal had found that future modifications to the Constitution that included provincial powers were 'thereby withdrawn from future British parliamentary competence except with the consent of the provinces'.[87]

Many accounts of convention define non-justiciability as a *principal* feature.[88] A convention is identified by the fact that it eschews judicial oversight. Thus, in delving into the issue, the Court entered the realm of custom and rules which are normally unwritten.[89]

[83] For an argument that the courts should hesitate to declare the substance of a convention *except* in an advisory opinion see Peter Oliver, 'Reform of the Supreme Court of Canada from Within: To What Extent Should the Court Weigh in Regarding Constitutional Conventions?' in Jennifer Smith and Nadia Verrelli, *Democratic Dilemma: Reforming Canada's Supreme Court* (Kingston, ON: McGill-Queens, 2013) 161.

[84] Statute of Westminster 1931, 22 Geo V, c 4 (UK).

[85] TRS Allan, 'Law, Convention, Prerogative: Reflections Prompted by the Canadian Constitutional Case' (1986) 45(2) Cambridge Law Journal 305.

[86] ibid.

[87] ibid at 310 citing (1981) 1 18 DLR (3d) 1.

[88] AV Dicey, *Law of the Constitution* (London: Macmillan; New York: St. Martin's Press, 1959) 23–24:

> The one set of rules are in the strictest sense 'laws', since they are rules which (whether written or unwritten, whether enacted by statute or derived from the mass of custom, tradition, or judge-made maxims known as the common law) are enforced by the courts; these rules constitute 'constitutional law' in the proper sense of that term, and may for the sake of distinction be called collectively 'the law of the constitution'.
>
> The other set of rules consist of conventions, understandings, habits or practices which, though they may regulate the conduct of the several members of the sovereign power, of the Ministry, or of other officials, are not in reality laws at all since they are not enforced by the courts. This portion of constitutional law may, for the sake of distinction, be termed the 'conventions of the constitution', or constitutional morality.

[89] In the *Patriation Reference* (n 42) the majority noted that conventions generally are unwritten but occasionally may be reduced to written form. It gave as an example the Statute of Westminster 1931.

In being willing to answer a question about a convention, the Court confirmed a particular role for itself in Canada's constitutional order. It emerged as a *provider of answers.* The Court confirmed that role while simultaneously denying that the role was attended by any real power. The Court eschewed any authority to ensure compliance with the convention should the Prime Minister decide to ignore it. Yet, it is impossible to believe that the Court thought that its answer would have *no* bearing on executive actors. The fact that the Court was split on the *content* of the convention rather belies that point.

So, in the reference the Court overcame what appeared to be a formidable institutional hurdle: how to address constitutional phenomena long considered injusticiable. It did so by stressing both the non-enforceability of its answer and the critical importance of providing one.

C. Consequences: Quebec Veto

In 1981 the federal and provincial governments resumed constitutional negotiations. On 4 November Prime Minister Trudeau suggested that whatever agreement emerged should be put to a popular referendum. Behind closed doors, eight provinces rejected that idea as politically divisive. But when the provinces reconvened, Quebec Premier René Lévesque broke with that group and stated his support for the idea.

At the end of the day on 4 November, Quebec was in a good strategic position. The other provinces did not wish to adjourn and decided that closing statements would be made the following morning. During the evening, they reached an agreement in principle about an amending formula based on the equality of provinces and a Charter of Rights with a legislative override. No Quebec delegates were present. The next morning, Lévesque was informed of the agreement. The Prime Minister was agreeable. And so the resolution was put forward to the UK Parliament with the consent of the federal government and only nine provinces.

The preceding events have achieved a particular, iconic status in Quebec. They have crystallised a perception of a sequence of manoeuvres that profoundly betrayed the province's interests and position in Confederation. The events have shaped much of the subsequent federal–provincial constitutional dialogue.[90]

Quebec's opposition began as soon as the federal–provincial agreement was announced on 5 November 1981. As the precise sequence of events would prove significant it is recounted in some detail.

[90] For example, shortly following patriation, Quebec applied the Charter's override clause (s 33) to every law in effect in the province, ensuring their immunity from constitutional scrutiny where any alleged violation concerned ss 2 or 7–15. The override would remain in effect for five years. Its validity was largely confirmed (an attempt to make the override apply retroactively was rejected): *Ford v Quebec (AG)*, [1988] 2 SCR 712.

On 18 November Prime Minister Trudeau tabled a motion in the House of Commons to secure a parliamentary resolution for the new package. The following week, the Quebec legislature decreed that the motion 'would have the effect of substantially reducing the powers and rights of Quebec and of its National Assembly without its consent'; that 'it has always been recognized that no change of this kind could be made without the consent of Quebec'; and that the province was thereby registering a 'formal' veto of the agreement.[91]

On 9 December the Governor General advised that the motion tabled in Parliament had received the assent of both chambers and he therefore would pass it on to the Queen. Simultaneously, Quebec put a reference to its Court of Appeal.[92]

On 22 December the UK government introduced in the Westminster Parliament 'A Bill to Give Effect to a Request of the Senate and House of Commons of Canada' – the Canada Act 1982. The Quebec Court of Appeal heard oral argument on the reference from 15 to 17 March 1982. The UK Bill was passed on 25 March and received royal assent on 29 March. The latter was the date on which the Canada Act 1982 came into force.[93]

On 7 April the Quebec Court of Appeal unanimously stated a negative answer to the reference. The following week, the Attorney General of Quebec appealed to the Supreme Court and two days later Chief Justice Lamer stated a constitutional question on terms identical to those in the Court of Appeal.[94]

On 17 April 1982 the Constitution Act 1982 was proclaimed in force by the Queen.

Once again, the Supreme Court was urged not to answer the question.[95] The Court noted that while the matter was before the lower court, the process of patriation was still under way. In that Court, the Quebec government conceded that any answer would have, at most, political not legal consequences. The Court

[91] Decree No. 3214-81 cited in *Quebec Veto* (n 39) at 705.

[92] Decree No 367-81, cited *ibid* at 793-794. The questions were:

> Is the consent of the Province of Quebec constitutionally required, by convention, for the adoption by the Senate and the House of Commons of Canada of a resolution the purpose of which is to cause the Canadian Constitution to be amended in such a manner as to affect:
>
> i) the legislative competence of the Legislature of the Province of Quebec in virtue of the Canadian Constitution;
> ii) the status or role of the Legislature or Government of the Province of Quebec within the Canadian federation;
>
> and, does the objection of the Province of Quebec render the adoption of such resolution unconstitutional in the conventional sense?

[93] The history is recounted in the Supreme Court's opinion, ibid at 794.

[94] As noted in Chapter 3, a provincial reference does not proceed to the Supreme Court by an Order-in-Council, but an appeal. At the time, constitutional questions in all matters were set by the Chief Justice. That left the Court with discretion to vary the questions put to the provincial court of appeal. In practice, however, the Court invariably accepted the provincial government's wording (though, as discussed in Chapter 4, that does not prevent it from re-interpreting questions, or occasionally declining to answer them).

[95] *Quebec Veto* (n 39).

of Appeal decided it was nonetheless necessary to address what it perceived to be an important underlying issue of legitimacy.

By the time the matter reached the Supreme Court in June of 1982, it was truly moot. The Canada Act 1982 had been passed by the UK Parliament and its attendant constitutional documents proclaimed by the Queen. Canada argued that that fact, alone, weighed against providing an answer. The question, it said, was 'purely political'.

Pointing to the analysis of the majority in the *Patriation Reference*, the Court (which spoke *per curiam*) dismissed any attempt to invoke what has been called a 'political questions' doctrine to refuse to answer. Though the questions in *Quebec Veto were* 'political', they also possessed a legal character. On that basis, they deserved to be answered. The mootness issue, however, was different. The legality of the Constitution Act 1982, the Court acknowledged, was 'neither challenged nor assailable'.[96] The new amendment procedure contained therein (Part V) made Quebec's argument irrelevant. However, at the time of the provincial reference, the matter was not moot. The opinion had been appealed to the Supreme Court as of right (pursuant to provisions in the Supreme Court Act, mentioned in Chapter 3). As an 'appeal', the matter now fell under the Court's jurisdiction. The Court retained the discretion to refuse to dispose of it on the basis of mootness, but it was also free to conclude that the particular circumstances made it more desirable to proceed. In the circumstances, the Court decided that an answer was warranted.[97]

With respect to the substantive issue, Quebec argued that there was a convention against amending the Constitution in a way that substantially reduced its powers, without its consent. It said that the *Patriation Reference* had not actually settled the issue of whether there was a convention of provincial unanimity because the majority had decided that it had not been asked that precise question. The Court rejected that argument. It pointed out that, while the majority in the *Patriation Reference* had indeed read the conventional question as *not* directed towards 'unanimous consent', the majority had made various statements clearly rejecting that there was such a convention.[98]

Quebec also argued that a principle of 'duality' in Canadian federalism recognised Quebec's special role within Canadian Confederation – the province was 'the stronghold of the French-Canadian people' and the 'living heart of the French presence in North America'.[99] It was intolerable that such a momentous change to the country's governing framework could occur without Quebec's consent.

[96] ibid at 806.

[97] ibid

[98] ibid at 807–08, citing the majority's endorsement of the argument of Saskatchewan, which argued not for unanimity but for substantial agreement (*Patriation Reference* (n 38) at 886) as well as noting that 'while the precedents taken alone point at unanimity, the unanimity principle cannot be said to have been accepted by all the actors in the precedents'. Ibid at 901.

[99] Factum of AG Quebec in *Quebec Veto* (n 43) at 813 (emphasis in original).

The Supreme Court acknowledged that a commitment to duality appeared in an 'abundance of material, speeches made in the course of parliamentary debates, reports of royal commissions, opinions of historians, political scientists [and] constitutional experts'.[100] 'There can be no doubt', it continued, 'that many Canadian statesmen, politicians and experts [have] favoured [it]'.[101] But its mere existence was insufficient. Duality might be a political fact, but there was no evidence that federal or other provincial actors had *recognised* it to entail a privileged role for Quebec in the amending process. The Court stated, further, that the arguments in favour of a unanimity rule made by several provinces in the *Patriation Reference* was 'incompatible with a special power of veto for Quebec'.[102]

Ultimately, the Court concluded that the events leading up to patriation and the Constitution Act ·1982, which lacked Quebec's agreement, did not breach any other conventional rules and, therefore, could not be assailed on that basis. *Quebec Veto* confirmed that the Court viewed the Constitution Act 1982 as having been, in effect, legitimately entrenched in such a way as to include *all* the actors in Confederation. Essentially, the Court confirmed Quebec's obligation under the Constitution as a matter of law, to which its political sense of exclusion would have to bend.

The legacy of the 1982 patriation continues to reverberate. The sense of betrayal in Quebec has waxed and waned, but never dissipated. Two attempts were made to secure a new package to which Quebec would assent. Both (the Meech Lake and Charlottetown Accords) ultimately failed.[103] A second provincial referendum, held on 30 October 1995, resulted in a razor-thin majority opting to remain within Canada.

Some years after that referendum, the federal government initiated a reference on the circumstances under which a province might secede from Canada. The resulting opinion (discussed in Chapter 8) would prove to be one of the most important in Canadian legal history.[104]

* * *

Through their advisory role, Canadian courts exerted a powerful influence on the events attending constitutional rebirth in Canada. While ultimate emancipation from the UK may well have been achieved through a 'solo' federal effort, it was unquestionably better for the country that federal and provincial actors achieved a measure of unification that became the basis on which Westminster could, eventually, cede its authority.

By the time of the patriation struggle, the reference function was well entrenched in Canadian law. Nonetheless, the events recounted above harnessed

[100] ibid at 814.
[101] ibid.
[102] ibid at 815. Yet, both conventions could coexist. Neither logically precludes the other.
[103] The Meech Lake Accord of 1987; the Charlottetown Accord of 1992.
[104] *Reference re Secession of Quebec*, [1998] 2 SCR 217.

the power in a new way. Although the Court did not instigate the constitutional battle, its opinions came to occupy the heart of it. Dispensing with traditional boundaries of justiciability, the Court accepted that it was in a unique position and, implicitly, that it had a responsibility to illuminate the tricky merging of legal and political principle that was required to negotiate changes of such magnitude. It should be noted that the Court permitted the delivery of the *Patriation* opinion to be televised – a well-intentioned moment that was unfortunately destroyed when an audio cable was disturbed and the broadcast did not have any sound.[105] The decision to 'go live' – which has never been repeated – indicates the Court's awareness of the gravity of the occasion.

Change rarely comes easily, or without cost. The cost of patriation was the exclusion of Quebec and, with it, the ability to easily cast the occasion as a nationally unifying event. Ultimate responsibility for that exclusion rests with the political actors who were content to proceed without the agreement of all of the provinces. Nonetheless, the Court's advisory opinions were instrumental to those decisions.

Not only did this period of rebirth and rupture confirm the Court's critical role, but it also highlighted a particular aspect of that role. The Court emerged as a provider of answers, as a definitive word in disputes over fundamental aspects of Canadian law and politics. The use of advisory opinions might have been perceived as less intrusive given that the Court's power was expository in nature. But, as would become apparent in the ensuring years under the Constitution Act 1982, the Court's primary role under a system of constitutional supremacy is a declaratory one. Thus, the peculiar nature of the advisory opinion would find a complement in the Court's assumption of additional authority in its numerous, landmark constitutional decisions.[106]

[105] Mandel (n 47) 29.

[106] Note, though, that the dissent in the *Patriation Reference* stated that the appropriate route would be to simply declare the federal government's unilateral action ultra vires.

7

Interpretation and Rights

This chapter deals with the implications of advisory opinions for rights issues. Its focus is the period following the entrenchment of the Constitution Act 1982, in particular the Charter of Rights and Freedoms. The Charter changed the nature of constitutional accountability from being primarily about jurisdiction to including the relationship between citizen and state.

Constitutional reform brought questions similar to those arising after the elimination of Privy Council appeals (discussed in the previous chapter). There was uncertainty about the weight to be accorded to pre-1982 case law. The Supreme Court decided that while it would consider such cases it was not bound by them. A number of those earlier cases, it said, presumed certain things about the nature of rights, and about the state's duties to respect those rights, that were ill-suited to the current constitutional project.[1]

The Constitution Act 1982 deeply affected the status of the judiciary and changed the parameters of constitutional litigation. Yet, the Act barely mentioned the courts.[2] The general role played by advisory opinions did not change: courts continued to hear references and to issue extremely important opinions. But references began to diminish as a proportion of overall constitutional cases.

Today, constitutional law operates in a markedly different context. The manner in which cases get to courts, how they are litigated, and the available remedies have all undergone shifts. For example, there has been a relaxation of many of the procedural rules governing how and when courts hear issues. Doctrines that were initially developed to constrain courts' ability to adjudicate, such as standing, mootness and ripeness, have been relaxed.

There has also been a significant expansion in the courts' remedial powers. At one time, Canadian courts faced a relatively simple binary choice: whether to rule

[1] *R v Therens*, [1985] 1 SCR 613 at para 48 ('[T]he *Charter* must be regarded, because of its constitutional character, as a new affirmation of rights and freedoms and of judicial power and responsibility in relation to their protection'); *R v Big M Drug Mart Ltd.*, [1985] 1 SCR 295 at para 113 [*Big M Drug Mart*]. ('[T]he concept of "freedom of religion" under the *Canadian Bill of Rights* … cannot easily be transferred to a constitutional document like the *Charter* and the fundamental guarantees it enshrines').

[2] Despite being a topic of discussion, the Court largely was left out of the 1982 package: Warren J. Newman, 'The Constitutional Status of the Supreme Court of Canada' (2009) 47 SCLR (2d) 429, 432. The exception was Part V, which prescribes formulae for amendment. Section 41(d) states that changes to the Court's 'composition' are governed by the so-called 'unanimity' formula, which requires the consent of both Houses of Parliament and all 10 provincial legislatures. Section 42 states that all other amendments 'in relation to … the Supreme Court of Canada' require the consent of Parliament and seven of the 10 provinces comprising at least 50 per cent of the population of all of the provinces.

that a law was ultra or intra vires.[3] Now, they have many more kinds of remedies at their disposal. Indeed, their constitutional remedies may well render Canadian courts among the most assertive in the world. The Canadian Supreme Court has declared that courts may sever offending portions from statutes or read in others.[4] It has read into laws complex interpretations,[5] limits,[6] and exemptions[7] that are not obvious from the text of a particular statute. In addition, the courts have suspended the effect of their remedies for anywhere from six months to, increasingly, one or two years – in effect suspending the Constitution itself.[8] (And, none of these remedies is limited to the apex court.) The result has been a dramatic expansion of judicial power.[9]

What is striking about the above developments is how many of them come not from conventional litigation, but from advisory opinions. They illustrate, in part, the ever-narrowing space between references and cases.

This chapter looks at opinions that have affected rights through the articulation and, in some cases, reformulation of numerous doctrines. The doctrines are in some instances substantive and in others procedural or structural. They include non-originalist interpretation; suspended declarations; relaxed uses of extrinsic evidence; the durability of constitutional provisions and the rejection of a hierarchy among them; and the framework for the revision of precedent.

This chapter, then, is primarily about constitutional litigation. As such, it seems fitting to begin by examining a much earlier reference, which also has status as a 'rights' case and which has indelibly shaped the narrative of such litigation.

Prologue: Process and Persons

Perhaps one of the best-known of all advisory opinions, *Edwards v Attorney General (Canada)* [10] (or the *Persons Case*) concerned whether the BNA Act allowed for the appointment of women to the Senate of Canada. Under section 24 of that Act,

[3] They also could impose variations of these, such as holding an otherwise valid provincial law 'inoperative' or 'inapplicable' by virtue of its conflict with a valid federal law or a federally controlled entity (the doctrines of, respectively, paramountcy or inter-jurisdictional immunity).

[4] *Schachter v Canada*, [1992] 2 SCR 679.

[5] *R v Butler*, [1992] 1 SCR 452; *Canadian Foundation for Children, Youth and the Law v Canada (Attorney General)*, [2004] 1 SCR 76, 2004 SCC 4.

[6] *R v Keegstra*, [1990] 3 SCR 697; *Saskatchewan (Human Rights Commission) v Whatcott*, 2013 SCC 11, [2013] 1 SCR 467.

[7] *R v Sharpe*, [2001] 1 SCR 45, 2001 SCC 2.

[8] Bruce Ryder, 'Suspending the Charter' (2003) 21 SCLR (2d) 267; Robert Leckey, 'Suspended Declarations of Invalidity and the Rule of Law' UK Constitutional Law Blog (12 March 2014) https://ukconstitutionallaw.org/.

[9] That is not to say, though, that Canadian courts routinely apply such remedies, or even that they are particularly inclined to overturn legislation. But their very availability is a striking and dramatic development.

[10] *Edwards v Attorney General (Canada)* [1930] AC 124, 1929 UKPC 86 (*Persons Case*).

the Governor General may 'summon qualified persons' to become members, but it was disputed whether 'persons' included women.[11]

The *Persons Case* emerged out of a growing feminist movement.[12] By the early twentieth century, women had gained the suffrage;[13] been admitted to the professions;[14] and been elected to the House of Commons.[15]

The Canadian Supreme Court concluded that women were not eligible. 'Never', the Chief Justice said, 'from 1867 to the present time has any woman ever sat in the Senate of Canada, nor has any suggestion of women's eligibility for appointment to that House until quite recently been publicly made'.[16]

The majority opinion in the *Persons Case* has become synonymous with chauvinism and hostility to women in public life.[17] But Anglin CJ insisted that the Court was 'in no wise concerned with the desirability or the undesirability of the presence of women in the Senate, nor with any political aspect of the question submitted'.[18] It merely was considering whether section 24 ought to bear the same meaning as in 1867.

The Judicial Committee considered the matter and released an opinion on 18 October 1929. Not only did the Committee overturn the Supreme Court, it also diverged sharply from decisions reached in comparable British cases.

The Committee stated that '[while t]he exclusion of women from all public offices is a relic of days more barbarous than ours … it must be remembered that the necessity of the times often forced on man customs which in later years were not necessary'.[19]

[11] The matter was taken up by Emily Murphy, Henrietta Muir Edwards, Nellie McClung, Louise McKinney and Irene Palby. Murphy, the first female magistrate in the British Empire, had long faced similar arguments; on her very first day in her new role a lawyer argued that '[she] was not a "person" and was therefore not able to perform the duties of a magistrate'. Monique Benoit, 'Are Women Persons?' www.collectionscanada.gc.ca/publications/002/015002-2100-e.html. *R v Cyr* (1917), 12 Alta LR 320, 38 DLR 601 (SC(AD)).

[12] Marguerite E Ritchie, 'Alice through the Statutes' (1975) 2194) McGill Law Journal 685–708; Olive M Stone, 'Canadian Women as Legal Persons – How Alberta Combined Judicial, Executive and Legislative Powers to Win Full Legal Personality for All Canadian Women – The Jubilee of Henrietta Muir Edwards and Others v. Attorney-General for Canada decided October 18, 1929' (1979) 17(3) Alberta Law Review 331–71.

[13] By 1918, all Canadian women except those in Quebec could vote.

[14] Susan Altschul and Christine Carron, 'Chronology of Some Legal Landmarks in the History of Canadian Women' (1975) 212(4) McGill Law Journal 476–94.

[15] 'Women are Eligible for Upper Chamber Privy Council Rules', *Toronto Daily Star*, 18 October 1929, cited in Robert J Sharpe and Patricia McMahon, *The Persons Case: The Origins and Legacy of the Fight for Legal Personhood* (Toronto: Osgoode Society, 2008) 106, 184. Perhaps ironically, the first women MP, Agnes McPhail, regarded the Senate as 'a menace to good government'.

[16] ibid at 284–85.

[17] Mary Jane Mossman, 'Feminism and Legal Method: The Difference it Makes' (1987) 3 Wisconsin Women's Law Journal 147; Sharpe and McMahon (n 14).

[18] *Reference re meaning of the word 'Persons' in s. 24 of British North America Act*, [1928] SR 276 [*Persons Case – SCC*] at 281–82.

[19] ibid at 3.

The word 'persons' was 'ambiguous' and not assisted by historical references. The fact that no woman had served in the Senate was not particularly relevant, since 'custom would have prevented the claim being made'.[20] Moreover, it was wrong 'to apply rigidly to Canada of today the decisions … which commended themselves, probably rightly, to those who had to apply the law in different circumstances, in different centuries to countries in different stages of development'.[21]

The Judicial Committee described BNA Act as the governing framework for a nation situated within 'the Britannic system' which 'embrace[s] countries and peoples in every stage of social, political and economic development and undergoing a continuous process of evolution'.[22] A final court of appeal such as the Committee must 'take great care … not to interpret legislation meant to apply to one community by a rigid adherence to the customs and traditions of another'.[23] It then observed:

> *The [Act] planted in Canada a living tree capable of growth and expansion within its natural limits.* The object of the Act was to grant a Constitution to Canada. 'Like all written constitutions it has been subject to development through usage and convention'.
>
> Their Lordships do not conceive it to be the duty of this Board – it is certainly not their desire – to cut down the provisions of the Act by a narrow and technical construction, but rather to give it a large and liberal interpretation so that the Dominion to a great extent, but within certain fixed limits, may be mistress in her own house, as the provinces to a great extent, but within certain fixed limits, are mistresses in theirs.[24]

The passages have come to epitomise the Canadian approach to constitutional interpretation. Many think of the 'living tree' metaphor as the core of Canadian constitutionalism, representing a rejection of so-called 'originalism' and the embrace of the 'progressive' interpretative approach.[25]

The passages, though, have a broader context. The Board approached the issue as one of statutory interpretation and not, as is sometimes attributed to it, high constitutional theory. As the Committee noted, 'there are statutes and statutes'.[26] The strict construction appropriate to, say, a taxation law would 'subvert' the intent of an Act 'passed to ensure the peace order and good government of a British

[20] ibid at 7.

[21] ibid at 8. The Board continued: 'Referring therefore to the judgment of the Chief Justice and those who agreed with him, their Lordships think that the appeal to Roman Law and to early English decisions is not of itself a secure foundation on which to build the interpretation of the British North America Act of 1867'.

[22] ibid at 8.

[23] ibid.

[24] The quoted provision is attributed to the eighth Prime Minister of Canada, Sir Robert Borden (Canadian Constitutional Studies, (1922), p. 55) (emphasis added).

[25] For an excellent account and defence of originalism (albeit within the US context) see Ilan Wurman, *A Debt Against the Living* (Cambridge: Cambridge University Press, 2017).

[26] Marshall Rothstein, 'Checks and Balances in Constitutional Interpretation' (2016) 79(1) Saskatchewan Law Review 1.

Colony'.[27] The BNA Act was better interpreted in a 'large, liberal and comprehensive spirit'.[28]

The Committee even acknowledged the advisory nature of its opinion. Considering the argument that it ought not to interfere with the Senate's discretion to decide upon qualifications, it said:

> We are asked for advice on the general question, and that, I think, we are bound to give. *It has, of course, only the force of an advisory opinion.* The existence of this jurisdiction of the Senate does not, I think, affect the question of substance. We must assume that the Senate would decide in accordance with the law.[29]

Thus, notwithstanding the 'heavy burden' on the appellants, the Committee overturned the Supreme Court decision and ruled in their favour.[30]

Some accounts of the *Persons Case* mistakenly describe Emily Murphy as having 'discovered' the reference procedure.[31] Murphy was perfectly aware of the nature of section 60 of the Supreme Court Act. She did not characterise her petition as ground breaking.[32] Rather, she correctly assessed that the (by now well-established) advisory function might serve the interests of citizens as well as government.[33] (This point is revisited in Chapter 10).

In other words, the *Persons Case* was an early instance of 'test case' litigation. In seeking a reference, Murphy made a savvy choice. Appreciating the obstacles facing the federal government obstacles, she suggested a more palatable option.

[27] See WPH Clement, *The Law of the Canadian Constitution*, 3rd edn (Toronto: Carswell, 1916) 347.

[28] *St. Catherines Milling and Lumber Co. v The Queen* (1888) 14 App Cas 46 at 50.

[29] ibid at 14 (emphasis added). But see the criticism of this point by Henderson, *infra* note 183 at 626: 'It is well known that the Canadian Senate was designed for the protection of Provincial and minority rights. It is therefore easy to understand the reason why, while provision is made in the BNA Act for alteration by the Parliament of Canada of the qualifications or disqualifications of persons entitled to be elected to the House of Commons, the Imperial Parliament alone is empowered to alter the Constitution of the Senate. If at the time of Confederation provision was made for a Senate which did not include women, the fact that women subsequently became eligible for membership in the House of Commons has no bearing whatever upon the question of their eligibility for membership in the Senate'.

[30] ibid at 14.

[31] The reference was found on numerous sites accessed on 3 January 2017 including the Wikipedia entry about Emily Murphy: https://en.wikipedia.org/wiki/Emily_Murphy ('In order for her question to be considered, she needed at least five citizens to submit the question as a group'. The sentence is noted 'citation needed'); the Historica Canada site, www.historicacanada.ca/content/heritage-minutes/emily-murphy ('She found a section of the Supreme Court Act that allowed any five interested persons the right to petition the government for a ruling on a constitutional point'); the Canadian Encyclopedia site, www.thecanadianencyclopedia.ca/en/article/persons-case/ ('According to Section 60 of the *Supreme Court Act*, a group of five persons could petition the government to direct the Supreme Court to interpret a point of law in the *BNA Act*'). At the time, the advisory function was found in s 60: 54-55 V, c 25, s 4; 6 E VII, c 50, s 2.

[32] See also Sharpe and McMahon (n 15) 106.

[33] It is appropriate to note that many of Murphy's views on other social issues, including race, would be unacceptable today; and her status as a feminist trailblazer is a complicated one. See ibid; and Mary Jane Mossman's book review of the same in (2009) 40:1 *Ottawa Law Review* 159, 163.

It took time for the *Persons Case* to make its mark. In the 1931 *Aeronautics Reference*, the federal solicitor general described the opinion as having articulated 'rules of progressive construction'.[34] But, aside from a few other Privy Council decisions,[35] it went virtually unmentioned until 1979.[36] In its own time, academic discussion of the reference was uniformly negative.[37] British scholar Berriedale Keith said that 'no decision of the Privy Council is probably harder to defend as sound in law'.[38] GF Henderson was equally cutting, charging that the case was 'not written in strict accordance with well understood legal principles'; that the federal government had manipulated the situation to secure its preferred outcome; and that the JCPC had by 'judicial legislation … altered the constitution of the Senate of Canada'.[39]

More positive regard began to emerge in the 1970s, a time of greater awareness of women's rights and an increasing role for feminist advocacy. After being mentioned in some early Charter decisions,[40] *Edwards* quickly assumed more prominence. The reference enjoyed an intriguing duality. It was used to chart a different path to constitutional interpretation compared to the more formalist approach of the Supreme Court of the 1970s. At the same time, being so deeply rooted in the country's legal history, it may have rendered the Court's momentous interpretative choices, a number of which are explored later in this chapter, less radical.

To be sure, some continue to dispute whether the reference actually rejected 'originalist' interpretation, at least as that term is understood today.[41] Early complaints that the ratio of the opinion has been overstated persist.[42] The latter

[34] John T Saywell, *The Lawmakers: Judicial Power and the Shaping of Canadian Federalism* (Toronto: Osgoode Society, 2002) 193. The reference was also discussed in Chapter 5.

[35] *British Coal Corporation v The King* [1935] AC 500 at 518 (PC) (Parliament had authority to eliminate appeals to the JCPC in criminal cases; 'in interpreting a constituent or organic statute such as the [*BNA*] *Act*, that construction most beneficial to the widest possible amplitude of its powers must be adopted'); *Re Regulation and Control of Aeronautics in Canada* [1931] UKPC 93; *A-G Ontario v A-G Canada* [1947] AC 127 [*Re Privy Council Appeals*] at 154 (Parliament could abolish altogether Privy Council appeals; 'It is … irrelevant that the question is one that might have seemed unreal [in 1867]. To such an organic statute the flexible interpretation must be given which changing circumstances require').

[36] *Att. Gen. of Quebec v Blaikie et al.*, [1979] 2 SCR 1016.

[37] George F Henderson, 'Eligibility of Women for the Senate' (1929) IX Canadian Bar Review 617.

[38] A Berriedale Keith, 'The Privy Council Decisions: A Comment from Great Britain' (1937) XV Canadian Bar Review 428, 429. Keith noted with apparent relief that the 'unfortunate precedent has not been followed'.

[39] Henderson (n 37) 628.

[40] *Hunter et al. v Southam Inc.*, [1984] 2 SCR 145; *Law Society of Upper Canada v Skapinker*, [1984] 1 SCR 357; *Re BC Motor Vehicle Act*, [1985] 2 SCR 486 [*Re Motor Vehicle*].

[41] Leonid Sirota and Benjamine Oliphant, 'Originalist Reasoning in Canadian Constitutional Jurisprudence' (2017) 50(2) University of British Columbia Law Review 505. Bradley Miller, 'Beguiled by Metaphors: The "Living Tree" and Originalist Constitutional Interpretation in Canada' (2009) 22 The Canadian Journal of Law and Jurisprudence 331.

[42] Henderson (n 37) 619.

point is a fair one, though it occasionally is twinned with a defensive and unpersuasive account of women's actual position in society.[43]

The critiques of the *Persons Case* are reminiscent of the debates in the United States over the soundness of the *Brown v Board of Education (Topeka)* landmark decision.[44] Although it is possible to legitimately object to the judicial craft in each, and many commentators do, few take the next step and claim that the decision should be cast aside.[45] In Canada, such a position would be repudiated by all but the most implacable defenders of constitutional minimalism.[46] The hesitation to fully back the implications of such a critique illustrates the opinion's power. For, while the reference may attract debate over its precise contours, and future applications, there is in almost all quarters an acceptance of its legacy and continuing force.

It is intriguing to consider whether the *Persons Case* was enabled by the advisory function *itself*. Henderson noted that, as compared to the Supreme Court, the JCPC was 'entitled, if not obliged, to advise His Majesty on grounds of public policy and to take into account matters of political expediency'.[47] In his view, such a body 'has no limitations at all, is not bound to follow precedent, nor to determine matters upon grounds of law alone'.[48] The reference framework, so the argument goes, permitted the Board to disregard the true state of affairs: it was freed from the tedious but necessary task of considering a factual context.[49]

The allegation is intriguing.[50] It can be extended to references in general. In effect, the argument is the flip side of the executive 'capture' discussed in Chapter 4 – suggesting that, quite contrary to the notion that references constrain courts by making them subject to executive requests, they may actually free courts to consider issues in a much broader way. This argument will be revisited in Chapter 10.

[43] See EA Driedger's remarkable screed against the Constitution Act 1982: 'The Canadian Charter of Rights and Freedoms' (1982) 14 Ottawa Law Review 366, 373.

[44] *Brown v Board of Education (Topeka)* 347 US 483 (1954) (holding that state laws mandating racial segregation in public schools offend the US Constitution's guarantee of equal protection).

[45] Ilan Wurman, *A Debt Against the Living* (Cambridge: Cambridge University Press, 2017) 108–16, devotes a chapter to how *Brown* is entirely reconcilable with an originalist approach to the Constitution. See also Michael W McConnell, *The Originalist Case for* Brown *v* Board of Education (1995) 19 *Harvard Journal of Law and Public Policy* 457 and his 'Originalism and the Desegregation Decisions' (1995) 81 Virginia Law Review.

[46] See the memorandum by then-law clerk William Rehnquist in which he argued that *Brown* ought to have been decided in the state's favour: 'A Random Thought on the Segregation Cases' (1952), www.gpo.gov/fdsys/pkg/GPO-CHRG-REHNQUIST/pdf/GPO-CHRG-REHNQUIST-4-16-6.pdf.

[47] ibid.

[48] ibid.

[49] JF Davison, 'The Constitutionality and Utility of Advisory Opinions' (1937–38) 2 University of Toronto Law Journal 254, 275–76; FE LaBrie, 'Constitutional Interpretation and Legislative Review (1950) 8 University of Toronto Law Journal 298, 347.

[50] Gerald Rubin, 'The Nature, Use and Effect of Reference Cases in Canadian Constitutional Law' (1959) 6 McGill Law Journal 168, 184.

An Age of Rights

The Constitution Act 1982 was ushered in via an advisory opinion. The *Patriation Reference* was the first opportunity for the judiciary to contemplate, if not directly engage, with the proposed new order. While it may overstate things to claim that the advisory function, per se, influenced the result, the patriation experience demonstrates how critical that function could be. The Supreme Court did not shy away from the monumental task set before it. It took as given that it should answer the questions.

The new constitutional order thrust the courts into a different role vis-à-vis individual rights and freedoms; as well as vis-à-vis the rights guaranteed for Canada's historic linguistic minorities and its aboriginal peoples.[51] In previous decades, civil liberties and individual rights had been moderated through application of common law rules, principles of statutory interpretation, or the assertion of subject matter boundaries. Such techniques occasionally could promote results that were consistent with personal rights and freedoms. But they were not effective against a government determined to implement draconian policy that fell within its enumerated powers.

The Constitution Act 1982 changed that. Its rights guarantees provided an irreproachable basis for subjecting legislation and state action to review. And, in being identified as the 'supreme law of the land', the Constitution implicitly affirmed the role of the courts as the primary arbiters of its guarantees.[52]

Of course, the Court had many other decisions to make. A plethora of questions awaited: about interpretative approaches, about judicial deference to other branches and about threshold litigation issues such as standing and application. But the majority of those issues were self-executing. They could be influenced, but not dictated, by forces external to the Court.[53]

Given the uncertainty over how the Constitution Act 1982 would be interpreted, one might think that the reference function would have provided a relatively straightforward way to clarify some of those issues. Yet it did not. On Charter issues, governments largely waited for inter partes litigation to be initiated. While the governments would be in the defensive position of respondent they also could

[51] Charter, ss 16–23; Constitution Act 1982, s 35.

[52] It is often stated that s 52 (the supremacy clause) affirms the role of the courts to review the other branches for constitutional compliance. On its face, s 52 does nothing of the sort. While it affirms the principle of constitutional supremacy, it does not lead inexorably to a corresponding principle of judicial supremacy. Nonetheless, it is difficult to dispute that, by 1982, the implications of inserting such a clause would have been well understood, especially in light of the review function the courts had been performing for over a century.

[53] It is true that to the extent that they are amenable to inclusion in the Supreme Court Act or other legislation such as the Criminal Code, issues such as standing and jurisdiction (as opposed to application of the Charter) were within the control of the legislature. And, indeed, changes to the Supreme Court Act continued post-1982.

attempt to strike out claims on the basis either that would-be claimants lacked standing or that the Charter simply did not apply.

In inter partes litigation, because parties must begin at the bottom of the judicial hierarchy, cases can take years to reach the final court of appeal (if, indeed, they get there at all). The Supreme Court released its first Charter case, *Skapinker*, in 1984.[54] By 1989, the Court had issued its 100th Charter decision.[55] Among them are just five advisory opinions. But that low number masks their influence. They include[56] the most important constitutional moments of the first Charter decade: *BC Motor Vehicle*,[57] *Manitoba Language Rights*,[58] and *Re Bill 30*.[59] Each has been cited in hundreds of subsequent decisions and opinions and their core holdings largely[60] have remained intact.[61]

Waiting for litigation to arise through rights claims can greatly affect the direction of early jurisprudence. An example is *R v Big M Drug Mart*,[62] a landmark decision on freedom of religion. The case involved a federal law mandating the closure of commercial enterprises on the Christian Sabbath. Because of the law's preference for Christianity, the case could easily have supported arguments based on the Charter's equality rights guarantees. But the relevant provision, section 15, was not yet in effect at the time the rights dispute arose.[63] The absence of a separate equality rights claim in *Big M* proved determinative to the subsequent treatment of the fundamental freedom of religion, and the textually separate right to equality of law without religious discrimination. The latter right has largely been eclipsed by the former – such cases are overwhelmingly decided on the basis of the freedom of religion.[64]

It is impossible to know what 'might have been' had a government initiated a reference on the scope of section 15's equality rights. But it is an intriguing question. And, it works in reverse as well. One can see how when considering the Court's pronouncement on another Charter right of supervening importance – section 7 of the Charter – in the *Motor Vehicle Reference*.

[54] *Law Society of Upper Canada v Skapinker*, [1984] 1 SCR 357. The first case under s 35 was *R v Sparrow*, [1990] 1 SCR 1075.

[55] FL Morton, Peter H Russell and Michael J Withey, 'The Supreme Court's First One Hundred Charter of Rights Decisions: A Statistical Analysis' (1992) 30(1) Osgoode Hall Law Journal 1.

[56] Rounding out the five are *Reference Re Public Service Employees Relations Act (Alta.)*, [1987] 1 SCR 313 and *Reference Re Workers' Compensation Act, 1983 (Nfld.)*, [1989] 1 SCR 922.

[57] *Re B.C. Motor Vehicle Act*, [1985] 2 S.C.R. 486 *[Re Motor Vehicle]*.

[58] *Reference Re Manitoba Language Rights*, [1985] 2 SCR 347 [*Re Manitoba Language*].

[59] *Reference Re Bill 30, An Act to Amend the Education Act (Ont.)*, [1987] 1 SCR 1148.

[60] The *Public Service Employees* reference was influential in carving out a narrow approach to labour rights but has subsequently been abandoned for a more expansive view: *Saskatchewan Federation of Labour v Saskatchewan*, 2015 SCC 4, [2015] 1 SCR 245.

[61] It has been observed that, of those five advisory opinions, only one was initiated by the federal government (*Manitoba Language*); the others were appealed as of right from provincial courts of appeal under s 36 of the Supreme Court Act.

[62] *Big M Drug Mart* (n 1).

[63] Section 15 came into force on 17 April 1985.

[64] See C Mathen, 'What Religious Freedom Jurisprudence Reveals About Equality' (2009) 6(2) Journal of Law and Equality 163.

A. Fundamental Justice and Criminal Fault (*Motor Vehicle*)

The *Motor Vehicle Reference* began as a provincial advisory opinion about section 94(2) of the Motor Vehicle Act.[65]

The Act imposed a minimum seven day term of imprisonment on any individual who operated a motor vehicle while (a) under a driving prohibition or (b) his driver's licence was suspended.[66] Under section 94(2), the offence did not require the Crown to prove fault; the offence was satisfied by proof of driving with either of the two conditions. In fact, the defendant could not even raise fault as an issue, for example by proving that he had exercised 'due diligence'.[67] As such, the offence was one of absolute liability.

The reference asked about the law's consistency with the Charter overall, as opposed to any of its specific rights. But there was general recognition that the matter primarily[68] involved section 7, which reads: 'Everyone has the right to life, liberty and security of the person and the right not to be deprived thereof except in accordance with the principles of fundamental justice'.[69]

From the start, section 7 had generated interpretative and political concerns. Its wording is similar to that found in the Canadian Bill of Rights[70] (a federal statute), which provides 'the right of the individual to life, liberty, security of the person and enjoyment of property, and the right not to be deprived thereof except by due process of law' and the US Constitution, which guarantees against deprivations of 'life, liberty or property, without due process of law'.[71] Section 7 departs from those comparator provisions in that it does not mention the term 'due process'. Its operative phrase is 'the principles of fundamental justice'.[72]

The meaning that courts would give to 'fundamental justice' was a matter of much debate. There were fears that the Canadian judiciary would follow the example of the United States Supreme Court in its so-called *Lochner*[73] period, when it

[65] *Reference re Section 94(2) of the Motor Vehicle Act*, 1983 CanLII 268 (BC CA), 147 DLR (3d) 539 [*Re MVA (1983)* cited to CanLII].

[66] Motor Vehicle Act, RSBC 1979, c 288, as amended by the Motor Vehicle Amendment Act 1982, 1982 (BC), c 36.

[67] *R v Sault Ste. Marie*, [1978] 2 SCR 1299.

[68] Also mentioned, but not determinative, was s 11(d) of the Charter: '11. Any person charged with an offence has the right … (*d*) to be presumed innocent until proven guilty according to law in a fair and public hearing by an independent and impartial tribunal'.

[69] Charter, s 7.

[70] Passed in 1960, the Bill of Rights articulates certain rights and freedoms as standards for federal legislation. However, it does not permit courts to strike down inconsistent laws; all federal laws shall not 'abrogate, abridge or infringe' the rights therein described. Though it remains in force, the Bill largely has been superseded by the Charter. Bill of Rights SC 1960, c 44; RSC 1985.

[71] US Constitution, Amendments V, XIV.

[72] The Canadian Bill of Rights does use the phrase 'fundamental justice' in the context of the right to a fair hearing, but it is narrowly interpreted: *R v Duke*, [1972] SCJ No 67, [1972] SCR 917 (SCC).

[73] *Lochner v New York*, 198 US 45 (1905) [*Lochner*]. The case is almost universally discredited and identified with the worst excesses of judicial power. Geoffrey R Stone, Louis Michael Seidman and Cass R Sunstein, *Constitutional Law* (New York: Aspen, 2001) 718, citing B Siegan, *Economic Liberties and the Constitution* (Chicago: University of Chicago Press, 1980) 23.

applied a concept called 'substantive economic due process'[74] to invalidate both state and federal laws aimed at promoting social welfare. The US Court eventually changed course but not before falling into disrepute.[75] That said, the Court did not abandon the interpretative technique, albeit employing it to very different effect in endorsing, inter alia, a fundamental right to 'privacy' in *Griswold v Connecticut*[76] and *Roe v Wade*.[77]

When a Special Joint Committee of Parliament debated the text of the Constitution Act 1982, federal officials testified that the meaning of 'fundamental justice' was like 'natural justice'.[78] They did not believe that it reasonably could be used in a *Lochner*-type fashion.[79]

The interpretation of section 7, then, raised two issues: the proper meaning of 'fundamental justice', and the legitimate bounds of judicial review. In a brief, *per curiam* opinion, the British Columbia Court of Appeal rejected the idea that section 7 protects only procedural due process. Such a narrow approach did not account for the section's constitutional status. The Constitution Act 1982 provides the courts with 'jurisdiction to look at not only the *vires* of the legislation and whether the procedural safeguards required by natural justice are present but to go further and consider the content of the legislation'.[80]

The BC Court also stated that proof of fault is a fundamental penal principle based on 'revulsion against the punishment of the morally innocent'.[81] Section 7 elevated that requirement to a 'principle of fundamental justice'. In the instant case, where the province had simply sought to reverse the effect of an earlier judicial decision,[82] it had not demonstrated that the law was a 'reasonable limit' under section 1.[83]

[74] Under this concept, an individual's liberty of contract and rights in property are protected against unwarranted economic interference. The locus of the inquiry is not the *manner* in which rights or liberties are infringed but the state choice to infringe those rights in the first place.

[75] During the *Lochner* era (from 1905 to about 1930), the Supreme Court invalidated about 200 economic regulations, though it upheld a roughly equivalent number. In response, President Roosevelt threatened to increase the Court's composition from nine to 15. See Franklin Delano Roosevelt, 'A "Fireside Chat" Discussing the Plan for Reorganizing the Federal Judiciary' (Washington, DC, 9 March 1937) in Robert Jackson, *The Struggle for Judicial Supremacy* (New York: Knopf, 1941) 343–44.

[76] *Griswold v Connecticut*, 381 US 479 (1965) ('penumbra' of the Constitution protects a right of 'marital privacy'; States may not criminalize contraceptives).

[77] *Roe v Wade* 410 US 113 (1973) (decision to terminate pregnancy before foetal viability protected against state intrusion under the fundamental right to 'privacy').

[78] *Re Motor Vehicle* (n 57). 'Natural justice' entails largely procedural protections such as the right to make representations, and to receive reasons.

[79] The Deputy Minister of Justice, for example, said: 'We assume that the Court would look at that much like a Court would look at the requirements of natural justice, [which] is quite familiar to courts and [to which] they have given a good deal of specific meaning. We would think that the Court would find in that phraseology principles of fundamental justice a meaning somewhat like natural justice or inherent fairness'. Cited in *Re Motor Vehicle*, ibid at para 36.

[80] *Re MVA (1983)* (n 65) at para 9.

[81] ibid, para 22 citing *Sault Ste Marie* (n 67).

[82] *R v Prue; R v Baril* (1979), 1979 CanLII 227 (SCC), 46 CCC (2d) 257, 96 DLR (3d) 577, [1979] 2 SCR 547.

[83] Section 1 of the Charter provides: 'The *Canadian Charter of Rights and Freedoms* guarantees the rights and freedoms set out in it subject only to such reasonable limits prescribed by law as can be demonstrably justified in a free and democratic society'.

On appeal, the Supreme Court[84] acknowledged the sensitivity around judicial overreach – the fears that the Charter would usher in a judicial 'super legislature'.[85] It characterised such concerns as having been rendered moot by the political fact of entrenchment.[86] The Court rejected any suggestion that it should allow 'the American debate to define the issue'.[87] While lessons provided by that country would be helpful, they could not definitively settle the meaning of particular provisions in Canada's Constitution.

Rather than a binary choice between categories of protection, the Court stated, the question required a 'purposive approach' that could ensure the provisions' full benefit.[88] The purposive approach was inconsistent with a strictly procedural interpretation of a Charter right.[89]

Because the patriation process produced a robust record on the meaning to be accorded to various Charter provisions,[90] including statements by public officials, the Court had to consider the proper role, if any, of extrinsic evidence. Recall that, in the *Inflation Act Reference*, the Court had decided that, after years of refusing to receive such evidence, it now would.[91] In *Re Motor Vehicle* it affirmed that approach but said that the minutes of constitutional debates would carry minimal evidentiary weight. In part, this was because of the difficulty of ascertaining the intentions of an individual within a group versus the group itself.[92] But, equally,

[84] The reference was heard by seven judges. Lamer J wrote a majority opinion for five. McIntrye and Wilson JJ wrote separate concurring reasons. Lamer J's opinion has eclipsed all other judicial pronouncements on the issue.

[85] *Re Motor Vehicle* (n 57) at para 15.

[86] ibid: 'It ought not to be forgotten that the historic decision to entrench the *Charter* in our Constitution was taken not by the courts but by the elected representatives of the people of Canada. It was those representatives who extended the scope of constitutional adjudication and entrusted the courts with this new and onerous responsibility. Adjudication under the *Charter* must be approached free of any lingering doubts as to its legitimacy'.

[87] ibid at para 17.

[88] ibid at para 20.

[89] ibid at para 26: 'it would be wrong to interpret the term "fundamental justice" as being synonymous with natural justice. To do so would strip the protected interests of much, if not most, of their content and leave the "right" to life, liberty and security of the person in a sorely emaciated state. Such a result would be inconsistent with the broad, affirmative language in which those rights are expressed and equally inconsistent with the approach adopted by this Court toward the interpretation of *Charter* rights in *Law Society of Upper Canada v Skapinker*, [1984] 1 SCR 357, *per* Estey J, and *Hunter v Southam Inc.*'.

[90] Adam Dodek (ed), *The Charter Debates: the Special Joint Committee on the Constitution, 1980–81, and the Making of the Canadian Charter of Rights and Freedoms* (Toronto: University of Toronto Press, 2018).

[91] See the discussion in Chapter 5. *Re: Anti-Inflation Act*, [1976] 2 SCR 373; *Re Residential Tenancies Act, 1979*, [1981] 1 SCR 714; and *Re: Authority of Parliament in relation to the Upper House*, [1980] 1 SCR 54.

[92] *Re Motor Vehicle* (n 57) at paras 51–52: 'the *Charter* is not the product of a few individual public servants, however distinguished, but of a multiplicity of individuals who played major roles in the negotiating, drafting and adoption of the *Charter*. How can one say with any confidence that within this enormous multiplicity of actors … the comments of a few federal civil servants can in any way be determinative? Were this Court to accord any significant weight to this testimony, it would in effect be assuming a fact which is nearly impossible of proof. In view of the indeterminate nature of the data, it would in my view be erroneous to give these materials anything but minimal weight'.

the Court thought it essential that the Charter not be 'frozen in time to the moment of adoption with little or no possibility of growth, development and adjustment to changing societal needs'.[93] Drawing on the *Persons Case*, and referring explicitly to the Charter as a 'living tree', the Court insisted that the latter document must 'have the possibility of growth and adjustment over time', and that historical materials 'not stunt its growth'.[94]

Section 7's protected interests (life, liberty and security of the person) are qualified by the principles of fundamental justice which also required elucidation. Some of those principles existed at common law, and others had been recognised through international agreements. What united them was the sense that they are 'essential elements of a system for the administration of justice … founded upon human dignity and the rule of law'.[95] Crucially, the principles did not 'lie in the realm of general public policy but in the inherent domain of the judiciary as guardian of the justice system'.[96] Requiring as a precondition of criminal conviction that the Crown prove fault was one such principle.[97]

In *Re Motor Vehicle* the Supreme Court sought to accomplish two things: (1) explain how a section described during constitutional debate as providing only a heightened due process protection could enable substantive review; and (2) quell criticism of such review undertaken by the courts. While the Court's accomplishment of those goals has been subject to debate,[98] there is no question that it set forth a powerful template for all future section 7 jurisprudence and a robust defence of its new role.

For a number of reasons, the *Motor Vehicle Reference* is a notable advisory opinion.

First, the Court grounded the principles of fundamental justice in the common law. The principles were defined as those that the *courts* have, over time, come to recognise as essential to the administration of justice. The primary way to uncover them is through *judicial* decisions. Strikingly, with respect to a Charter section the boundaries of which were seen as *particularly* threatening to the separation

[93] ibid at para 53.
[94] ibid at para 53.
[95] ibid at para 30.
[96] ibid at para 31.
[97] The Court did not engage in a lengthy discussion of s 1. But, but in a passage that has proven to have extraordinary staying power, it endorsed a strict threshold for justifying a s 7 violation. Discussing when 'administrative expediency' might count as 'reasonable limit', Justice Lamer noted that only cases arising out of 'exceptional conditions, such as natural disasters, the outbreak of war, epidemics, and the like' would qualify. Ibid paras 30–31. Over time, the initial narrow articulation of a particular justification (administrative expediency) morphed into a general judicial reluctance to use s 1 to uphold s 7-infringing laws. No Supreme Court majority has ever done so.
[98] Peter Hogg criticised the Court for proclaiming proof of fault as a principle of fundamental justice given that absolute liability had been common in criminal offences: Peter W Hogg *Constitutional Law of Canada* (5th edn sup) 47.10(b). But Don Stuart strongly praised it: 'Four springboards from the Supreme Court of Canada: Hunter, Therens, Motor Vehicle Reference and Oakes – asserting basic values of our criminal justice system' (1987) 12(2) Queen's Law Journal 131–54.

of powers, the Court proclaimed itself the guarantor of those boundaries. It could have defined the principles as those already enumerated in the Charter's legal rights. But it settled on a much broader approach.

Second, the issue in the *Motor Vehicle Reference* may well have benefited from being considered as a reference instead of during the inter partes litigation that otherwise would have been required. A provincial highway traffic charge against a single individual does not easily afford opportunities for the kind of analysis that a reference can produce. That is likely to be the case for most absolute liability offences. The questions around the scope of section 7 were well known, as were the fears of its overreach. Some provinces had been perturbed by the prospect of Charter review from the beginning. While a live case would have vigorously debated the basic unfairness of absolute liability, the more sweeping constitutional argument may have been somewhat muted.

Such arguments would have arisen eventually.[99] But the dynamic created by the reference may well have motivated the courts to take a firm stand at the first opportunity, in a proceeding where their input had been sought by some of the very actors which earlier had opposed that judicial role in setting constitutional norms.

Finally, the *Motor Vehicle Reference* may have been an early portent of the collapse of meaningful distinctions between references and cases. Once they determined that the law was deficient under section 7, the BC and Supreme Courts declined to canvass other possible infringements of fair trial rights under section 11(d).[100] On one hand, that approach could be defended as a sensible one rooted in judicial economy and restraint. On the other, given the underpinnings of a 'fair trial' that were at issue, it is striking that the courts fell back on a well-established feature of live cases, namely 'say only what is necessary to resolve the dispute'.

B. The Rule of Law (*Manitoba Language*)

Another early reference opinion with similarly broad impact is *Re Manitoba Language Rights*. The Manitoba Act had enabled the province's entry into Confederation in 1870. In so doing, it authorised the use of both English and French in the legislature and the courts and required that statutes 'be printed and published' in both languages.[101] Yet, Manitoba continued to publish its laws solely in English.

[99] Important, precedent-setting rulings in regulatory offences include *R v Wholesale Travel Group Inc.*, [1991] 3 SCR 154; *Lévis (City) v Tétreault*; *Lévis (City) v 2629-4470 Québec Inc.*, [2006] 1 SCR 420, 2006 SCC 12.

[100] An argument under s 12 of the Charter – which guarantees against cruel and unusual punishment or treatment – also had been raised but was not considered beyond the first instance court.

[101] Manitoba Act 1870, RSC 1970, App II.

Indeed, in 1890 the province enacted a law – the Official Languages Act – that established English as the official language.[102]

Despite numerous court rulings finding the Official Languages Act to be ultra vires,[103] the unilingual laws remained in place.[104] After Manitoba unsuccessfully tried to initiate a constitutional amendment to change its obligation, the federal government launched a reference. It noted the importance of resolving the matter 'as expeditiously as possible'.[105]

It is rare to find a constitutional issue so starkly presented. In *Manitoba Language Rights*, the constitutional obligation was clear[106] and the province's actions dilatory at best.[107] The Supreme Court noted that the protections in the Manitoba Act were 'a specific manifestation' of Franco-Manitoban linguistic rights for which, as guardian of the Constitution, the judiciary bore responsibility.[108]

The legal conclusion was unsurprising. But it raised another issue. By virtue of the Constitution's supremacy clause, almost all laws enacted by the Manitoba legislature after 1980 were surely null. That, the Court said, would lead to chaos. '[C]ourts, administrative tribunals, public officials, municipal corporations, school boards, professional governing bodies, and all other bodies created by law … would be acting without legal authority'.[109] The composition of the Manitoba Legislature would be in doubt. Further, all rights and obligations owing to statute would be subject to challenge.

Such a result would be incompatible with the 'unwritten postulate [that forms] the very foundation of the Constitution' – the rule of law.[110] The rule of law, the

[102] An Act to Provide that the English Language shall be the Official Language of the Province of Manitoba 1890 (Man.), c 14.

[103] *Pellant v Hebert*, St Boniface Co Ct, 9 March 1892, reported at (1981) 12 RGD 242. See also *Bertrand v Dussault*, 30 January 1909, County Court of St Boniface (unreported), reproduced in *Re Forest and Registrar of Court of Appeal of Manitoba*, (1977) 77 DLR (3d) 445 (Man. CA), at 458–62; *R v Forest*, (1976) 74 DLR (3d) 704 (Man. Co Ct); *Attorney General of Manitoba v Forest*, [1979] 2 SCR 1032.

[104] It appears that at least some of the early disregard was owing to the relative obscurity of the decisions: *Re Manitoba Language* (n 58) at 733. That cannot be the case for the later decisions, of course, nor for the province's enactment of An Act Respecting the Operation of Section 23 of the Manitoba Act in Regard to Statutes 1980 (Man.), c 3, which authorised 'the bilingual promulgation of legislation in two stages: (i) the enactment of a statute in one official language only; and (ii) subsequent translation into the other official language'. *Re Manitoba Language*, ibid at 776.

[105] ibid at 728–29.

[106] That is not to say there was no debate at all. In particular, arguments arose over whether the provisions of the Manitoba Act were 'directory' rather than 'mandatory'. If 'directory', failure to comply with them would not render the actions taken under that failure a nullity. In *Bilodeau v Attorney General of Manitoba*, [1981] 5 WWR 393, a majority of the Manitoba Court of Appeal relied on that distinction to uphold the validity of certain impugned laws. The Supreme Court rejected it as appropriate for constitutional provisions: *Manitoba Language*, ibid at 741.

[107] After 1982 the province complied with the bilingual requirement, but only with respect to new public legislation. Amendments and private acts continued to be published in English only. *Manitoba Language*, ibid at 734.

[108] ibid at 744–45.

[109] ibid at para 56.

[110] ibid at para 66. Note that the rule of law is mentioned in the Constitution Act 1982, but only in the Preamble: 'Whereas Canada is founded upon principles that recognize the supremacy of God and the rule of law'.

Court said, requires 'the creation and maintenance of an actual order of positive laws which preserves and embodies the more general principle of normative order'.[111] In other words, by giving effect to the Constitution in this case the Court at the same time would seriously undermine it.

Destroying 'the positive legal order which has purportedly regulated the affairs of the citizens of Manitoba since 1890' was unacceptable.[112] Yet that is what the Constitution seemed to require. Could the competing demands be reconciled? The Court concluded that they could, by 'declaring' the laws invalid but permitting them to have continued force and effect for the minimum period of time necessary for re-issue of the offending statutes in both languages.[113]

The Court noted that in other jurisdictions, facing situations of civil war,[114] insurgency[115] and constitutional transition,[116] courts have invoked the 'doctrine of necessity' to ensure the continuity of some kind of legal system. The doctrine was 'not used in these cases to support some law which is *above* the Constitution',[117] but to maintain the rule of law which is the foundation of *any* Constitution.[118] While those precedents involved actions taken by the executive or legislative branches, not the courts themselves, their subsequent confirmation on judicial review demonstrated that 'the courts will not allow the Constitution to be used to create chaos and disorder'.[119]

Manitoba Language Rights was a stunning constitutional moment. It continues to reverberate today. The spectre of lawlessness was undoubtedly powerful, and the Court's rationale that there must be some interval during which existing (albeit invalid) laws would continue seems reasonable. But the Court's assertion that it *alone*[120] could prevent anarchy is an extraordinary assertion of judicial supremacy.

[111] ibid at para 60.

[112] As the Court noted, "the rule of law [is] a fundamental postulate of our constitutional structure" (*per* R and J., *Roncarelli v Duplessis*, [1959] SCR 121, at p. 142)'. Moreover, 'the principle is clearly implicit in the very nature of a Constitution'. Ibid at paras 63–64.

[113] ibid at para 107: '... the Constitution requires that temporary validity and force and effect be given to the current Acts of the Manitoba Legislature from the date of this judgment, and that rights, obligations and other effects which have arisen under these laws ... are deemed temporarily to have been and continue to be effective and beyond challenge. It is only in this way that legal chaos can be avoided and the rule of law preserved'.

[114] *Texas v White*, 74 US 700 (1868); *Horn v Lockhart*, 84 US 570 (1873); *United States v Insurance Companies*, 89 US 99 (1874); *Baldy v Hunter*, 171 US 388 (1898).

[115] *Madzimbamuto v Lardner-Burke* [1969] 1 AC 645 (PC); *Special Reference No. 1 of 1955*, PLR 1956 WP 598.

[116] *Attorney General of the Republic v Mustafa Ibrahim* [1964] Cyprus Law Reports 195.

[117] *Manitoba Language* (n 58) at paras 105–06.

[118] ibid.

[119] ibid.

[120] The Attorney-General of Manitoba, for example, argued that instead of judicial invalidation, the Lieutenant-Governor could protect linguistic rights through the power of reservation. Some interveners even suggested the federal power of disallowance. The Court rejected such arguments because 'it would make the executive branch of the federal government, rather than the courts, the guarantor of constitutionally entrenched language rights'. Ibid at paras 69–70.

Since the opinion, the Pandora's box of suspended declaration has never been closed – indeed, its lid has been torn off. Suspended declarations have moved further and further from the initial *in extremis* justification offered in the reference.[121] Suspensions have, rather, become so *pro forma* that it is their absence that is now noteworthy.[122] The Court has delayed the effect of its rulings where, for example, a law is under-inclusive and a finding of invalidity would negatively affect existing beneficiaries.[123] Somewhat more worrisome, the technique has appeared in the explicit furtherance of what is called constitutional 'dialogue' as a method to allow Parliament breathing room to consider its response to criminal prohibitions found to be invalid.[124] The Court frames its decisions in such cases as rooted in deference to the legislative policy-making function. But it does so by enabling the continued application, up to and including criminal punishment, of laws that have been found to be in violation of the Constitution. The phenomenon seems an odd fit for the Constitution's so-called 'guardian'.

Moreover, it seems significant that such an outsize development in remedial jurisprudence should have occurred in a type of proceeding – an advisory opinion – that that is characterised by its total *separation* from remedies.[125] Chapter 10 revisits the Reference, and what it reveals about advisory opinions more generally.

The situation inspiring the language reference was grave: a province in continuing dereliction of a constitutional duty imposed by explicit political agreement. While English-only legislation did not pose an overt threat to law and order, it damaged the system's perceived commitment to constitutionalism and the rule of law. For a province to remain in such a position risked undermining the state's ability to insist on compliance with other aspects of the new framework. Clearly, it also risked exposing the basic vulnerability of the courts: absent obedience from other actors, they have little other than moral suasion to 'enforce' their opinions.

[121] Robert W Kerr, 'The Remedial Power of the Courts After the Manitoba Language Rights Case' (1986) 6 *Windsor Yearbook of Access to Justice* 252, 267: 'Since the laws continued in force by the Court in the Manitoba Language Rights case represent the status quo in Manitoba, the action taken by the Court is consistent with traditions of judicial conservatism. There is no guarantee that this case marks the beginning of an era of judicial activism in framing remedies for unconstitutional government action. The case does provide a jurisprudential basis for such activism. With the task of remedying violations of the Canadian Charter of Rights and Freedoms in its formative stages, this decision could be the key to a creative approach by the courts to constitutional remedies in the future'.

[122] In a recent decision, an Ontario Superior Court judge immediately struck down an income tax rule requiring charities to devote no more than 10 per cent of their time to 'political activities'. The fact that he did *not* suspend the ruling was considered noteworthy. *Canada Without Poverty v AG Canada*, 2018 ONSC 4147.

[123] *Schachter v Canada*, [1992] 2 SCR 679.

[124] *Canada (Attorney General) v Bedford*, 2013 SCC 72, [2013] 3 SCR 1101 [*Bedford*]; *Carter v Canada (Attorney General)*, 2015 SCC 5, [2015] 1 SCR 331.

[125] Note that suspensions are employed by specialist constitutional courts in some countries, such as Austria. Anna Gamper and Francesco Palermo, 'The Constitutional Court of Austria: Modern Profiles of an Archetype of Constitutional Review' (2008) 3 Journal of Comparative Law 64.

The *Motor Vehicle* and *Manitoba Language Rights* references dealt with matters of high theory, addressing issues in need of clarification in the wake of the Constitution Act 1982. While the questions could have been pursued through inter partes litigation, the advisory function provided some advantages.

Most other references on rights issues during this period tended to arise out of more contingent factors. They revealed governments not especially eager to seek the Court's advice on matters arising specifically under the Constitution Act 1982. Rather, the opinions functioned as episodic reminders of the reference power and its potential to shape constitutional doctrine.

C. Competing Constitutional Interests (*Bill 30*)

Manitoba Language Rights involved an essential part of the Confederation bargain: minority rights.[126] Another post-1982 reference, *Re Bill 30*, also took up this issue, albeit under the rubric of the relationship between section 93 of the Constitution Act and the new Charter.[127] Section 93 grants each province the exclusive power to make laws in relation to education provided that such laws do not impinge upon any existing guarantees for 'Denominational Schools'.[128] In other words, the 1867 Confederation pact included preferential treatment for some religious groups. The Charter, in contrast, guarantees citizens both freedom of religion, and equality without state discrimination on the basis of religion.

For 80 years, it was thought that section 93 guaranteed funding only to primary schools.[129] In 1985, when the province of Ontario proposed to extend that funding through the secondary level, it put a reference to the Court of Appeal asking whether to do so would be consistent with section 93 and with the Charter. A 3–2 majority of the Court of Appeal said that such funding was valid. The matter was then further appealed to the Supreme Court.

The Court concluded that section 93 authorised Ontario to offer funding beyond the primary schools level. Section 93(3) extends protection to schools established *after* the date of Union. Combined with the plenary power granted under section 93(1), that means that a province is not bound to offer only such support as existed at Confederation.

[126] Sir Charles Tupper put the matter thus: 'without this guarantee for the rights of minorities being embodied in that new constitution, we should have been unable to obtain any confederation whatever'. Speech before the House of Commons, 3 March 1896.

[127] *Reference re Bill 30, An Act to Amend the Education Act (Ont.)*, [1987] 1 SCR 1148 [*Re Bill 30*]. Dale Gibson, 'Are Some Supreme Laws More Supreme than Others?: Reference re Bill 30, An Act to Amend the Education Act' (1988) 67(1) Canadian Bar Review 142–53.

[128] Rights to the same effect were entrenched under s 17 of the Alberta Act, RSC 1985, App II, No 20, and Saskatchewan Act, RSC 1985, App II, No 21, s 22 of the Manitoba Act 1870, RSC 1985, App II, No 8, and Term 17 of the Terms of Union of Newfoundland with Canada as confirmed by the Newfoundland Act, RSC 1985, App II, No 32.

[129] *Tiny Separate School Trustees v The King*, [1927] SCR 637.

Re Bill 30's most important conclusions were with respect to the interaction between the denominational rights guaranteed under the CA 1867 and the minority rights additionally protected by the Charter. In a system that guarantees (a) state neutrality with respect to religion and (b) an individual right to access public benefits on a non-denominational basis, such preferential treatment ordinarily would be constitutionally suspect. If so, Confederation's protection of denominational education would be inconsistent with the Charter and, possibly, with the entire constitutional vision of patriation. *Re Bill 30*, then, presented an important early indicator of the Charter's potential, scope and its effect on the rest of the Constitution.

The Court concluded that the Charter did not support a collateral attack on section 93.[130] Justice Estey, writing for two judges, stated that the Charter was 'not envisaged in our jurisprudence as providing for the automatic repeal of any provisions of the Constitution of Canada'. While action taken under the Constitution Act 1867 was subject to Charter review, 'sub-section 93(3) expressly contemplates that the province may legislate with respect to a religiously-based school system funded from the public treasury'.[131]

Justice Wilson went even further than this, stating that 'the rights or privileges protected by s. 93(1) are *immune* from Charter review'.[132] She appeared to rest that conclusion on the primacy of those older rights to the Confederation bargain:

> The Confederation compromise in relation to education is found in the whole of s. 93, not in its individual parts. What the province gives pursuant to its plenary power the province can take away, subject only to the right of appeal to the Governor General in Council. But the province is master of its own house when it legislates under its plenary power in relation to denominational, separate or dissentient schools. This was the agreement at Confederation and, in my view, it was not displaced by the enactment of the *Constitution Act, 1982*.[133]

The Court's resolution of *Bill 30* was an important early sign of judicial deference for pre-Charter constitutional arrangements. The Court signalled that it would not be a vehicle for rolling back those Confederation-era protections. In subsequent cases, the Court would hew to that early non-interventionist attitude.[134]

D. Revisiting Past Decisions (*Prostitution*)

In the 1990 *Prostitution Reference*, the Court was asked to analyse the criminal offences of keeping a common bawdy house; and communicating in a public

[130] This was done in Newfoundland in 1998: Constitution Amendment, 1998 (Newfoundland Act) (see SI/98-25) and the Constitution Amendment, 2001 (Newfoundland and Labrador) (see SI/2001-117); and Quebec in 1997: Constitution Amendment, 1997 (Quebec) (see SI/97-141).

[131] *Re Bill 30* (n 127) at para 80.

[132] ibid at para 62 (emphasis added).

[133] ibid at para 63.

[134] *Adler v Ontario*, [1996] 3 SCR 609; *Ontario English Catholic Teachers' Assn. v Ontario (Attorney General)*, [2001] 1 SCR 470, 2001 SCC 15.

place for the purpose of engaging in prostitution.[135] The issue arose following a provincial court decision holding that the communicating offence was inconsistent with section 7 of the Charter and therefore of no force or effect.[136] The trial judge also made reference to the interaction of those provisions with section 2(b) of the Charter (which guarantees freedom of expression) but agreed with previous rulings finding such behaviour to be not 'expression', which is protected, but 'conduct', which is not.[137] The matter was pursued as a reference to the Court of Appeal for Manitoba[138] before being appealed to the Supreme Court.

A majority of the Court found that the laws were inconsistent with section 2(b) but saved under section 1; and consistent with section 7.[139] Writing for three judges, Dickson CJC concluded that, while soliciting was prima facie protected under section 2(b), the impugned law was a reasonable limit. Keeping a common bawdy house, he said, did not implicate a person's freedom of expression. And, while both laws subjected individuals to the risk of imprisonment, neither breached section 7's principles of fundamental justice.[140]

The evidentiary record before the Court was sparse.[141] The trial record and appeal book included just one 1985 parliamentary report on the subject.[142] A single non-governmental intervener, the Canadian Organization for the Rights of Prostitutes, appeared. The reference contains relatively little in the way of social science information about the actual conditions of the sex trade, or the law's negative effects on the class of workers most likely to be affected.

For two decades, the reference was treated as settled law.[143] Then, in 2012, the Supreme Court considered a new challenge to the same provisions[144] as well as one other: the crime of living on the avails of prostitution. In the new case, *Bedford*,[145] the lower courts accepted that they were, in principle, bound to follow the *Prostitution Reference*.[146] They did not rest any of their analysis of precedent or

[135] *Reference re ss. 193 and 195.1(1)(c) of the Criminal Code (Man.)*, [1990] 1 SCR 1123 [*Prostitution Reference*].

[136] *R v Cunningham* (1986), 31 CCC (3d) 223 (Man. Prov. Ct.). The judge also mentioned s 2(b) of the Charter.

[137] ibid at para 42.

[138] *Re Constitutional Questions Act*, 1987 CanLII 991 (MB CA).

[139] The matter was heard before seven judges but one, McIntyre J., did not take part in the opinion.

[140] Lamer J reached the same conclusions, but also stated that 'liberty' does not protect the right to practise a 'profession'. L'Heureux-Dubé and Wilson JJ dissented. They thought s 195's infringement of expression was not a proportional limit because it was insufficiently tailored in light of the restriction it placed on an otherwise legal, constitutionally protected activity.

[141] 'Prostitution' was the term expressly used by Parliament in the relevant provisions. In the wake of the decision in *Bedford v Canada* and consequent legislation, the Code now refers to 'providing or obtaining sexual services for consideration': Criminal Code, s 213, 2014, C 25 s 14.

[142] Special Committee on Pornography and Prostitution. *Pornography and Prostitution in Canada*: report of the Special Committee on Pornography and Prostitution, Ottawa, 1985.

[143] In *R v Downey*, [1992] SCJ No 48, [1992] 2 SCR 10 (SCC), the Court narrowly upheld a reverse onus in s 212(1)(f) of the Criminal Code, which prohibits living on the avails of prostitution. The issue of how a reference could be so regarded is the subject of Chapters 9 and, especially, 10.

[144] Criminal Code, ss 210, 212(1)(f) and 213(1)(c).

[145] *Bedford* (n 124).

[146] ibid at paras 31, 41.

stare decisis on the fact that the precedent derived from a reference rather than a case. That aspect of the decision is discussed in the Chapter 10.

A major difference between the *Prostitution Reference* and *Bedford* was the latter's enormous record, including over 25,000 pages of evidence and numerous affidavits. The trial judge characterised it as both richer and based on research that had not been available in the reference.[147] Her findings as to the law's effects on sex workers, as well as conclusions about the effects of legal regimes in other jurisdictions, appeared to be supported by powerful evidence. In comparison, the *Prostitution Reference*'s treatment of the same issues reads as very sparse.

That difference is not necessarily due to the reference function, as the proceeding itself originated in a trial which appears to have involved relatively little social science argument. It also would have been open to the Supreme Court to appoint an *amicus curiae* to present argument it felt was lacking. Certainly, references may involve enormous amounts of material, as evidenced by the mammoth record compiled for the *Polygamy Reference*, in part because it was heard by a trial-level court.[148]

But *Bedford* was 'test case' litigation, a phenomenon that emerged in the wake of the Charter and is specifically oriented towards rights claims. As a test case, it was initiated by advocates to challenge a law they viewed as highly unjust, not by claimants seeking to derive a personal benefit. The named plaintiffs were selected (by counsel) for their ability to illustrate one or more important effects of the law. The case also featured much greater participation by non-parties, with over two dozen interveners. By contrast, the *Prostitution Reference* featured five Attorneys General and only one non-government group.

Of the two judicial engagements with prostitution, *Bedford* is, indeed, richer and more developed. However, the reasons for that may have less to do with the nature of the litigation than the time and context in which it arose. In particular, the trajectory of section 7 case law had expanded far beyond its conceptualisation in either the *Motor Vehicle* or *Prostitution* references. Evidence-gathering techniques were employed, to devastating effect, to bring home the enormous risks borne by sex workers permitted to exchange sex for money so long as they kept themselves hidden from view and socially unobtrusive. The Conservative government of Prime Minister Stephen Harper, which had pursued policies and rhetoric openly hostile to judicial review on Charter grounds, aggressively defended the laws in zero-sum terms. The trial judge engaged in an exhaustive, expert review. All combined to produce a dramatic result.

Given the differences between the two proceedings, it is interesting to note how *Bedford* dealt with the apparent 'precedent' created in the *Prostitution Reference*. How could the conclusions in the reference be, as it were, re-litigated? Essentially, in *Bedford* the Supreme Court embraced a modification to the normal rules of

[147] ibid at para 17.
[148] *Reference re Section 293 of the Criminal Code of Canada*, [2011] BCJ No 2211, 279 CCC (3d) 1.

stare decisis, providing a template on which older decisions may be revisited in the wake of previously unavailable evidence or sufficiently important legal shifts so as to make the prior conclusions apt for revisiting. That process is discussed more in Chapter 10 for it reveals a Court mostly unconcerned with any real distinction between reference opinions and cases.

E. The Intersection of Individual Rights, Federalism and Politics (*Same-Sex Marriage*)

I have already noted how references are sometimes the product of contingency. A good example of this is *Same-Sex Marriage*.[149] Aspects of the reference were discussed in the chapter on the separation of powers and are taken up again in the book's final two chapters. Here, the reference is examined for its tricky occupation of a contested space in a federal system.

The matter was initiated by the federal government in the wake of successive LGBTQ victories in the early 2000s (in inter partes litigation)[150] that had challenged the opposite-sex-limited, common law definition of 'marriage'. While gay marriage did not yet enjoy widespread public support, the federal government grew reluctant to continue to oppose it outright.[151] Thus, instead of appealing the losses, the government put three questions directly to the Supreme Court: one on the federal authority to pass draft legislation (the Civil Marriage Act) recognising the capacity of same-sex couples to marry; one on the draft law's 'consistency' with the Charter; and one on the freedom of religious officials to refuse to solemnise them. Some months later, a fourth question was added: whether the common law definition of marriage was itself inconsistent with the Charter.[152] Its initial omission was odd. Only after significant public pressure did the federal government agree to it, and it declined to present argument about it.

The reference attracted 25 interveners. It was a constitutional cause célèbre – viewed as the culmination of a decades-long struggle towards equality for LGBTQ persons. Yet, the Court's disposition of the reference was curious.

[149] *Reference re Same-Sex Marriage*, [2004] 3 SCR 698, 2004 SCC 79 [*Same-Sex Marriage*].

[150] *Hendricks c Québec (PG)*, [2004] RJQ 851 (CA); *Halpern v Toronto (City)*, (2003) 65 OR (3d) 161 (CA); *EGALE Canada v Canada (AG)*, (2003) 13 BCLR (4th) 1, 2003 BCCA 251. At common law, marriage was defined as 'the union of one man and one woman for life, to the exclusion of all others': *Hyde v Hyde*, (1866) LR 1 P & D 130 at 133.

[151] As late as 1999, the federal government had agreed to a parliamentary motion affirming the idea 'that marriage is and should remain the union of one man and one woman to the exclusion of all others' Hansard (8 June 1999) 15960. Prior Supreme Court rulings had contained opinions sympathetic to an opposite-sex-only definition of marriage: *Miron v Trudel*, [1995] 2 SCR 418 at 448–52, Gonthier J, dissenting; *Egan v Canada*, [1995] 2 SCR 513 at 535–39, La Forest J. Even in *M v H* – a near unanimous judgment for a same-sex, common-law spouse – the majority specified that it was not dealing with 'marriage': [1999] 2 SCR 3 at para 134, Cory and Iacobucci JJ.

[152] Order in Council PC 2004-28 (26 Janaury 2004) cited in *Reference re Same-Sex Marriage* (n 164) at para 3.

The Court answered the first question, whether the legislation fell within Parliament's *exclusive* jurisdiction, largely in the affirmative. As the Court noted: the legislation clearly pertained to 'civil marriage'; section 92(27) of the Constitution Act 1982 reserves to the provinces power over 'Solemnization of Marriage'; and it has been settled law since 1912[153] that the question of who may marry – in other words, capacity – falls within federal, not provincial jurisdiction.

The Court's answer about Question 1 drew on such well-established law that it is fair to wonder why the government even felt moved to ask it. Two reasons come to mind. Note, first, that the government did not raise the general issue of which level of government has the jurisdiction over 'capacity to marry'. It asked whether *the proposed legislation* was 'within the exclusive authority of Parliament'. An affirmative answer would nullify jurisdictional objections from the provinces, some of which were likely happy to use a more politically neutral reason (protecting their authority under the division of powers) than the much starker position of asserting opposition to same-sex marriages per se.[154]

Second, in the lower court cases, it had been argued that the word 'marriage' must be understood in its historical context at the time of Confederation. One trial-level judge accepted that argument, holding that absent formal amendment to the division of powers, neither Parliament nor a province could change the word 'marriage' beyond its 1867 meaning.

Once again drawing on the *Persons Case*, the Supreme Court rejected the idea that marriage was a 'frozen concept'. Such an argument ran 'contrary to one of the most fundamental principles of Canadian constitutional interpretation: that our Constitution is a living tree which, by way of progressive interpretation, accommodates and addresses the realities of modern life'.[155]

That answer assisted the federal government in neutralising another tool wielded by opponents of same-sex marriage. While Canadian jurisprudence has rarely accepted the tenets of originalism,[156] with something like marriage it could have had broader public appeal. Some, perhaps many, members of the public would likely have agreed that 'marriage' is subordinate to a long-standing *social* conception of the term that is quite beyond the power of a legislature to critically redefine.[157] The Supreme Court's answer to Question 1 made that argument more difficult to advance.

[153] *In Re Marriage Laws*, (1912) 46 SCR 132.

[154] This is exactly what happened. Those provinces most outspoken in defence of 'traditional marriage' – such as Alberta – quickly conceded that they could not avoid the federal law. For example, the provinces could not use the notwithstanding clause (s 33 of the Charter), because s 33 is unavailable to a legislature with respect to a law that falls outside its powers. Katherine Harding, 'Alberta plans to fight gay marriage', *The Globe and Mail* (10 December 2004) http://www.globeandmail.com.

[155] *Same-Sex Marriage* (n 150) paras 21–23.

[156] Peter Hogg, *Constitutional Law of Canada* (Toronto: Thomson Carswell, 1997) 15–45; *Re Motor Vehicle Reference* (n 57).

[157] See n 151 and surrounding text.

The Court did find fault with section 2 of the legislation, which read: 'Nothing in this Act affects the freedom of officials of religious groups to refuse to perform marriages that are not in accordance with their religious beliefs'. The federal government claimed that section 2 merely attempted to balance the competing interests at stake when a rite often performed by religious officials is extended to include gay and lesbian couples. Though the government argued that the section was declaratory, the Court concluded that it created a legal exemption. Section 2 therefore was ultra vires because only the provinces have the jurisdiction to determine who may solemnise (or be excused from solemnising) civil marriage.

Nonetheless, the final version of the Bill contained a very similar provision.[158] The government said that it was meant simply to reflect the fact that

> religious officials are already protected by the Canadian Charter of Rights and Freedoms from being compelled to perform marriages that would be contrary to their religious beliefs, as confirmed by the Supreme Court of Canada in its opinion on the marriage Reference.[159]

But it is arguable that section 3 and, possibly, section 3.1, of the federal law are inconsistent with the *Same-Sex Marriage Reference.*

Question 2 of the reference asked whether extending capacity to marriage is 'consistent' with the Charter. The government's choice of words suggested that it was 'hedging' its bets: obtaining the Court's approval without ever putting before it the key question (Question 4). The Court said that section 1 of the draft legislation directly responded to the findings of several lower courts that the traditional definition of marriage violates the Charter,[160] and that the law's preamble stated a clear intent to honour the Charter's equality guarantee.[161] The combination, the Court said, meant that the legislation's purpose, 'far from violating the Charter, flows from it'.[162]

Few scholars questioned the constitutionality of section 1 of the draft legislation; yet some of the interveners did raise Charter-based objections. These were mostly weak arguments that the proposed legislation violated the equality rights

[158] Civil Marriage Act SC 2005, c 33:

> 3. It is recognized that officials of religious groups are free to refuse to perform marriages that are not in accordance with their religious beliefs.
>
> 3.1 For greater certainty, no person or organization shall be deprived of any benefit, or be subject to any obligation or sanction, under any law of the Parliament of Canada solely by reason of their exercise, in respect of marriage between persons of the same sex, of the freedom of conscience and religion guaranteed under the *Canadian Charter of Rights and Freedoms* or the expression of their beliefs in respect of marriage as the union of a man and woman to the exclusion of all others based on that guaranteed freedom.

[159] Federal Department of Justice (Canada), Fact Sheet, 'Civil Marriage Act' (1 February, 2005).

[160] *Same-Sex Marriage* (n 149) at para 41.

[161] ibid at para 42.

[162] ibid at para 43.

and religious freedoms of persons who opposed same-sex marriage for religious reasons.[163] Expanding the definition of marriage, supposedly, would create an 'impermissible conflict of rights'[164] in spheres other than its solemnisation. The Court rejected the argument as hypothetical, but not before noting that the Charter provided sufficient means for dealing with such conflict.

Because critics of the legislation invoked the spectre that same-sex marriage ceremonies would be forced on unwilling religious officials, the third question was especially salient. The Court advised that such compulsion emanating from the state clearly would violate section 2(a) of the Charter and that, '[a]bsent exceptional circumstances which we cannot at present foresee, such a violation could not be justified under s. 1'.[165] Section 2(a) also was held to protect against 'the compulsory use of sacred places for the celebration of such marriages and … being compelled to otherwise assist in the celebration of same-sex marriages'.[166]

While *Same-Sex Marriage* confirmed that persons affiliated with religious institutions may not be compelled to perform same-sex marriage ceremonies, it did not address related issues, such as how to deal with civic officials who assert religiously based refusals to perform same-sex ceremonies. Such matters fell to the provinces. The federal Minister of Justice urged them to accommodate such persons.[167] In a follow-up reference, Saskatchewan asked its Court of Appeal whether it would be lawful to permit a marriage commissioner to refuse to solemnise a marriage on religious grounds. In *Re Marriage Commissioners*,[168] the Saskatchewan Court of Appeal advised that *permitting* such an exemption would itself be contrary to the Charter equality rights of same-sex couples.

Finally, there was Question 4 – the principal issue. The federal government, though, was not eager to get an answer to it. Nor, as it turns out, was the Supreme Court eager to provide one. Instead, the Court asserted a number of factors that made it 'unwise and inappropriate' to answer the question.

The Court suggested, though it did not explicitly cite, a mootness problem: the government had indicated that it would 'proceed by way of legislative enactment, regardless of what answer we give to this question'. It raised a fairness issue: 'the parties to previous litigation had relied upon the finality of the judgments they obtained through the court process' and had acquired vested rights. And, finally, it said, answering the question could 'undermine the uniformity that would be achieved by the adoption of the proposed legislation'.[169]

The government's stated goal was to ensure uniformity in the treatment of same-sex couples. But the Court pointed out that were it to hold that the Charter

[163] Factum of the Intervener Canadian Conference of Catholic Bishops paras 52–61.
[164] *Same-Sex Marriage* (n 149) at paras 50–54.
[165] ibid at para 58.
[166] ibid at para 59.
[167] Certain provinces regarded an exemption of this sort as contrary to public policy: 'Don't give officials a licence to discriminate', Editorial, *The Globe and Mail* (7 January 2005) A14.
[168] *Marriage Commissioners Appointed Under The Marriage Act (Re)*, 2011 SKCA 3 (CanLII).
[169] *Same-Sex Marriage* (n 149) at paras 65–69.

did *not* compel the inclusion of same-sex couples within the state institution of marriage, the resulting 'confusion' would threaten that goal. The confusion would emanate from the uncertain status of a reference opinion issued by an apex court that conflicted with a 'final judgment', on the same issue, of a lower one. That line of argument, one of the clearest indicators that the Court itself views reference opinions as being authoritative statements of law, is further discussed in Chapter 10.

The Court's refusal to answer Question 4 had little impact on the social and political impetus to recognise marriage equality. To be sure, opponents used it to continue their campaign. But, the federal government relied on the structural and division-of-powers arguments to secure passage of the Civil Marriage Act, an important policy accomplishment in the Charter era.

Perhaps, by proceeding via a reference rather than an appeal, the federal government deprived both advocates, and the public at large, of a landmark legal decision. The *Same-Sex Marriage Reference* lacks some of the sweeping pronouncements about equality and human dignity displayed in other marriage rulings such as the United States Supreme Court's majority decision in *Obergefell v Hodges*.[170] It is impossible, though, to know exactly how the 2005 Canadian Supreme Court would have answered Question 4. While the trajectory of the Court's LGBTQ equality case law favoured the claimants, prior cases had stopped well short of recognizing same-sex marriage.[171] Perhaps the Court would have divided on the core issue of whether the Charter compelled the redefinition of marriage to include same-sex couples – similar to its division in other cases. It is plausible that at least some of the Court's members would want to avoid appearing divided on such an important rights issue, especially when it seemed highly likely that Parliament would pass legislation in favour of the rights claimants – and settled instead for a 'non-answer'.[172]

That is not to say that the question was not worth answering, or that the Court gave persuasive arguments for refusing to do so.[173] But, in terms of jurisprudential impact, the *Same-Sex Marriage Reference* is a somewhat muted victory for equality rights. Its greater significance lies in the Court's further articulation of its power to refuse to answer, and what its reasons may reveal about the nature of reference authority. That aspect of the reference is discussed in other chapters.

* * *

[170] *Obergefell v Hodges* 576 US _ (2015).

[171] Above n 157.

[172] Admittedly, this analysis requires that (a) at least a significant proportion of the judges believed that the issue was an important one and (b) at least a majority preferred to not answer the question rather than risk a divided opinion. I stress the need for a majority who favoured the claimants because had there been a majority against expanding the definition of 'marriage' one might expect that belief to have manifested in an opinion that attempted to set the (legal) record straight.

[173] For a critique of the court's refusal, see Carissima Mathen, 'Mutability and Method in the *Marriage Reference*' (2005) LV University of New Brunswick Law Journal 43, 53–54.

This chapter canvassed some of the most significant Canadian advisory opinions dealing with rights and rights-related issues. It began with the 1929 *Persons Case*, which, despite occasional criticism, continues largely to define the Court's approach to constitutional interpretation. It then moved to the dramatically different era ushered in by the Constitution Act 1982. In that era, characterised by explicitly entrenched individual and group rights, the Canadian Supreme Court has assumed increasing power. Some of that power was proclaimed through advisory opinions in which the Court outlined its approach to the new order and, just as importantly, its place within it.

The Charter era has not been marked by nearly as many rights-related references as references about the division of powers or other institutions. In the main, governments have been content to wait for such issues to make their way through the system as ordinary litigation. There is a happenstance quality to the references that belies any sort of systemic approach. (That includes the intriguing fact that the post-1982 period has yet to inspire any references dealing specifically with indigenous peoples.) Some of the reasons for initiating, and not initiating, references are canvassed in the book's final two chapters.

All the same, the advisory opinions that have emerged have been noteworthy for their impact. In particular, they are distinctive in their tendency to confirm certain tendencies and developments in constitutional litigation writ large. That focus, in extremely significant, norm-setting litigation, continues in the next chapter.

8

Institutions

This chapter deals specifically with three advisory opinions that have profoundly affected institutional elements of political and legal governance. The *Secession*, *Senate Reform* and *Supreme Court Act References* all concern roles and relationships. In the Supreme Court's own words, they 'combine legal and constitutional questions of the utmost subtlety and complexity with political questions of great sensitivity'.[1]

The references engage fundamental constitutional doctrines, in particular, the relationships between and among federal-provincial actors. *Quebec Secession* confronted an existential question about the permanence of the federation itself. *Senate Reform* examined the legitimate expectations surrounding change to the upper house. *Supreme Court Act* addressed federalism somewhat less directly, by considering the implications of a commitment to constitutionalism for the apex court and the conditions under which its composition and essential features can be changed. The latter two, in particular, considered the required balance between ensuring reasonable prospects for formal constitutional change and the proper provincial input regarding that change.

The references also dealt with significant issues vis-à-vis the separation of powers and, in particular, the role of the Court and the bounds of Parliamentary discretion to enact change at a constitutional level. In all three, the Court can be seen at the centre of debate over constitutional norms. It was asked to, and did, provide answers in highly contested disputes that were inescapably political. While the Court's answers have proved controversial, they are accepted by nearly all relevant actors[2] as articulating the rules and principles applicable to them. Thus, the opinions below demonstrate, to an unmistakeable degree, the Court's deep production of constitutional norms; its confidence in its constitutional role; and its embrace of its advisory role. Moreover, they show the ordinariness of that role in the sense of their reception by everyone.

Rupture, for Real: Quebec Secession

The first opinion, *Reference re Secession of Quebec*,[3] is known both within Canada and internationally. It was the product of a long-simmering national tension thrust into high and urgent relief.

[1] *Reference re Manitoba Language Rights*, [1985] 1 SCR 721 at 728, cited in *Secession Reference* (n 3) at para 1.

[2] As discussed below, Quebec is a special case.

[3] *Reference re Secession of Quebec*, [1998] 2 SCR 217 [*Secession Reference*].

As discussed in Chapter 6, a prime motivation for constitutional reform in the 1980s was to counteract separatist sentiment in Quebec. It was especially problematic that the province did not consent to the Constitution Act 1982.[4] In response, the federal government initiated additional constitutional negotiations in what ultimately were unsuccessful attempts to bring Quebec into the Constitution in a political sense, thereby repairing the damage wrought to the federation.[5]

The failed accords[6] exacerbated the situation and likely contributed to a razor-thin result in the 1995 Quebec referendum[7] on sovereignty-association.[8] The Quebec government had introduced a Bill so that, should the referendum be positive, the legislature would issue a unilateral declaration of independence (UDI). A lawyer named Guy Bertrand challenged the Bill on the grounds that it threatened his constitutional rights.[9] Somewhat remarkably, a Superior Court judge agreed with the substance of that argument, though he declined to issue an injunction.

After the separatist side lost the Quebec referendum by a very narrow margin. Bertrand sought a permanent injunction against the issuance of any future UDI. A judge decided that the claim was not hypothetical and identified several issues as appropriate for judicial comment and resolution. Those issues were then taken up by the federal government, which put the following questions to the Supreme Court:

1. Under the Constitution of Canada, can the National Assembly, legislature or government of Quebec effect the secession of Quebec from Canada unilaterally?
2. Does international law give the National Assembly, legislature or government of Quebec the right to effect the secession of Quebec from Canada unilaterally? In this regard, is there a right to self-determination under international law that would give the National Assembly, legislature or government of Quebec the right to effect the secession of Quebec from Canada unilaterally?
3. In the event of a conflict between domestic and international law on the right of the National Assembly, legislature or government of Quebec to effect the secession of Quebec from Canada unilaterally, which would take precedence in Canada?

[4] See the discussion of the *Patriation* and *Quebec Veto References* in Chapter 6.

[5] Meech Lake Constitutional Accord, 1987; Charlottetown Consensus Report, 1992.

[6] See the account in Michael Behiels, 'Canada's Supreme Court, Constitutional Principles, Federalism, and the 1998 Quebec Secession Reference Case: Toxic Wine in a Very Old Bottle?' (2013) 31(2) National Journal of Constitutional Law 129–59; Nadia Verrelli, 'Searching for an Amending Formula: the 115-Year Journey' in E MacFarlane (ed), *Constitutional Amendment in Canada* (Toronto: University of Toronto Press, 2016) 19.

[7] The first referendum was held in 1980.

[8] The 1995 referendum question was: 'Do you agree that Quebec should become sovereign after having made a formal offer to Canada for a new economic and political partnership within the scope of the bill respecting the future of Quebec and of the agreement signed on June 12, 1995?'.

[9] D Schneiderman, *The Quebec Decision: Perspectives on the Supreme Court Ruling on Secession* (Toronto: Lorimer, 2009) 83.

Dubbed 'the case of the century',[10] the reference transfixed the public.[11] The proceedings heightened the tension over national unity.[12] All of Quebec's major political parties objected to the hearing on the basis that it dealt with subjects inappropriate for judicial comment. The province refused to appear at the Supreme Court, necessitating the appointment of an *amicus curiae*, noted separatist André Joli-Coeur, to make submissions that might capture Quebec's position.[13]

The hearing itself involved 13 separate interveners.[14] In the end, the Court advised that Quebec could not achieve secession on its own.[15] Further, being neither oppressed nor subject to colonial rule, Quebec could not pursue secession under international law. The *per curiam* opinion concluded that, as there was no conflict between international and domestic law, it was unnecessary to answer the final question.

The primary question was whether a Canadian province may unilaterally secede from the federation. But the Court's discrete resolution of that issue has in subsequent years been eclipsed by a number of ancillary ones relating to (a) the reference function, (b) unwritten constitutional principles and (c) the conditions under which orders of government are compelled to negotiate, in good faith, a desire by one actor to secede. The discussion below focusses on the first two of those points.

The *amicus curiae* raised threshold arguments about the reference function.[16] In doing so, he recited the familiar objections to advisory opinions made in the 1912 *Reference re References*.[17] The Supreme Court found it appropriate 'In light of the significant changes in the role of this Court since 1912' to revisit the conclusions of the earlier opinion.[18]

[10] Simone Chambers, 'Contract or Conversation? Theoretical Lessons from the Canadian Constitutional Crisis' 1998 26(1) Politics and Society 143.

[11] Florian Sauvageau, David Schneiderman and David Taras, *The Last Word* (Vancouver: UBC Press, 2006) 91.

[12] 'Ottawa plots new betrayal: Bouchard', *The Gazette* (13 May 1997) Al 1, cited in H Wade MacLauchlan, 'Accounting for Democracy and the Rule of Law in the Quebec Secession Reference' (1997) 76 Canadian Bar Review 155, 156.

[13] Pierre Bienvenu, 'Secession by Constitutional Means' (1999–2000) 21 Journal of Public Law and Policy 1, 22. The Order-in-Council was issued on 30 September 1996. The Court approached Joli-Coeur about acting as *amicus* in July 1997.

[14] Interestingly only two provinces (Manitoba and Saskatchewan) participated.

[15] The Court defined the term 'unilateral' thusly: 'In one sense, any step towards a constitutional amendment initiated by a single actor on the constitutional stage is "unilateral". We do not believe that this is the meaning contemplated by Question 1, nor is this the sense in which the term has been used in argument before us. Rather, what is claimed by a right to secede "unilaterally" is the right to effectuate secession without prior negotiations with the other provinces and the federal government'. *Secession Reference* (n 3) at para 86.

[16] For further discussion, see Bruce Ryder, 'A Court in Need and a Friend Indeed: An Analysis of the Arguments of the Amicus Curiae in the Quebec Secession Reference' (1998) 10 Constitutional Forum 9–13.

[17] *Re References by Governor-General in Council*, (1910) 43 SCR 536, affirmed on appeal to the Privy Council, [1912] AC 571 [*Reference re References*].

[18] *Secession Reference* (n 3) at para 6.

In the end, the Court confirmed that the reference function was well within the bounds of the Constitution.

The *amicus* argued that, in order to be valid, an advisory function must find express mention in the Constitution. He cited as examples India (where it does, and is thus recognised) and the United States (where it does not, and is shunned).[19] The Court rejected the comparison to the US Constitution because the latter's 'Article III' expressly describes a *limitation* on federal courts (they can decide only 'cases and controversies').[20] The US example could not support the argument that, absent specific textual support, a judicial advisory role is unjustified in *any* constitutional system.[21] Additionally, the Canadian Constitution 'does not insist on a strict separation of powers'. Therefore, 'Parliament and the provincial legislatures may properly confer other legal functions on the courts, and may confer certain judicial functions on bodies that are not courts'.[22]

The *amicus* also urged the Court to conclude that, because they entailed consideration of international law, the reference questions lay outside section 53 of the Supreme Court Act in any event.[23] The Court rejected that submission as well. The reference questions, it noted, were directed at least partially to constitutional interpretation, or to legislative and executive powers. They thus fell within the very broad class of questions that may be referred to the Court.

Lastly, the *amicus* argued that the questions were theoretical, political and not ripe – in other words, non-justiciable.[24] Therefore, even if not expressly excluded from consideration by section 53, the nature of the questions was such that the Court should decline to answer them.

The Court first said that the concept of justiciability applies differently to advisory opinions than to cases, precisely because the Court 'is acting in an advisory capacity'. Hypothetical questions clearly may be asked, for example concerning the constitutionality of proposed legislation. That indicated that the function was one which 'engages the Court in an exercise it would never entertain in the context of litigation'. Because 'a reference does not engage the Court in a disposition of rights … the Court may deal on a reference with issues that might otherwise be considered not yet "ripe" for decision'.[25]

The Court's disposition of the justiciability questions is one of the few times it has specifically discussed the difference between advisory opinions and ordinary cases. It observed that many references involve hypothetical questions. A court *may* refuse to answer such a question where to do so 'would take the Court beyond

[19] ibid at para 12.
[20] ibid at para 13, citing *Muskrat v United States*, 219 US 346 (1911) at 362.
[21] ibid at paras 113, 15.
[22] ibid at para 15.
[23] Section 53 is reproduced in Chapter 3.
[24] *Secession Reference* (n 3) at para 24.
[25] ibid at para 25.

its own assessment of its proper role in the constitutional framework'; or where an answer required the Court to stray beyond legal interpretation.[26] (Then again, the Court did not acknowledge that the Supreme Court Act imposes on it a duty to answer.)

Answering the questions would not 'usurp any democratic decision that the people of Quebec may be called upon to make' but merely would articulate aspects of the legal framework under which such a decision would occur. Furthermore, any extralegal aspects were severable from the clear legal context.[27] Given the 'fundamental public importance' of the questions, and similar to what the majority said in the *Patriation Reference* (discussed in Chapter 6), the Court found it appropriate to provide an answer.

Turning to the questions themselves, the Court noted that the Constitution has a basic structure that functions as its architecture: a series of interlinked provisions upon which the proper interpretation of the Constitution depends. Crucial to that structure are unwritten principles, 'the vital unstated assumptions upon which the [constitutional] text is based'.[28]

The Court stressed that unwritten principles are central to the Canadian Constitution. Such principles 'assist in the interpretation of the text and the delineation of spheres of jurisdiction, the scope of rights and obligations, and the role of our political institutions'.[29] They 'may in certain circumstances give rise to substantive legal obligations' which can be 'very abstract and general' or 'more specific and precise'. They are 'not merely descriptive, but are also invested with a powerful normative force [that is] binding upon both courts and governments'.[30]

The Court identified four such principles – federalism, democracy, constitutionalism and the rule of law, and respect for minorities – relevant to the question at hand.[31] Elaborating on each of them in turn, the Court explained that they function in 'symbiosis', that none can be 'defined in isolation', nor may it any 'trump or exclude the [others'] operation'.[32]

The Court determined that there was no basis in either Canadian or international law to justify Quebec seceding by means of a unilateral act.[33] In particular, while 'secession' was not expressly mentioned in Part V of the

[26] ibid at para 26, citing *Reference re Canada Assistance Plan (BC)*, [1991] 2 SCR 525, at 545.

[27] ibid at paras 27–28.

[28] ibid at para 49. For critique of the Court's use of architecture, see E Macfarlane, 'Unsteady Architecture: Ambiguity, the Senate Reference, and the Future of Constitutional Amendment in Canada' (2015) 60(4) McGill Law Journal 883–903.

[29] ibid at para 52.

[30] ibid at para 54.

[31] Six years later, the Court recognised a fifth defining principle: 'respect for human rights and freedom': *R v Demers* [2004] 2 SCR 489, 2004 SCC 46 at para 83.

[32] ibid at para 49.

[33] The Court did, though, acknowledge that a de facto secession could be achieved, depending upon 'effective control of a territory and recognition by the international community'. Ibid at paras 106, 143. See also Andrew Orkin and Joanna Birenbaum, 'The Aboriginal Argument: The Requirement of Aboriginal Consent' in Schneiderman (n 9) 83.

Constitution Act 1982, it nonetheless would constitute an amendment of the Constitution.[34] Secession, thus, is governed by cooperative negotiating mechanisms set in place precisely to effect formal constitutional change.[35]

The Court could have concluded its 'advice' at that point. It instead engaged in an extended analysis of what would happen in the event of a referendum result *for* secession (perhaps the ultimate 'hypothetical').[36]

A provincial vote in favour of secession would trigger a duty on all parties, it said, to negotiate with each other 'in good faith'. This new step relied entirely on the interaction of the unwritten principles. In the event of a 'clear repudiation of the existing constitutional order' together with 'the clear expression of the desire to pursue secession' there would be a 'reciprocal obligation on all parties to Confederation to negotiate constitutional changes to respond to that desire'.[37]

The reference was groundbreaking.[38] Some applauded.[39] Others expressed deep concern. It was complained that the Court had 'pulled the duty to negotiate out of rarified air'.[40] It was pointed out, too, that the duty had not been argued by any of the parties,[41] suggesting in effect that the Court had gone off on an intellectual frolic.

Having articulated a duty to negotiate, the Court disavowed any responsibility for its oversight. The 'initial impetus for negotiation' was properly 'subject only to political evaluation'. Thus, '[o]nly the political actors would have the information and expertise to make the appropriate judgment' as to how to resolve the various questions that would arise.[42]

Perhaps the disavowal signalled the Court's awareness that it was on less-than-solid constitutional ground.[43] Yet it is unclear that such a monastic stance would persist if, in a situation of *actual* pending secession, parties sought the

[34] *Secession Reference* (n 3) at para 84.

[35] ibid at para 97. The Court did not specify whether the general or unanimity formula would apply. But, in light of the *Senate Reference* (2014) (n 67) it seems unquestionable that the consent of all Confederation actors (unanimity) would be required.

[36] Patrick J Monahan, 'The Public Policy Role of the Supreme Court of Canada in the Secession Reference' (1999) 11 National Journal of Constitutional Law 65, 66.

[37] *Secession Reference* (n 3) at paras 87, 88, 90. The Court did acknowledge that such negotiations might not succeed. But it did not endorse 'the proposition that, at the end of the day, good faith in negotiation extends to actually offering or acceding to secession', Sujit Choudhry and Robert Howse, 'Constitutional Theory and The Quebec Secession Reference' (2000) 13 Canadian Journal of Law & Jurisprudence 143.

[38] Jose Woehrling, 'The Quebec Secession Reference: Some Unexpected Consequences of Constitutional First Principles' in Schneiderman (n 9) 124.

[39] Robert A Young, 'A Most Politic Judgement' in Schneiderman, ibid at 107.

[40] John D Whyte, 'The Secession Reference and Constitutional Paradox' in Schneiderman, ibid at 133.

[41] Monahan (n 36) 103.

[42] *Secession Reference* (n 3) at para 100. Note that at para 105, the Court did note the possibility of further involvement respecting questions that had not been posed, ie, regarding secession attempts that flowed other than from a unilateral declaration of secession.

[43] 'Introduction' in Schneiderman (n 9) 9.

Court's advice. After all, the Court has willingly addressed other issues deemed similarly 'political' and, indeed, non-justiciable – such as the constitutional conventions at work in the *Patriation Reference*. Additionally, a number of elements of the duty-to-negotiate framework – for example, what counts as a 'clear question' or a 'clear majority' – do not seem far removed from the Court's core 'judicial competence'.[44] The Court insisted that any negotiations should be oriented towards *amendment*, not *rupture*, of the Constitution – a Constitution of which the Court asserts that it is the guardian. All of that warrants at least some scepticism at its vow of silence.[45]

The *Secession Reference* is one of the most important advisory opinions the Court has ever issued. Its influence extends far beyond the discrete issue of secession.[46] As with so many other examples discussed in this book, the *Secession Reference* is notable for asserting, at a level that has proven especially resistant to contestation, certain 'truths' about the Canadian constitutional framework.

During oral arguments, the Court appeared most taken with somewhat tangential issues, including: what if negotiations were to break down? what about the territorial interests of aboriginal peoples in Quebec? what about other minority groups?[47] Many of those issues were raised not by the principal parties, but by third-party interveners.[48]

The Court may have been attracted to such issues because it recognised that a bare answer that Quebec could not proceed unilaterally would be politically damaging, including to itself.[49] If so, that may help to explain its acknowledgment of Quebec's place within Canadian society and the Constitution. The Court could 'rehabilitate' itself in the eyes of Quebecers, who could see the justices' open-mindedness, and their concern to develop solutions able to take into account the interests of all groups'.[50] (Whether those ought to have been their preoccupations is another matter.)

[44] Choudhry and Howse (n 37) 160.

[45] That is not to dispute the immense difficulties that would obtain, for example, if the Court's composition favours Quebec over the rest of Canada.

[46] For example, during the 2015 federal election, leaders pressed each other on the standard for determining a successful secession vote. When Justin Trudeau criticised the leader of the New Democratic Party for stating that he would accept the normal majority standard (50 per cent plus one), Trudeau was challenged for his own number. Trudeau responded: 'Nine. Nine justices of the Supreme Court have set the standard'. The moment is thought to have contributed to public acceptance of him as a serious candidate for Prime Minister. Andrew Coyne, 'The moment Trudeau had Mulcair's number', *National Post*, 14 October 2015.

[47] 'Introduction' in Schneiderman (n 9) 7.

[48] ibid.

[49] Consider the following comments of Quebec Premier Lucien Bouchard: 'With the scarcely concealed aim of raising fear among Quebecers, the federal government unilaterally asked nine judges of its own Supreme Court, nine persons whose federalist faith is not in doubt, to pronounce themselves on the Canadian federalist arguments'. Speech delivered on 21 August 1998. Reprinted in Schneiderman (n 9) 95.

[50] Sauvageau, Schneiderman and Taras (n 11) 124. Some of the 'praise' was no doubt performance in the service of saving face. For a contrary view, see Josee Legault 'How to Deny Quebec's Right

In any reference, the court is at the centre of inquiry. But the *Secession Reference* demonstrated the Court's growing comfort with providing critical benchmarks for political actors engaged in a highly perilous discourse concerning 'momentous questions that go to the heart of our system of constitutional government'.[51]

History is not always kind to courts that act as though they can, by sheer force of will, avert pressing political crises or the disintegration of legal orders.[52] Yet, the *Secession Reference*'s legacy is not so stark. That is most likely due to the following factors.

First, and perhaps most importantly, both sides were able to claim victory. Federalists took heart from the Court's rejection of a unilateral right to secede; the fuzziness around what constitutes a 'clear mandate'; and the rejection of a simple majority standard (50 per cent plus 1) to trigger the duty to negotiate. They could take heart, as well, in the opinion's clear preference for an orderly process, informed by rule of law considerations, under which political actors were expected to act in the best interests of all citizens.[53] The Prime Minister called the opinion 'a victory for all Canadians'.[54] At the same time, sovereigntists quickly seized upon the duty on the rest of the country to negotiate in good faith, as well as the endorsement of their right to self-determination (albeit not an absolute right to achieve it).[55]

Second, the Court's articulation of a duty to negotiate closely tracked public opinion about what a 'yes' vote would require.[56] It was an easy-to-understand, 'best option' to avoid further political and social conflict should such a contentious situation ever arise. It also mirrored simultaneously emergent norms about a federal duty to exercise utmost good faith in required negotiations with indigenous persons.

to Self-Determination', *The Globe and Mail*, 21 August 1998, reprinted in Schneiderman (n 9) 115, denouncing the opinion as 'dominating federalism'.

[51] *Secession Reference* (n 3) para 1.

[52] See *Dredd Scott v Sandford*, 60 US 393 (1857) (holding that black persons are not 'citizens of the United States'; finding unconstitutional the Missouri Compromise).

[53] Part of the federal government's response was to pass An Act to give effect to the requirement for clarity as set out in the opinion of the Supreme Court of Canada in the Quebec Secession Reference SC 2000, c 26. The Clarity Act sets out processes and procedures by which the House of Commons will determine that any referendum question concerning the proposed secession of a province is 'clear'. It also enjoins any Minister of the Crown from proposing a constitutional amendment to effect provincial secession 'unless the Government of Canada has addressed, in its negotiations, the terms of secession that are relevant in the circumstances, including the division of assets and liabilities, any changes to the borders of the province, the rights, interests and territorial claims of the Aboriginal peoples of Canada, and the protection of minority rights'.

[54] Speech delivered by Prime Minister Jean Chretien on 21 August 1998, reproduced in Schneiderman (n 9) 92.

[55] 'The reality is that the federalists learned yesterday from the Supreme Court that the clear, reasonable and logical process proposed to the citizens of Quebec by the sovereignists is legitimate and that they will have to negotiate its implementation after a winning referendum.' Bouchard (n 49) 100.

[56] Vuk Radmilovic, 'Strategic Legitimacy Cultivation at the Supreme Court of Canada: Quebec Secession Reference and Beyond' (2010) 43(4) Canadian Journal of Political Science 843, 850.

Third, the notion of 'unwritten constitutional principles', though hardly free from controversy,[57] had by then become a familiar part of constitutional adjudication. As discussed below, the notion has featured in several subsequent references that also have articulated essential components of the nation's institutional relationships.

Sujit Choudhry and Robert Howse have noted the inadequate theoretical justification for many of the reference's claims. Given the Court's express reliance on 'unwritten principles' for the duty to negotiate, they write, it is difficult to gainsay that the Court simply wrote a 'secession clause' into the Constitution.[58] Such a result could nonetheless be defended if one views the events leading to the opinion as evidence of a need for 'extraordinary constitutional interpretation' in which 'the text assumes secondary importance'.[59]

Choudhry and Howse consider whether the fact that the Court was 'invited' to weigh in gave it additional authority that it 'might not possess when deciding cases and controversies'.[60] That said, they found the response to the *amicus* arguments about the reference function lacking. The Court 'remained largely unforthcoming with any general theory about the significance of the reference for the balance of judicial and political action in charting the future evolution of constitutional law and politics'.[61]

One must be careful here not to ignore the broader context behind the opinion's admittedly concise discussion of the reference function. References already had attracted close to a century of jurisprudence and practice. To be sure, it had been some time since a party to Confederation had objected so strenuously to the advisory function. But, assuming that the *amicus curiae* could be taken to be speaking for that party (Quebec), which had utilised references for its own advantage, it is difficult to countenance such objections.[62] The *amicus* arguments about the nature of the specific reference questions, however, were different. In that respect, the Court can be critiqued as adopting inconsistent positions on so-called 'political questions' and its willingness to state an opinion on them.

The *Secession Reference* shows yet again how the advisory function can play a defining role in moments of high constitutional drama. Although the country was not facing a formal demand to separate, the events leading up to the proceedings

[57] Peter Oliver, 'Reform of the Supreme Court of Canada from Within: To What Extent Should the Court Weigh in Regarding Constitutional Conventions?' in Jennifer Smith and Nadia Verrelli (eds), *Democratic Dilemma: Reforming Canada's Supreme Court* (Kingston, ON: McGill-Queens, 2013) 161.

[58] Choudhry and Howse (n 37) 155.

[59] ibid at 156–57. See also Jonathon W Penney, 'Deciding in the Heat of the Constitutional Moment' (2005) 28 Dalhousie Law Journal 217–60.

[60] ibid 156.

[61] ibid.

[62] *Re Objection by Quebec to a Resolution to amend the Constitution*, [1982] 2 SCR 793. Understandably, perhaps, the Court did not avert to this fact!

may be viewed as the sort of 'last resort'[63] circumstance in which the function might be particularly salient.

For Canadian federalists, the 1995 referendum result was extremely discomfiting. The nation was seized with uncertainty, dread and (most alarmingly) growing regional hostility. Arguably, the federal government had two choices: assert its own authority so as to prevent secession, or seek authority from a different source. The first option would 'confront the Schmittean extra-legalism of the Quebec separatists with a unilateral claim of the "enemy" (the federal authorities) about legitimacy'.[64] It would reinforce the idea 'that what was at stake was merely a clash of wills, unresolvable by any agreed or shared legal principles or conception of legitimacy'.[65] The reference function provided an opening for an alternate narrative in which certain legal principles, albeit offered at a level of high abstractness, could draw support from rival interests and, over time, lessen the prospect of dangerous confrontation.

One can see the *Secession Reference* as simultaneously providing clarity about, *and* the parameters for, future contestation. It would be joined, a decade-and-a-half later, by two opinions arising in the context of similarly potent disputes. It is to these opinions, the *Senate Reform (2014)* and *Supreme Court Act References*, that I now turn. Together, they take up the threads of the *Secession Reference*; they foreground the Court once again in the process of constitutional discovery; and they entrench a sense of strong regard and protection for provincial interests in foundational questions of political and constitutional governance.

Amendment, Actors and Judicial Supremacy

Both the *Senate Reform* and *Supreme Court Act References* deal with the Constitution's amending formula. Located in Part V of the Constitution Act 1982, and as discussed in Chapter 6, the formula was a principal driver of patriation. The formula ultimately adopted also had been one of the factors that prompted Quebec's isolation as the province did not view the process as adequately protecting its interest and position in Confederation. Part V prescribes multiple amendment routes which produce ambiguity and uncertainty.[66] It seems to have been tailor made for judicial intervention.

[63] See the discussion in Chapter 3.
[64] Choudhry and Howse (n 37) 166.
[65] ibid at 166.
[66] SA Scott, 'Pussycat, Pussycat or Patriation and the New Constitutional Amendment Processes' (1982) 20 University of Western Ontario Law Review 247, 292–98; Adam Dodek, 'Uncovering the Wall Surrounding the Castle of the Constitution: Judicial Interpretation of Part V of the Constitution Act, 1982' in E MacFarlane (ed), *Constitutional Amendment in Canada* (University of Toronto Press, 2016) 42. See also Kate Glover, 'Hard Amendment Cases in Canada' in Richard Albert, Xenophon Contaides and Alkmene Fotiadou (eds), *Foundations and Traditions of Constitutional Amendment* (Oxford: Hart Publishing, 2017) 273.

A. Frozen in Time: Senate Reform

The *Senate Reform Reference (2014)*[67] was the result of a series of efforts, over many decades and by various political actors, to change the Upper House of the federal Parliament.[68] As of 1982, such changes would have to take into account Part V of the Constitution Act 1982, which mentions the Senate in a number of places.[69]

The Conservative government of Prime Minister Stephen Harper, which held power from 2006 to 2015, had long advocated for a Senate that it called 'equal, elected and effective'.[70] At a minimum, that required the elimination of near-life incumbency (Senators hold office until age 75), and appointments that reflected some form of democratic input rather than executive fiat. To those ends, the government introduced a number of Bills[71] that sought to, inter alia, change the tenure of Senators to renewable eight-year terms, and institute a framework of 'consultative elections'.[72]

Quebec referred the validity of one of those bills to its provincial court of appeal.[73] In 2013 that court concluded that Parliament could not unilaterally

[67] *Reference re Senate Reform*, 2014 SCC 32, [2014] 1 SCR 704 [*Senate Reform*].

[68] The *Upper House* reference is discussed in Chapter 6. See also the account by David E Smith, *The Canadian Senate in Bicameral Perspective* (Toronto: University of Toronto Press, 2000) C3; and the example of PE Trudeau's Bill C-60, Constitutional Amendment Bill (1978), which, among other things, proposed to replace the Senate with a House of the Federation selected through 'indirect election by provincial legislative assemblies and the House of Commons' ibid 52.

[69] CA 1982 Part V. Unanimous consent is required for changes reducing a province's Members of Parliament below a certain level related to the number of its Senators; and the general formula is required to change 'the powers of the Senate and the method of selecting Senators'; however, and somewhat confusingly, Parliament is permitted to 'exclusively make laws amending the Constitution … in relation to … the Senate'. The 'general formula', sometimes called the '7/50 rule', requires the consent of both houses of Parliament, and resolutions passed by at least seven provinces representing at least 50 per cent of the population of the provinces.

[70] The 'Triple E Senate' was a key plank of the Conservative Party of Canada platform. See Conservative Party of Canada, *Stand Up for Canada* (2006); Conservative Party of Canada, *The True North Strong and Free: Stephen Harper's Plan for Canadians* (2008); Conservative Party of Canada, *Here for Canada: Stephen Harper's Low-Tax Plan for Jobs and Economic Growth* (2011).

[71] Bill S-4, Constitution Act 2006 (Senate tenure); Bill C-7, An Act Respecting the Selection of Senators and Amending the Constitution Act, 1867 in Respect of Senate Term Limits, 1st Sess, 41st Parl, 2011 (first reading 21 June 2011); Bill C-20, An Act to Provide for Consultations with Electors on their Preferences for Appointments to the Senate, 2nd Sess, 39th Parl, 2007 (first reading 13 November 2007). All three bills died on the Order Paper.

[72] *Senate Reform* (n 67) at paras 8 and 9:

> Under Bill C-20, the names of the winners of national consultative elections would be submitted to the Prime Minister of Canada, for consideration by him or her when recommending nominees to the Governor General for vacant Senate seats.
>
> Similarly, Bill C-7 provides that Senators would sit for a non-renewable nine-year term and sets out a model statute for provincial and territorial legislation creating consultative elections. It provides that the Prime Minister "must" consider names from the lists of successful candidates: cl. 3. Its appended model statute states the principle that Senators "should be chosen" from among those candidates: cl. 1 of the Schedule.

[73] *Projet de loi fédéral relatif au Sénat (Re)*, 2013 QCCA 1807 (CanLII) [*Quebec Senate Reference*].

change Senators' terms of office, or introduce consultative elections. Such changes would require application of the general amending formula. Although the Bill did not touch the question of Senate abolition, the court added that abolition would require unanimous provincial consent.[74]

The federal government then initiated its own reference. It sought to confirm that most of its proposed changes (including enacting term limits, abolishing the requirement that Senators hold real property worth $4,000, and instituting consultative elections) could be achieved through federal law alone sheltered under the Parliamentary amendment power.[75] The government also put abolition squarely on the table, arguing that it could be accomplished under the general or 7/50 rule.[76]

Lasting three days, the hearing attracted all 10 provinces, two of the three territories, individual Senators and several francophone organisations. The Court appointed an unusual, joint *amicus curiae* composed of a law dean from Quebec and a senior member of the British Columbia bar.

A number of provinces opposed the federal legislation. Ontario, Quebec, Nova Scotia, New Brunswick, Prince Edward Island, Manitoba, and Newfoundland and Labrador argued that because the Senate was integral to the original Confederation bargain, *all* of the proposed changes required some form of provincial consent.[77] Alberta and British Columbia supported the federal government.[78] As it often does in such proceedings, Saskatchewan adopted a more nuanced position.[79]

The hearing was a spirited affair. The issues mooted included how, exactly, Canada might become a dictatorship(!); which amending formula was required to abolish the House of Commons; and whether, if the Prime Minister could use non-binding elections to appoint Senators, the same applied to the appointment of superior court judges. Clearly the proceedings were not so much about Senate reform as about the parameters of constitutional amendment and the constitutive elements of the country's politics, self-governance and democracy.

[74] ibid at para 29. Changes to the amending formula are expressly included under s 41.

[75] The consultative election questions were framed as follows:

2. Is it within the legislative authority of the Parliament of Canada, acting pursuant to section 91 of the *Constitution Act, 1867*, or section 44 of the *Constitution Act, 1982*, to enact legislation that provides a means of consulting the population of each province and territory as to its preferences for potential nominees for appointment to the Senate pursuant to a national process as was set out in Bill C-20, the *Senate Appointment Consultations Act*?
3. Is it within the legislative authority of the Parliament of Canada, acting pursuant to section 91 of the *Constitution Act, 1867*, or section 44 of the *Constitution Act, 1982*, to establish a framework setting out a basis for provincial and territorial legislatures to enact legislation to consult their population as to their preferences for potential nominees for appointment to the Senate as set out in the schedule to Bill C-7, the *Senate Reform Act*?

[76] See n 69.

[77] Submissions of Attorneys General at www.scc-csc.ca/case-dossier/info/af-ma-eng.aspx?cas=35203.

[78] ibid.

[79] ibid.

During the hearing, then Chief Justice Beverley McLachlin remarked on the emphasis, in written argument, on 'what the founding fathers thought'. It reminded her, she said, of 'American originalism'.[80] Numerous provinces had argued that imposing shorter term limits and non-binding elections would affect the Senate's ability to perform its original purpose, namely ensuring that legislation passed by the Commons receives 'sober second thought'. Therefore, they argued, provincial input to its reform was absolutely required. The entire point of the Senate, they claimed, was its unelected status – enabling it to fulfil a function quite distinct from the elected House of Commons. That independent character, the provinces insisted, had acted as a predicate for their entry into Confederation.

In an unsigned opinion, the Court largely agreed with those provinces. It concluded that the proposed changes required more than simply ushering a Bill through Parliament. Most required following the 7/50 rule.[81] Abolition required unanimity.[82]

Borrowing from and building upon the language of the *Secession Reference*, the Court cited the need to respect the Constitution's underlying architecture.[83] Architecture, it said, provides a basic structure to the Constitution that extends beyond 'discrete textual provisions'.[84] Therefore, if a proposed change affects that architecture, it must fit into the schema of Part V.

The Senate was 'a core component of the Canadian federal structure of government'[85] – designed, in part, to respond to provincial concerns about a central body (Parliament) enacting laws for the entire country. Those provincial concerns prompted the incorporation of a regionalist perspective into Parliament. Thus, changes to the Upper House could well implicate the Constitution's architecture.

The Court then interrogated the discrete changes against both textual and structural elements of the Constitution. With respect to consultative elections, the Attorney General of Canada argued that the chief consideration should be whether such processes affected either the text of the Constitution Act 1867 or the actual appointment mechanism.[86] If neither was affected, the Attorney General said the initiative should not even count as an amendment. The Court found that argument to privilege form over substance.[87] So long as any changes

[80] Carissima Mathen, 'Living Originalism', *CBA National Magazine*, 9 December 2013, www.nationalmagazine.ca/Articles/November/Living-originalism.aspx.

[81] The Court held that, because of specific wording, changes to the property qualifications of Quebec Senators require the consent of Quebec's legislative assembly. *Senate Reform* (n 67) at para 86.

[82] ibid at para 3.

[83] To be sure, the concept of constitutional architecture had been mentioned before: see *Secession Reference* (n 3).

[84] *Senate Reform* (n 67) at para 27.

[85] ibid at para 77.

[86] ibid at para 41. The Attorney General argued in the alternative that if consultative elections required a constitutional amendment, they would fall under the unilateral federal power in s 44.

[87] *Ibid*, at para 52.

engaged 'the interests of the provinces in the Senate as an institution forming *an integral part of the federal system*', they would require the general amending formula.[88]

Using similar reasoning, the Court found that abolition of the Senate requires unanimity.[89]

A curious element was the Court's consideration of whether Parliament may unilaterally impose senatorial term limits. In the *Upper House Reference* (discussed in Chapter 6), the Court had declined to answer a similar question because no particular tenure had been proposed. It noted merely that '[a]t some point, a reduction of the term of office might impair the functioning of the Senate in providing what Sir John A. Macdonald described as "the sober second thought in legislation"'. It went on to state that the imposition of compulsory retirement at age 75 had not changed the essential character of the Senate.[90]

What the Court in the *Upper House Reference* omitted to mention is that the life term for Senators had been changed in 1965 *without* the explicit consent of the provinces.[91] Given that the Court took no issue with that prior act, it was reasonable to think that, if substituting a life tenure with one ending at 75 had not changed the Senate's 'essential character', then perhaps the same might apply to instituting terms for Senators not linked to their age.

In the 2014 reference the federal government put to the Court whether Parliament could unilaterally change the age limit to any of the following: fixed term limits of eight, nine or 10 years, fixed term for the life of a set number of Parliaments (two or three); or a renewable term.[92]

The Court interpreted the question and its sub-parts as asking whether section 44 was a residual clause that encompassed all changes to the Senate not explicitly mentioned in Part V. This it rejected. Furthermore, 'the current duration of senatorial terms [was] directly linked' to the idea that the Senate was intended to function as a 'complementary legislative body of sober second thought'. That Senators 'are appointed roughly for the duration of their active professional lives', the Court said, enables the Upper House 'to function with independence in conducting legislative review'.[93]

The Court concluded that any 'significant change' to tenure would thus affect the Senate's fundamental nature and role and could only be achieved under the general amending procedure.[94] What, though, counted as significant? The Court refused to say. The issue was a 'policy' decision that 'engages the interests of the provinces and requires their input'.[95]

[88] ibid at para 75 (emphasis added).
[89] ibid at paras 106–107.
[90] *Re: Authority of Parliament in relation to the Upper House*, [1980] 1 SCR 54.
[91] Constitution Act 1965, SC 1965, c 4. The change was effected unilaterally under s 91(1).
[92] *Senate Reform* (n 67) at para 5.
[93] ibid at para 79.
[94] ibid at paras 79–80.
[95] ibid at para 82.

Political scientist Emmett MacFarlane has criticised the Court for dodging the question, noting that its 'refusal to engage in a line-drawing exercise here is problematic to the extent that line-drawing is precisely what was being asked of it'.[96] He notes that the government clearly sought the Court's guidance as to whether 'certain types of term limits might be enacted under section 44 even if other types could not'. By declining to answer the question, 'the Court sidestepped a contradiction and logical flaw in its approach'.[97]

The *Senate Reference* has greatly reduced the prospect of large-scale reform to the Upper House without provincial input. Prime Minister Stephen Harper did not push ahead with his desired changes, declaring instead a 'moratorium' on future appointments until such time as the provinces indicated a willingness to engage in discussions around real reform.[98] The refusal was almost certainly unconstitutional and itself became the subject of a legal challenge which was ruled moot after the 2015 election produced a change of government.[99] That, though, was the extent of any 'resistance'. All future discussion of the Senate has proceeded on the assumptions that any changes to it must respect the precepts laid out in the reference.

B. Self-entrenchment

The second advisory opinion of 2014, the *Supreme Court Act Reference*,[100] affected the Court itself. It arose after Prime Minister Harper nominated[101] Marc Nadon to replace the outgoing jurist Morris Fish in 2013. Nadon, a semi-retired Federal Court of Appeal judge, was thought to reflect the government's preference for a particular judicial ideology – conservative, restrained and rights-sceptical.[102]

[96] MacFarlane (n 28) 897.

[97] ibid.

[98] Jason Fekete, 'PM Harper slaps moratorium on Senate appointments ahead of election', *Ottawa Citizen*, 28 July 2015, https://ottawacitizen.com/news/national/stephen-harper-slaps-moratorium-on-senate-appointments-ahead-of-election-calls-on-provinces-to-accept-reforms-or-abolition).

[99] *Alani v Canada (Prime Minister)*, 2016 FC 1139 (CanLII).

[100] *Reference re* Supreme Court Act, *ss. 5 and 6*, 2014 SCC 21, [2014] 1 SCR 433 [*Supreme Court Act Reference*].

[101] The terminology of a 'candidate' who has been 'nominated' by the Prime Minister came into vogue during the preceding decade when Supreme Court candidates started to appear before parliamentarians to answer questions. But, as acknowledged by a previous Liberal Minister of Justice, MPs cannot 'approve' the selection. See Carissima Mathen 'Choices and Controversy: Judicial Appointments in Canada' (2007) 58 University of New Brunswick Law Journal 52, 62.

[102] Interview of John Gomery (10 May 2014) on *The House*, CBC Radio: www.cbc.ca/player/News/Politics/Audio/ID/2455409481; Kirk Makin, 'The coming conservative court: Harper to reshape judiciary', *Globe and Mail*, 13 May 2011, www.theglobeandmail.com/news/politics/the-coming-conservative-court-harper-to-reshape-judiciary/article595398/ (30 April 2016). See also Mathen, 'Judicial Appointments' (n 101) 60, noting how, as Leader of the Official Opposition, Stephen Harper accused the former Liberal government of stacking the Court with judges sympathetic to the push

More worrying for the government was the possibility of technical barriers. The problem was that Justice Morris Fish hailed from Quebec. As discussed in Chapter 6, the Supreme Court Act (in section 6) requires that 'At least three of the judges shall be appointed from among the judges of the Court of Appeal or of the Superior Court of the Province of Quebec or from among the advocates of that province' (the provision allocating the other seats, section 5, uses less constrained language).[103] At the time, Justice Nadon was not serving on a Quebec court, nor a member of the Bar of Quebec. He was the first-ever section 6 appointee to hail from the Federal Court.

The government was aware of the issue.[104] On the day of Justice Nadon's nomination, the Minister of Justice released a memorandum, written by a retired Supreme Court judge, that supported Nadon's eligibility. The government also said that a second retired judge, as well as a noted constitutional scholar, supported that opinion.[105]

Justice Nadon was sworn in as a puisne justice on 7 October 2013. The next day, a Toronto lawyer filed suit seeking judicial review of the appointment. The government of Quebec publicly supported the challenge. Justice Nadon delayed taking up his new duties and the Court stated it would not have contact with him until the matter had been resolved.[106]

for same-sex marriage. In 2007 the Prime Minister said: 'We want to make sure we're bringing forward the laws to make sure we crack down on crime, that we make our streets and communities safer … We want to make sure our selection of judges is in correspondence with those objectives'. House of Commons Debates, No 110 (14 February 2007) 1400.

[103] 5. Any person may be appointed a judge who is or has been a judge of a superior court of a province or a barrister or advocate of at least ten years standing at the bar of a province.

…

6. At least three of the judges shall be appointed from among the judges of the Court of Appeal or of the Superior Court of the Province of Quebec or from among the advocates of that Province.

And in French:

5. Les juges sont choisis parmi les juges, actuels ou anciens, d'une cour supérieure provinciale et parmi les avocats inscrits pendant au moins dix ans au barreau d'une province.

…

6. Au moins trois des juges sont choisis parmi les juges de la Cour d'appel ou de la Cour supérieure de la province de Québec ou parmi les avocats de celle-ci.

[104] Tobi Cohen, 'Peter MacKay insists Conservatives are not moving Canada toward US-style justice', *National Post*, 17 August 2013, http://news.nationalpost.com/2013/08/17/peter-mackay-insists-conservatives-are-not-moving-canada-toward-u-s-style-justice/. In his November 2013 testimony before the Standing Senate Committee in Legal and Constitutional Affairs, the Minister of Justice stated that the government 'anticipated that there could be difficulty': House of Commons, The Standing Senate Committee on Legal and Constitutional Affairs, 'Evidence' (27 November 2013), www.parl.gc.ca/content/sen/committee/412/LCJC/51062-e.HTM [hereinafter House of Commons, 'Evidence'].

[105] Only the memorandum written by Ian Binnie was publicly disclosed. Access to information requests by Members of Parliament shed some but not much light on the other external opinions.

[106] See www.thestar.com/news/canada/2013/11/03/supreme_court_quarantines_marc_nadon_until_challenge_heard.html#; www.scc-csc.gc.ca/case-dossier/info/dock-regi-eng.aspx?cas=35586. See also www.thestar.com/news/canada/2013/11/03/supreme_court_quarantines_marc_nadon_until_challenge_heard.html.

The situation was deteriorating. On 22 October 2013 the government introduced two declaratory clauses so sections 5 and 6 of the Supreme Court Act would permit the appointment of anyone who *had been* a barrister or advocate of at least 10 years standing.[107] Since declaratory legislation is retroactive,[108] sections 5 and 6 would be interpreted as having *always* permitted the appointment of such person. In other words, Nadon would *always* have been eligible.[109]

On the same day that it introduced clauses 471 and 472, the government *also* put to the Supreme Court the following questions:

> 1. Can a person who was, at any time, an advocate of at least 10 years standing at the Barreau du Québec be appointed to the Supreme Court of Canada as a member of the Supreme Court from Quebec pursuant to sections 5 and 6 of the *Supreme Court Act*?
> 2. Can Parliament enact legislation that requires that a person be or has previously been a barrister or advocate of at least 10 years standing at the bar of a province as a condition of appointment as a judge of the Supreme Court of Canada or enact the annexed declaratory provisions as set out in clauses 471 and 472 of the Bill entitled *Economic Action Plan 2013 Act, No. 2*?

It is highly unusual for a government to seek to pass declaratory legislation at the same time that it initiates a reference.[110] Appearing before a House of Commons Committee, the Justice Minister defended the move as necessary to obtain 'clarity'.[111] He did not explain why the declaratory legislation, which is after all directed at future judicial interpretation, failed to provide all the clarity that could be required. Seeking an advisory opinion about provisions that have already been reshaped by the legislature's declaratory power seems redundant. The government most likely was caught off guard by the speed at which events unfolded.[112] Declaratory legislation would be attractive to a government eager to constrain a court's interpretative powers, while the reference acknowledged the symbolic and political importance of the Supreme Court's approval.

The government's strategy backfired. In a 6–1 opinion,[113] the Court advised that candidates filling the reserved seats are limited to jurists currently serving on certain Quebec courts, and Quebec bar members.[114] It concluded, further, that the

[107] Economic Action Plan 2013 Act, No. 2 (Bill C-4), SC 2013, c 40 [Economic Action Plan 2013 Act], ss 471, 472.

[108] *Régie des rentes du Québec v Canada Bread Company Ltd.*, [2013] SCJ No 46, [2013] 3 SCR 125, 2013 SCC 46, at para 48 (SCC).

[109] Clauses 471 and 472 received Royal Assent on 12 December 2013.

[110] The last time that any government introduced legislation at the same time as it sought an opinion about its validity was the *Reference re: Anti-Inflation Act (Canada)*, [1976] SCJ No 12, [1976] 2 SCR 373, but the legislation was not declaratory.

[111] House of Commons, Standing Committee on Justice and Human Rights (21 November 2013) at 0920. See also House of Commons, 'Evidence' (n 104).

[112] C Mathen, 'The Shadow of Absurdity and the Challenge of Easy Cases: Looking Back on the *Supreme Court Act Reference*' (2015) 71 SCLR (2d) 161 at 169–70.

[113] Justice Marshall Rothstein recused himself. I discuss the circumstances of this recusal in ibid 170–71.

[114] See Michael Plaxton and Carissima Mathen, 'Purposive Interpretation, Quebec, and the *Supreme Court Act*' (2013) 22 Constitutional Forum 15.

declaratory legislation attempted to alter the Court's 'composition' contrary to the amending procedures set out in Part V of the Constitution Act 1982.[115] As a result, Marc Nadon's appointment was void *ab initio*.

To many observers, it was not evident why a Federal Court jurist would be ineligible for appointment. But the Court stressed that one must look beyond what appears to be the most obvious reading, to pinpoint that which best accords with parliamentary intention and is consistent with relevant interpretative factors.

The majority stated that sections 5 and 6 of the Supreme Court Act fulfil distinct functions. Section 5 guarantees minimum legal expertise for the Court as a whole. But section 6 reflects 'the historical compromise that led to the creation of the Supreme Court',[116] protecting 'both the *functioning* and the *legitimacy* of the Supreme Court as a general court of appeal for Canada'.[117] The section was intended to guarantee expertise with respect to *Quebec's* legal traditions. But also, and as discussed in Chapter 2, section 6 was adopted to assure the province in a deeper sense of the legitimacy of such appointees.

The majority thus concluded that the distinct function of section 6 required candidates who were not only 'qualified to represent Quebec on the Court, but … *were perceived by Quebecers as being so qualified*'.[118] While the exclusion of past Quebec advocates did not 'perfectly advance' that objective,[119] it provided a sufficient to explain the textual differences between sections 5 and 6.

Therefore, Justice Nadon was not eligible. Section 6, though, was a part of ordinary legislation. Even if the existing framework presented an obstacle to Nadon J's appointment, there appeared to be a relatively straightforward corrective: amend the statute.[120]

The government's choice to pre-emptively pass declaratory legislation proved fateful not only to the outcome, but also to the status of the Court itself. That is because the Court had to both interpret sections 5 and 6, *and*, potentially, determine the scope of Parliament's authority to set that interpretation. Once the Court concluded that Nadon J was ineligible according to the terms of sections 5 and 6, Question 2 required the Court to decide whether it was open to Parliament to fiddle with certain aspects of the Supreme Court itself – forcing the Court to venture into the complicated territory of Part V.[121]

[115] Justice Moldaver, who dissented from the Court's interpretation of s 6, did not take express issue with the discussion of Part V; and he agreed that changes to the Court's composition are embraced under s 41(d), though he declined to opine on whether the specific professional standard articulated in s 6 would qualify. But he thought it unnecessary to answer the second question since he found that Justice Nadon had always been eligible for appointment under s 6. *Supreme Court Act Reference* (n 100) at para 114.

[116] ibid at para 48.

[117] ibid at para 49 (emphasis in original).

[118] ibid at para 56 (emphasis added).

[119] ibid at para 57.

[120] Of course, there would still be the question of what to do with Nadon J himself, as in the normal course such changes would not have retroactive effect.

[121] Even if the reference had dealt solely with the interpretative issue, it is possible that broader constitutional questions would have arisen. But, without a reference question clearly requiring such analysis

Like the interpretative question regarding section 6, the specific issue regarding Part V had never been addressed. As noted earlier in this book, the Supreme Court Act was enacted, and has been amended numerous times, as ordinary federal law.[122] Although mentioned in Part V of the Constitution Act 1982, the Supreme Court appears nowhere else in the written text. Some scholars had suggested that Part V's mention of the Court was aspirational – it would take effect only in the event of a *future* decision to entrench the Court.[123]

The Court rejected the 'aspirational' argument.[124] It did so not on the basis that Part V had *itself* entrenched the Court, but on the basis that Part V merely *recognised* the fact that the Court *already had become* entrenched. That recognition, the Court stated, was predicated on and driven by the country's essential federal character. Since the 1949 abolition of Privy Council appeals, the Court had come to perform a role necessary in any federal system. It acted as the impartial arbiter of jurisdictional disputes.[125] From then on, 'the continued existence and functioning of the [Supreme Court] became a key matter of interest' to all actors in the federation.[126] Consequently, in negotiating the 1982 package, the relevant actors 'accepted that future reforms would have to recognise the Supreme Court's position within the architecture of the Constitution'.[127]

Thus, the declaratory legislation sought to change the Court in a way that could only be done through constitutional amendment. For changes to the Court's composition (which the Court took to include the eligibility criteria in section 6 of the Supreme Court Act) section 41 of Part V prescribes unanimity. Changes to the Court's other 'essential features' require the general formula.

The Supreme Court routinely considers highly controversial issues.[128] And those decisions provoke spirited reaction.[129] Even so, the reaction to the reference was particularly sharp. While it obeyed the letter of the ruling, the government

it is quite possible that the Court would decline to answer such questions on the basis it would be premature to do so.

[122] Supreme and Exchequer Court Act, SC 1875, c 11, s 4; and subsequent legislation.

[123] This has been referred to as the 'empty vessels' theory and one of its proponents includes Peter Hogg in his *Constitutional Law of Canada*, 5th edn, Supp (Toronto: Thomson Carswell, 2007) 4–21 cited in *Supreme Court Act Reference* (n 115) at para 97.

[124] Justice Moldaver did not take express issue with this part of the majority's decision, though he disagreed somewhat on the relevant formula that would apply to specific changes. Ibid at paras 113–14. I think, therefore, that the analysis is fairly attributed to 'the Court'.

[125] ibid at para 83, citing *Reference re Securities Act*, 2011 SCC 66, [2011] 3 SCR 837.

[126] *Supreme Court Act Reference* (n 100) at para 85.

[127] ibid at para 87.

[128] See *Carter v Canada (Attorney General)*, 2015 SCC 5, [2015] 1 SCR 331 [*Carter*] and *Canada (Attorney-General) v Bedford*, 2013 SCC 72, [2013] 3 SCR 1101 [*Bedford*]; *Reference re Senate Reform*, [2014] SCJ No 32, [2014] 1 SCR 704, 2014 SCC 32 (SCC); *Tsilhqot'in Nation v British Columbia*, [2014] SCJ No 44, [2014] 2 SCR 256, 2014 SCC 44 (SCC); *R v Nur*, [2015] SCJ No 15, 2015 SCC 15 (SCC).

[129] Grant Huscroft, 'The Supreme Court should leave assisted suicide to Parliament' *Toronto Star*, 10 October 2014, www.thestar.com/opinion/commentary/2014/10/10/supreme_court_should_leave_assisted_suicide_to_parliament.html; Tristan Hopper, 'Peter MacKay slams Supreme Court for quashing mandatory minimum gun sentences', *National Post*, 22 April 2015.

made it clear that it considered the Court's opinion to be utterly misguided. Ministers continued to defend their interpretation of section 6, relying on Moldaver J's dissenting opinion as well as the prior endorsements by former justices and eminent scholars.[130] Some government members went so far as to impugn the integrity of the Chief Justice.[131]

Public commentary on the ruling was mixed.[132] But criticism emerged from unusual sources such as former Supreme Court justices[133] and the Chief Justice of the Federal Court of Appeal.[134] The reference left many persons unconvinced that it was the 'right answer'.[135] That likely was a reaction to several factors: the internal

[130] The Prime Minister's Office issued the following comment: 'This legal advice was reviewed and supported by another former Supreme Court justice as well as a leading constitutional scholar, and was made public. None of these legal experts saw any merit in the position eventually taken by the Court'. Mark Kennedy, 'Harper refused "inappropriate" call from chief justice of Supreme Court on Nadon appointment, PMO says', *National Post*, 1 May 2014, http://news.nationalpost.com/news/canada/canadian-politics/harper-refused-inappropriate-call-from-chief-justice-of-supreme-court-on-nadon-appointment-pmo-says. Additionally, former Justice Michel Bastarache testified, with the author, before the Senate Committee on Legal and Constitutional Affairs on 21 November 2013. Justice Bastarache opined that both ss 5 and 6 included past advocates.

[131] John Ivison, 'Tories incensed with Supreme Court as some allege Chief Justice lobbied against Marc Nadon appointment', *National Post*, 1 May 2014, http://news.nationalpost.com/news/canada/canadian-politics/tories-incensed-with-supreme-court-as-some-allege-chief-justice-lobbied-against-marc-nadon-appointment. As discussed above, the Chief Justice *had* raised concerns about how s 6 would bear on the appointment of a federal court judge (after the government's short list revealed that four of the six candidates were from that bench) but she did so when the process was still underway and long before Nadon was selected: Kennedy (n 150); Julius Melnitzer, 'ACTL weighs in on Harper-McLachlin spat', *Financial Post*, 8 May 2014, http://business.financialpost.com/legal-post/actl-weighs-in-on-harper-mclachlin-spat.

[132] Grant Huscroft, 'The Supreme Court's faulty logic on Nadon', *National Post*, 25 March 2014, http://news.nationalpost.com/full-comment/grant-huscroft-the-supreme-courts-faulty-logic-on-nadon; Andrew Coyne, 'Flaky Supreme Court ruling meets dubious appointment', *National Post*, 24 March 2014, http://news.nationalpost.com/full-comment/andrew-coyne-on-marc-nadon-flaky-supreme-court-ruling-meets-dubious-appointment; Leonid Sirota, 'What You Wish For', 22 March 2014, https://doubleaspectblog.wordpress.com/2014/03/22/what-you-wish-for/. More positive commentary included Paul Daly, quoted in Sean Fine, 'Supreme Court's rejection of Nadon is a legal marker and a political blow', *The Globe and Mail*, 21 March 2014, www.theglobeandmail.com/news/politics/supreme-courts-rejection-of-nadon-is-a-legal-marker-and-a-political-blow/article17625541/; Adam Dodek, quoted in John Geddes, www.macleans.ca/politics/ottawa/q-a-supreme-court-of-canadas-rejects-a-harper-appointment/; Carissima Mathen, 'Nadon ruling hits like an earthquake', *Ottawa Citizen*, 21 March 2014, A8.

[133] See the comments by former Justice John Major in Sean Fine, 'Harper says he will "respect" Supreme Court's blocking of Nadon', *The Globe and Mail*, 25 March 2014.

[134] See the extraordinary speech made by the Chief Justice of the Federal Court: Cristin Schmitz, 'Chief Justice Noel's remarks spark debate over how far to go', *The Lawyers Weekly*, 26 December 2014, www.lawyersweekly-digital.com/lawyersweekly/3432?pg=3#pg3.

[135] I borrow this term from legal theory, but its use is not intended to enter into that debate. See, among many others, HLA Hart, *The Concept of Law* (Oxford: Oxford University Press, 1997); Ronald Dworkin, *A Matter of Principle* (Cambridge MA: Harvard University Press, 1985); Joseph Raz, 'Authority and Justification' (1985) 14 Philosophy and Public Affairs 3; John Mackie, 'The Third Theory of Law' reprinted in Marshall Cohen (ed), *Ronald Dworkin and Contemporary Jurisprudence* (London: Duckworth, 1984); Brian Bix, *Law, Language and Legal Determinacy* (Oxford: Clarendon Press, 1995).

division within the opinion; the particular nature of 'finality' that attended it; and the fact that the answer was unexpected.

Justice Michael Moldaver dissented from the majority's interpretation of section 6.[136] In particular, he wrote, the majority's insistence that bar membership under section 6 must be 'current' created an absurdity: a person could simply 'rejoin' the Quebec bar for a 'single day' and, thereby, become eligible for appointment. He thought that the majority's refusal to address whether that was in fact the case essentially acknowledged that its opinion made 'no practical sense'.[137]

Normally, a 6–1 split would not be highly significant. But in the exceptional context of the reference, it carried more weight than usual. First, it lent credence to the view that the majority had evaded certain issues.[138] Additionally, and especially to critics of the opinion, Moldaver J's dissent did not really stand alone. It vindicated previous opinions by persons who might be considered of equivalent stature to the majority: former justices, and the most prominent constitutional scholar in the country.[139]

Supreme Court rulings are 'final' in the sense that they are not subject to appeal, and act as a powerful precedent. In Chapter 10, I will present the view that references share in this sense of finality. If that is so, then the *Supreme Court Act Reference* would constitute an especially powerful moment. Additionally, the outcome was not necessarily within the contemplation of most participants and observers. The original question put to the Court concerned what the executive clearly assumed was ordinary legislation.[140] But, once the declaratory legislation was introduced, the stakes became much higher.[141] The Court's conclusion transformed the 'Quebec Rule' into a constitutional dictate. Such a move could be perceived as an effort by the Court to insulate section 6 from subsequent meddling. And that perception could foster suspicion of its answer to Question 1.

The reference also concerned an issue – constitutional amendment – that may attract a more powerful *degree* of finality. In terms of constitutional design, amendment rules represent the most direct expression of a society's *political* will. Arguably, they are also the most tied to expectations of predictability. The process governing amendment would seem to be entitled to a powerful presumption of

[136] Though he dissented from the main opinion, Justice Moldaver did not take issue with the majority's analysis of Part V; and he expressly agreed that changes to the Court's composition are embraced under s 41(d).

[137] *Supreme Court Act Reference* (n 100) at paras 152–53.

[138] Mathen, 'Shadow' (n 112); n 72 and surrounding text.

[139] ibid; n 105 and surrounding text.

[140] Of course, there would still leave the question of what to do with Nadon J himself, as in the normal course such changes would not have retroactive effect. The matter is discussed in Chapter 10.

[141] Prior to the release of the opinion, I mused that one way out of the conundrum would be for the Court to decide Question 1 in the government's favour and to decline to answer Question 2. Now, even without the declaratory provisions, it is possible that broader constitutional questions would have arisen. But, without a reference question clearly requiring such analysis, it would have been possible for the Court to issue one of its 'refusals'.

stability, and against change. Thus, while it is theoretically possible that the Court will articulate reasons[142] to justify eventually departing from rulings about the amending formula, the prospect seems unlikely. If that is true, then the *Reference* seems to be 'untouchable'. Any misgivings about the substance of the decision would no doubt be heightened by the attendant degree of finality.

The final reason that the *Supreme Court Act Reference* drew such sharp criticism, of course, is what it actually said. Many persons, it seems, perceived the reference to be an 'easy case'.[143] On policy grounds, there seemed to be no 'good' reason to exclude Federal Court judges from appointment under section 6. The reference was initiated *after* Nadon J (a competent jurist) had been sworn in. And the Court was reviewing the exercise of a highly discretionary executive power. Very few people anticipated that the Court would actually *reject* Nadon J.

The *Supreme Court Act Reference* is surely one of the oddest advisory opinions discussed in this book. From rather mundane beginnings, it morphed into a high-stakes battle over the power and legacy of the Court itself. Though it was criticised on a number of bases, those bases did *not* include the fact that it was merely an advisory opinion. There seems to have been no real dispute over the idea that the Supreme Court legitimately had a role to play in such an important conflict. All objections were to *how* it did so, and the attendant consequences.

* * *

The three references discussed in this chapter have had profound consequences for Canadian law and politics. They have set the parameters under which a variety of types of constitutional change, large and small, may be pursued.

Through them all runs the increasingly magisterial stance of the apex court. That stance is enhanced not only by the seriousness of the issues upon which it is called to give guidance or provide finality. It is affected, too, by the very fact of that calling – of the *other* institutions of the state expecting the Court to pronounce, to clarify, and to dispose. Even a Prime Minister (Stephen Harper) who was notably suspicious of judicial power nonetheless saw fit to refer to it critically important questions. And, when the results received were entirely contrary to his and his government's express preferences, he nonetheless acknowledged them as obligatory, as have all subsequent actors. Why would someone generally opposed to robust judicial review turn to the Court in that way? And what could motivate them to acquiesce in the result? The next and final two chapters take up those, and related, questions.

[142] *Carter* (n 128); *Bedford* (n 128); *R v Bernard*, [1988] SCJ No 96, [1988] 2 SCR 833 (SCC).

[143] To be clear, I dispute the notion that the *Reference* was, even initially, an easy case. Section 6 of the Supreme Court Act presented an issue of first impression, in a context of great uncertainty. The issue depended upon non-obvious interpretative factors. For a fuller discussion, see Mathen, 'Shadow' (n 112).

9

Actors, Advice and Law

The next two chapters examine how advisory opinions fit into the broader picture of law and jurisprudence. I explore a tension that lies at the core of the advisory opinions, one that has never been fully explained. That tension provokes examination of the reasons why actors in a system treat advisory opinions in the way that they do – both in terms of deciding to trigger the function and, then, once the opinion has been received, treating it as a reason for action, forbearance or decision. In this chapter, I consider non-judicial actors, generally in the executive branch. In Chapter 10, I move to the courts themselves.

The chapters are complementary – intended to function as a single, broader discussion. For example, a significant reason that non-judicial actors treat references in a particular way is how judicial actors treat them. That examination is left for the next chapter, in part because it requires a lengthy analysis and, in part, because there is value in considering separately those reasons that directly invoke the courts, and those which do not.

The Core Tension

In Canada advisory opinions are now so common and familiar that a tension at their very core has receded from view. The tension arises from the asymmetry between references' formal and practical status. Formally, such opinions are not 'binding' – they do not, on their face, provide independent reasons for compliance by other actors or, indeed, by the courts. This is at least in part because, as discussed earlier in this book, advisory opinions lack many of the elements thought to be necessary for courts' ordinary adjudicative functions. Recall that references do not arise through a live case, do not require a particular conflict or 'adversarial' quality between parties, and do not require a current or pending legal issue. They are initiated on the sole say-so of the executive and can include any question under the sun.[1] Those features complicate the question of what, exactly, an advisory opinion is, and, in particular, whether it counts as 'law'.

[1] Recall that the Supreme Court Act grants the federal Cabinet the broadest possible scope by including as permissible questions 'important questions of law or fact' and states that *any* question shall be 'conclusively deemed to be an important question'. Supreme Court Act RSC 1985 c S26 s 53.

Once we move from the formal to the practical, however, the picture needs adjustment. In the 'here and now', advisory opinions do resemble cases. Although they need not involve legal questions, most advisory opinions do; they stay within well-defined parameters of legal inquiry. (Though, admittedly, with regard to particular references[2] reasonable people can disagree about how far those parameters extend). And, advisory opinions are heard through a process that is very similar to ordinary appeals. Further, advisory opinions and cases appear indistinguishable in terms of their substantive content, or how they are treated once issued. None of that means, necessarily, that advisory opinions *are* binding law. But it complicates the picture.

This chapter proceeds as follows. First, it considers why a non-judicial actor might wish to trigger an advisory opinion at all. Second, it suggests reasons that, having done so, those actors would then treat the resulting opinion as something with which they must comply.[3] It might appear that once the first question has been covered, the second is unnecessary. I mean to show why that is not so – why the reasons that might explain the first phenomenon are not necessarily the reasons that could explain the second. In the course of discussing the second set of reasons (why comply?) I will delve into the nature of legal authority. which, I believe, has insights for the issues under discussion.

Some of the reasons that non-judicial actors might pursue an advisory opinion mirror those for ordinary litigation. The same can be said for the reasons that parties other than the initiator will seek to participate in them. I do not argue that such reasons are, necessarily, *exclusive* to the advisory function. But their combination and permutation within the context of references merits special consideration.

Why Pursue?

The initiation of advisory opinions depends, in part, on the political context in which various actors operate. In Canada, that includes the fact that only executive actors who are part of the government formally initiate such questions. It also includes whether a particular government enjoys a majority or minority of the seats in the legislature to which executive actors are responsible, and the broader social context of a particular legal dispute. The scope of the power to legislate in respect of chartered banks is entirely different from an alleged wrongful

[2] Consider, for example, the *Patriation* and *Secession References* discussed in Chapters 6 and 8.

[3] Obviously, such compliance is dependent upon what that actor perceives an opinion to say. Reference opinions can be quite clear – for example, when the court advises that a particular law is ultra vires. But they may also contain elements that require interpretation – for example, the *reasons* that the court concludes that a law is ultra vires. This chapter presumes that actors do not stray far from what they *believe* is the generally accepted interpretation of the court's conclusions. That does permit some room for debate, however.

conviction, or a dispute over freedom of religion. Likely to figure in the decision, too, is the actor's overall attitude towards the courts; and, where relevant, their assessment of the underlying legal dispute.

Advisory opinions are sought for numerous reasons. Sometimes, though not frequently, they are undertaken as a preparatory step to law making. As discussed in Chapter 5, they have been used as a tool in federalism disputes – a way to secure advantage against another government, or to inject legitimacy into an executive or legislative decision. More recently, they may reflect a desire to harness the significant authority of the judicial branch. The discussion below groups reasons together in four categories: doctrinal guidance; co-ordination; strategy; and imprimatur.

A. Doctrinal Guidance

A common reason for an advisory function is that it can provide *doctrinal guidance*. It arises when, sensibly enough, the actors who initiate advisory opinions wish to obtain *advice*. Depending on the situation, an actor may welcome guidance of all sorts – moral, political, ethical and/or legal. But, while courts sometimes are associated with moral/ethical leadership, their raison d'être is to provide guidance on legal principles and to determine answers to legal questions – which is why the guidance may be understood as 'doctrinal'. Where a problem of legal dimension spurs uncertainty or tension among important political groups, a state actor may look for ways to resolve it. To be sure, actors sometimes will deliberately avoid such guidance, precisely because they do *not* want to know the limits on their choices. One might think of this as a sort of policy-oriented 'wilful blindness'. But, more often, actors seek answers.

Most references discussed in this book have involved, to some degree, the pursuit of such guidance. References pertaining to criminal law, particularly as it interacts with the Charter of Rights, fall within this category. Consider the *Motor Vehicle Reference*,[4] which, in light of the new demands imposed by the Charter's reference to 'the principles of fundamental justice', sought clarity about the nature of criminal responsibility; or the *Prostitution Reference*, where the Court had to determine whether long-standing prohibitions on aspects of the sex trade were constitutionally valid.[5] And, the Minister of Justice's stated intention to seek a Supreme Court opinion about the validity of the 2017 Genetic Discrimination Act almost surely reflected a sincere desire by her to clarify certain doubts about the law (even if she had other reasons as well).[6]

[4] *Re BC Motor Vehicle Act*, [1985] 2 SCR 486 (also discussed in Chapters 7 and 10).

[5] *Reference re ss. 193 and 195.1(1)(c) of the Criminal Code* (Man.), [1990] 1 SCR 1123 (also discussed in Chapters 7 and 10).

[6] See the discussion in Chapters 4 and 5.

An issue may be sufficiently controversial or dubious that other actors are unlikely to take *any* steps without judicial reassurance. Consider the 2014 reference on Senate reform.[7] Most provinces were leery of entering into formal negotiations that might change the Senate. Following the controversial 1982 constitutional reforms, and the subsequent failed negotiations of Meech Lake and Charlottetown, amendment had become politically unfeasible.[8] Federal and provincial governments were unwilling to devote much energy to it. As a result, Prime Minister Harper sought to avoid the more stringent routes to amendment,[9] and to shift what changes he could to ordinary legislation or executive decision. But since taking that step outright would invariably prompt objections, Harper first sought judicial guidance. (Admittedly, the federal government also was dealing with a provincially initiated reference in lower courts; but it very likely would have turned to the Supreme Court anyway.)

B. Co-ordination

The initiation of a reference may relate to the *co-ordination*[10] of social aims and projects. Co-ordination, of course, runs in tandem with other reasons, but is set off here for its functional and pragmatic element. The idea is to seek co-ordination to minimise occasions for conflict, risk and uncertainty. An actor may well be neutral about the outcome. Co-ordination of litigation, especially, may not serve as an end in itself, but to dispel any uncertainty surrounding a policy or law in order that separate institutional and political actors can make informed decisions regarding, say, *other* policies and laws.

An actor may confront a dispute that is likely to spur multiple sites of litigation. The problem is heightened in a federal state where the matter involves a question of subnational jurisdiction, or is the subject of suit in a court which has many regional counterparts each operating with equivalent authority. In such a situation, an actor may desire an opinion from the apex court as quickly as possible, to tamp down the uncertainty flowing from multiple rulings. In Canada, all such decisions ultimately are appealable to the same court, so the actor can simply speed up the process by which that institution weighs in.

Such ultimate determination likely will be desired for urgent national issues. The *Anti-Inflation Act Reference* (discussed in Chapter 5) clarified the validity of extraordinary federal measures to impose wage and price controls. The law

[7] *Reference re Senate Reform*, 2014 SCC 32, also discussed in Chapter 8.

[8] See Emmett Macfarlane (ed), *Constitutional Amendment in Canada* (Toronto: University of Toronto Press, 2016) ch 3.

[9] Namely, amendments requiring the application of either the 7/50 or unanimity rule. See Constitution Act 1982, Part V, ss 38, 41.

[10] Edna Ullman-Margalit, 'Coordination Norms and Social Choice' (1977) 11 Erkennmis 143; John Finnis, 'Law as Co-ordination' (1989) 2 Ratio Juris 97, 101. The discussion in this chapter does depend on a conclusion vis-à-vis whether coordination supports or mandates an obligation to obey the law.

encouraged co-operative measures between orders of government to align provincial and federal controls; and all of the provinces either entered into such arrangements or instituted parallel controls. Given the significant impact on various parties, litigation was inevitable. The federal government wanted an opinion about the law's validity as soon as possible. And, indeed, it was able to obtain that opinion, from the country's highest court, in only nine months – an impossibly brief period for ordinary litigation.

An actor, conversely, might want to frustrate co-ordination. It may try to avoid a situation in which other actors build their own practices, policies and legislative regimes around the policies and legislation of another government, treating it as a fait accompli. The actor could wish to discourage the sense that the challenged policy or legislation is treated as a 'fixed point' around which everyone else should coalesce. An advisory function may prove useful in that way as well.

C. Strategy

A number of reasons for initiating a reference can be characterised, generally, as *strategic*.

i. Pre-emption

One such reason to pursue a reference is pre-emption. By initiating a proceeding, an actor can 'leapfrog' existing or anticipated litigation; or debate about an issue outside of a judicial process. Executive actors can initiate proceedings in the highest court in their respective jurisdictions – Canadian provinces in courts of appeal and the federal government in the Supreme Court. In contrast, ordinary litigation must begin in the lowest judicial body, generally, a trial court. Pre-emption provides both speed and usurpation of existing proceedings, which may be highly valuable. (At other times, though, a government may find it preferable to have the matter considered first in lower courts.)

Recall from Chapter 8 the dispute that arose over the validity of the Prime Minister's appointment to the Supreme Court of Federal Court of Appeal Justice Marc Nadon. Nadon was appointed under section 6 of the Act, which reserves three of the court's nine seats for Quebec jurists and advocates. Almost certainly, pre-emption motivated the federal government's subsequent reference.

The government was aware of a potential problem, but initially decided not to seek judicial advice to clarify the matter. Instead, it commissioned a memo from a *former* Supreme Court judge, Ian Binnie, attesting to Nadon's eligibility for the seat – which it proceeded to release alongside the announcement. And it noted that another former justice agreed with him.[11]

[11] That judge was Louise Charron. In fact, she was the person first approached to offer an opinion but, as she had not rejoined the bar, could not be cited by the government as having provided a

It was only after Toronto lawyer Rocco Galati filed an application for judicial review of the appointment, Nadon recused himself from all Supreme Court work, and the Quebec legislature passed a resolution indicating its concern with his appointment that the federal government initiated a reference (while also taking the unusual step of passing declaratory legislation that intended to render the appointment retroactively permissible). One can appreciate that the federal government had the sense that the issue was getting away from them. The reference was the best way to pre-empt the litigation (it also was a way to regain control, a separate reason discussed below).

Pre-emption is especially available to the federal government, because it alone can proceed directly to the Supreme Court, while the provinces must first resort to their courts of appeal. However, it is possible that, by initiating a reference first, a province may successfully pre-empt a federal reference simply by making it awkward for the federal government to initiate its own proceeding.

ii. Displacement

A related but different reason to pursue is that, by occupying the space formerly devoted to intra-party conflict, pre-emption may perform a function of displacement. It may deflect pressure, discord or strife between competing power sites that risks lasting social and political damage. Before the reference, the conversation might mix issues of legality with debates about the merits of the policy/law. Once the reference is initiated, the question is more likely to become 'would such a policy/law be legal or constitutional?' with the merits of the policy less prominent. Recall the struggle (recounted in Chapter 5) between the federal and Alberta governments over the Social Credit movement. The federal government was of the view that Alberta's legislation put at risk Canada's standing in international markets. Nonetheless, it hesitated to respond with the blunt cudgel of disallowance. Instead, the Prime Minister suggested a reference. After initially rejecting the idea, Alberta agreed. Arguably, the federal government was able to displace the bulk of the conflict onto a 'cooler' platform – one that involved legal argumentation before a (more) neutral tribunal. (Importantly, Canadian political actors had by that time developed a practice of treating advisory opinions as binding.)

The *Secession Reference* probably falls within this category as well. As discussed in Chapter 8, the reference was initiated after the launch of a lawsuit in Quebec seeking an injunction against a Unilateral Declaration of Independence.[12] But, given the overall context including the political aftermath of the 1995 referendum, one can see why the federal government would have been willing and even eager to shift the focus from seemingly intractable political opponents to the halls of the Supreme Court.

legal opinion. Interview with author on 17 May 2018 and recounted in Carissima Mathen and Michael Plaxton, *The Nadon Chronicles* (working title) (forthcoming UBC Press, 2019).

[12] See Chapter 8.

Today, such a tactic may have diminished applicability to the extent that litigation before the Supreme Court is viewed as highly political too. It is also highly visible. In recent years, the Court has made specific efforts to increase its accessibility to the broader public, making available case materials, and streaming its hearings on the internet. Diverting an issue to the Court may not necessarily result in less attention paid to it. But it may still change the tenor of the conversation. To the extent that the Court itself becomes the focus, any resulting displacement may yet be useful.

iii. Positioning

A number of references discussed in this book show how an advisory function enables an actor to send a particular message. For example, the federal government's use of references as a pre-condition to disallowance allowed it to demonstrate a degree of humility. That can be a valuable political tool that not only blunts an opponent's force, but also functions as particular public messaging. In the disallowance cases, by seeking judicial advice before taking direct action, the federal government acknowledged that nullifying provincial laws would have very negative consequences. Of course, in order to be fully effective, the federal government must be seen as willing not only to seek out the advice, but to comply with it. Still, as noted in Chapter 5, the discussion among federal actors in the late nineteenth century supports the idea that the reference power could function to channel intergovernmental resentment in a way that was perceived as helpful to the federation's overall stability.

A second example of this positioning is the decision by the British Columbia government to pursue a reference with respect to its opposition to the Trans Mountain Extension (TMX) (discussed in Chapter 5.) While it was not the only reason, public comments by provincial leaders have stressed their fealty to judicial review and the rule of law, and their wish to obtain clarity on the matter as soon as possible so that both the province *and* its opponents may know how to proceed.[13]

References can provide a method for institutional actors to challenge one another in a kind of 'power play'. Barry Strayer argued that this sort of interaction was an inevitable by-product of federalism.[14] Governments frequently initiate references about legislation and policy pertaining to their jurisdictional rivals. In the *Firearms Reference*, for example, a number of provinces questioned the validity of a federal gun registry – an extremely polarising initiative that divided citizens and provinces alike.[15] Recent provincial use of the reference function regarding

[13] www.cbc.ca/news/canada/british-columbia/bc-reference-case-pipeline-1.4624848.

[14] Barry L Strayer, *The Canadian Constitution and the Courts: The Function and Scope of Judicial Review* (Toronto: Butterworths, 1988).

[15] *Reference re Firearms Act* (Can), [2000] 1 SCR 783.

federal environmental and resource development initiatives (recounted in Chapter 5) appears to use the advisory function not just to thwart federal goals, but to assert provincial autonomy and policy choices in the face of a clear and countervailing federal decision.

iv. Avoidance

References allow governments to avoid 'hot potatoes'.[16] Subtly different from the displacement tactic, the motivation is to avoid damage to the initiating actor itself. By diverting a controversial issue to the judiciary, its political 'heat' will follow. (Admittedly, the same could be said for litigation generally.) One example is the use of references to deal with alleged wrongful convictions. Such matters are highly sensitive. They are invariably complicated, often spanning years and involving governments which may be far removed from the initial events and decisions. They pose significant evidentiary, jurisdictional and legal challenges. In that context, the use of the advisory function can help to re-characterise an acute political controversy as unambiguously legal. Of course, given that they represent a profound failure of the criminal justice system, wrongful convictions *are* legal. But the choices made and discretion exercised that contribute to such failures are often political. Post hoc judicial review taking the form of a reference can be characterised strictly as remediating legal errors. Courts generally seek to avoid making broader comments.

An interesting example is the case of Wilbur Coffin, convicted of murder, whose leave to appeal application was denied by Supreme Court Justice Douglas Abbott.[17] Abbott J, who had no prior criminal experience, was a controversial appointment directly from a federal Cabinet position (something that would be unthinkable today). Abbott's dismissal of the leave application was received extremely badly. It not only confirmed many Canadians' concern about an unfair case, but it also cemented suspicions that the Court was staffed with sub-par appointees who were indifferent to basic issues of fairness.

The reason why this is an interesting example is that at least part of the controversy emanated from the Court's own action. But, in a trial widely perceived as unfair, the negative perception redounded to the government as well. In response to the increasing outcry, the federal government referred to the Court the question:

> If the application made by Wilbert Coffin for leave to appeal to the Supreme Court of Canada had been granted on any of the grounds alleged on the said application, what disposition of the appeal would now be made by the Court?[18]

[16] Matthew A Hennigar, 'The Canadian Government's Litigation Strategy in Sexual Orientation Cases' in James B Kelly and Christopher P Manfredi (eds), *Contested Constitutionalism: Reflections on the Canadian Charter of Rights and Freedoms* (Vancouver: UBC Press, 2009) 209; Kate Puddister, *Inviting Judicial Review: A Comprehensive Analysis Of Canadian Appellate Court Reference Cases*, PhD thesis, McGill University, Montreal, December 2015, ch 5.

[17] *R v Coffin*, [1956] SCR 191.

[18] ibid.

The question was extraordinary. It invited the Court to engage in counter-factual reasoning. It also provided an opportunity for the entire bench to vindicate one of its colleagues. And it permitted the Court to counter stinging criticism in a criminal matter. (Whether the Court actually accomplished those aims is debatable.[19])

Another strategic reason to pursue references is the control that they permit (which can also involve co-ordination and pre-emption). First, the proceedings provide the actor greater choice over timing. References permit actors to speed up or slow down the dynamics of a dispute. In the *Manitoba Egg Reference*[20] the province of Manitoba created a constitutional controversy out of whole cloth because those provinces most directly implicated in competitive agricultural marketing (Quebec and Ontario) were slow to pursue the issue in court. That frustrated Manitoba's desire to determine the validity of such protectionist regimes. Through its reference, Manitoba was able to obtain that guidance regardless of its lack of direct standing.

A possible example of 'slowing down' is the Canadian Justice Minister's statement in 2017 that she would refer the constitutionality of a genetic discrimination law to the Supreme Court (a law she had opposed but which had nonetheless been passed). Some critics charged that the Minister wished simply to delay full and effective implementation of the Bill, reasoning that private parties most affected by the law would be slow to change their policies in advance of the advisory opinion.[21]

A further example of how references can draw out policy disputes is the British Columbia government's decision to refer questions relating to TMX. At the time, the private owner of the pipeline had become increasingly skittish over the prospect of lengthy delays. Though it has not admitted as such, the British Columbia government – which was newly elected and had a constituency that was largely opposed to the project – likely wanted to increase that unease.[22]

An important aspect of control includes the right to frame the questions. In an ordinary case, the moving party sets the questions, but is subject to cross-appeal where the respondent can pose questions of its own. Additionally, in constitutional matters, the Supreme Court (and other courts) must ultimately approve all questions. In references, by contrast, the questions are set by the

[19] The Court split. Five judges would have upheld the conviction, while two would have vacated it and ordered a new trial. One month later, Coffin was hanged. An inquiry commissioned in 1964 determined that his trial was fair. In the ensuing decades, though, a growing number of persons and groups have asserted his innocence and the matter is generally viewed as a low point for Canadian criminal justice. Ibid.

[20] *Attorney-General for Manitoba v Manitoba Egg and Poultry Association et al.*, [1971] SCR 689. See the additional discussion in Chapter 5.

[21] As noted in Chapter 4, the issue will first be considered in a reference initiated by Quebec to the provincial court of appeal.

[22] In fact, in order to speed things up again, the federal government subsequently announced that it would buy the entire project: Rachel Aiello, 'Feds spending $4.5B to buy Trans Mountain pipeline', CTV News, 28 May 2018, www.ctvnews.ca/politics/feds-spending-4-5b-to-buy-trans-mountain-pipeline-1.3949663.

initiating actors and, save for the Court's rarely exercised discretion to refuse to answer, they generally are left undisturbed.

As I argued in Chapter 4, question setting is a significant advantage.[23] The very nature of judicial inquiry emphasises line drawing and 'narrow casting'. The question 'Do I have the power to create entity X?' is different from the question 'Do I have the power to create any entity that falls into category Y?'; and both again are different from the question 'What are the defining characteristics of entity X and category Y and do they fall within my existing jurisdiction over subject matter Z?' The nature of a question determines the precedential power of the answer: the more narrow and fact centric a question is, the less likely it is to have what the philosopher Ronald Dworkin called 'gravitational force'[24] – the ability to generate principles of broad and future application.

Thus, an initiating actor enjoys the chance to derive maximum advantage from the proceeding by tailoring the questions. The actor can highlight those parts of an issue it deems most crucial, and (try to) avoid those it deems to be inconvenient, distracting or dangerous. The provincial references in the *Patriation Reference* are good examples of this.

Recall that in the *Same-sex Marriage Reference*[25] the federal government did not want to ask the Supreme Court what was, after all, the central question: whether limiting civil marriage to persons of the opposite sex violated the Charter's equality guarantees. As discussed in Chapter 7, the reference questions related to federalism, and to a possible conflict between equality and religious freedom.

In trying to explain the government's curious strategy, some have pointed to the 'conversion' among Liberal Party of Canada leaders to a position favouring marriage equality. The argument is that the government no longer wanted to openly oppose the claimants (quite separate from the fact that it likely would have lost). At the same time, the government was reluctant to reverse its previously argued position in court. Possibly, party leaders anticipated negative pushback from MPs. And yet, the government wished to get the input of the Supreme Court on some ancillary issues (division of powers) that it viewed as relevant. Nothing but the reference function would permit such a bald sidestepping of the central issue. An appeal would have dealt with it squarely, by cross-appeal if necessary.

The exclusion of the central question was, itself, controversial.[26] Only after being subject to significant political pressure did the federal government agree to

[23] The practice varies between federal references (which are initiated directly before the Supreme Court) and appeals of provincial reference opinions. Because the latter are styled as appeals, there is the opportunity for the Court to set the questions. In practice, the Court virtually always accepts the questions considered in the lower court.

[24] Ronald Dworkin, *Taking Rights Seriously* (Cambridge, MA: Harvard University Press, 1977) 113.

[25] *Reference re Same-Sex Marriage*, [2004] 3 SCR 698, 2004 SCC 79.

[26] ibid.

put the issue of marriage equality to the Court. As noted in Chapter 4, the Court asserted an independent power to refuse to answer that question.

The power to set questions is not ironclad and may itself be subject to political pressure. But the *Same-Sex Marriage Reference* suggests that governments likely perceive significant benefit in being able to tailor a proceeding. Choice of timing is also valuable; through it, the government can avoid (or exploit) politically volatile events and public sentiment. In earlier times, the government even facilitated the participation of other parties (today such measures have been largely subsumed by the Court's own processes.[27]

As a reference's primary mover, a government can also greatly shape the evidentiary record. In the *Manitoba Egg Reference*, by structuring questions around its own Order in Council that presumed certain facts, Manitoba circumvented the introduction of contrary evidence. The lack of a factual context is, of course, no impediment to a reference. That appears to have been a factor in the British Columbia government's unusual decision to refer the validity of section 293 of the Criminal Code (polygamy) to a trial court.[28]

D. Imprimatur

The last reason I will explore is the idea that having the court weigh in on an issue has a value all its own. Through references, actors can trade on the special legitimacy and power of the court which they, largely, lack. This can be described as seeking the court's imprimatur.

There are, of course, a variety of circumstances in which an imprimatur may be sought.

Sometimes, a dispute is unlikely to be the subject of ordinary litigation. It might present difficulties in terms of securing standing before the court, or not be ripe. The *Patriation Reference* concerned an issue (the Prime Minister's ability to trigger the consideration of the Westminster Parliament for an amendment of the Constitution Act 1867) about which it would have been difficult to identify

[27] This is discussed further in Chapter 10.

[28] *Reference re: Section 293 of the Criminal Code of Canada*, 2011 BCSC 1588. The reference was discussed in the Introduction to this book. The Crown used the following reasoning for the reference:

> Pursuing a reference through B.C. Supreme Court gives us the option to introduce evidence and witnesses, which will put a human face on polygamy in contrast to the more abstract nature of a reference to B.C. Court of Appeal. Proceeding by way of reference is consistent with the earlier advice of senior lawyers Richard Peck and Leonard Doust. …
>
> British Columbians and Canadians deserve and want to know whether valid laws are in place that prohibit polygamous relationships, particularly when those relationships involve minors. I am asking the court for its direction so the justice system, in B.C. and in Canada, can address the serious social harms that can result from the practice of polygamy.

R v Blackmore, 2018 BCSC 367 at para 35.

a party able to launch a lawsuit in the ordinary course.[29] It therefore made sense for the provinces opposed to such action to initiate a reference to their respective courts of appeal. Although the provinces may also have wanted doctrinal guidance, it was useful to draw the court into a dispute that it otherwise would not readily enter.

This motivation operates best when the actor seeking clarification thinks it is reasonable that an opponent will pursue a course of action injurious to its interests (in the case of patriation, constitutional amendments that would diminish provincial powers). Suppose, though, that is not the case. Might an actor seek clarification about its *own* decision? Partly, the answer lies in whether continued uncertainty or claims of diminished legitimacy could hamper the actor's ability to fully pursue certain ends. Additionally, in a federal system where both orders of government can refer questions, an actor may wish to seek such guidance prior to a similar move being employed by a jurisdictional adversary (which, being a tactical consideration as well, was discussed above).

An imprimatur may also be pursued in the form of a reference because the underlying matter *has* been finally adjudicated and other possible avenues (such as a royal commission of inquiry) have, for whatever reason, been rejected or put off. This could partially explain the use of references to examine wrongful convictions such as those of Stephen Truscott[30] and Donald Marshall.[31] The matters were not amenable to ordinary appeal. In 2002 Parliament amended the Criminal Code to permit the federal Minister of Justice to refer such matters to the relevant provincial court of appeal, and they are treated as appeals. (Such references also serve other purposes, discussed below.)

In the *Same-sex Marriage Reference*,[32] the federal government found itself at a crucial juncture. Having decided not to appeal lower court losses to the

[29] The argument about the level of difficulty is based on the standing rules at the time. Possibly, a litigant today could make a claim for public interest standing. But such a grant is discretionary and certainly not guaranteed. See *Finlay v Canada (Minister of Finance)*, [1986] 2 SCR 607; *Canada (Attorney General) v Downtown Eastside Sex Workers United Against Violence Society*, 2012 SCC 45, [2012] 2 SCR 524. Standing is further discussed in Chapters 1 and 10.

[30] *Reference Re: Steven Murray Truscott*, [1967] SCR 309 [*Re Truscott*]. Similar to the *Coffin* reference, the Governor in Council asked: 'Had an appeal by Steven Murray Truscott been made to the Supreme Court of Canada, as is now permitted by Section 597A of the *Criminal Code* of Canada, what disposition would the Court have made of such an appeal on a consideration of the existing Record and such further evidence as the Court, in its discretion, may receive and consider?'
Section 597A, 1960–61, c. 44, s. 11 provided:

> Notwithstanding any other provision of this Act, a person
>
> (*a*) who has been sentenced to death and whose conviction is affirmed by the court of appeal, or
> (*b*) who is acquitted of an offence punishable by death and whose acquittal is set aside by the court of appeal,
>
> may appeal to the Supreme Court of Canada on any ground of law or fact or mixed law and fact.

[31] Prime Minister Jean Chretien referred the matter to the appeal division of Supreme Court of Nova Scotia, which quashed Marshall's conviction (though not without making negative comments about him that proved to be quite controversial: (1983) 57 NSR (2d) 286. An authoritative account of the entire case is provided in *MacKeigan v Hickman*, [1989] 2 SCR 796.

[32] *Reference re Same-Sex Marriage*, [2004] 3 SCR 698, 2004 SCC 79.

Supreme Court, it drafted a law that would enshrine an expanded definition of marriage. But the executive controlled only a minority of seats in the legislature. The issue of marriage equality was just beginning to enjoy broad public support. The government's own caucus was divided.[33] The dynamics were unstable. Bringing the matter to the Supreme Court was a way to obtain its imprimatur without having to shoulder the political burden of trying to overturn lower court rulings with which a number of the government's supporters agreed.

It is striking that even actors who regard the courts with suspicion have recognised the value in the judicial voice. The *Senate Reform* and *Supreme Court Act* references of 2014 come to mind. There were a multitude of reasons to have pursued either reference. I suggest that the federal government also believed that the Court's endorsement would help it move forward on particularly fraught issues of federal–provincial conflict. That the government had, over more than a decade, repeatedly displayed its impatience with judicial review makes its decisions highly illuminating on the power of the court's advisory function.

Having considered the reasons why non-judicial actors seek advisory opinions, it might be thought redundant to go on to explore why those same actors would comply with the resulting opinion. But, as argued below, those reasons deserve separate consideration.

Why Not Comply?

It is surely noteworthy when one arm of government approaches another for assistance in clarifying a question of law. It is not surprising, then, that advisory opinions would be considered important. But Canadian advisory opinions go somewhat further than that. They are taken as legal directives – conveying statements that constitute reasons for action, compliance and/or forbearance.

It is difficult to find an example of an actor initiating a reference and later disavowing the 'advice' received. Disavowal does not occur even among those who opposed the reference going ahead in the first place. Recall that in the *Secession Reference*, Quebec refused to participate. Yet, when the opinion was released, the province was content to cite those portions that supported its political aims – namely, the duty on the rest of Canada to negotiate in good faith. While that may have been at least partly a strategic posture, Quebec likely did not think it fruitful to attack the opinion in any event.

That point leads to another. Actors can indicate that they are not persuaded of the soundness of *any* judicial ruling. In Canada, such moments are relatively rare[34]

[33] Matthew Hennigar, 'The Canadian Government's Litigation Strategy in Sexual Orientation Cases', 9, www.cpsa-acsp.ca/papers-2004/Hennigar.pdf, citing Brian Laghi, 'MPs' debate mirrors national turmoil', *The Globe and Mail*, 17 September 2003, A4.

[34] Some examples, taken from the rather fractious period of the Stephen Harper government, are recounted in C Mathen, 'A Recent History of Government Responses to Constitutional Litigation' (2016) 25(3) Constitutional Forum 101–08.

but they can and do happen. But the *pedigree* of the directive (ie, whether it comes from a decision or an advisory opinion) does not appear relevant to that choice. Political actors do not say things like:

> While we thank the Court for its opinion, it is of course just that: an opinion. The opinion was not issued in the course of an appeal and, thus, it has no force or effect. Therefore, we do not consider ourselves bound to follow it as a general rule. Even if we did, we do not have a duty to follow the opinion if we *also* have grave reservations – which we do here – about its soundness as a matter of law.[35]

Instead, Canadian political actors treat advisory opinions as containing reasons for action that apply to them, and they modify their behaviour accordingly. They do so even where the opinion completely contradicts a prior asserted position; they have displayed only modest respect for the court that issued it; and they and/or others perceive the opinion as misguided.

The above attitude is particularly striking given the factors that would seem to militate against it, to provide reasons to *not* comply, or, at least, to not *readily* comply. First, and perhaps most obviously, references are initiated to obtain 'advice' and occur apart from normal adjudicative processes. As stated in the *Reference re References*,[36] the function is separate from the Supreme Court's general appellate role and in performing that function the Court does not issue anything that is formally binding upon the parties.

Joseph Raz has distinguished the act of giving 'advice' from that of giving an 'order'.[37] A legally binding rule or order is a preclusive norm, in the sense that,

[35] Actors occasionally seek to avoid the result, but they virtually never do so in open defiance. See, for example, the decision by the government of Nova Scotia to call an election in 2017 a few months after the provincial court of appeal advised that three electoral districts had been eliminated in violation of the Charter's democratic rights. Despite the ruling, the election took place under the old map. *Reference re the Final Report of the Electoral Boundaries Commission*, 2017 NSCA 10, www.canlii.org/en/ns/nsca/doc/2017/2017nsca10/2017nsca10.html.

[36] *Re References by Governor-General in Council*, (1910) 43 SCR 536, aff'd [1912] AC 571.

[37] Joseph Raz, *The Authority of Law* (Oxford: Clarendon Press, 1979) 21–22: 'Consider the standard grounds for seeking advice. These are usually to gain information relevant to the solution of some practical problem facing one or for comparing one's own evaluation of the weight and importance of various factors with that of other people as a means of checking one's own views and calculations. But sometimes advice is sought for entirely different reasons. A person may be faced with a problem involving considerations concerning which he has little knowledge or understanding. He may turn to an expert, to an authority, for advice despite the fact that he has no way of assessing the reasons pointed out by the authority against other conflicting reasons of which he may be aware. He may decide to follow the advice given without trying to work out whether it indicates reasons that tip the balance. If he does so he is in fact excluding all the conflicting reasons of which he is aware from his considerations. He is regarding the advice both as a reason to perform the action he was advised to perform and for not acting on conflicting reasons. A person may be justified in holding the advice he received to be a protected reason, even though advice is not given with an intention to be taken as a protected reason'. The point is further developed below. For an earlier treatment, see Thomas Hobbes, *Leviathan, or the Matter, Forme and Power of a Commonwealth Ecclesiasticall and Civil* [1651] (Oxford: Basil Blackwell, 1946) ch xxv. See also Mark D Walters, 'Judicial Review of Ministerial Advice to the Crown' (2016) 25(3) Constitutional Forum 33.

if taken properly by the subject to whom it applies, it precludes that subject from engaging in an independent assessment of the substantive reasons for action that the rule embodies. Advice, Raz says, is different. The adviser offers substantive reasons that the recipient is expected to weigh him or herself; and the fact that the adviser has offered those reasons for action does not preclude the recipient from assessing, independently, the conclusions reached.

Thus, while an adviser intends his advice to be taken as correct, he or she does not necessarily intend for it to be taken as a reason for action.[38] It stands to reason, then, that those receiving the advice do not make a category mistake if they choose to apply their own independent judgement, and not simply regard the advice as a set of self-contained reasons. (Raz does allow that advice can be taken as a reason for action even if it is not intended that way.)[39]

In light of the above point it is useful to remember that references are launched by actors with significant legal and political authority of their own. Executive and legislative actors routinely issue directives (laws, regulations, policies) which *others* treat as reasons for actions.

In addition, these actors possess a level of knowledge and experience comparable to the court's. In an era marked by explicit constitutional guarantees and the ever-present possibility of judicial review, non-judicial actors routinely and proactively assess statutes and other decisions for constitutional compliance. It has become standard for Canadian government lawyers to vet government Bills for constitutional compliance.[40] In 2017 the federal Justice Minister introduced legislation to formalise that duty, extending it to *all* government Bills, whether introduced by her or not.[41]

Executive and legislative actors frequently grapple with the implications of proposed legislation in formal debate, as well as in the Committee process where smaller groups of MPs or Senators study proposed legislation. They also consider policy issues unconnected to specific Bills.[42] Standing committees of the House and Senate, respectively, apply their judgement to proposed legislation in order to address potential policy and/or legal problems; clarify points of ambiguity; and remove or minimise constitutional concerns. It is evident that such actors engage

[38] ibid at 15.

[39] ibid.

[40] To be sure, the resulting conclusions have not always been faithful to meaningful compliance thresholds. During the tenure of Prime Minister Stephen Harper, such review was alleged to be extremely lax; indeed, some scholars charged that the government was content to introduce legislation that was 'manifestly unconstitutional'. See Jennifer Bond, 'Failure to Report: The Manifestly Unconstitutional Nature of the Human Smugglers Act' (2014) 51(2) Osgoode Hall Law Journal 377.

[41] Bill C-51, An Act to amend the Criminal Code and the Department of Justice Act and to make consequential amendments to another Act, 42nd Parliament, 1st Session, www.parl.ca/LegisInfo/BillDetails.aspx?Language=E&billId=9002286.

[42] See, for example, 'Delaying Justice is Denying Justice: Final report of the Standing Senate Committee on Legal and Constitutional Affairs', Senate of Canada, 14 June 2017, https://sencanada.ca/content/sen/committee/421/LCJC/reports/Court_Delays_Final_Report_e.pdf.

in legal discussion and debate, that they have substantive legal expertise, and that they believe their own opinions to be worthy of serious consideration.

In other words, the legislature and executive almost certainly consider themselves equipped to engage in highly technical analyses of the implications, constitutional or otherwise, of their law-making roles or of the interpretation of their directives. (Indeed, the legislative branch enjoys significant latitude to control that interpretation through declaratory legislation.)[43]

Additionally, formal power holders in both branches routinely receive advice from bureaucrats; internal legal advisers; individual members of Parliament; external counsel; and members of the public. And those power holders just as routinely decide which of those sources they will take up, which they will contest and which they will ignore.

Thus, when a court issues an advisory opinion that relates directly to the authority or actions of another branch, the dynamics are different from a situation involving private parties, or a 'sovereign' and its 'subjects'. The institutions are, roughly speaking, equals.[44] They enjoy a degree of interplay and mutual regard. There may even be a sense of interdependence. The courts in Canada, for example, rely on the executive branch to appoint their members; and on the legislative branch to set the terms for their operations. There are, of course, strong protections – both legal and political – against undue interference of those branches in judicial affairs. But, in the absence of voluntary agreement, ensuring compliance is costly. Thus, judicial forbearance may be something of a virtue.[45]

Another point that weighs against compliance is the fact that non-judicial actors have public duties at least equal to those of courts, duties that extend further than the obligation to uphold the rule of law. Where the actor has a sincere belief that the directive is wrong, he or she may well be expected to back up that substantive disagreement with action. The Canadian constitution itself provides a route for such disagreement: section 33 of the Charter of Rights permits the legislative branch to maintain a law in place notwithstanding that it violates certain rights and freedoms.[46] Section 33 can be invoked at any time – including *after* a court

[43] *Régie des rentes du Québec v Canada Bread Company Ltd.*, 2013 SCC 46, [2013] 3 SCR 125.

[44] Admittedly, when it comes to legal interpretation, the judiciary enjoys a decided advantage and there are not many who advocate for an equivalent power in either of the other branches. The only point being made here is that those actors might not necessarily feel that way. For a trenchant critique of the court's privileged position see Dennis Baker, *Not Quite Supreme: The Courts and Coordinate Constitutional Interpretation* (Kingston and Montreal: McGill-Queen's University Press, 2010).

[45] In 2017 Chief Justice Paul Crampton of the Federal Court made a public plea for more funding from the executive branch. He argued that courts should not have to go, hat in hand, to the government for adequate monies to ensure their efficient operations, and called for greater involvement of Parliament. *CTV News*, '"It's not right": Federal judge accuses government of chronic underfunding', 27 June 2017, www.ctvnews.ca/politics/it-s-not-right-federal-judge-accuses-government-of-chronic-underfunding-1.3479238.

[46] Charter, s 33:

> (1) Parliament or the legislature of a province may expressly declare in an Act of Parliament or of the legislature, as the case may be, that the Act or a provision thereof shall operate notwithstanding a provision included in section 2 or sections 7 to 15 of this Charter.

finds that a particular law is unconstitutional.[47] It can, therefore, be used to deliberately disregard a legal directive.

While political actors in Canada have only occasionally used the notwithstanding clause,[48] those occasions have included responses to court decisions. And, while the political reaction has been mixed, there is a general sense that the clause remains an available (albeit controversial) option for the various Canadian legislatures to consider. Extrapolating from that, it is at least possible that an executive or other actor could offer a careful, focussed explanation of the difference between 'advisory' and other judicial opinions; and could join that to a substantive case for why a particular opinion ought not to be followed.

Finally, compared to an individual, the executive or legislature simply has more room to respond. Suppose that a reference returns an answer that a law is ultra vires. The government that proposed the law has a variety of options. It can accept the directive and abandon the law altogether. But it also can enact a new or amended law that responds to the core of the directive or tries to reframe the issue. In Charter litigation (which admittedly has produced relatively few advisory opinions) such a move has been referred to as 'second-look' legislation.[49]

The above factors might complicate the pull by institutional actors to disregard advisory opinions. Yet, for the most part, they have not. Advisory opinions are treated by political actors as containing reasons for them to modify their behaviour, decisions and posture, and do not inspire different attitudes traceable to their pedigree *as* references. The final section examines possible reasons why.

Why Comply?

Political actors who initiate references have a choice to make about the resulting opinion: shall they treat them as containing reasons for action – as setting out

(2) An Act or a provision of an Act in respect of which a declaration made under this section is in effect shall have such operation as it would have but for the provision of this Charter referred to in the declaration.

[47] *Ford v Quebec (AG)*, [1988] 2 SCR 712. The Supreme Court did state that the clause cannot operate retroactively. Thus, as against an unfavourable ruling, s 33 cannot negate any previous state of invalidity, or any remedy imposed by the Court prior to the date of the actual resolution invoking the clause.

[48] Beginning in 2017, after many years where the clause was seen as more or less defunct, a number of provinces have been willing to use, or at least discuss using, the notwithstanding clause, including Saskatchewan, Ontario and Quebec. The long-term implications are uncertain. CBC News, 'Sask. government invokes notwithstanding clause over Catholic school ruling', 08 November 2017, www.cbc.ca/news/canada/saskatchewan/sask-notwithstanding-schools-1.4392895; Andrew Russell, 'Ontario Premier Doug Ford plans to invoke notwithstanding clause. Here's what you need to know', 10 September 2018, https://globalnews.ca/news/4438198/notwithstanding-clause-doug-ford-bill-5-toronto-city-council/; Les Perreaux, 'Legault to use notwithstanding clause to ban religious symbols for civil servants', *The Globe and Mail*, 2 October 2018, www.theglobeandmail.com/canada/article-francois-legault-to-invoke-notwithstanding-clause-to-ban-quebec-public/. The long-term implications are uncertain.

[49] Peter W Hogg, Allison A Bushell Thornton and Wade K Wright, 'Charter Dialogue Revisited – Or "Much Ado About Metaphors"' (2007) 45 Osgoode Hall Law Journal 1.

a rule or rules with which they must comply? There is little indication, though, that political actors, at least in Canada, regard that choice as real. Rather, they have developed a practice of complying with whatever a reference opinion says, or, at least, with what they believe it to say. It seems, in other words, that they do not regard advisory opinions as being merely 'advisory'.

The practice is all the more striking when one looks at the reaction by those same actors to other forms of 'advice' or 'guidance'. Consider proceedings such as Royal Commissions, which are entities set up to study a problem, determine facts and (sometimes) policy and, in many cases, make recommendations for the future. Almost invariably such commissions are headed by active or former judicial actors. But although their reports are often greeted with enthusiasm, the executive branch at best inconsistently follows their advice.[50]

Does anything meaningful distinguish an advisory opinion from a report by a Royal Commission? What about 'advice' like the memorandum authored by former Supreme Court justice Ian Binnie in the Nadon controversy?

The discussion below focuses on two sets of answers. The first is that, for political actors, advisory opinions simply count as 'law' in the way that cases do. I canvass some reasons why that might be the case. The second is that, even if advisory opinions do not properly count as 'law', non-judicial actors might nonetheless consider them to contain norm-generating reasons.

It might be supposed that the fact that advisory opinions are not binding automatically renders them 'not-law'. One could argue that, unless something is capable of generating compliance – binding someone – it falls outside of the law. The idea is roughly analogous to John Austin's theory that law consists primarily of *commands* backed by *sanctions*.[51] Wherever one finds a social group (or majority of it) displaying habitual obedience to commands from a sovereign that habitually obeys no one, one finds law.

Although the command theory does not hold much sway in current philosophical analyses of law,[52] it surely reflects important intuitions that people have when they think about what they understand law to be. One of those intuitions is that law can *modify* a person's behaviour from what they initially may have intended to do. A legal prohibition against, say, tax fraud can cause a person to change their decisions around tax filings, out of fear of the potential consequences. Law's ability to impose sanctions for its breaches creates a dynamic that is essential to the regulation of some human activity.

[50] Grant Hoole, 'Commissions of Inquiry in Canada' in Scott Prasser and Helen Tracey (eds), *Royal Commissions and Public Inquiries: Practice and Potential* (Ballarat, Vic: Connor Court, 2014) 331. Commissions are discussed in the next chapter.

[51] John Austin, *The Province of Jurisprudence Determined and the Uses of the Study of Jurisprudence* (London: Weidenfeld and Nicolson, 1954) 13; HLA Hart, *The Concept of Law* (Oxford: Oxford University Press, 1994) 100.

[52] For an argument that legal obligation does depend on a sense of sanction, see Frederick Schauer, *The Force of Law* (Cambridge MA: Harvard University Press, 2015).

The command theory is powerfully simple. But, in most human societies, that very simplicity renders the theory too crude to be workable. One of its chief deficiencies, as HLA Hart argued, is that not all law fairly can be characterised as 'orders'.[53] Law does not, invariably, seek to force people to act in a certain way. Sometimes, law confers upon private persons the power to do things (to contract or to make a will); or it grants immunity; or it allocates jurisdiction to institutions like courts and legislatures. Hart argued that, in modern legal systems, a good deal of 'law' is concerned with such non-prohibitory but still essential components of human social life. Thus, instead of being concerned primarily with orders, law is more accurately described as a system of rules.

Part of the dynamic that law creates is that it has authority over people. Joseph Raz has insisted that authority is the central claim of law – the quality that distinguishes it from other power-exerting mechanisms.[54] Raz argues that law does not merely command that it *must be* obeyed – even if it often has the resources to enforce that command. The ability to apply force to a non- or pre-compliant person is insufficient. Any person with sufficient means and determination can exact compliance in numerous situations that no one would accept as lawful. In the classic example, a gunman who 'compels' a victim to turn over money certainly controls her, but that control is not sensibly described as an exercise of 'authority'. What makes law distinctive, Raz says, is its insistence, not just that it *must* but that it *ought to* be obeyed – that its authority is legitimate. (Note that this is different from whether law's claim is also *actually* justified – ie., de jure as well as de facto.)

The idea that advisory opinions are perceived as authoritative is a possible and plausible explanation of why non-judicial actors might think that such opinions constitute a form of law. In order to more fully explain why, it is necessary to canvass understandings of authority that do not depend upon the mere ability to impose sanctions for non-compliance. For such an understanding, I turn again to Raz, whose model of authority has been highly influential.[55] I should note from the outset that there are at least two ways to understand authority vis-à-vis the reference function, namely, the authority of the court which issues the opinion, and the authority of the opinion itself. For the purposes of the following discussion, I generally do not distinguish between the two. As will become clear in the next chapter, I think that they are sufficiently integrated that such a distinction is unhelpful.

[53] I will leave aside, for now, Hans Kelsen's powerful argument that law consists primarily of directives to authorities as to when to apply sanctions to those who breach its dictates. Hart addresses it and attempts to show why it is unpersuasive (n 51) 35–42.

[54] Raz (n 37) 28–29.

[55] Which is not to say that it lacks critics. See Robert Ladenson, 'In Defense of a Hobbesian Conception of Law' in Joseph Raz (ed), *Authority* (New York: New York University Press, 1990) 32; Stephen Perry, 'Law and Obligation' (2005) 50 American Journal of Jurisprudence 278; John Finnis, 'Law and What I Should Truly Decide' (2003) 48 American Journal of Jurisprudence 107.

To illustrate his argument about authority, Raz used the example of an arbitrator.[56] An arbitrator's authority lies in the fact that conflicted parties agree to be bound by her decision. But her authority as an 'arbitrator' is not solely established by the *fact* of such agreement. It involves additional concepts.

First, in resolving the dispute the arbitrator is expected to apply certain processes of reasoning and judgement. Parties could agree to resolve their dispute on the basis of something, like a coin toss, that is unrelated to the underlying dispute. They could even entrust the management of that coin toss to a third party, and call that party an 'arbitrator'. But the ensuing process would not, in any meaningful sense, correspond to what 'arbitration' generally is understood to be. Arbitration entails a decision maker drawing on factors that are related to the dispute (Raz calls these 'dependent reasons').

In other words, the authority of the decision rests partly on *how* it is made – the idea that, in reaching it, the arbitrator privileges certain sorts of considerations and downplays or excludes others. (None of that, by the way, means that the arbitrator's decision is necessarily final. It can be authoritative alongside some mechanism of further review. It does, though, provide at least one criterion for such review.)

The second important concept is that the arbitral decision functions so as to *replace* or *pre-empt* the reasons for action that the parties might otherwise have. Even though the arbitrator herself has relied on those other (dependent) reasons, once the decision is issued, it becomes the prime reason for those parties who are bound (either by agreement or by some other norm) to follow it.

As a social practice, of course, law is not dependent upon parties' discrete agreements to be bound by anything. One must find a substitute for that agreement. For Raz, the substitute is provided by a concept he calls the 'normal justification thesis'. Under that thesis, someone or something has authority over another person if

> the alleged subject is likely better to comply with reasons which apply to him if he accepts the directive of the alleged authority as authoritatively binding and tries to follow them, than if he tries to follow the reasons which apply to him directly.[57]

In other words, part of what makes law authoritative is that people accept its directives without first interrogating them. For example, people accept posted speed limits as authoritative regardless of whether they, independently, would choose to observe the same limit. Now, accepting the speed limit as authoritative does not then entail or require perfect compliance with it. Indeed, as most of us can attest, perfect compliance is a fiction! But, if the thesis holds, almost everyone accepts the limit as an authoritative directive with which they are *supposed* to comply. And they accept that the state may hold them accountable for exceeding a posted speed limit simply on the basis that they failed to observe it. (Of course,

[56] Raz anticipates and defends against the argument that his model applies primarily to adjudicative authorities but not others: Joseph Raz, 'Authority, Law and Morality' (1985) 68(3) Monist 295, 298.

[57] ibid at 299.

that does not preclude disputing either the issuance of a particular ticket, or its prescribed punishment.)

Together, those two elements form the 'service' conception of authority. Law mediates between people and the 'right reasons' governing for their behaviour. Society accepts that mediation function because the persons who are its members accept that they are better off accepting legal directives (the NJT).

Only certain kinds of entities can claim legal authority. The entity must be one whose directives are per se identifiable as authoritative, without requiring independent evaluation. Authorities, thus, generally have a certain institutional permanence and immediately identifiable characteristics – in the case of a legislature, say, a set of rituals that signifies the due passage of statutes. Additionally, the authority in question 'must be capable of forming an opinion on how its subjects ought to behave, distinct from the subjects' own reasoning about their reasons for action'.[58] It has a distinctive capacity for reasoning.

Advisory opinions appear to satisfy many of the above accounts of authority. They are issued in the form of directives that rely explicitly on reasons that apply to the issue put before the court. Indeed, as noted in Chapter 3, the duty to provide reasons was inserted as a feature in 1891, after a few early references where the Supreme Court issued only a bare answer.

Advisory opinions make use of independent judgement. As we have seen throughout this book, they contain a court's analysis of how particular rules apply in particular situations or to particular parties. Indeed, the court's advice has weight, at least in part, because the judiciary is presumed to be competent, indeed, is thought *especially suited*, to employ independent judgement. The norms and structural features of judicial independence also help to ensure that the court is able to draw upon its own judgement and is not unduly harnessed to, or dependent upon, the judgements of others.

An advisory opinion (for example, a conclusion that a law is ultra vires) also replaces the reasons that the parties otherwise have for deciding upon a particular course of action. The advisory opinion does not just become a directive that the parties must follow. It *replaces* the reasons that those parties may have had to pursue that or a different course of action. While the parties may object to one or more aspects of the reasons, they invariably treat it as changing the terms of the debate. For example, if the advisory opinion issues from a lower court, and is appealed, generally the advisory opinion will be the focus of that appeal. Importantly, even if one of the party 'wins', they will accept the directive's reasons for reaching that result instead of continuing to insist on their own.

The courts themselves are recognised legal authorities. They make rulings and produce directives that bind the actions of others, and they are broadly viewed as having the legitimacy to do so. Whether the advisory opinions they issue bear the indicia of authority is a different question. To be sure, advisory opinions are styled

[58] Andrei Marmor, *Positive Law and Objective Values* (Oxford: Clarendon Press, 2001) 54.

differently from cases (for example, Anglo-American practice is to use the title '*Re X*' as opposed to '*X v Y*'). They do not require a pre-existing dispute (even if, in fact, they may occur in the context of an underlying legal conflict). While efforts are made to ensure that opposing arguments are received, advisory opinions need not involve someone who stands in opposition to the initiating actor. They do not produce a judgment, but rather an opinion setting out the answers to questions. Nor do they issue formal remedies (although, as discussed in the next chapter, the point has less force than might be supposed) such as powers of *certiorari*, trial *de novo*, *mandamus* or injunction.

Yet, advisory opinions unquestionably bear strong similarities to cases. Once initiated, both follow a similar trajectory. The docket for the *Senate Reform Reference* shows a myriad of motions, filings and correspondence among the various parties, involving various judges of the Court. The reference was set down for hearing in the Fall 2013 term, alongside dozens of regular appeals; formed one of the entries on the Court's docket; was heard in the same courtroom; was live-streamed on the internet; was later archived for future access; and was subject, just prior to its release, to a 'media lock-up', which the Court employs for particularly important rulings.[59]

Most importantly, advisory opinions engage in very similar *reasoning* to cases. Indeed, were one to hide the style of cause, and perhaps the first paragraph setting out the litigation history, one would be hard pressed to tell the difference between an advisory opinion and an ordinary decision. Owing, partially, to that, advisory opinions are treated as containing statements of law by the courts themselves. (These points are extensively developed in the next chapter.)

If advisory opinions are 'law' like any other authoritative directive from a court, then non-judicial actors will face heavy pressure to comply with them. The most important of those pressures is the normative idea of the rule of law. Its core principle is that everyone, individual and institution alike, is subject to law's dictates and authority – regardless of whether a particular subject of the law is itself an authority. In countries that adhere to it, the rule of law is a powerful, culture-creating ethos. It explains, at least in part, why legislatures and executive actors regularly comply with court dictates to release someone from prison; initiate a new trial; cease applying a law found to be unconstitutional; or pay damages. To the extent that the dictates found in advisory opinions are regarded as the same kind of dictate as any other court ruling, there would seem to be the same pressures on those actors to follow the dictates found in references.

[59] In a lock-up, the media is given an advance briefing of the decision so that it and accompanying news stories may be publically released simultaneously: SCC Case Information, In the Matter of a Reference by the Governor in Council concerning reform of the Senate, as set out in Order PC 2013-70, dated 1 February 2013, Docket Number 32503, www.scc-csc.ca/case-dossier/info/dock-regi-eng.aspx?cas=35203.

Thus, there is an argument to be made that advisory opinions *are* a form of law, or at least that there are reasons why non-judicial actors would treat advisory opinions as such. But what if those actors do not accept that advisory opinions are law? What if they take the Supreme Court at its word that advisory opinions are not binding? Or, what if they have not formed a decided view on the matter?

Even then, there are a number of reasons why an actor could still believe that advisory opinions contain reasons for action with which it should comply.

The most obvious reason, perhaps, is that the actor perceives that an advisory opinion is likely to be treated as authoritative by the court itself. If that is so, then gainsaying the result is only postponing the inevitable. The anticipation, by non-judicial actors, of the reception of advisory opinions by judicial ones is, in fact, a highly salient point. But, given the division in this and Chapter 10 of considerations relating to those two sets of actors, a fuller discussion is saved for that chapter.

Another reason is that seeking advice from a court (or participating in such a process) is likely to generate pressure – both self-generated and external – to comply with any advice that is received. It would be strange for one to initiate a proceeding – before a body that is generally considered authoritative, routinely issues authoritative directives, and of whom one has requested something that very much *looks* like a directive – only to subsequently disregard the resulting opinion. Doing so would create the perception that the actor was trying to 'game' the process – seeking a judicial imprimatur for purely transactional reasons but unwilling to absorb the cost of a negative result. It would risk at least some reputational and political damage.

No doubt, such damage is at its peak for initiating actors. The self-initiated nature of the advisory process might create an obligation to comply with the ruling regardless of what it says. But the pressure clearly extends, in some form, to all actors whose subsequent actions are implicated by the substance of the directive.

It is also possible that the 'advice' itself exerts a pull to comply. Raz, for example, notes that advice, though often pursued to gain relevant information in order to solve a practical problem or to compare one's own interpretation with another, may be sought for other reasons. To wit,

> A person may be faced with a problem involving considerations concerning which he has little knowledge or understanding. He may turn to an expert, to an authority, for advice despite the fact that he has no way of assessing the reasons pointed out by the authority against other conflicting reasons of which he may be aware.[60]

In such a case, a person may be inclined to follow the advice given 'without trying to work out whether it indicates reasons that tip the balance'.[61] He would, if he

[60] Raz (n 37) at 21–22.
[61] ibid.

did so, treat the advice as pre-empting any conflicting reasons he holds or would arrive at. Depending on the circumstances, then, a person can hold the advice to be a reason for action even though advice is not given with that intention.

An example of the above dynamic, in the reference context, would be an actor seeking advice on a new or unexplored issue. As discussed in earlier chapters, many references – including those relating to the advisory function itself, to basic questions of division of powers, and to the treaty power – presented a situation of interpretation, in the context of a new and unfamiliar legal order, such that an actor would find it prudent to treat the resulting opinion as 'binding', even if it were not, and even if the actor did not quite accept the dependent reasons for the court's conclusion. In the modern era, examples include the *Senate Reform Reference*, which was the first opportunity for the Supreme Court to consider Part V of the Constitution Act 1982; the *Supreme Court Act Reference*, which dealt with an interpretative question of first impression; and the *Patriation Reference*, which considered the implications of domestic constitutional reform in the context of a federal–provincial dispute.

An actor may also treat a reference opinion as binding because she holds the institution that issued it in high regard. Such regard can reflect either genuine deference or rational self-interest. As to the first, the actor may have developed an attitude towards the court that is deferential and respectful. He may regard the court as generating norms and principles worth following. He may hold as a default view that court opinions are a reason to act in one way instead of another. An analogy may be drawn with HLA Hart, who theorised that a system of law requires an 'internal point of view' about the law. As Scott J Shapiro puts it, the internal point of view is 'a practical attitude of rule acceptance';[62] it exists with respect to a rule when 'one intends to conform to the rule, criticizes others for failing to conform, does not criticize others for criticizing, and expresses one's criticism using evaluative language'.[63] While Hart was speaking in terms of legal rules, it is possible that a person could develop such a point of view about other (ie, non-legal) types of directives. The regard for courts, in general, is an important part of the rule of law in countries like Canada. It should not be surprising if it were difficult to disaggregate that regard based on whether a court pronouncement takes the form of a reference versus a decision in inter partes litigation.

Finally, there is almost certainly a degree of self-interest at work. Self-interest could provide incentives for compliance to the extent required to preserve the authority of the courts writ large. There is a strategic element to this and, also, a healthy dose of realism. Simply put, an actor who declines to follow a reference

[62] Scott J Shapiro, 'What is the Internal Point of View?' (2006) 75 Fordham Law Review 1157, 1159. For an excellent discussion of Hart's practice theory of rules, see Joseph Raz, *Practical Reason and Norms*, 42nd edn (Oxford: Oxford University Press, 1975) 9–58.

[63] Shapiro (n 62) 1163.

opinion increases the likelihood that her rivals will as well. Such a situation of uncertainty will have negative repercussions for political stability and for peaceful resolution of all manner of disputes – intergovernmental, government–citizen, citizen–citizen. To be sure, the force of this reason presupposes a general orientation towards social peace and a disinclination to use raw force to achieve political ends. The potency of both are demonstrated by actors' overwhelming tendency – no matter their political stripe – to seek out peaceful resolution (which, of course, does not preclude pointed, even vociferous, disagreement).

* * *

Together with Chapter 10, this chapter deconstructs a basic tension in the understanding of reference opinions: their formally, non-binding status does not correlate, meaningfully, to how they are received and, in particular, to the fact they are thought to contain reasons for action. With respect to the non-judicial actors that were the focus here, the explanation for that tension relates to a number of factors. One is the set of reasons why an actor would initiate such a proceeding. Those reasons might seem to make unnecessary the question of why compliance follows. But, given other broad characteristics of those non-judicial actors, the reasons do not fully explain the attitudes, not just of initiating actors, but of others. A second factor is comprised of institutional and systemic factors that plausibly would convince non-judicial actors to treat court reasons as counting as 'law'. These involve the nature of authority, the complex relationship among different state institutions, and the similarities between advisory opinions and cases. A third is that, even without reaching a definitive conclusion about the precise nature of advisory opinions and, in particular, whether they are properly regarded as 'law', such actors likely experience other pressures or incentives to treat advisory opinions in particular ways.

The missing element from the above discussion is the role and the attitude of the courts themselves. That factor, and concluding observations, are the subject of the next and final chapter.

10

The Advisory Court

The previous chapter discussed the significant pull that advisory opinions exert on non-judicial actors. It suggested that those actors view opinions as either being akin to law, or possessed of qualities that warrant similar treatment as law. Some of the reasons for treating advisory opinions in that way are political. Some relate to the legal culture in which the actors find themselves (ie, one that prioritises and privileges judicial statements). And some are rooted in pragmatic considerations regarding the anticipated consequences of failing to so treat them.

One of those considerations is that, in important ways, a Canadian advisory opinion and a judicial decision are substantively *indistinguishable*. It makes little difference, to a party's future legal position, whether a judicial resolution has emerged from one proceeding and not the other. That is because courts themselves do not draw such distinctions. The advisory opinion about the nature of Charter rights in, say, the *Motor Vehicle Reference* receives no less regard than rulings in ordinary 'live' cases such as *R v Oakes*[1] or *R v Therens*.[2] Courts treat the former reference as an authoritative statement of law. It was a statement that had clear and obvious effect not only on the offence at issue, but on all similar ones. Furthermore, the broader principles articulated in that reference – concerning the general interpretative approach to the Charter, the scope of section 7's protection, and the relationship between section 7 and section 1 – are also received as authoritative statements of law, as statements that 'bind' judicial actors including the Supreme Court itself.[3]

That binding-ness is the focus of this chapter. I argue that advisory opinions have become part of the broader set of rulings that make up the common law. As such, they are subject to the force of *stare decisis* – a powerful norm that undergirds how the courts engage with law. It is that feature that best explains why advisory opinions generally are indistinguishable from rulings in live cases.

Chapter 3 recounted how Canadian and British jurists viewed the idea of a general appellate court exercising an advisory function. Those jurists insisted that part of what made it possible for them to tolerate that additional role (in a

[1] *R v Oakes*, [1986] 1 SCR 103 (the use of reverse onuses on elements of a criminal offence prima facie violates the presumption of innocence; approach to Charter justification and proportionality).

[2] *R v Therens*, [1985] 1 SCR 613 (police detention must be prescribed a legal rule).

[3] Like most apex courts, the Supreme Court of Canada is not bound by its own precedents, but generally expends considerable effort to respect them.

constitutional sense) was precisely the fact that advisory opinions are *not* binding. They did not seriously consider that parties *or* courts would experience any notable pressure to regard such 'advice' as affecting the future legal status quo.

Of course, that was not to be. Advisory opinions quickly assumed a status that other forms of commissioned 'advice' lacked. Recall the controversy that swirled around Prime Minister Harper's appointment of Marc Nadon to the Supreme Court (the *Supreme Court Act Reference*). In an attempt to defend the appointment, the government approached former Supreme Court judges to provide opinions about his eligibility. One of them, Ian Binnie, did so via a written memorandum; another Louise Charron, permitted the government to share her agreement with it. Yet another, Michel Bastarache, appeared before a Parliamentary Senate Committee to make the same point. In the reference opinion, the Court paid little heed, and certainly gave no deference, to those various instances of support by their former colleagues.[4] While such materials are not necessarily ignored, courts do not treat them as reasons that must be respected.[5]

The first section of this chapter explores how advisory opinions came to occupy the same procedural space as cases. Both have been and are pursued as a legal form of inquiry, subject to formal (if not exactly identical) rules of procedure. They attract similar parties (understood generally) undertaking similar analysis. They produce similar work product. Advisory opinions make extensive use of written reasons, which follow conventional norms governing (appellate) adjudication; and they are subject to the same norms of intra-court engagement regarding the preparation of opinions and the freedom of individual judges to decide how to signal their view (including concurring with and dissenting from a majority conclusion).

Next, the chapter argues that advisory opinions fit into the body of precedent in a way that other forms of 'advice' do not. I offer a series of examples to show that Canadian courts regard advisory opinions like judicial decisions. The phenomenon is heightened by the fact that the courts have tended to downplay the importance of live issues as an adjudicative precondition. Whereas issues like direct standing and mootness were once policed fairly strongly, that no longer tends to be the case. At times, it appears, the chief factor in whether a court will consider a constitutional case is not whether the matter is properly before the court, but, simply, whether the court wishes to hear it. That observation is greatly strengthened by

[4] Justice Ian Binnie wrote the memorandum, and Justice Louise Charron, as reported by the government, expressed her agreement with his opinion. Only Ian Binnie's advice was publicly disclosed. Access to information requests by Members of Parliament shed some, but not much, light on these external opinions. Results of such inquiries are on file with the author. Michael Plaxton and Carissima Mathen, 'Purposive Interpretation, Quebec, and the *Supreme Court Act*' (2013) 22(3) Constitutional Forum 15. Indeed, in an appearance before Parliament, I (mistakenly) predicted that the 'Binnie memorandum' would receive at least some focus in the Court's opinion.

[5] Randy Kozel argues that 'a judicial proposition that is treated as persuasive carries no force beyond that which might accrue to an amicus curiae brief or a scholarly treatise'. Randy J Kozel, 'The Scope of Precedent' (2014) 113 Michigan Law Review 179, 186.

the doctrine of *public interest standing*, under which constitutional challenges may proceed without a directly affected litigant.[6]

The chapter concludes by suggesting that advisory opinions complement and enhance the idea that, especially in modern rule-of-law states, the primary role of high courts is to *provide answers*. It is, therefore, unsurprising that courts would hesitate to either (a) shed their adjudicative posture when crafting an advisory opinion, or (b) treat such opinions as less significant than ordinary case law. This is buttressed by the fact that in some references the courts do not even distinguish what they are doing in terms of remedial effect, which further illustrates the fungible nature of declaratory 'judgments' versus declaratory 'statements'.

Process

In thinking about why Canadian courts themselves do not seem to pay much heed to whether a matter has been initiated as an advisory opinion or a case, it is useful to look at the history of the function and certain procedural choices that attended them from earliest days. (Some of this was covered in Chapters 2 and 3.)

Advisory opinions carry many of the procedural *trappings* of cases. References, especially in Canada but also in similar jurisdictions where they are used, take their cues from the traditions of adversarial litigation. The point may seem highly formalist. After all, previous chapters dealt, at some length, with the differences between advisory opinions and appeals, especially regarding how they are initiated. I have argued that such differences can be important, for example, with respect to the separation of powers. Here, however, I mean to approach the issue from the opposite direction, looking at choices made long ago that tended to place advisory opinions within the same *conceptual and practical space* as cases.

In the British system, advisory opinions were envisioned as judicial matters, even if the 'courts' rendering them were nothing like the courts that exist today. There was for centuries no clear judicial hierarchy.[7] Any operating judiciary was part of the executive and, thus, an instrument of sovereign power (I leave aside the evolution of courts of equity). In Norman times, a King's Council, the *Magnum*

[6] *New Brunswick (Minister of Health and Community Services) v G (J)*, [1999] 3 SCR 46 at paras 41–48; *M v H*, [1999] 2 SCR 3 at paras 43–44. See, generally, Thomas Cromwell, *Locus Standi: A Commentary on the Law of Standing in Canada* (Toronto: Carswell, 1986).

[7] Neil Duxbury, *The Nature and Authority of Precedent* (Cambridge: Cambridge University Press, 2008). For example, eighteenth-century London had approximately 70 law courts presided over by some 800 judges: Patrick Colquhoun, *A Treatise on the Police of the Metropolis* 383–88 (5th edn) cited in M Todd Henderson, 'From Seriatim to Consensus and Back Again: A Theory of Dissent' [2007] *Supreme Court Review* 283, 297. See also James Oldham, *English Common Law in the Age of Mansfield* (Chapel Hill, NC: UNC Press, 2004) 366, stating that 'Decisions from another court would be looked to only as advisory or as a means of persuasion'.

Concilium, delivered advice in direct response to the sovereign's need (indeed, it was obligated on pain of punishment to do so). The 'Great Council' gradually developed into the *Curia Regis*, a sprawling collection of noblemen who, during the Tudor years especially, operated quite apart from Parliament.

Such bodies were 'judicial' in the sense that they had a character independent of the monarch they served.[8] But their advice did not 'bind' that monarch. He was the source of all authority and legitimacy: the 'fount of justice' referred to in earlier chapters. The idea that a separate body could engage in decisions capable of binding even the King took centuries to develop.[9]

The early Council opinions, though offered as 'advice',[10] were highly formalised. They engaged in a particular style of argumentation – an assessment of facts and principles based in a type of expertise and an avowed neutrality to the outcome. Indeed, courts expressed dismay when the sovereign appeared overly eager to draw them into disputes outside formal legal processes – they feared that doing so would imperil their neutrality. Recall two (cautionary) examples cited in the *Reference re References*:[11] the idea of the Lords requesting specific advice, from judges, of 'what the law is, in order to better inform itself how if at all the law should be altered;'[12] and the reservation, expressed by Lord Mansfield in the 1759 court martial of Lord Sackville, that while the judges were content to express an opinion, they would nonetheless 'be ready, without difficulty, to change [that] opinion' should further circumstances or evidence warrant it.[13]

By the time of the Judicial Committee's formal creation by enactment in 1833, parliamentary power had grown significantly, with a corresponding diminution of purely sovereign authority. Parliament, itself a type of court, may have perceived little need to seek the 'advice' of the judicial branch – the most important members of which were part of its ranks anyway.[14] And, although the executive branch remained a central actor, Parliament's increasing prominence may have made

[8] JJ Beauchamp, *The Jurisprudence of the Privy Council* (Montreal: Periaud, 1891) 4, noting a cite in *MacQueen* for a case in which Edward I lost a civil suit before the Council and was 'condemned'. It is important to recognise, too, the abuse of the advisory function by the House of Stuart, which led to its overall marginalisation in English constitutional law. Itzhak Zamir, *The Declaratory Judgment* (London: Stevens and Sons, 1962) note 62.

[9] The sovereign bowed to political pressure by setting up, under the authority of Parliament, the Court of the Exchequer. 27 Elizabeth ch 8.

[10] In the context of the JCPC, the principle was stated as follows: 'Although the Queen is never present at the hearing, or at the rendering of judgments, she is considered, by a fiction of law, as present and presiding over the Court, and the Lords, sitting as judges, are only her advisers'. Beauchamp (n 8) vii.

[11] *In re References by the Governor-General in Council*, (1910) 43 SCR 536 at 547 (SCC), aff'd [1912] AC 571 (PC).

[12] ibid at 8.

[13] ibid at 8–9; see also the Record of Proceedings: 12 December 1911, at 11; www.bailii.org/uk/cases/UKPC/1912/1912_35(image5).pdf.

[14] Jeffrey Goldsworthy, *The Sovereignty of Parliament: History And Philosophy* (Oxford: Oxford University Press, 1999) 45.

the practice less urgent. Thus, as we saw in Chapter 2, despite the retention of an advisory function for the Judicial Committee of the Privy Council, the function was rarely used in a domestic context – restrained treatment that continues today.[15]

Nonetheless, the allocation of advisory opinions to the court seems to have influenced its structure. Section 4 of the Judicial Committee Act provided a straightforward link to the JCPC's 'ordinary' processes: stating the questions/issues in advance; receiving written submissions; entertaining oral argument and permitting interaction with the bench; maintaining a continuity of membership on the panel; and issuing reasons accompanying the answers to the question.[16] Advisory opinions did not stray from those processes.

A separate possible factor was the JCPC's practice of issuing a single opinion meant to represent it as a whole. Dissenting or concurring opinions were not permitted until 1966.[17] Certainly, it was never required that each judge pronounce an individual opinion – what are known as *seriatim* rulings – which characterised the vast majority of other UK courts. The practice of issuing a single opinion may have lent those opinions a special character and invested them with greater weight.[18] Indeed, in other contexts, the move from *seriatim* to *per curiam* rulings has been described as an explicit attempt to consolidate judicial power.[19]

To be clear, I am not arguing that those processes *necessarily* invested advisory opinions with authority. My point simply is that such features – which were common to all appeals – may have set in motion a process by which such opinions would be viewed as part of the court's general work.

Early references did not entail a set of specific procedures. Indeed, that was noted as an early flaw. Advisory opinions were afforded cursory oral submissions although during the Canadian Supreme Court's first 15 years that was the case for most matters.[20] They also often failed to include reasons. As recounted

[15] Beauchamp (n 8) 8. That said, some newer applications for the advisory function have been enacted. Consider the ability to refer certain matters involving the devolved legislatures of Wales and Scotland. Alan Trench, 'The United Kingdom's New Supreme Court' in Jennifer Smith and Nadia Verrelli (eds), *Democratic Dilemma: Reforming Canada's Supreme Court* (Kingston, ON: McGill-Queens, 2013) 205; Paul Craig and Mark Walters, 'The Courts, Devolution and Judicial Review' [1999] Public Law 274.

[16] See the description of the Committee's general procedure, including a quote from Lord Brougham, in Beauchamp (n 8) 22–23.

[17] Judicial Committee (Dissenting Opinions) Order, 1966 (UK) CSI 1966, No 1100.

[18] *Seriatim* opinions were the practice in England for centuries. For a fascinating account of how their deficiencies in mercantile law prompted reform, albeit short lived, by Lord Mansfield, see Todd Henderson (n 7).

[19] See the battles between Thomas Jefferson and Chief Justice John Marshall (with input, too, from James Madison) when the Chief Justice started issuing United States Supreme Court decisions as single rulings: Letter from Thomas Jefferson to Justice William Johnson (6 June 1823) in Henry A Washington), *Writings of Thomas Jefferson* 7th edn (Washington, DC: Taylor & Maury, 1853–1854) 293–98; letter from James Madison to Spencer Roane, 2 September 1819, http://presspubs.uchicago.edu/founders/documents/a1_8_18s15.html.

[20] Barry Strayer, *Judicial Review of Legislation in Canada* (Toronto: University of Toronto Press, 1968) 183.

in Chapter 3, the perceived deficiency was resolved by amendments under which the Court was required to 'hear and consider [the reference], and to answer each question so referred';[21] and to certify 'its opinion upon each such question, with the reasons for each such answer'[22] along with any dissents. In addition, a reference opinion was to be 'pronounced in like manner as in the case of a judgment upon an appeal to the Court'.[23]

The changes made plain Parliament's intent: procedurally, advisory opinions were to resemble ordinary appeals. Note that, in 1875, Canada already had departed from what was the JCPC practice of single opinions, and was permitting 'any judge or judges of the said Court who may differ from the opinion of the majority' to 'certify a [separate] opinion' to the Governor in Council.[24]

The reporting of advisory opinions also cemented their link to cases. Early *Supreme Court Reports*, which contain accounts of the oral submissions, hint at the governing dynamic. They suggest that the process for advisory opinions and appeals was largely the same. The point is illustrated when looking at such early hearings as the the *Manitoba Education Reference*. The reference arose out of an attempt to tax a minority Catholic population to pay for its denominational schools.[25] A few years earlier,[26] the JCPC had upheld Manitoba's right to abolish such schools.[27] After Catholics sought to appeal the province's decision to the Governor in Council, the federal government referred the matter to the Supreme Court.[28]

The overall approach to the dispute was similar to appeals, like *Citizens Insurance Co v Parsons*,[29] occurring at the same time. That is to say, counsel in both matters vigorously represented the various interests at stake and offered argument to support their respective positions. And members of the panel engaged with the submissions and issued opinions reflecting their individual judgement[30] of the questions posed.

[21] 54–55, Vict., c 25 (1891) (Can), s 4.

[22] ibid.

[23] ibid.

[24] Bill C-31, An Act to establish a Supreme Court, and a Court of Exchequer, for the Dominion of Canada, 2nd Session, 3rd Parliament, 38 Victoria, 1875 (second reading 26 February 1875), s 57.

[25] *In re Certain Statutes of the Province of Manitoba relating to Education*, (1894) 22 SCR 577 [*Manitoba Education Reference*].

[26] *City of Winnipeg v Barrett*, [1892] AC 445, rev's'g *Barrett v City of Winnipeg*, (1891) 19 SCR 374.

[27] See the discussion in John T Saywell, *The Lawmakers: Judicial Power and the Shaping of Canadian Federalism* (Toronto: Osgoode Society, 2002) 75–76. Saywell refers to the JCPC's analysis as so unpersuasive that even members of the Board occasionally seemed to admit as much.

[28] Section 93 of the Constitution Act 1867 provides for denominational schools for Protestant and Catholic minority populations in certain provinces and further provides that 'an Appeal shall lie to the Governor General in Council from any Act or Decision of any Provincial Authority affecting any Right or Privilege of the Protestant or Roman Catholic Minority of the Queen's Subjects'.

[29] *Citizens' and The Queen Ins. Cos. v Parsons; Western Ins. Co. v Johnston*, (1880) 4 SCR 215. The case examined the scope of s 91(2) of the Constitution Act 1867 specifically, which order of government could make laws over the subject matter of insurance.

[30] I use the word in its functional, as opposed to strictly legal, sense.

In the *Manitoba Education Reference*, the Solicitor General appeared for the federal government, and the Catholic petitioners were represented by private counsel. But, at the first appearance, no one indicated an intention to argue for Manitoba. That caused the panel some disquiet:

> TASCHEREAU J.: – You represent Manitoba Mr. Robinson? It is just as well to know whom you represent.
>
> THE CHIEF JUSTICE: – You appear under the statute?
>
> *Mr. Robinson*: – I appear, under the statute, by direction of the court.
>
> *Mr. Wade*: – I appear on behalf of the Province of Manitoba. *I desire to state, that while Manitoba appears here it is simply to acknowledge that the Province has been served with a copy of the case by the Clerk of the Privy Council, and not to take any part in the argument*; I appear, out of deference to the court, to acknowledge that the Province has been served.
>
> I might say further, my lords, as to Mr. Robinson, that the Province does not know him in the matter.[31]

Eventually, a Queen's Counsel was appointed for that purpose who 'fully and ably' argued the matter.[32]

Clearly, the judges thought that the matter required the presentation of opposing views. As previously noted, the Supreme Court Act was amended to provide for such participation generally, by giving notice to Attorneys General and permitting other parties to apply to intervene (in addition to the Court occasionally appointing *amicus curiae*). In the *Manitoba Education Reference* the Court expected someone to present the (likely) position of Manitoba. That is, the Court thought it natural that, in order to properly examine the questions, the proceeding should fairly reflect the fact that it concerned a dispute. That element was provided for by exhaustive submissions for and against the validity of Manitoba's decision, which the Court used as a basis for its eventual opinion.

The opinion itself displays entirely recognisable legal reasoning. As was the practice, the four judges wrote separately. They refer to textual sources including the British North America and Manitoba Acts. The opinions exhaustively examine the most plausible meaning of terms like 'provincial authority' and 'any right or privilege of the Protestant or Roman Catholic minority of the Queen's subjects in relation to education'. They refer to the United States Constitution as well as jurisprudence interpreting that document.[33] They also refer to previous decisions interpreting the Constitution of Canada, noting that the task required examining 'the circumstances under which that statute was passed, the condition of the different provinces, their relations to one another, as well as the system of government

[31] *Manitoba Education Reference* (n 25) at 625 (emphasis added).

[32] ibid at 652.

[33] *Trustees of Dartmouth College v Woodward*, 17 US 518 (1819) (state not at liberty to rescind contract).

which prevailed in those provinces and countries'.[34] And the respective opinions specifically mention the earlier decision in which the JCPC reached a conclusion that, on a largely similar point, went against the Catholic minority.[35]

As mentioned in Chapter 3, Justice Taschereau was perturbed by the entire affair. He doubted the Court's jurisdiction to hear the case at all. His doubt extended to whether the proceeding was permitted under the Supreme and Exchequer Court Act.[36] The problem, as he saw it, was:

> This court is evidently made, in the matter, a court of first instance, or rather, I should say, an advisory board of the federal executive, substituted, *pro hac vice*, for the law officers of the crown, and not performing any of the usual functions of a court of appeal, nay, of any court of justice whatever.[37]

Given that no party had raised an argument about jurisdiction, Taschereau J was prepared to answer the questions but not before observing:

> [O]ur answers to the questions submitted will bind no one, not even those who put them, nay, not even those who give them, no court of justice, not even this court. We give no judgment, we determine nothing, we end no controversy; and, *whatever our answers may be, should it be deemed expedient … by the Manitoba executive to impugn the constitutionality of any measure that might hereafter be taken* by the federal authorities, … whether such measure is in accordance with or in opposition to the answers to this consultation, *the recourse, in the usual way, to the courts of the country remains open to them*.[38]

Manitoba had not seen fit to offer argument precisely because the reference opinion would not keep anyone from challenging such legislation in the future.[39] Indeed, Taschereau J said, the petitioners might have followed the same course, unless they were assured that the federal government would actually exercise its asserted power. The ultimate outcome was uncertain as it depended upon a decision that no court could compel or enjoin Canada from taking. In his opinion, a reference in such a matter was 'futile'.[40]

From its earliest days, the advisory opinion generated expectations, entirely similar to cases, of written and oral argumentation, and legal reasoning. Some judges *were* bothered by the Court exercising such a function and concerned about its distorting future effects. But their concerns did not pose a meaningful bar. Advisory opinions quickly became part of the Court's docket and were accorded the same treatment, procedurally, as cases.

[34] *Manitoba Education Reference* (n 25) at 666.
[35] ibid at 673.
[36] ibid at 677.
[37] ibid at 677.
[38] ibid at 678 (emphasis added).
[39] ibid.
[40] ibid.

At the beginning of this chapter, it was noted that advisory opinions have enjoyed a type of regard not typically found with other kinds of 'advice', for example, the memorandum commissioned from former Supreme Court Justice Ian Binnie on whether a federal court judge (Marc Nadon) was eligible to be appointed to one of the Court's 'Quebec' seats. Although not a complete answer, the history of advisory opinions may provide part of one. In the case of the Nadon memorandum, Justice Binnie could be viewed as acting as a lawyer more than as a judge. He was 'hired' by the government; he developed his opinion in private; he was not expected to, nor did he, receive arguments addressing all sides of the issue; and the opinion was released in order to bolster the government's position. Indeed, had Binnie come to a conclusion contrary to the government's position, there would have been no clear obligation on the government to release it. The circumstances, in other words, were not 'judicial' in the way that advisory opinions have evolved to be.

Authority, Precedent, *Stare Decisis*

Advisory opinions are now such a common and accepted part of the structure of Canadian precedent that most people and institutions – courts included – rarely distinguish them from case law. In scores of cases the courts have relied upon, cited, taken issue with and distinguished advisory opinions just as they do other decisions. There is not an appreciable difference in judicial treatment of the two kinds of legal reasoning.

Now, it is difficult to say whether it is *because* courts employ similar reasoning in both advisory opinions and cases that they treat past advisory opinions in that way; *or*, that courts apply similar reasoning when they engage with reference questions precisely because they anticipate that, in the future, those opinions will be accorded the same weight as cases. The two may well be mutually reinforcing. Nonetheless, both are important to grasping the peculiar status of advisory opinions in Canadian law.

One indicator of that status is how advisory opinions appear in the Supreme Court's arrangement of its work product. When the Supreme Court of Canada releases what it calls 'judgments in appeals' (a category that includes references), the decisions explaining those judgments are organised in a set manner. First, the citation, date and docket number are given. Then, the full style of cause is noted, followed by the judges constituting the panel (*coram*), and a breakdown of how the judges voted. That is followed by a brief summary and a longer headnote, prepared by Court staff. Decisions then list materials cited in the following order: *Cases*; *Statutes and Legislation*; and *Authors*.

It should not be a surprise to the reader that advisory opinions are listed under 'Cases'. Admittedly, it would be difficult to squarely fit them into either of the other two categories. But it is not insignificant that they are included alongside decisions in live cases.

The classification is not just a procedural quirk. It mirrors the way that advisory opinions are actually used, *as sources of law*, in cases themselves. They are *not* treated like historical curiosities, Commissions of Inquiry,[41] repositories of academic or learned counsel, indications of legislative intent, or evidence of some broader point of social science. The courts treat such opinions as generating *legal rules*. Moreover, it is evident that, when deciding references, Canadian courts view themselves as engaged, and *do* engage, in common law legal reasoning drawing on precedent, analogy and principle.

The above point is readily established. First, consider an early reference dealing with the scope of the criminal law power. The *Reference re Validity of Section 5 (a) Dairy Industry Act* examined a federal law that prohibited the manufacture, importation or sale of margarine.[42] At the time, the Judicial Committee had defined the scope of the federal criminal law power, very broadly, as 'a prohibition attended by penal consequences (punishment)'.[43] The province claimed that such a definition allowed the federal government to invade obviously provincial areas of jurisdiction by simply enacting a law that took a particular form.[44] In what is known as the *Margarine Reference*, Justice Rand accepted that argument, noting that a valid exercise of the criminal law power must also identify a particular 'evil' that the law in question is intended to address. The prohibition must be 'enacted with a view to a public purpose which can support it as being in relation to criminal law [such as] [p]ublic peace, order, security, health, [and] morality'.[45]

The *Margarine Reference* was a key moment in the division of powers. It responded to a perceived imbalance between the federal power to create crimes and the provincial power to regulate other key aspects of human behaviour such as those relating to property and human rights. It has been cited[46] in dozens of subsequent cases and its core idea – that the subject matter of 'criminal law' encompasses both a form *and* a purpose – has never been rejected.

The next few examples involve key moments in Canada's Charter jurisprudence. The first revisits the *Motor Vehicle Reference*[47] and its subsequent influence.[48]

Recall that the *Motor Vehicle Reference* considered the constitutional validity of absolute liability offences. Under this type of crime, the Crown need only prove a prohibited act – the accused's state of mind is irrelevant. One such offence, driving under a suspended licence, was attacked as unconstitutional. While the offence was relatively mundane, the underlying issues were not. As the Court noted, they

[41] See, for example, the use of the *Report of the Special Committee on Hate Propaganda in Canada* (Ottawa: Queen's Printer, 1966) in *R. v. Keegstra*, [1990] 3 S.C.R. 697.

[42] *Reference re Validity of Section 5 (a) Dairy Industry Act* [1949] SCR 1 [*Margarine Reference*].

[43] *Proprietary Articles Trade Association et al v Attorney-General for Canada et al* [1931] AC 310.

[44] See the discussion of this concern in *RJR-MacDonald Inc. v Canada (Attorney General)*, [1995] 3 SCR 199, 1995 CanLII 64 (SCC) at para 28.

[45] *Margarine Reference* (n 42) at 49–50.

[46] It has also been criticised: F.R. Scott, 'Centralization. and Decentralization in Canadian Federalism'"(1951) 29 Canadian Bar Review 1095.

[47] *Re BC Motor Vehicle Act*, [1985] 2 SCR 486 [*Motor Vehicle Reference*].

[48] *R v Vaillancourt*, [1987] 2 SCR 636.

included 'fundamental questions of constitutional theory, including the nature and the very legitimacy of constitutional adjudication under the Charter as well as the appropriateness of various techniques of constitutional interpretation'.[49]

The Court analysed numerous factors – text, legislative intent, comparative constitutional history, the role of the courts and the nature of criminal responsibility.[50] It stated that judicial interpretation of the Charter should not be limited by how those who drafted the document expected that interpretation to proceed. It resisted what it called an attempt to 'Americanize' the process, noting that legal and political issues in the two countries were very different. It straightforwardly defended the judiciary's role in setting fundamental norms of interpretation and, effectively, constitutional obligation. In the result, it determined that absolute liability offences carrying a risk of imprisonment violate section 7 of the Charter.[51]

R v Vaillancourt, decided some years later, dealt with a possible extension of the *Motor Vehicle* rule. There, a defendant to a robbery was charged with murder because his accomplice had killed someone with a gun. Prior to the robbery, Vaillancourt had insisted that the accomplice unload the gun but (unbeknownst to him) the accomplice failed to do so. Vaillancourt was charged under a definition of murder that applied to death caused during certain ongoing criminal activity regardless of the defendant's intent to cause or foresight of death.[52] In deciding the case, the Court noted:

> [Our] decision in *Re B.C. Motor Vehicle Act* [stated] that absolute liability infringes the principles of fundamental justice … [The decision] thus elevated *mens rea* from a presumed element in *Sault Ste. Marie* [to a constitutionally required one] …
>
> As a result of the foregoing, [the impugned provision] violates both s. 7 and s. 11(*d*) of the *Charter*, and I would declare [it] to be of no force or effect.[53]

As seen above, the Court cited the *Motor Vehicle Reference*. In the same paragraph, Justice Lamer noted that the *Reference* itself expanded on a point of law articulated in an earlier case called *R v Sault Ste Marie*[54] (namely, the fundamental role of fault in criminal offences). Nothing in either the specific paragraph or the broader decision distinguishes, on the basis of advisory status, the *Reference* from any other case.

In both matters, the Court identified broad principles and applied them to produce legal rules. Those rules plainly were intended to guide future interpretation. The Court's identification, in the reference, of a 'substantive' element to

[49] *Motor Vehicle Reference* (n 47) at para 10.
[50] That analysis is recounted in Chapter 7.
[51] *Motor Vehicle Reference* (n 47).
[52] Such a variation of the offence is sometimes called 'felony' or 'constructive murder' – where the death of a human being arises in the circumstances of another criminal offence.
[53] *R v Vaillancourt* (n 48) at paras 25–28, 43.
[54] *R. v. Sault Ste. Marie*, [1978] 2 SCR 1299.

section 7 of the Charter meant that the section would extend beyond so-called 'due process' claims. That conclusion permitted future courts to scrutinise the actual content of criminal offences in future cases, including *Vaillancourt*. The Court held that the definition of the crime of 'murder' had to respect certain principles – namely that particular crimes carrying a very high degree of stigma must include a fault element properly reflective of that fact. On any measure, that is a very robust conception of individual rights and a remarkably assertive instance of judicial review. And it originated in an advisory opinion.

Next, one can look to the Court's consideration of the questions posed in the *Same-Sex Marriage Reference*. Recall that the federal government refused to appeal a successful constitutional challenge holding that the use of 'marriage' as a legal term had to include couples of the same sex. Instead, the government drafted legislation to enshrine that definition and then referred the Bill to the Court. The initial questions did not put to the Court the central question of whether the Charter's equality guarantees actually compel a gender-neutral definition of civil marriage. Eventually, after criticism and political pressure, the government included that question.[55]

Citing three reasons, the Supreme Court declined to answer it. First, the government had stated its intention to proceed with the legislative enactment 'regardless of what answer we give to this question'. (Note that the stated commitment did not include any willingness to *ignore* a constitutional dictate; the government simply indicated that it was prepared to expand the definition and there was no plausible constitutional argument against its doing so.) Given that intention, the Court said, 'an opinion on the constitutionality of an opposite-sex requirement for marriage serves no legal purpose … and [could] have serious deleterious effects'.[56]

Second, the parties to the previous litigation had already entered into civil marriages in reliance upon 'the finality of the judgments they obtained through the court process'.[57] Those persons thus had acquired 'vested rights' that outweighed any benefit that might accrue from an answer to the fourth question.[58] There was no precedent, the Court said, 'for answering a reference question which mirrors issues already disposed of in lower courts where an appeal was available but not pursued'.[59]

Finally,

> [c]onsideration of the fourth question has the potential to undermine the uniformity that would be achieved by the adoption of the proposed legislation. The uniformity argument succeeds only if the answer to Question 4 is 'no'. By contrast, a 'yes' answer would throw the law into confusion. *The decisions of the lower courts in the matters*

[55] The four questions are set out in Chapters 4 and 7.
[56] *Reference re Same-sex Marriage*, [2004] 3 SCR 698, 2004 SCC 79 at para 65.
[57] ibid at para 66.
[58] ibid.
[59] ibid at para 68.

> *giving rise to this reference are binding in their respective provinces. They would be cast into doubt by an advisory opinion which expressed a contrary view, even though it could not overturn them*. The result would be confusion, not uniformity.[60]

The Court was concerned about the 'confusion' that might spring from a reference opinion it issued that conflicted with final lower court judgments on the same issue.[61] The Court, plausibly, also may have anticipated that 'confusion' would result because such an advisory opinion would exert some force on those lower courts in future cases.[62] While the reference opinion would not affect the law in the provinces in which final judgments had issued, it would nonetheless create an anomaly.

But *why* would there be such an anomaly? After all, if a reference is merely 'advice', its answer is one of many – ike those found in treatises and other scholarly work – that can be considered and then dismissed. It would seem that the 'anomaly' holds only if an answer *in a reference* either *is* an authoritative statement of law, or all of the relevant actors *including* courts invariably will treat it as such.

A plausible explanation for the anomaly lies in the doctrine of *stare decisis*. If an advisory opinion is subject to *that*, there is no doubt that the *Same-Sex Marriage Reference* could create confusion. Lower courts would consider themselves bound to respect the dictates laid out by the Supreme Court, even if they had already issued a 'final' (because it was not further appealed) answer in a case raising the same issue. (They would be in the same position as if they had issued a judgment that had not been appealed, but a similar matter had proceeded to the Supreme Court from a different jurisdiction.)

Interestingly, one way – indeed, perhaps the clearest way – to surmount the anomaly would be to recognise, and attach special significance to, the fact that an answer *did* come from a reference. And there is a hint in the reference that the Court came close to doing so – namely, in saying that a contrary answer could not 'overturn' earlier, finally decided lower court opinions. But, while that might look like an important concession, in the opinion's overall context it is better viewed as an afterthought. Had the statement enjoyed *true* persuasive value, the fact that references are non-binding should have settled the issue as to whether, in law, it would create 'confusion' to answer the fourth question. The Court did not acccept that. The fact that its answer was not formally *binding* could not overcome the confusion that would result precisely because its 'advice' *would be taken as an authoritative statement of law*.

[60] ibid at para 69 (emphasis added).

[61] I have never been persuaded by this analysis: C Mathen, 'Mutability and Method in the Marriage Reference' (2005) LV *University of New Brunswick Law Journal* 43, 53–54.

[62] I thank Paul Daly for raising this point with me.

Next, consider the 2013 case of *Canada v Bedford*.[63] In *Bedford*, a number of plaintiffs challenged the validity of three criminal offences related to the sex trade.[64] In a 1990 reference about two of those laws, the Supreme Court advised that they were constitutional.[65] Nonetheless, the *Bedford* trial judge, Justice Susan Himel, decided that all three laws were unconstitutional.

Himel J accepted that she ordinarily was bound to follow the pronouncements of a higher court. She then went on to articulate and apply a theory of *stare decisis* that could in some circumstances attenuate that obligation.[66] The theory, though, had *nothing* to do with whether the prior rule had appeared in a reference. None of the parties made that argument either.

The lack of distinction between a prior decision and a prior advisory opinion carried over to the Supreme Court. In considering the weight to be accorded to the *Prostitution Reference*, the Court focussed not on the opinion's advisory status, but on its *doctrinal differences* from *Bedford*. It is hard to think of a more striking illustration of the nature of an advisory opinion. For example, the Court pointed out that the 1990 reference had focussed on section 7's 'liberty' interest, but *Bedford* was far more concerned with the provision's guarantee of 'security of the person'. The Court also noted that, during the intervening 23 years, section 7's 'principles of fundamental justice' had evolved to include such concepts as over-breadth and gross disproportionality, such that the 1990 opinion could no longer be taken as an authoritative statement with regard to that particular constitutional right.[67]

The Court concluded that, based on certain 'newer' principles of fundamental justice encompassed within section 7, the impugned laws did violate the claimants' security of the person. It was therefore not necessary to determine whether the precise ratio articulated in the earlier *Prostitution Reference* – namely, that the

[63] *Canada (Attorney-General) v Bedford*, 2013 SCC 72, [2013] 3 SCR 1101 [*Bedford*]. Note that this was a constitutional challenge initiated by private litigants.

[64] The offences were keeping a common bawdy house; soliciting in a public place, for the purpose of prostitution; and living on the avails of a prostitute. Criminal Code, ss 210, 212(1)(f) and 213(1)(c). They were challenged as being in violation of s 7 of the Charter, which states: 'Everyone has the right to life, liberty and security of the person, and the right not to be deprived thereof except in accordance with the principles of fundamental justice'.

[65] *Reference re ss. 193 and 195.1(1)(c) of the Criminal Code (Man.)*, [1990] 1 SCR 1123 [*Prostitution Reference*]. The reference considered whether the bawdy-house and solicitation laws violated s 2(b) (freedom of expression) and s 7 of the Charter. The Court found that the laws were inconsistent with s 2(b) but could nonetheless be upheld as a 'reasonable limit' under s 1, and were not inconsistent with s 7.

[66] *Bedford* (n 63) at paras 31, 41.

[67] The Supreme Court held that, while the *Prostitution Reference* focused on s 7's 'liberty' interest, *Bedford* was argued on the basis of its guarantee of 'security of the person'. The Court also held that, since 1991, the 'principles of fundamental justice' had evolved to include the principles of over-breadth and gross disproportionality: ibid at paras 45, 47. In addition, because the Court found that all of the impugned laws violated s 7 (and were not justified as 'reasonable limits'), it deemed it unnecessary to revisit whether the laws ran afoul of s 2(b) of the Charter–the key *ratio* from the *Prostitution Reference*.

solicitation offence constituted a 'reasonable limit' on the Charter guarantee of freedom of expression should be followed. But its analysis of *stare decisis* suggests that it *made no difference* that the earlier rule had been articulated in an advisory opinion. The Court made a point of observing that 'Certainty in the law requires that courts follow and apply authoritative precedents'. It further noted that '*While reference opinions may not be legally binding*, in practice they have been followed'.[68] Over several passages, the Court treated the *Prostitution Reference* as a binding precedent, implying that it could only be departed from if it was formally *overruled*.[69] In other words, the Court treated the *Prostitution Reference* as entitled to the same consideration and deference as any of its decisions. The Court further stated that one of the issues (the communication provision's effect on freedom of expression) had been 'decided' in 1990. The Court did all this even as it insisted that references are not 'legally binding'.

In 2018 a trial judge relied upon the above language to justify following a reference opinion in the case of *R v Blackmore*.[70] *Blackmore* was the direct result of the *Polygamy Reference* discussed in the introduction to this book. The first Canadian criminal polygamy prosecution in over 50 years, *Blackmore* followed a protracted period of uncertainty during which the British Columbia Attorney General's office sought to confirm whether section 293 of the Criminal Code was consistent with the Charter.[71] Ultimately, the BC government initiated a rare, trial court reference, in which a single judge advised that the offence was constitutional (save for its application to underage persons).[72] In a subsequent trial against a long-time polygamist and Mormon leader, Winston Blackmore, the question arose of how the trial judge ought to deal with that advisory opinion.

The *Blackmore* judge decided that under the principle of 'comity', he was expected to 'follow the decision of another judge of the same court, except in certain limited circumstances'.[73] Applying the analysis in *Bedford*, he found that the *Polygamy Reference* was akin to 'the decision of another judge'.[74] As there was no basis, in the *Bedford* exceptions, on which he could depart from *the Polygamy*

[68] ibid at para (emphasis added).
[69] ibid at paras 38, 40, 46, 47.
[70] *R v Blackmore*, 2018 BCSC 367 [*Blackmore*].
[71] For further discussion, see Carissima Mathen, 'Reflecting Culture: Polygamy and the Charter', in Benjamin Berger and James Stribopoulos (eds), *Unsettled Legacy: Thirty Years of Criminal Justice under the Charter* (Toronto: LexisNexis, 2012) 389.
[72] *Reference re: Section 293 of the Criminal Code of Canada*, 2011 BCSC 1588 (CanLII) [*Polygamy Reference*].
[73] *Blackmore* (n 70) at 299, citing *Re Hansard Spruce Mills Ltd.*, [1954] 4 DLR 590 (BCSC) at 592. In the latter case, comity was described as a principle under which judges should not depart from a ruling by a fellow judge unless '(a) [s]ubsequent decisions have affected the validity of the impugned judgment; (b) it is demonstrated that some binding authority in case law, or some relevant statute was not considered; (c) the judgment was unconsidered, a *nisi prius* judgment given in circumstances familiar to all trial Judges, where the exigencies of the trial require an immediate decision without opportunity to fully consent authority'.
[74] *Blackmore* (n 70).

Reference, the trial judge concluded that he was obligated to treat section 293 of the Code as constitutionally valid. Therefore, a conviction was permissible. *Blackmore* is particularly interesting because it shows that, to some courts, an advisory opinion *at the lowest judicial level* is nonetheless captured within the doctrine of precedent.

In the above examples we see that, when considering the opportunity to depart from a prior advisory opinion, or to distinguish its precedential weight from prior case law, courts simply do not do so.

It may be instructive here to consider again the special phenomenon of Commissions of Inquiry. Commissions are framed as 'advice-seeking' exercises, initiated by the Executive, and frequently headed by jurists.[75] But, as mentioned in Chapter 9, their reports are not accorded the same regard as advisory opinions.[76] Part of the answer may be procedural. Inquiries do not involve the courts per se and their processes are not adversarial in the conventional sense (although they often invite submissions from interested parties). But there probably are deeper reasons at work. While both references and commissions seek answers, commissions seem to be viewed as speaking directly *to* the initiating actors, while references have an additional audience: the judiciary. Commissions normally are not asked specific legal questions, but are given either an investigative mandate requiring them to draw specific conclusions of fact; or a brief that touches on broad questions of public policy that courts are less likely to address. The specificity of an inquiry's mandate also makes it less likely that a commissioner will feel bound to rely on previous material although he or she does gather evidence. Commissions are instituted for a single, limited purpose. While they may benefit from previous fact-finding, they do not operate in a precedent-based system. They do not depend for their effectiveness on a sense of being part of a larger whole, one that is invested in the coherence and stability of the law as a system of rules and principles.

Finally, it is worth mentioning that advisory opinions are treated as part of the body of precedent independent of the degree of judicial consensus that attends them. That is to say, references issuing from a divided panel compel the same degree of compliance as those proceeding from a unanimous one. In the *Patriation Reference* (discussed in Chapter 6), the Court split along not one but

[75] Originating as a British 'function of royal prerogative', and long since codified, Canadian commissions are created by the executive. Grant Hoole, 'Commissions of Inquiry in Canada' in Scott Prasser and Helen Tracey (eds), *Royal Commissions and Public Inquiries: Practice and Potential* (Ballarat: Connor Court, 2014) 331.

[76] But see Prime Minister Justin Trudeau's promise to implement all of the recommendations (within federal jurisdiction) of the *Truth and Reconciliation Commission* (Winnipeg: Truth and Reconciliation Commission of Canada, 2015): http://nctr.ca/assets/reports/Calls_to_Action_English2.pdf; John Paul Tasker, 'Justin Trudeau announces 3 steps to help enact Truth and Reconciliation calls to action', *CBC News*, 15 December 2016, www.cbc.ca/news/politics/trudeau-indigenous-leaders-trc-1.3897902.

two issues.[77] The *Supreme Court Act Reference*[78] was decided 6–1 and the dissent was vigorous.[79] There have even been 5–4 splits, such as in the *Reference re Assisted Human Reproduction Act*.[80] If advisory opinions were truly exercises in seeking 'advice', one might expect it to matter that a particular opinion did not attract unanimity. Yet, it does not.

One can dispute whether *any* split judicial decision ought to carry the same weight as a unanimous one.[81] But, to the extent that such authority is unaffected by lack of unanimity, that point holds for references just as surely as it does for cases. It is yet another indicator of the status of advisory opinions.

Providing Answers

The previous section explored how advisory opinions have become part of ordinary precedent – taking their place alongside case law in providing guidance to future courts. This final section draws upon different concepts relating to what it is reasonable to regard as a primary function of Canadian courts, and, arguably, courts in similar systems. The first is that Canadian courts tend to consider the *issue* in a case as more important that the *parties* bringing it to them. The second is that when they declare particular answers, those answers have the same effect as a formal declaration issued at the conclusion of an appeal. And the third has to do with remedies and the fact that the supposedly strongest distinction between references and live cases – the lack of true remedial force in the former – is somewhat weaker than has been supposed.

There is a complicated relationship between somewhat competing forces at work here. While Canadian courts have tended to be willing to relax standing requirements (discussed in greater detail below), they are still most comfortable in an environment where there is some opposition between the parties that *do* appear. Thus, to the extent that references may expand the scope of ordinary litigation, it is also the case that adversarial norms have worked themselves into references as well. Both factors are consistent with the 'providing answers' premise, as well as the fact that the 'pull' of advisory opinions with respect to those answers would be no different than the pull of case law.

[77] The splits, one 7–2 and the other 6–3, were over whether (a) it was *legal* for Parliament to seek constitutional change on its own and (b) there was nonetheless a *convention* requiring 'substantial provincial consent' for constitutional change affecting provincial powers.

[78] *Reference re Supreme Court Act, ss. 5 and 6*, 2014 SCC 21, [2014] 1 SCR 433 [*Supreme Court Act Reference*].

[79] See the discussion in C Mathen, 'The Shadow of Absurdity and the Challenge of Easy Cases: Looking Back on the *Supreme Court Act Reference*' (2015) 71 Supreme Court Law Review 161, 184–85. To be sure, there was some reliance by government ministers on the dissenting opinion, but that was offered more as a defence of undertaking the reference at all.

[80] *Reference re Assisted Human Reproduction Act*, 2010 SCC 61, [2010] 3 SCR 457.

[81] For related discussion of this point, see Jeremy Waldron, *Political Political Theory* (Cambridge MA: Harvard University Press, 2016), ch 10.

A. Abstract Review

Often, courts are thought to do something improper when they engage in 'abstract review' outside of the confines of a particular case. In the acid words of one judge: 'The Courts are neither a debating club nor an advisory bureau'.[82] Courts 'decide only live, practical questions', they have no concern with 'hypothetical, premature or academic' ones, and they do not 'exist to advise litigants as to the policy which they should adopt in the ordering of their affairs'.[83]

The very existence of an advisory function complicates that point of view. An additional element in Canada is that changes to the law of standing – or, who has the right to seek resolution from the court – have made the need for a concrete 'dispute' more tenuous *even in ordinary cases*.

Though the two may be technically differentiated,[84] standing works as an essential component of justiciability because it narrows the ability of the court to hear cases. Traditionally, standing is satisfied if a prospective litigant alleges a direct injury. In constitutional law, establishing direct standing would require that a claimant has suffered a violation of her personal constitutional rights. Applying that threshold, any *potential* wrongdoing would lie beyond the jurisdiction of the court. Actual injury is required. Standing traditionally also employs a fairly narrow understanding of what counts as an 'injury'. For example, in the division of powers context, it is the orders of government that are thought to be 'injured' by ultra vires legislation passed by a rival government – not the multitudes of persons affected by such laws.

In societies committed to constitutional norms and obligations, a strict application of direct standing may lie in tension with the idea that persons have a legitimate interest in ensuring the validity of *all* laws.[85] Accepting that ensuring constitutional compliance is a good thing, the idea that one first must establish personal harm or injury seems unnecessary, even counter-productive. One could also argue for a broader understanding of 'injury' that applies when society as a whole must tolerate extra- or unconstitutional laws.

And, indeed, a number of courts *have* stopped insisting on the strictest possible understanding of direct standing. In *Norris v Ireland*, the European Court of Human Rights considered a man's claim that his human rights were threatened by an Irish law criminalising 'homosexuality' even though the risk of prosecution was remote.[86] The Court found that Norris's fear of prosecution whenever he engaged

[82] *Macnaughton v Macnaughton's Trustees* [1953] SC 387 at 392.

[83] *Rusbridger & Anor, R (on the application of) v Her Majesty's Attorney General* [2003] UKHL 38 [35] [*Rusbridger*].

[84] Lorne Sossin, *Boundaries of Judicial Review: The Law of Justiciability in Canada*, 2nd edn (Toronto: Thompson Reuters, 2012) ch 1.

[85] *R v Oxfordshire County Council ex p P* [1996] ELR 153, cited in David Elvin, 'Hypothetical, Academic and Premature Challenges' [2006] Judicial Review 307, 313.

[86] *Norris v Ireland* (1989) 13 EHRR 186.

in same-sex relations was sufficient to grant him standing. In India, beginning in the 1980s, the courts issued a series of decisions that 'practically eliminated standing requirements and procedural formalities'. Instead the courts held that 'where a legal wrong is caused to a person' who is 'by reason of poverty, helplessness or disability or social or economically disadvantaged position, unable to approach the court for relief' *anyone* can seek judicial direction.[87]

The Canadian Supreme Court has stated that because the Constitution is the country's supreme law, a person subject to a law may challenge its validity on any basis, whether directly connected to that person or not. Thus, a retail pharmacy chain successfully argued that a federal prohibition on Sunday commercial activity infringed the Charter guarantee of 'freedom of religion'. The corporation, Big M Drug Mart, was not recognised as potentially enjoying such a right; nevertheless, it could argue that the law infringed the rights of other, natural persons.[88] Similarly, in *R v Morgentaler*,[89] a male physician charged with performing illegal abortions successfully argued that the prohibitions violated the Charter rights of pregnant women – rights that he could not enjoy.

No doubt, the expansion of direct standing is significant (the narrower version remains, for example, a highly potent gatekeeper in jurisdictions like the United States).[90] But it is surpassed by an even more striking idea, under which there need be no concrete link between a litigant and the impugned law.

That idea is given effect through the doctrine of *public interest standing*. Though articulated in Canada prior to the Charter,[91] the doctrine achieved its full effect afterwards. Like most constitutionally entrenched Bills of Rights, the Charter created many more sites of possible litigation. Initially, the Canadian Supreme Court expressed concern that a too-broad approach to interest standing would overwhelm the courts with well-meaning but misguided 'busybodies'.[92]

[87] *S.P. Gupta v. Union of India*, AIR 1982 SC 149, 189. See also Michael D Gilbert and Mauricio A Guim, 'Active Virtues', 28 July 2018 (unpublished manuscript on file with author); Manoj Mate, 'The Rise of Judicial Governance in the Supreme Court of India' (2015) 33 Boston University International Law Journal 169, 178; SP Sathe, 'Judicial Activism: The Indian Experience' (2001) 6 Washington University Journal of Law and Policy 29, 63.

[88] *R v Big M Drug Mart Ltd.*, [1985] 1 SCR 295, successfully challenging the Lord's Day Act, RSC 1970, c L-13, s 4. The Supreme Court has since affirmed that religious freedom has an organisational aspect and may be exercised by legal entities acting on the behalf of individuals. It has not yet endorsed the idea that the right may be enjoyed by corporations. See *Loyola High School v Quebec (Attorney General)*, 2015 SCC 12, [2015] 1 SCR 613.

[89] *R v Morgentaler*, [1988] 1 SCR 30.

[90] Antonin Scalia, 'The Doctrine of Standing as an Essential Element of the Separation of Powers' (1983) 17 Suffolk University Law Review 881; *United States v Windsor*, 133 S Ct 2675, 2675–76 (2013); *Hollingsworth v Perry*, 133 S Ct 2652, 2667–68 (2013). Even in the US, though, the practice of test case litigation whereby a dispute is manufactured in order to obtain judicial relief has a long and storied history.

[91] *Thorson v Canada (Attorney General)*, [1975] 1 SCR 138; *Nova Scotia (Board of Censors) v McNeil*, [1976] 2 SCR 265; *Canada (Minister of Justice) v Borowski*, [1981] 2 SCR 575; and *Finlay v Canada (Minister of Finance)*, [1986] 2 SCR 607.

[92] *Hy and Zel's Inc. v Ontario (Attorney General)*, [1993] 3 SCR 675; *Paul Magder Furs Ltd. v Ontario (Attorney General)*, [1993] 3 SCR 675; June Ross, 'Standing in Charter Declaratory Actions' (1995) 33(1) Osgoode Hall Law Journal 151.

It therefore set out a stringent test: so long as a potential litigant with direct standing could be imagined, a court should not award public interest standing.[93]

Over the next two decades, that position softened. In a Charter challenge to public health care, the Court granted standing to a doctor and a patient when (a) neither was at direct risk of injury and (b) many *other* potential plaintiffs had suffered the alleged harm caused by the program's deficiencies.[94] The Court waved away the sorts of objections that would have been a complete bar 20 years earlier.[95] It did the same in a case where a non-profit organisation and a former sex worker sought to challenge several prostitution-related offences.[96] None of the plaintiffs had been charged and there was a similar (though not identical) challenge already under way in Ontario. Under the traditional test, the plaintiffs were thus poor candidates for public interest standing. Nonetheless, the Court allowed their claim to proceed.[97]

Given that cases involving public interest standing only operate in the absence of ordinary parties, they have parallels to references. While a great many persons may be affected by the impugned law, they are not before the court.[98] And yet, such cases are completely authoritative, with absolutely no appreciable difference from a case pursued through direct standing.

To be sure, the less the focus is on specific injured parties, the more likely it is that a public interest case will involve limited facts.[99] But, in constitutional litigation, the facts themselves may be quite limited. In making this point, as part of his larger 'case against judicial review', Jeremy Waldron argues that by the time a case reaches the appellate level, 'almost all traces of the original flesh-and-blood rights holders have vanished', 'argument such as it is revolves around the abstract issue of the right in dispute' and 'the [apex court] almost always addresses the issue in general terms'.[100]

[93] The test required: (a) a serious issue about the invalidity of the impugned legislation; (b) a litigant with a 'genuine interest' in the question; and (c) the lack of any other manner in which the question might arise before a court.

[94] *Chaoulli v Quebec (Attorney General)* [2005] 1 SCR 791 [*Chaoulli*]. It was argued that the prohibition of the purchase of private insurance contracts led to serious delay in receiving treatment, potentially jeopardising the health and even the lives of some patients.

[95] Though dissenting in the result, Justice Ian Binnie provided the following defence of a broader approach to public interest standing: 'From a practical point of view, while individual patients could [bring their own cases to court], it would be unreasonable to expect a seriously ailing person to bring a systemic challenge to the whole health plan, as was done here. The material, physical and emotional resources of individuals who are ill, and quite possibly dying, are likely to be focussed on their own circumstances. In this sense, there is no other class of persons that is more directly affected and that could be expected to undertake the lengthy and no doubt costly systemic challenge to single-tier medicine'.

[96] *Canada (Attorney General) v Downtown Eastside Sex Workers United Against Violence Society*, 2012 SCC 45, [2012] 2 SCR 524.

[97] Further discussion of both of these cases may be found in Carissima Mathen 'Access to *Charter* Justice' in Peter Oliver, Patrick Macklem and Nathalie Des Rosiers (eds), *Oxford Handbook of the Canadian Constitution* (New York: Oxford University Press, 2017).

[98] *Gupta v Union of India* (n 87).

[99] Kent Roach, *Constitutional Remedies in Canada*, 2nd edn (Toronto: Canada Law Book, 2012) ch 12-10 (ch 12, p 10, looseleaf).

[100] Waldron (n 81) 220.

It is true that appellate constitutional decisions tend to be removed from the facts. But that is more a function of the way that higher courts tend to defer to lower ones *about* facts. Indeed, recent successful Charter challenges have involved voluminous materials, argued before a trial judge who used fact finding techniques to determine which legal arguments had merit.[101] When such rulings are appealed, a higher court generally will shun re-engaging in the factual analysis because it cannot do so in a meaningful way without considering the evidence supporting that analysis itself – and that would require enormous expenditures of judicial resources.

Public interest litigation and advisory opinions do differ in certain respects. Litigants depend upon the courts to grant them leave – unlike executive actors, who can initiate a reference and, generally, expect their questions to be answered. And, public interest cases are inherently 'adversarial' because it is the litigant's very desire to *challenge* state action that motivates their claim. Those differences, though, do not justify treating only public interest cases as part of the common law subject to the rules of precedent and *stare decisis*. The fact that the initiating power is located in one branch rather than another (ie, the executive rather than the court) seems a poor basis on which to base the authority of a resulting expression of legal analysis and argument. And, as already discussed, over the last century-and-a-half advisory opinions have proceeded both under a clear expectation, including by the courts, of an adversarial context, and against the backdrop of the political reality that the questions posed in them will, invariably, draw interested and opposing points of view.

The development of public interest standing demonstrates a judicial willingness to extend the boundaries of the litigation process. It is defended as an instance of the idea that the courts can thus act as a bulwark against the risk that, due to the absence of a directly affected litigant, a state actor might otherwise continue to evade scrutiny for unconstitutional acts. But one could also argue that its particularly robust application in Canada is the *product* of a system in which the courts have long been engaged in abstract review – in reference opinions. The point is necessarily speculative but perhaps the Court's comfort in its advisory function has encouraged it to be more tolerant of the idea that citizens, and not just government actors, should have the opportunity to obtain its advice on constitutional issues.

Whether through public interest litigation, or advisory opinions, abstract review can also be seen as an endorsement of the concept of the declaratory action. Under it

> no 'injury' or 'wrong' need have been actually committed or threatened in order to enable the plaintiff to invoke the judicial process; he need merely show that some legal interest or right of his has been placed in jeopardy or grave uncertainty, by denial, by

[101] *Bedford* (n 63) is an example, as is *Carter v Canada*, [2015] 1 SCR 331.

> the existence of a potentially injurious instrument, by some unforeseen event or catastrophe the effect of which gives rise to dispute, or by the assertion of a conflicting claim by the defendant.[102]

That phenomenon, among others, is addressed below.

B. Answers, Declarations, Remedies

When a court issues an advisory opinion, it answers questions. One might say, it 'declares' those answers, especially as they relate to legal rules, rights, powers or responsibilities. Because references lack formal remedial power, they are not described as 'judgments'. Nonetheless, the functions performed by the court appear to be similar. That may well be a good reason why statements of law provided by a court in an advisory opinion would receive much the same treatment, to at least some extent, as the statements of law issued by a court in a live case. It is less surprising, still, when one considers that courts already have a well-developed practice of issuing declaratory judgments in ordinary litigation.

The long history of declaratory judgments cannot be fully canvassed here. But briefly, in England, the judgment emerged from the inherent jurisdiction of the Court of Chancery.[103] In the mid-nineteenth century, after decades of avoidance, English courts began to issue such judgments more broadly. Judgments against the Crown were more complicated[104] but possible; in 2002 a British Law Lord stated that 'in exceptional circumstances' an individual might properly seek a declaration that certain proposed conduct is lawful and might 'name the Attorney General as the formal defendant to the claim'.[105]

The theory that 'no Act of Parliament, be it as repugnant to the rules of common law or natural justice as it may, can be declared illegal or void on any ground whatsoever' is of long standing.[106] But it is peculiarly applicable to those systems, such as that of the UK, that lack an expressly enacted Constitution. For those that do have such an instrument, the court's power to declare legislation void if it conflicts with the Constitution is of equally long standing.[107] In Canada, such a power is thought to have first drawn strength from the Colonial Laws Validity Act, which provided that colonies' domestic laws could stand to the extent they

[102] Edwin Borchard, *Declaratory Judgments*, 2nd edn (Cleveland, OH: Banks-Baldwin Law Publishing Co, Chicago, 1941) 27.

[103] Itzhak Zamir, *The Declaratory Judgment* (London: Stevens and Sons, 1962) 7.

[104] But see *Imperial Tobacco Limited v Attorney General* [1981] AC 718.

[105] *Regina (Pretty) v Director of Public Prosecutions* [2002] 1 AC 800 at [116].

[106] Stanley A de Smith, *Judicial Review of Administrative Action*, 4th edn (London: Stevens and Sons Ltd, 1980) 367–57; Goldsworthy (n 14).

[107] *Marbury v Madison* 5 US 137; 1 *Cranch* 137; WA Wynes, *Legislative, Executive and Legal Powers in Australia*, 2nd edn (Sydney: Law Book Co, 1956) 586–89.

were *not* repugnant to Imperial ones.[108] However, it can also be described simply a function of the rule-of-law requirement that state actors and institutions can only do that which is authorised by law.

Declaratory judgments are sought in all manner of cases. Public law scholars have noted their utility in administrative and constitutional litigation. Indeed, administrative law declarations are increasingly popular despite the fact that the declaration does not invalidate the act, lead to damages or, even, 'impose any ongoing obligation'.[109] They are popular because the state actors to which they are directed tend to comply with them. In the constitutional context, declaratory relief has been noted as superior to injunctive relief due to its ability 'to respond to either past or future violations'[110] by stating 'in general terms what is necessary to achieve compliance with the Constitution and allow the government flexibility to decide' how to achieve that compliance.[111]

The similarity between declaratory judgments and advisory opinions has long been noted. (That very similarity has been used to criticise advisory opinions.[112]) Regardless of whether one views declaratory judgments as desirable per se, their presence in constitutional litigation signals that a court can be called upon to state a general principle of law or right, and have that statement count as a source *of* law. If that is so, then it is unsurprising that a court called upon to *provide answers* to questions of law, or of right, should perceive itself (and be perceived) as engaging in a sufficiently similar function that those answers, too, count as sources of law.

The idea is tied to the effect of a court providing answers. The link between that function and constitutional supremacy in the Canadian context is explored below. But it is useful to think about its effect outside of that specific supremacy. A good example is the Canadian Supreme Court's opinion about constitutional convention in the *Patriation Reference*.[113] As discussed in Chapter 6, once the Court concluded that there was a convention requiring 'substantial provincial consent' before certain changes to the Constitution could be pursed, the Prime Minister returned to the negotiating table. The *Patriation Reference* is particularly intriguing because, to the extent that it dealt with conventional rules, it seems that the *most* it could do was to confirm a certain state of affairs. Yet, its result was immediate, and profound.

[108] 28 & 29 Vict c 63. See also the discussion in Chapter 2.

[109] Farrah Ahmed, Richard Albert and Adam Perry, 'Judging Constitutional Conventions' (Oxford Legal Studies Research Paper No 59/2017) citing Mark Elliott and Jason Varuhas, *Administrative Law*, 5th edn (Oxford: Oxford University Press, 2017) 455.

[110] Of course, whether there is a real risk of violation is a question of fact. For a sceptical treatment of that question, see *Rusbridger* (n 83) (declining to make a declaratory judgment regarding an 1848 treason law because the risk of charges – which had not been laid in 100 years – was not a serious one).

[111] Roach (n 99) ch 12.

[112] Borchard (n 102) 561: 'The special ground asserted has been that the declaratory judgment imposes on the courts powers non-judicial in character and that it requires them to decide cases that are moot or to render advisory opinions, or, in some instances, even, that judgments that carry no execution are unconstitutional'.

[113] *Re: Resolution to amend the Constitution*, [1981] 1 SCR 753.

The power of a court's statements is also demonstrated by the significance attached to obiter commentary even where a claim is dismissed. An example is the UK House of Lords' decision in *Rusbridger*.[114] A newspaper publisher who engaged in 'a press campaign advocating the peaceful and constitutional replacement of the monarchy by a republican form of government' sought assurances from the Attorney General that he and his writers would not be punished under the 1848 Treason Act.[115] When the Attorney General refused, Rusbridger sought a declaration that the older law was 'incompatible' with the European Convention right to freedom of expression.

Noting that declaratory judgments should be awarded only in 'exceptional circumstances', the Court refused to award one. But, in opinion after opinion, the Lords made it clear what they thought of the impugned law. The 1848 Act was 'a relic of a bygone age [that] does not fit into the fabric of our modern legal system. The idea that section 3 could survive scrutiny … is unreal'.[116] It was 'plain as a pike staff … that no one who advocates the peaceful abolition of the monarchy and its replacement by a republican form of government is at any risk of prosecution'.[117] '[N]o Attorney-General or Director of Public Prosecutions would or could authorise a prosecution for such advocacy without becoming a laughing stock'.[118] If an Attorney General was at all inclined to test the validity of the 1848 Treason Act, the tenor of the Lords' comments surely would dissuade him or her from doing so.

That leads to the question of remedy. Advisory opinions do not trigger the Court's ordinary remedial power. The Court *delivers* an *opinion*. It *answers questions*. It does not *strike down* legislation; *sever* certain clauses; *read down* a provision; or *order* an Executive actor to do something. In the main, courts have tended to follow the conventional rule that their remedial authority is not available when they issue an advisory opinion. There are, though, counter-narratives.

The first example, admittedly, is modest. In the course of their opinions, courts often do slip into language more suited to cases. For example, in the *Motor Vehicle Reference* Justice Lamer appears, almost casually, to invoke a constitutional remedy:

> In the result, I would dismiss the appeal and answer the question in the negative, as did the Court of Appeal, albeit for somewhat different reasons, *and declare* s. 94(2) of the Motor Vehicle Act, R.S.B.C. 1979, as amended by the Motor Vehicle Amendment Act, 1982, inconsistent with s. 7 of the Canadian Charter of Rights and Freedoms.[119]

[114] *Rusbridger* (n 83).

[115] The specific provision made it a felony to 'deprive or depose the Queen from the Crown'. Ibid at para 4.

[116] ibid at para 28.

[117] ibid at 40.

[118] ibid. Similar comments may be found in *In the matter of an application by the Northern Ireland Human Rights Commission for Judicial Review (Northern Ireland)* [2018] UKSC 27.

[119] *Motor Vehicle Reference* (n 47), at para 97 (emphasis added).

Lamer J did not just answer the question – he 'declared' the particular law to be invalid.

Lamer J also described the matter before him as an 'appeal', but that is most likely because, having originated as a provincial reference, the matter proceeded under section 36 of the Supreme Court Act.[120] The Supreme Court itself styles such proceedings as references rather than cases. But it also occasionally refers to them as 'appeals'.[121] There is, thus, some semantic ambiguity. A possible explanation lies in the fact that the Court's overall jurisdiction is appellate. So long as direct access to a reference remains an exceptional function within the sole purview of the federal government, it makes sense that the route for provincial references would be analogous to, and referred as, an appeal. That does not suggest a difference in kind between the two types of references.

In any event, other Canadian references show that the Court's tendency to slip into remedial language is not confined to provincial matters. In the Governor in Council-initiated *Supreme Court Act Reference* a majority concluded that the Act did not permit the appointment of a Federal Court judge to fill one of the three seats reserved for Quebec. In the course of a great deal of discussion regarding the Court and the Act, including much legislative and other history, the Court also turned its attention to the judge, Marc Nadon, at the centre of the dispute. It stated: 'The *practical effect* is that the appointment of Justice Nadon and his swearing-in as a judge of the Court were void *ab initio*. He *remains* a supernumerary judge of the Federal Court of Appeal'.[122]

The above statement lies some way from mere 'advice' or 'opinion'. Rather, it reads as a statement of the status of an individual – that is, a declaratory judgment. It should be noted that Justice Nadon was not represented at the hearing. On that ground alone, for the Court to proclaim on his legal status would seem to trench on procedural fairness. It is very likely that the majority wished only to ensure that he could return to his prior position on the Federal Court of Appeal. The issue, though, is whether *in the context of its advisory function* that decision was the Court's to make.

It appears that the Order in Council appointing Justice Nadon was never revoked. In fact, by law Supreme Court judges 'hold office during good behavior' and are removable only by the Govenor General acting on a request from Parliament.[123] Obviously Justice Nadon's situation in no way was a breach of good

[120] Supreme Court Act, RSC, 1985, c S-26. Similarly, the provincial Constitutional Questions Act, RSBC 1996 Chapter 68 s 6 provides in respect of appeals that 'The opinion of the Court of Appeal or the Supreme Court is a judgment of the Court of Appeal or of the Supreme Court, as the case may be, and an appeal lies from it in the manner of a judgment in an ordinary action'. The 'Supreme Court' referred to is the British Columbia Supreme Court, a superior court of inherent jurisdiction.

[121] And, it appears that in certain references parties other than the government have been able to further appeal the matter to the Supreme Court: *Reference re Bill 30, An Act to Amend the Education Act (Ont.)*, [1987] 1 SCR 1148. The reference was discussed in Chapter 7.

[122] *Supreme Court Act Reference* (n 73) at para 6. The quoted passage followed the Court's summary answers to the questions (emphasis added).

[123] Supreme Court Act (n 120), section 9.

behaviour, so his appointment could not be vacated on that basis. Prudence, then, might have dictated that the government initiate some sort of *live* proceeding to obtain a declaration (perhaps from the Federal Court) that the *Order in Council* was void *ab initio*. That it did not do so neatly illustrates the real-world impact of advisory opinions. For the OIC certainly has been *treated* as if it were revoked. It likely was not even considered by the government in what would otherwise have been a risky course of action: appointing someone else to the seat. (Indeed, Justice Nadon has joked that he may still be a member of the Supreme Court.[124])

Another powerful example of a remedial effect is found in *Re Manitoba Language Rights*.[125] Previously discussed in Chapter 7, the reference arose when all of Manitoba's statutes, which had been published solely in English, were challenged as being in clear conflict with a constitutional rule requiring the province to print and publish its laws in French and English.[126]

The Supreme Court thought it intolerable that an entire jurisdiction's laws could be rendered null. The prospect threatened the constitutional postulate of the rule of law which requires 'the creation and maintenance of an actual order of positive laws …'.[127] In order to reconcile what appeared to be diametrically opposing demands of the Constitution, the Court decided to 'declare' the laws invalid but suspend that declaration for the minimum period of time necessary for translation, re-enactment, printing and publication.[128] This would be the first of many such 'suspended declarations'.[129]

Re Manitoba Language Rights was a stunning assertion of judicial supremacy. It is, then, ironic that such a critical development in constitutional remedies occurred *in the context of an advisory opinion*, which is not supposed to engage remedies at all! *Re Manitoba Language Rights* contains absolutely no consideration of whether its status *as* a reference could help to avoid the constitutional conundrum that the Court found so troubling. The word 'advisory' does not even appear in the opinion. The word 'binding' does, twice, but on an unrelated issue.[130]

[124] Taken from an interview with Marc Nadon on 4 June 2018 as described in Carissima Mathen and Michael Plaxton, *The Nadon Chronicles* (working title) (forthcoming, UBC Press, 2019).

[125] *Re Manitoba Language Rights*, [1985] 1 SCR 721 [*Re Manitoba Language*].

[126] Manitoba Act, 1870, RSC 1970, App II

[127] *Re Manitoba Language* (n 125) at para 60.

[128] ibid at para 107: '… the Constitution requires that temporary validity and force and effect be given to the current Acts of the Manitoba Legislature from the date of this judgment, and that rights, obligations and other effects which have arisen under these laws … are deemed temporarily to have been and continue to be effective and beyond challenge. It is only in this way that legal chaos can be avoided and the rule of law preserved'.

[129] For discussion and critique, see Bruce Ryder, 'Suspending the Charter' (2003) 21 Supreme Court Law Review 267. At the time, Ryder observed that the Court had strayed very far from the initial moorings of the suspended remedy, noting its approach as 'casual' (p 271). The situation arguably has only worsened since then. Robert Leckey, 'The Harms of Remedial Discretion' (2016) 14(3) International Journal of Constitutional Law 584.

[130] Binding-ness was cited in relation to the de facto doctrine, which some interveners claimed would resolve the difficulty. *Re Manitoba Language Rights* (n 125) at 755–56.

Unlike the *Motor Vehicle Reference*, there is not even the textual fig leaf provided by a provincial 'appeal'. The Governor in Council referred the questions to the Court directly.

If references are merely advisory, why would the Court need to 'suspend' the effect of its answer that, yes, Manitoba's laws had been enacted in an unconstitutional manner? Could not the reference simply have been accepted as a signal (albeit an urgent one) that the legislature had best attend to the problem? There is little question that Court assumed, at least implicitly, that its answer would be akin to a declaration of invalidity. Nor is there much doubt that, had it in fact issued a declaration, the consequences would indeed have been catastrophic.

Owing to the nature of the Constitution's supremacy clause, the Court's assumption probably was inevitable. Section 52(1) of the Canadian Constitution-states that the Constitution 'is the supreme law of Canada, and any law that is inconsistent with [it] is, to the extent of the inconsistency, of no force or effect'. Since the clause was entrenched in 1982, Canadian courts have invoked it as a justification for numerous kinds of remedies. Yet, viewed strictly on its own terms, the supremacy clause says nothing at all about courts. It does not expressly authorise the extremely broad panoply of remedies that the Supreme Court has arrogated to itself, up to and including suspending the effect of its judgments. Section 24 of the Charter does contain such enabling language but it is limited to individuals who have 'established' a violation of their Charter rights – seemingly confining its scope to inter partes litigation.[131] That section is of no assistance in a situation such as *Re Manitoba Language Rights*. Given that the supremacy clause does not specifically refer to the courts but is still taken to have permitted the practice of judicial review, there must be something about the statement of supremacy per se that generates that effect.

What that is, I suggest, is fidelity to a special idea. A constitutionally ordered society is bound by a higher law. Actors should *care* about whether their actions (generated either at the level of a democratic formal assembly or by a single executive actor) are consistent with the Constitution. They should *want* to comply with it; and they should take seriously indicators that they have not. Those indicators need not come exclusively from the courts – they can, for example, come from pre-legislative review by government lawyers. But when they *do* come from the courts in the course of their ordinary adjudicative function, all actors are bound to comply with those interpretations, including any remedies issued therefrom,

[131] Charter s 24:

> 24. (1) Anyone whose rights or freedoms, as guaranteed by this Charter, have been infringed or denied may apply to a court of competent jurisdiction to obtain such remedy as the court considers appropriate and just in the circumstances.
>
> (2) Where, in proceedings under subsection (1), a court concludes that evidence was obtained in a manner that infringed or denied any rights or freedoms guaranteed by this Charter, the evidence shall be excluded if it is established that, having regard to all the circumstances, the admission of it in the proceedings would bring the administration of justice into disrepute.

subject, of course, to any exceptions or qualifications themselves allowed under the Constitution, such as principles of proportionality, processes of justification, or extraordinary *non obstante* powers.

Courts, especially, though not only, those that exercise judicial review, bear a great responsibility when they provide answers to legal questions. They must, of course, exercise their judgement, analysis and discretion to the very best of their ability. But they must also police the boundaries of their powers, ensuring, for example, that when they do change the traditional limits on their dispute mechanisms – such as by expanding the basis for standing – they do not risk imperilling the broader acceptance of their judicial role.

And here, I think, is where the role of advisory opinions may be best understood. Courts strive for coherence in the corpus of legal rules with which they engage. Sometimes, that coherence is impossible to obtain, such as where the courts have no control over their production as is obviously the case for statutes. But where they *do* exercise that control, they must, and do, ensure that, so far as possible, those roles avoid gaping inconsistency. To fail to do so would damage their ability to exercise that role.

Thus, the declaratory *power* that a court invokes in a live case appears indistinct, in any meaningful sense, from the declaratory *function* of that court when it sits in a reference and acts as the *provider of answers*. It is a by-product of a court firmly ensconced in the common law tradition. The influence, power and, yes, authority of an advisory opinion in a constitutionally limited system is consistent with the broader parameters of that constitutionalism. It reflects perhaps more clearly than any other feature the status of the court. That status is sufficiently weighty to extend authority and binding-ness to all of the pronouncements made by the court in a proceeding where it has been asked to determine what the law is.

* * *

This chapter argued that advisory opinions do not count as something appreciably different from cases. The courts cite references alongside both ordinary and constitutional decisions, and use the rules and principles articulated therein in their subsequent legal reasoning. Indeed, at times it appears that the Canadian Supreme Court forgets that it *is* sitting in its advisory rather than appellate capacity, such as when it declares a law invalid, or suspends that declaration – neither of which, technically, have any effect. The chapter explained why courts might view advisory opinions in that way, and why their attitude matters.

Here, we can return briefly to Raz, whose analysis is helpful in setting up, but does not completely encompass, the authoritative nature of advisory opinions. If a reference opinion were simply 'advice', then political actors and judges would inquire into the substantive reasons for the advice and re-weigh those reasons (giving suitable deference to the status of the advisor) and reach an independent decision about whether to follow the advice or not. But no actors treat reference opinions in that way. Rather they treat them as authoritative: if the opinion sets out a rule of law, that rule should be followed as a reason for action independently and separately from an assessment of its underlying justificatory reasons. It would seem, then, that if reference opinions are treated this way, they are authoritative statements of law.

But this account is not quite complete. It is not just that political actors and judges accept the authority of the Court according to, say, the normal justification thesis, but rather that they seem to regard advisory opinions as fitting into the interpretive discourse of the law in the ordinary way. Some advisory opinions do state crisp rules that can exclude reference to underlying reasons or principles. Others, though, operate in hard cases where the rules are contested, and the answer not at all evident. The value (and authority) of such opinions stems not just from the fact that they were issued by an apex court, but that they involve the substantive interpretation of reasons or principles that animate the law. They are treated as ordinary precedents in the ordinary common law way, and appear to have authority for that reason.[132]

[132] I am grateful to Mark Walters for helping me to frame these final points.

Conclusion

We are familiar with the idea that courts decide cases. When they do, courts employ powerful remedies that can profoundly affect society. The limits on that function are a set of proscriptions to ensure that courts do not interfere excessively in human affairs.

Those limits, which I described as a doctrine of justiciability, are integrally linked to what a court is, and, especially, how it functions in the overall machinery of the state. When a court does more than adjudicate live disputes, that can be cause for concern. It may appear to put at risk the separation of powers. The phenomenon of references – judicial hearings that do not involve live disputes – seems to take courts beyond adjudication and thus, has been rejected in some legal systems as a step too far.

In this book, I have argued that the strict divide between references and cases can be misleading. In constitutionally bound rule of law states, other state actors – namely, members of the executive and the legislature – are expected to limit their exercise of political power in conformity with prior articulated norms and rules. In the vast majority of those states, the courts are an important way that such norms are recognised and laws are scrutinized.

The courts can perform that role in a number of ways. They may consider such issues as part of their ordinary adjudicative function, issuing declarations of invalidity with (usually) immediate effect. Or, courts may operate in a separate sphere, performing *only* a role of abstract constitutional review. Traditionally, it has been thought important to keep those functions separate, either by rejecting abstract review or by confining it to separate courts. More unusually, the same courts perform both functions. Canadian courts fall in that category. The interrelation between those functions, residing in a single judicial body, is what inspired this book.

In Anglo-American systems the advisory function arose out of an ancient relationship between sovereign and council. In Canada, the role originally was conceived of, and especially concerned with, issues, such as arbitrating federalism, that were thought likely to challenge and complicate the development of a fledgling national polity. At the same time, it was not thought that references would have much purchase in the broader legal system.

That early view proved mistaken. A number of factors led to the absorption of references in the courts' general jurisprudence. One is the 'on the ground reality' that such opinions were not structured to be very different from cases. The main distinction – that a reference is triggered by another state actor in the possible absence of a live dispute – was complementary to the court's main function. Another factor is that the questions put to courts concerned some of the most important legal issues of the day, at times usurping existing litigation. References thus could not help but have very broad impact. And a third factor is the underlying common law tradition in which the Supreme Court, and other courts, work. That tradition grants great interpretative power to the courts mediated through a judicial hierarchy modelled on norms of precedent.

The advisory opinions produced by the Supreme Court and other Canadian courts clearly engage similar modes of analysis as in their adjudication. References rest comfortably within the larger body of law that courts treat as precedent and, therefore as authoritative sources of law within that common law tradition. And, in constitutional matters references perform the same function – *providing answers* – that undergirds much of law, and certainly constitutional law. Perhaps cognisant of the powerful pull, still, of ideas of justiciability, courts expect advisory opinions to present a 'dispute' – and most, practically speaking, do. But, the Canadian Supreme Court does not seem overly preoccupied with *who* participates in, or initiates, that dispute. It is content to be asked for its advice by actors expected to act in (reasonably) good faith; and it rarely declines to provide it. Moreover, the Court has developed rules, like the doctrine of public interest litigation, for constitutional disputes which have relaxed strict notions of standing. This permits the judicial branch to perform a quasi-advisory role in broadly framed challenges to legislation.

By 1982, Canadian references were operating in a system governed by the supremacy of a written Constitution covering both division-of-powers and individual rights. The interpretation of those provisions was entrusted to the judiciary. While the exclusivity of that interpretative role is contested, the continuing prevalence of the advisory function indicates that both non-judicial and judicial actors recognise the role as one that courts should play.

The advisory function is not without challenges. The executive control over the initiating function can shield from true accountability decisions to refer, or not to refer. Reference questions may be put to the court in unhelpful ways to further explicitly political goals. Though ordinary citizens have access to a similar form of review through public interest standing, access to the courts remains out of reach for many. Even if granted the opportunity to participate in a reference, many individuals find it financially prohibitive to do so in a meaningful way. And the blurred lines around a reference's remedial effect may create uncertainty.

That said, on the whole the advisory function fits remarkably well in a system committed to constitutional norms and limits. Its power resides in the effect of a court stating something to be 'the law'. References engage a declaratory function in perhaps its purest sense – not in the service of mediation of a particular dispute, but with the intention of clarifying a point of uncertainty so that everyone knows how the law may be applied to their future projects and decisions.

The Canadian experience may prove instructive – in both the positive and negative sense – to other systems contemplating new political arrangements. Additionally, it may be a helpful point of reference in much older systems that are being forced to reckon with the role of courts in new and unfamiliar ways.[1]

[1] Byron Karemba, 'Brexit, the Reference Jurisdiction of the UKSC and the New Separation of Powers', UK Constitutional Law Blog, 30 July 2018, https://ukconstitutionallaw.org/. See also the August 2018 decision to permit the French cour de cassation to ask for advisory opinions from the European Court of Human Rights (ECtHR). The French Court made its first such request in October 2018, asking the ECtHR whether the refusal to accept a birth certificate duly issued in a foreign country for a child born through surrogacy violates the right to respect for privacy and family life under the European Convention on Human Rights (available at https://www.jurist.org/news/2018/10/europe-rights-court-asked-to-weigh-in-on-france-surrogacy-case/).

INDEX

AOs = advisory opinions/references

Aberhart, William 84–5
aboriginal rights 122, 162, 164, 165
absolute liability 140–4, 214–15
abstract review of legislation 25, 83, 222–6, 234–5
accessibility of Supreme Court to public 186
adjudicative and advisory function, same court with 3, 7, 60, 205–6
adversarial proceedings 35, 221, 225
advisory, definition of 58–60, 197
Aeronautics Reference 81–2, 136
Aimé-Dorion, Antoine 39
Alberta
firearms registration and licensing 99
patriation 123
Senate, reform of the 169
Social Credit Legislation 84–7, 109, 185
Trans Mountain Expansion (TMX) 105
alcohol regulation 66
Allan, TRS 125
amicus curiae 49, 160–1, 166, 169
answers, Supreme Court as *see* **provider of answers, Supreme Court as**
apex courts 31–44 *see also* **Supreme Court**
appeals 12, 109–13 *see also* **general appeal courts exercising advisory functions**
binding nature 4
civil appeals 41
criminal appeals 41, 69, 110, 115
Crown prerogative 32, 112, 113
early controversies over Supreme Court 3, 7, 50, 60
JCPC 32–3, 39, 41, 43–4, 111–12
jurisdiction 42–4, 46, 69
number of appeals 91
provinces, direct appeals from 43, 46
terminology 229
wrongful convictions 187–8
appointments *see* **appointments to Senate; appointments to Supreme Court; women to the Senate, appointment of**
appointments to Senate
consultative elections 168–70
executive, by 168–9
Senate Reform Reference 172–9, 206, 213
term limits 168–72
women 132–7, 143, 153, 157
appointments to Supreme Court
avoidance of controversy 187–8
conservatism 114
constitutional development 108, 114, 116
declaratory legislation 174–5, 185, 230
denominationalism 114
eligibility 172–9, 184–5, 206
executive, by 26–7, 172–9, 184–5, 195, 206, 213
arm's length select committees 27
legislature, lack of involvement of 26–7
ideology 172
increase in number of judges 91
judicial consensus, degree of 221
pre-emption 184–5
provinces 114, 116, 172–9
Quebec, requirement for three judges from 172–9, 184–5, 206, 213
Supreme Court Act Reference 158, 167, 172–9, 184–5, 192, 203, 229–30
arbitrators, authority of 199
Aristotle 21
assisted dying 75
assisted human reproduction 99–100, 221
Atkin, Lord 82
Attorneys-General 1–2, 49, 88
Austin, John 197
Australia, separation of powers in 62
authority
arbitrators 199
cases and AOs, resemblance between 205

precedent 217–18, 232–3
service conception of 200

Bagehot, Walter 23
Balfour Declaration 80, 110
Bastarache, Michel 206
Bennett, WAC 91–2, 109
Bertrand, Guy 159
Bickel, Alexander 36
bigamy 87–8
Re Bill 30 139, 148–9
binding nature of advisory opinions 5, 58–60, 181, 205–33 *see also* **compliance; compliance, reasons for**
abstract review 222–6, 234–5
cases and AOs, resemblance between 205, 206–15, 232, 232, 234–5
common constitutional law, advisory opinions as part of 205, 232–3, 235
declarations 225–30, 232, 234–6
general appeal courts exercising advisory functions 58, 205–6
other forms of advice, difference from 296
precedent 205, 206–7, 213–21, 232–3, 235
process 207–13
provider of answers, Supreme Court as 207, 221–32, 235
remedies 226, 228–30
rule of law 207, 227, 230, 233–4
standing 206–7, 222–5, 232, 235
Binnie, Ian 184, 197, 206, 213
Blackstone, William 23
Blake, Edward 48–9, 83–4
Britain *see* **United Kingdom**
British Columbia
due process 141
employment of Chinese and Japanese aliens 80
fishing rights 52
jurisdiction 43
mineral rights 91–2
polygamy 190, 219
Senate, reform of the 169
Trans Mountain Expansion (TMX) 105–6, 186, 188
British North America Act 1867 116–18, 190–1
amendments 116–17, 190–1
formal requests to UK 118
Westminster Parliament, consideration of 190–1
Confederation 37, 39–40
Constitution Act 1982 149
criminal law 99
disallowance power 83, 85
early controversies over Supreme Court 54
environment 104–5
federal-provincial disputes, role of AOs in 38, 51–4, 117–18
general appeal courts exercising advisory functions 51–4
Imperial Parliament, matters left to oversight of 116–17
interpretation 132–7
JCPC 53–4
marriage, state regulation of 87
national identity 117
opposing views, presentation of 211–12
Quebec, agreement of 67
same-sex marriage 153
Senate Reform Reference 170
separation of powers 27
Supreme Court 37, 40, 41, 45
treaties 80
ultra vires 118

cabinet 23
Canada Act 1982 8, 115–30 *see also* **Constitution Act 1982**
entrenchment 115
entry into force 127–8
Quebec Veto Reference 126–9
separation of powers 64
Canadian Charter of Rights and Freedoms *see* **Charter of Rights and Freedoms**
carbon tax 104–5
Cartier, George-Etienne 39
cases and AOs, resemblance between 9, 180, 206–15
answers, status of 4–5
appeals, AOs distinguished from 207
authority 205
binding nature of AOs 205, 206–15, 232, 232, 234–5
British system, advisory opinions in 207–8, 234
Charter of Rights and Freedoms 205
classification 213–14
compliance 201, 204
criminal law 214
early controversies over Supreme Court 50, 59–60

emergency measures 95
format of AOs 213, 232
individual rights issues 132
Internet, streaming on the 201
legal rules, as generating 214
media lock-up 201
norms, access to the same 206
opposing views, presentation of 210–12
plaintiffs, absence of 4
precedent 213, 220
process 206, 207–9
reasoning, similarity of 201
reasons for conclusions 206
refusal to provide answers 4
reporting 210
rule of law 234
separation of powers 30, 62
sources of law, AOs as 214
submissions, making 4
terminology 10
threshold arguments on reference function 161–2
work product, appearance in arrangement of 213, 232

Charter of Rights and Freedoms 5, 142–4, 151, 214–16
accountability 131
Re Bill 30 139, 148–9
Bill of Rights, proposal for entrenched 117, 119, 122
compliance 195–6
conflict of rights 155
constitutionality of legislation 152–6, 189, 195–6
extrinsic evidence 142
freedom of expression 219
guidance, provision of doctrinal 182
inter partes litigation 138–9
interpretation 138–9, 142–3, 205
legislative override 126
living tree principle 143
maintenance of legislation which violates rights 195–6
notwithstanding clause 196
patriation 142–3
polygamy 1–2, 219
precedent 215–16
prostitution 74–5, 149–52
religion 139
same-sex marriage 73, 152–6, 189
second-look legislation 196
securities regulation 103
separation of powers 143–4
standing 223–5

checks and balances 23–4
Choudhry, Sujit 166
classification of AOs 9, 213–14
colonies
Balfour Declaration 80, 110
British Empire 80, 116
Colonial Laws Validity Act 1865 226–7
disallowance 38–9
marriage, state regulation of 88, 90
national identity 117
Supreme Court, constitutional development of 109

Colvin, Eric 124
comity 219–20
command theory 197–8
Commissions of Inquiry 220
common law systems 12–13
compliance 192–6 *see also* **binding nature of advisory opinions; compliance, reasons for**
Charter of Rights and Freedoms 195–6
disavowal 192–3
interdependence between branches 195
JCPC 35
order and advice, difference between 193–4
other sources of advice 195
politicians, disavowal by 192–3
rule of law 195
scrutiny of legislation 194–5
ultra vires rulings, actions following 196
vetting of constitutionality of bills 194

compliance, reasons for 9, 181, 196–204
action, reasons for 193–4, 196–7, 199, 202–3
advisory, meaning of 197
authority, legitimacy of 198–201, 202–4
cases and AOs, resemblance between 201, 204
command theory 197–8
deference 203
form of law, advisory opinions as a 4–5, 156, 198, 202, 204, 206, 213, 221, 232
high regard, compliance due to holding institution in 203
independent judgment 200
normal justification thesis 199, 233
not-law 197
orders, law as not being 198

other forms of guidance/advice, reaction to 197
political stability 204
pre-emption 199, 203
pressure to comply 202
rule of law 201
sanctions 197–8
self-interest 203–4
uncertainty, consequences of 204
composition of Supreme Court 41, 91, 108, 113, 115–16 *see also* **appointments to Supreme Court**
Confederation 7, 37–40
British legal tradition, formative aspects of 6–7, 31–7
denominational schools 148
Dominion of Canada 37
entrenchment 42
environment 104
federalism 38–40
federal-provincial disputes, role of AOs in 79–80, 98
post-confederation 79–90
secession 98
structure 38
Supreme Court, creation of 37–8
Constitution Act 1867 *see* **British North America Act 1867**
Constitution Act 1982
appointments to Supreme Court 167, 176
Charter of Rights and Freedoms 148–9
Constitution
development 115–16, 123, 126–30
secession 159, 162–3
federal-provincial disputes, role of AOs in 91
fundamental justice 140–1
individual rights issues 131, 138–41, 148–9, 157
interpretation 138–9
inter-provincial trade 96
patriation 167
Quebec Secession Reference 159, 162–3
Quebec Veto Reference 115, 123, 126–9
rule of law 148
same-sex marriage 153
Senate Reform Reference 167, 168, 203
Constitution of Canada 158–79
see also **Constitution Act 1982; constitutional development; constitutionality of legislation**
amendments 8, 115–28, 190–1
appointments to Supreme Court 176, 178–9
parameters 169–71
separation of powers 29, 64–5
appointments to Supreme Court 176, 178–9
architecture, effect on 170
common law, references as part of constitutional 9, 205, 232–3, 235
constitutional conventions 116, 128, 164
constitutionalism 23, 37, 116, 134, 147, 158, 162, 232
Crown prerogatives 116
declarations 227
democracy 162
entrenchment of individual rights and freedoms 37
federalism 162
guardian of the constitution, Supreme Court as 29
interpretation 132–9, 157, 172–8, 203, 211–12, 215
JCPC 39
judiciary, independence of 29
minorities, respect for 162
necessity 146
patriation from UK 5
positive law 146
rebirth and rupture 108, 129–30, 164
rule of law 145–8, 162, 230–1
secession of Quebec 158–67, 170
separation of powers 26–9, 30, 78
standing 223
status of courts 46
supremacy 145–6, 231, 235
treaties 80
ultra vires 145–8
unwritten rules and conventions 29, 116, 160, 162, 166
constitutional development 108–30, 164
1982, new constitutional era in 8
administrative changes 115
amendment process 8
appeals 109–13
appointments to Supreme Court 108, 114
British Empire 116
British North America Act 1867 116–18, 190–1
Canada Act 1982 8, 115–30
composition of Supreme Court 108, 113, 115–16

JCPC to Supreme Court, shift from 8, 110–13
new rights and procedures, institution of 8, 190–1
Patriation Reference 115, 118–26, 129–30, 162, 164, 189–91, 203
Quebec Veto Reference 115, 123, 126–9
Upper House Reference 115, 117–18
constitutionality of legislation 41, 45–6
absolute liability 214–15
abstract review of legislation 25, 83, 222–6, 234–5
Charter of Rights and Freedoms 152–6, 189, 195–6
compliance 194–5
criminal law 101
disallowance power 83
federal-provincial disputes, role of AOs in 49–50
judiciary 24
polygamy 1–2, 219–20
Quebec Secession Reference 160–1
same-sex marriage 152–6, 189, 192, 216
separation of powers 26–7, 61, 73
constitutions 11–13 *see also* **Constitution of Canada**
abstract review 25
interpretation 25
Matchless Constitution theory 23, 26
separation of powers 24–30
United States 25, 140, 161
unwritten constitutions 26, 29, 69, 226–7
context 9–10, 137, 181–2
control of proceedings 63, 188–9
controversy, avoidance of 187–90
co-ordination of social aims and projects 183–4
counsel 46, 211
Court of Chancery 226
courts with cases 11–30
adjudication, links with other arms of state of 6
function of courts 11–13
powers and limits of cases 13–20
separation of powers 6, 13, 20–9
criminal law
appeals 41, 69, 110, 115
cases and AOs, resemblance between 214
constitutionality of legislation 101
dispute, existence of 17–18
federal-provincial disputes, role of AOs in 8, 98–101, 186, 214
guidance, provision of doctrinal 182
JCPC 110, 214
presence of accused 17
prostitution 149–52
state as a party 17–19
ultra vires 99–101, 110
wrongful convictions 187–8, 191
Crown *see* **executive**
Curia Regis 31, 34, 208

declarations
abstract review of legislation 225–6
administrative and constitutional litigation 227
appointments to Supreme Court 174–5, 185
binding nature of AOs 225–30, 232, 234–6
common law 226–7
declaratory judgments versus declaratory statements 207
federal-provincial disputes, role of AOs in 231
freedom of expression 228
obiter commentary 228
provider of answers, Supreme Court as 221, 225–6
refusal of declarations 228
remedies 228–9
suspended declarations 147, 230
terminology 229
unilateral declarations of independence (UDI) 159, 185
unwritten constitutions 226–7
democracy 21, 162
denominational schools 148–9, 210–12
deterrence 18
Dickson, Brian 116
Diefenbaker, John 114
disallowance power 7–8, 41, 83–7
colonial legislation 38–9
displacement 185
early controversies over Supreme Court 49
Imperial Crown 38–9
national unity 86
political judgments 83
political parties 83
positioning 186–7
post-confederation 83–7
pre-emption 38–9
public messaging 186
reluctance to use disallowance 84

royal assent to provincial legislation, withholding 83
sovereignty 85
ultra vires 83–4
dispute, existence of 13, 15–18
distinction between cases and references *see* **cases and AOs, resemblance between doctrinal guidance, provision of** 182–3, 191–2
driving offences and fault
absolute liability 140–4, 214–15
cases and AOs, resemblance between 205
Charter of Rights and Freedoms 142–4, 151, 214–15
constitutional validity 214–15
declarations 228–9
fundamental justice, definition of 140–4, 182
interpretation 215
Motor Vehicle Reference 139, 140–4, 148, 151, 182, 214–16, 228–9
patriation 142–3
duality principle 128–9
due process 140–1, 143
Duff, Lyman 86
Dworkin, Ronald 189

early controversies over AOs 45–60
administration of law, interference with 54–5
advisory and appellate function in same body 3, 7, 60
advisory, definition of 58–60
appellate function of Supreme Court 3, 7, 60
binding but advisory, rulings as not being 58–60
Cabinet, questions from 47–8
cases and AOs, resemblance between 50, 59–60
Crown discretion 47
duty to hear references 50
federal jurisdiction 7, 49–57, 59
framing the function 45–8
general court of appeal, squaring advisory opinions with 50–7, 58
Governor in Council, proposal for referrals by 46–7, 50, 58
JCPC 51–7, 58–60
justiciability 54–5
limitations 49
notice 50
number of references 57
oral argument 48
permissible questions 50
prejudice 54–5
provinces, concerns of 7, 49–57, 59
reasons, provision of 48
References re References 51–7, 58
special cases 49
economic regulation 101–3
emergency measures 92–5
entrenchment 29, 37, 42, 114–15, 117, 119, 122
environment and development 103–6, 187–8
carbon tax 104–5
Paris Agreement 2016 104
POGG power 104
European Convention on Human Rights (ECHR) 12, 228
evidence
extrinsic evidence 94–5, 142
prostitution 150–2
Exchequer Court, proposal for 42
executive
appointments to Senate 168–9
cabinet 23
capture 7, 63, 137
Commissions of Inquiry 220
Crown immunity 25
Crown prerogative 32, 86, 112, 113
failure to seek a reference 74–5
initiation of AOs 7, 61, 62–70, 72–5, 235
JCPC 56
judiciary
alignment with 61
appointment 26–7, 172–9, 184–5, 195, 206, 213
arm's length select committees, appointment by 27
capture 63
independence 63
legislature, lack of involvement of 26–7
subordination of judiciary 62–3, 69
legislature
appointment of judiciary 26–7
overlap 72
separation of powers 23, 26, 31, 70–8
minority governments 72–5
presidential systems 62–3
separation of powers 20–9, 30, 62–78, 195

fair trial, right to a 144
fault 139, 140–4, 148, 151, 182, 214–16, 228–9

federal-provincial disputes *see also* **federal-provincial disputes, role of AOs in**
appeals 40
Constitution 39, 117–18
entrenchment of court, proposal for 39
religion 40
royal assent to provincial legislation, withholding 83
special cases on constitutional matters 46
federal-provincial disputes, role of AOs in 5, 79–107 *see also* **disallowance power**
appeals 50–7
Confederation 79–90, 98
constitutional dialogue 126
criminal law 8, 98–101, 186, 214
current battles 98–106
early controversies over Supreme Court 7, 49–57, 59
economic regulation 101–3
environment and development 103–6, 187–8
equality of provinces 126
general appeal courts exercising advisory functions 51–7
genetic discrimination 75–6, 100–1, 182
Inflation Act Reference 92–5, 142, 183–4
interpretation, norms of 8
inter-provincial trade 96–8, 188
JCPC 39, 53–7, 89–91
justiciability 125–6
marriage, state regulation of 87–90
natural resources 8, 91–2, 187
notification of hearings 49
Patriation Reference 119–26, 130, 190–1, 203
peace, order and good government (POGG) power 92
positioning 186–7
post-confederation 79–90
reasons for initiation of AOs 182
refusal to answer 89
rule of law 186
same-sex marriage 216–17
secession 98
separation of powers 54, 82, 84, 92, 95, 103, 105–7
Supreme Court, revamped 90–8
treaties 79–83
federalism 40–1, 158 *see also* **federal-provincial disputes**
Constitution, amendment of 64
cooperative federalism 102–3
early controversies over Supreme Court 7, 49–57, 59
federal trade and commerce power 101–2
paramountcy 101
separation of powers 25
unwritten constitutional principles 162
final court, Supreme Court as 90–1, 109–10, 113–14, 155–6, 216–17
finality of rulings 43–4, 155–6, 178–9
Finlay, Robert 54–5
firearms registration and licensing 99, 186
Fish, Morris 172–3
fishing rights 52
form of law, advisory opinions as a 4–5, 156, 198, 202, 204, 206, 213, 221, 232
format of AOs 213, 232
Fournier, Télesphore 42–3, 46–7
framing the question 188–90
France
civil law 39–40
validity of legislation 77
freedom of expression 219, 228
French and English Canada, divide between 42–3
function of courts 11–13
fundamental justice, principles of 140–4, 150, 182, 218–19

Galati, Rocco 185
general appeal courts exercising advisory functions 41–2, 109–10
binding nature of AOs 58, 205–6
definition 41
early controversies over Supreme Court 50–7, 58
federal-provincial disputes 40, 51–7
JCPC 53–7
separation of powers 62
genetic discrimination and insurance 75–6, 100–1, 182
German Federal Constitutional Court 35
good faith 160, 163, 165, 192
government *see* **executive**
Governor in Council 46–7, 50, 58, 68
Great Britain *see* **United Kingdom**
Guantanamo Bay 20
guardian of the constitution, Supreme Court as 29, 147, 164
guidance, provision of doctrinal 182–3, 191–2

Hamilton, Alexander 8, 24–5
Harper, Stephen 74, 151, 168, 172, 179, 183
Hart, HLA 8, 198, 203
Henderson, GF 136–7
Hogg, Peter 82, 110
House of Lords 55, 66, 71
Howse, Robert 166
human rights *see* **Charter of Rights and Freedoms; individual rights issues, implications of AOs for**

Imperial conferences 1926–30 110
imprimatur, seeking Supreme Court's 190–2, 202
independence of the judiciary
appointments 114
diminution in independence 63
entrenchment 29
executive 63
refusal to answer references 68–9
separation of powers 22, 24, 27, 29, 61, 63, 68–9
unwritten constitutional principle, as 29, 69
India 161, 223
indigenous rights 122, 162, 164, 165
individual rights issues, implications of advisory opinions for 131–57
cases and AOs, resemblance between 132
Charter of Rights and Freedoms 131, 138–9, 148–9, 157
competing constitutional interests 148–9
Constitution Act 1982 131, 138–9, 148–9, 157
constitutional litigation 8, 132
decrease in number of references 131
denominational schools 148–9
JCPC case law pre-1982, weight of 131
minority rights 144–9
Motor Vehicle Reference 139, 140–4, 148, 151, 214–15
Persons Case 132–7, 143, 153, 157
process 132–7
Prostitution Reference 149–52
religion, freedom of 139
remedial powers of Supreme Court, expansion in 131–2
rule of law (*Manitoba Language*) 144–8, 230–2
Same-Sex Marriage Reference 152–6, 189–92
ultra vires 132
Inflation Act Reference 92–5, 183–4
initiation of AOs *see also* **reasons for initiation of AOs**
executive
capture 7
separation of powers 7, 61, 62–70, 72–5, 235
failure to seek a reference 74–6
Governor in Council 68
Senate 71–2
separation of powers 7, 61, 62–77, 235
standing committees/independent parliamentary officers, by 77
inquisitorial systems 14
institutions 158–79
Constitution 158–79
federalism 158
provider of answers, role of Supreme Court as 8
provinces 158
Quebec Secession Reference 158–67, 170, 178, 185
Senate Reform Reference 158, 167–72, 192, 203
separation of powers 158, 161
Supreme Court Act Reference 158, 167, 172–9, 184–5, 192, 203, 206, 213
International Labour Organization (ILO) conventions 80–3
International Radiotelegraph Convention 1927 81–2
Internet, streaming on 186, 201
interpretation
British North America Act 1867 132–7
Charter of Rights and Freedoms 138–9, 142–3, 205
Constitution 132–9, 157, 172–8, 203, 211–12, 215
constitutions 25
living tree principle 134, 143, 153
norms 8
originalism 136–7, 153, 170
inter-provincial trade 96–8, 188
Ireland, criminalisation of homosexuality in 222–3

Jay, John 62
JCPC *see* **Judicial Committee of the Privy Council (JCPC)**
Jefferson, Thomas 24
Joli-Coeur, André 160
Judicial Committee Act 1833 32–6, 47–8

Judicial Committee of the Privy Council (JCPC) 7, 31–7
- abolition of jurisdiction 111–13
- advisory function 32–6, 209
- alcohol regulation 66
- appellate jurisdiction 32–3, 39, 41, 43–4
- clarification model 35, 37
- compliance with rulings 35
- Constitution 39
- creation 32
- criminal law 110, 214
- Crown, questions from the 56
- disallowance power 84
- dominions and colonies, appeals from 32
- early controversies over Supreme Court 51–7, 58–60
- economic regulation 102
- executive, advice to 33
- federal-provincial disputes, role of AOs in 39, 53–7, 89–91
- general appeal courts exercising advisory functions 53–7
- historical context 31–2
- House of Commons, advice to 32–3
- House of Lords, distinguished from advisory function of 55
- individual rights issues 131, 133–7
- inter-provincial trade 96
- JCPC 44
- Judicial Committee Act 1833 32–6
- Judicial Committee Act 1844 44
- judicial restraint or passive model 36–7
- last resort approach 35–6
- Lord Chancellor 33–6
- marriage, state regulation of 89–90
- opposing views, presentation of 211–12
- Parliament, growth in power of 208–9
- participation, importance of 35
- *per curiam* rulings 102, 209
- prior opinions, weight given to 113
- procedure 209
- provincial courts, appeals from 111–12
- reasons 48
- reserve powers 47
- role 7, 31–7, 39
- single opinions, issuing of 209–10
- special cases on constitutional matters 46–7
- Supreme Court, shift to 8, 110–14
- treaties 81–2
- ultra vires 53, 56–7

judiciary *see also* **independence of the judiciary; judiciary and separation of powers**
- number of judges 41–2
- passive model 36–7
- restraint 36–7
- salaries 40
- supremacy 230–1

judiciary and separation of powers 21–9, 30
- AOs 26–30, 61–70, 78, 195
- appointments by executive 172–9, 184–5, 195, 206, 213
  - arm's length select committees 27
  - legislature, lack of involvement of 26–7
- cases and AOs, resemblance between 30
- checks and balances 23–4
- constitutional review of legislation 24, 26–7
- constitutions, interpretation of 25
- coordinate construction 24
- Crown immunity 25
- depoliticisation 22
- discipline 27
- executive 7, 61, 62–70
  - alignment with judiciary 61
  - subordination of judiciary 62–3, 69
- expansion of function 7, 28–9, 61, 68
- independence 22, 24, 27, 29, 61, 68–9
- initiation of cases 7, 61, 62–70
- legislature
  - appointments, lack of involvement in 26
  - judgments against 25
  - removal 27
- neutrality 22
- removal of judges by legislature 27
- resources 63
- security of tenure 22, 27
- sovereign immunity 25

justiciability 30, 234
- early controversies over Supreme Court 54–5
- federal-provincial disputes, role of AOs in 125–6
- JCPC 36
- patriation 130
- political and legal system, boundaries between 13–14
- *Quebec Secession Reference* 161–2, 164
- religion 15
- separation of powers 13, 62, 67
- standing 222

Keith, Berriedale 16
Kelsen, Hans 25
King of England
advice to King, provision of 33–4
appeals, prerogative right to hear 32
Curia Regis 31, 34, 208
King-in-Parliament 21
King's Council (*Magnum Conciliium*) 207–8
King's Court 32
Westminster Parliament 32
writs of error 32
King-Byng constitutional crisis 110

languages 139, 144–8, 230–1
English language as official language 144–8
Official Languages Act 1890 144–8
ultra vires 144
Laskin, Bora 115–16
law, status of AOs as 180–1, 205, 214
law-making, AOs as preparatory step to 182
legislature
appointment of judges 26–7
British Parliament, growth in power of 208–9
executive and separation of powers 23, 61, 70–8
independence 77
initiation of AOs 71, 77–8
JCPC 208–9
judges, removal of 27
judgments against legislature 25
review of legislation 26–7, 61
section 64 references 71
separation of powers 7, 20–9, 30, 70–8
exclusion of legislature 26, 61, 70–8
removal of judges 27
section 64 references 71
standing committees/independent parliamentary officers, initiation by 77
supremacy 22
validity of legislation 26–7, 61, 76–8
Lévesque, René 126
living tree principle 134, 143, 153
Locke, John 22
locus standi *see* **standing**
Lord Chancellor 33–6

Macdonald, John A 38–42, 44, 47, 83, 171
MacFarlane, Emmett 172
McIntyre, William 116
Mackenzie, Alexander 42
Mackenzie King, William Lyon 85
McLachlin, Beverley 99–100
Madison, James 21
Magnum Conciliium 207–8
Mallory, JR 84–5
Manitoba
carbon tax 105
denominational schools, taxation of 58, 210–12
inter-provincial trade in eggs 96–8, 188, 190
language rights 139, 144–8, 230–1
patriation 119–26, 123
prostitution 150
Senate, reform of the 169
Margarine Reference 214
marriage, state regulation of 87–90
bigamy 87–8
colonialism 88, 90
JCPC 89–90
polygamy 151, 190, 219–20
religion 87–8, 90
sovereignty 87–8
ultra vires 89
Marshall, Donald 191–2
Matchless Constitution theory 23, 26
mineral rights 91–2
ministerial responsibility 23
minority governments 72–5
minority rights 117, 122, 144–9, 162, 164, 165
modification of questions 63–4
Montesquieu, Charles de 22–3
mootness 16–18, 67–8, 128, 206–7
Motor Vehicle Reference 139, 140–4, 148, 151, 182, 214–16, 228–9
Mowat, Oliver 41
murder, role of fault in 215–16
Murphy, Emily 135

Nadon, Marc 172–5, 179, 184–5, 197, 206, 213, 229–30
national identity 109, 117
natural justice 22, 35, 141, 226–7
natural resources 8, 91–2, 187
necessity 146
negotiations
duty to negotiate 163, 165–6
good faith 165
indigenous rights 165
Quebec Secession Reference 163, 165–6

neutrality 12, 14, 22, 208
New Brunswick 119, 169
Newfoundland and Labrador 119–26, 169
normal justification thesis 199, 233
notwithstanding clause 196
Nova Scotia 169

obiter commentary 228
Ontario
  carbon tax 104
  denominational schools, funding for 148–9
  inter-provincial trade in eggs 96, 188
  jurisdiction 66
  patriation 119
  power contract cancellations 84
  public interest standing 224
  same-sex marriage 73
  securities regulation 102
  Senate, reform of 169
opposing views, presentation of 201, 210–12
orders, law as not being 198
originalism 136–7, 153, 170

Paris Convention Relating to the Regulation of Aerial Navigation 1919 81–2
parliament *see* **legislature**
participation, importance of 35
passive, courts as 13, 14–15
patriation 5, 118–30, 162, 164, 203
  amending formula 119, 122–6
  appointment of judges 167
  British North America Act 1867, amendment of 190–1
  Charter of Rights and Freedoms 142–3
  Constitution Act 1982 138, 167
  Constitution, amendment of 115, 118–26, 190–1
  declarations 227
  imprimatur, seeking Supreme Court's 190–1
  joint resolution of House and Senate, constitutionality of 119
  justiciability 130
  Patriation Reference 5, 115, 118–30, 138, 142–3, 162, 164, 189–91, 203, 227
  political role of Supreme Court 124
  Prime Minister 115, 118–26
  provider of answers, Supreme Court as 126, 130, 162
  provinces, opposition from 119–26, 130, 190–1, 203

peace, order and good government (POGG) power 92–5, 104
Pearson, Lester 91
***per curiam* rulings** 92, 102, 128, 141, 160, 209
Persons Case 132–7, 143, 153, 157
pipelines 105–6, 186, 188
politics
  context 181
  disallowance power 83
  law and politics, boundaries between 7
  political and legal system, boundaries between 13–14
  political questions doctrine 128
  political role of Supreme Court 124
  same-sex marriage 74, 152–6
  secession 163–6, 186
  separation of powers 22
polygamy 151, 190, 219–20
positioning 186–7
positive law 70, 146
powers and limits of cases 13–20
precedent
  appointments to Supreme Court 178
  authority 217–18, 232–3
  binding nature of AOs 205, 206–7, 213–21, 232–3, 235
  cases and AOs, resemblance between 213, 220
  Commissions of Inquiry 220
  departure from advisory opinions 220
  judicial consensus, degree of 220–1
  mootness 206–7
  persuasive value 217
  prostitution 150–2
  standing 225
  stare decisis 9, 151–2, 205, 217–19, 225
  unanimity, lack of 221
pre-emption of legislation 38–9, 184–6, 199, 203
prejudice 54–5
prerogatives 32, 86, 112, 113
presidential systems 62–3
Prime Minister 115, 118–26
Prince Edward Island 123, 169
private bills or petitions, restrictions to 71–2
private parties, disputes between 16–17
privilege 55
Privy Council, role of Judicial Committee of (JCPC) *see also* **Judicial Committee of the Privy Council (JCPC)**
procedure
  binding nature of AOs 207–13

cases and AOs, resemblance between 206, 207–9
Commissions of Inquiry 220
control of proceedings 63, 188–9
individual rights issues 132–7
JCPC 209
section 54 references 71
Prostitution Reference 149–52
Bedford case 150–1
Charter of Rights and Freedoms 74–5, 149–52
criminal offences 149–52, 218–19
constitutionality of legislation 218
evidence 150–2
failure to seek a reference 74–5
fundamental justice, principles of 150, 218–19
guidance, provision of doctrinal 182
interveners, number of 151
precedent 150–2, 218–19
provincial courts 149–52
security of the person 218–19
standing 224
test case litigation 151
protectionism 96–8, 188
provider of answers, Supreme Court as 7–8
binding nature of AOs 207, 221–32, 235
cases and AOs, resemblance between 207
declarations 221, 225–6
patriation 126, 130, 162
remedies 226–32
provinces 41, 45–7, 158 *see also* **federal-provincial disputes**
appeals 43, 46
appointment of judges 114, 116, 172–9
Constitution, amendments of 64–5
constitutionality of legislation 41, 45–6
counsel 46
Governor in Council 46–7, 50, 58, 68
inter-provincial trade 96–8, 188
prostitution 149–52
Senate Reform Reference 169–71
special cases on constitutional matters 46
Supreme Court, development of 109
public health care 224
public interest standing 207, 223–5, 235
Puri, Poonam 103

quality of Supreme Court 108–9, 113
Quebec *see also* ***Quebec Secession Reference; Quebec Veto Reference***
appeals 42–3
appointments to Supreme Court 158, 167, 172–9, 184–5, 192, 203, 206, 213
assisted human reproduction 99
Civil Code 42–3
Constitution 108
Constitution Act 1982 67
French civil law 39–40
genetic discrimination 75–6, 101
ILO conventions 82
inter-provincial trade in eggs 96, 98
JCPC 39–40, 89–90, 114
jurisdiction 39
marriage, state regulation of 73, 89–90
Padlock Act 84
Patriation Reference 119–26, 130
radio communications, jurisdiction over 81
reserved seats in Supreme Court 113, 173, 213, 229
Resolutions of 1864 38
same-sex marriage 73
section 54 references 71
Senate Reform Reference 169
separatism 117
Quebec Secession Reference
amicus curiae, appointment of 160–1, 166
compliance 192
Constitution 158–67, 170, 178, 185
displacement 185
duty to negotiate 163, 165–6
good faith 160, 163, 165, 192
indigenous rights 162, 164, 165
injunctions against issue of further UDIs 159
interveners, number of 160
minorities, respect for 162, 164, 165
political question, secession as 163–6
reference function, threshold arguments on 160–2
referendum on sovereignty-association 119, 159, 167, 185
refusal of references 67–8
self-determination 159, 165
unilateral declaration of independence (UDI) 159, 185
unilateral secession, constitutionality of 159–60, 162–3, 165
unwritten constitutional principles 160, 162, 166
Quebec Veto Reference
amending formula 126–8
Charter of Rights and Freedoms 126
Constitution Act 1982 115, 123, 126–9

duality principle 128–9
patriation 127–9
refusal to answer 128
Queen's Counsel, appointment of 211

Rand, Ivan 114
Raz, Joseph 193–4, 198–9, 202, 232
reasons for decisions *see also* **reasons for initiation of AOs**
adjudication, function of 12
British system, advisory opinions in the 209–10
cases and AOs, resemblance between 206
JCPC 48
refusal of references 9, 67
reasons for initiation of AOs
avoidance of controversy 187–90
co-ordination of social aims and projects 183–4
displacement 185–6
doctrinal guidance, provision of 182–3, 191–2
federalism disputes, tool in 182
imprimatur, seeking court's 190–2, 202
law-making, preparatory step to 182
non-judicial actors, by 8–9, 180, 181–92
political context 181
positioning 186–7
pre-emption of existing or proposed legislation 184–6
social context 181–2
strategic reasons 184–90
Reference re References
compliance 193
general appeal courts exercising advisory functions 51–7, 58
JCPC 55, 89
marriage, state regulation of 88–9
neutrality 208
Quebec Secession Reference 160
separation of powers 62
refusal to answer by Supreme Court
federal-provincial disputes, role of AOs in 89
House of Lords 66
independence of judiciary 68–9
justiciability 67
legal uncertainty 67
legal role, retention of 67–8
limits of jurisdiction, own determination of 68
mootness 16–18, 67–8, 128, 206–7
political questions doctrine 128
reasons 9, 67
same-sex marriage 155–6, 189–90
Senate Reform Reference 171–2
separation of powers 63–9
specificity, lack of 67
vagueness 67
religion
denominational schools 148–9, 210–12
freedom of religion 139, 223
judges 114
justiciability 15
marriage, state regulation of 87–8, 90
same-sex marriage 152–6
Sunday trading 223
remedies 13, 18–20
binding nature 4, 226, 228–30
civil cases 19
declarations 228–9
enforceability 13, 18–20
examples 19
expansion in remedial powers of Supreme Court 131–2
legal character 19–20
provider of answers, Supreme Court as 226–32
rule of law 147, 230–2
style of advisory opinions 201
victimisation 19
reporting of AOs 210
revolutions 22–3
rights *see* **Charter of Rights and Freedoms; individual rights issues, implications of AOs for**
Royal Commissions 197
rule of law
binding nature of AOs 207, 227, 230, 233–4
cases and AOs, resemblance between 234
compliance 195, 201
Constitution 145–8, 230–1
declarations 147, 227, 230–1
federal-provincial disputes, role of AOs in 186
judicial supremacy 230–1
Manitoba Language 144–8, 230–2
remedies 147, 230–2
ultra vires 144–8
unwritten constitutional principles 162
rule of recognition 124
Russell, Peter 42–3

Same-Sex Marriage Reference
Charter of Rights and Freedoms 73, 152–6, 189
common law definition of marriage, compatibility with Charter of 152, 155–6, 189
conflicts with lower court judgments 155–6, 216–17
draft legislation, constitutionality of 152–6, 189, 192, 216
federal jurisdiction 152–6
finality 155–6, 216–17
freedom of religious officials to refuse to solemnise marriages 152–6
imprimatur, seeking Supreme Court's 191–2
individual rights 152–6, 189, 191–2
interveners, number of 152
marriage, definition of 216–17
minority governments 73–4
originalist interpretation 153
persuasive value 217
politics 74, 152–6
provinces 152–6, 216–17
refusal to answer 155–6, 189–90, 216–17
religion, freedom of 152–6
stare decisis 217
ultra vires 154
Saskatchewan 59, 104, 155, 169
Schmitt, Carl 167
Scott, FR 82
secession 98 *see also* ***Quebec Secession Reference***
Second World War 109
section 54 references 71–2
securities regulation 101–3
security of tenure of judges 22
self-determination 159, 165
self-entrenchment by Supreme Court 176
Senate *see* **women to the Senate, appointment of;** ***Senate Reform Reference***
Senate Reform Reference
abolition of Senate 118, 169–71
amicus curiae, appointment of joint 169
appointments 168–72
British North America Act 1867 115, 117–18, 170
cases and AOs, resemblance between 201
composition 118
Constitution 158, 167–72, 192, 203
amendments 169–71
architecture, effect on 170
guidance, provision of doctrinal 182
imprimatur 192
interveners, number of 169
provincial consent 169–71
separation of powers 6, 20–9 *see also* **separation of powers and advisory function**
Australia 62
capture of courts by executive 7
Charter of Rights and Freedoms 143–4
checks and balances 23–4
constitutions 24–30
democracy, as safeguard against 21
depoliticisation 22
executive 20–9, 30, 62–3
federal-provincial disputes, role of AOs in 82, 84, 92, 95, 103, 105–7
judicial branch 21–9, 30
justiciability 13
King-in-Parliament 21
legislature 7, 20–9, 30
executive 23
natural law 22
role of 20–9, 30
supremacy 22
Matchless Constitution theory 23, 26
ministerial responsibility 23
natural law 22
presidential systems 62–3
revolutions 22–3
United Kingdom 21, 23, 26–8, 62
United States 23–5, 62
separation of powers and advisory function 26–30, 61–78
amendments of Constitution 29, 64–5
captive to executive, courts as 63
cases, focus on 30, 62
Constitution 26–9, 30, 64–5, 67–8, 78, 158, 161
constitutional review of legislation 26–7, 61, 73
control over process 63
delay 77
executive 62–78
alignment with judiciary 61
failure to seek a reference 74–5
initiation of cases 7, 61, 62–70, 72–5, 235
legislature 26, 31, 70–8
minority governments 72–5
overlap with legislature 72
subordination of judiciary 62–3, 69

existence of doctrine in Canada 26–9, 61, 78
failure to seek reference 74–6
general court of appeal with advisory function 62
guardian of the constitution, Supreme Court as 29, 147, 164
independence of judiciary 27, 29, 61, 63, 69
initiation of cases 7, 61, 62–77
inter-branch tension 26–30, 61, 78
issues Supreme Court has declined to deal with 28–9
judicial branch 26–30, 61–70, 78
  appointment by executive 26–7, 195
  cases, focus on 30
  constitutional review of legislation 26–7
  discipline 27
  executive 7, 61, 62–70
  expansion of function 7, 28–9, 61, 68
  independence 27, 29, 61, 68–9
  initiation of cases 7, 61, 62–70
  judicial review 26–7
  positive law 70
  removal of judges by Parliament 27
  resources 63
  security of tenure 27
  subordination to executive 62–3, 69
justiciability 62
legislature 70–8
  appointment of judges 26–7
  exclusion of legislature 61, 70–8
  executive 26, 61, 70–8
  independence 77
  initiation of cases by legislature 71, 77–8
  positive law 70
  removal of judges 27
  review of legislation 26–7, 61
  same-sex marriage 73–4
  standing committees/independent parliamentary officers, initiation by 77
  Supreme Court Act 1985 71
  validity of legislation 76–8
Margarine Reference 214
Matchless Constitution theory 26
modification of questions 63–4
provinces 64–6
Quebec Secession Reference 161
Reference re References 62
resistance or refusal to answer 63–9, 78
  independence of judiciary 68–9
  legal role, retention of 67–8
    limits of jurisdiction, own determination of 68
    Supreme Court Act Reference 69, 78
  section 54 references 71–2
  subordination of judiciary to executive 62–3, 69
  Supreme Court Act 1985 63, 68, 71
separatism 117 *see also* ***Quebec Secession Reference;*** **secession**
Shapiro, Martin 21
Shapiro, Scott J 203
Smith, RC 89
Snell, James G 114
social aims and projects, co-ordination of 183–4
Social Credit Legislation 84–7, 109, 185
Sossin, Lorne 14
South Africa, delivery of arms to 33
sovereign immunity 25
sovereignty 79–80, 85, 87–8
sovereignty-association, referendum on 119, 159, 167, 185
special cases on constitutional matters 46–7
standing
  abstract review of legislation 225–6, 235
  binding nature of AOs 206–7, 222–5, 232, 235
  Constitution 223
  direct standing 206–7, 222–4
  justiciability 222
  public interest standing 207, 223–5, 235
  stare decisis 225
  ultra vires 222
stare decisis 9, 151–2, 205, 217–19, 225
state as a party 16–19
status of advisory opinions as law 180–1, 205, 214
Statute of Westminster 86, 110–12, 125
Strayer, Barry L 82, 186
Strong, Henry 40–1, 45
style of advisory opinions 201
Sunday trading 223
Supreme and Exchequer Court Act 1875 3, 7, 42–4, 46–7, 49–50, 212
Supreme Court, constitutional development of 108–15
  administrative changes 115
  appeals 109–13
  appointments 108, 114
  colonialism 109
  composition 108, 113–16
  criminal cases, appeals relating to 110, 115

establishment 109–10
final court, as 109–10, 113–14
hierarchy 109–10
independence 114
JCPC 8, 110–14
jurisdiction 109–15
national identity 109
prestige 108, 113–14
quality 108–9, 113
re-location 114
Upper House Reference 115, 117–18
workload 115
Supreme Court Act Reference
appointment of judges by executive 158, 167, 192, 203, 213, 229–30
declaratory legislation, passing of 174–5, 185
eligibility 69, 172–9, 184–5, 206
ideology 172
pre-emption 184–5
Quebec, requirement for three judges from 172–9, 184–5, 206, 213
separation of powers 69, 78
Constitution 158, 167, 172–9, 184–5, 192, 203
declaratory legislation, passing of 174–5, 185
finality of rulings 178–9
ideology 172
imprimatur 192
interpretation 172–8, 203
precedent 178
pre-emption 184–5
Quebec, requirement for three judges from 158, 167, 172–9, 184–5, 192, 203, 206, 213
self-entrenchment by Supreme Court 176
separation of powers 68, 78
status of Supreme Court 175
Supreme Court Reports 210

Taschereau, Henri 40
terminology 10, 229
territorial waters 91–2
test case litigation 135, 151
threshold arguments on reference function 160–2
Trans Mountain Expansion (TMX) 105–6, 186, 188
treaties and conventions 79–83
Trudeau, Pierre Elliott 92–3, 115–17, 119, 127
Truscott, Stephen 191

ultra vires
compliance 196
Constitution Act 1867 53
Constitution, amendments to 118
criminal cases 99–101, 110
disallowance power 83–4
economic regulation 102
individual rights 132
inter-provincial trade 96–7
ILO conventions 81–2
JCPC 53, 56–7
languages 144
marriage, state regulation of 89
rule of law 144–8
same-sex marriage 154
standing 222
UK legislation as law for Canada 125
unilateral declarations of independence (UDI) 159, 185
unilateral secession, constitutionality of 159–60, 162–3, 165
United Kingdom *see also* **British North America Act 1867; King of England; Judicial Committee of the Privy Council (JCPC); Westminster Parliament**
advisory opinions in British system 207–8
Canada Act 1982 126–7
colonialism 80, 116
Confederation 6–7, 31–9
constitutional conventions 116
Crown prerogatives 116
federal-provincial disputes, role of AOs in 119
House of Lords 55, 66, 71
law for Canada, UK law as 124–5
ministerial responsibility 23
separation of powers 21, 23, 26–8, 62
Supreme Court, creation of UK 62
unitary British state, Supreme Court ties to 40
unwritten constitution 26, 116, 226–7
United States
Brown v Board of Education 137
checks and balances 23–4
Constitution 25, 140, 161
due process 140–1
federalism 25, 38
Guantanamo Bay 20
originalism 170
Presidents and Supreme Court, battles between 24–5

privacy 141
same-sex marriage 156
separation of powers 23–5, 62
Supreme Court 24–5, 140–1
treaties as part of supreme law 80
unwritten constitutions 26, 29, 69, 226–7
Upper House Reference 115, 117–18

Vaughan, Frederick 114

Waldron, Jeremy 224
Washington, George 62
Westminster Parliament
Canada Act 1982 127–8
Constitution, amendments of 64, 190–1
JCPC 33–4
King-in-Parliament 21
King's power 32
Patriation Reference 119, 190–1
Quebec Veto Reference 126
residual legislative power 38–9
rule of recognition 124
Wilson, Bertha 116
women to the Senate, appointment of 132–7
British North America Act 1867, interpretation of 132–7
constitutional interpretation 132–7, 157
context, lack of consideration of 137
executive capture 137
living tree metaphor 134, 153
originalist interpretation 136–7
Persons Case 132–7, 143, 153, 157
writs of error 32
wrongful convictions 187–8, 191

www.ingramcontent.com/pod-product-compliance
Ingram Content Group UK Ltd.
Pitfield, Milton Keynes, MK11 3LW, UK
UKHW021909150926
475560UK00003B/261

9 781509 922499